centrated his efforts to "urbanize" revivalism as part of a general struggle to adapt a traditional faith to a rapidly changing external environment. After his triumphant revival crusades of the 1870's, the impact of his style and message faded before the progressive liberal approach to religion which was to shape twentieth-century Protestantism.

The present biography of this great evangelist is far superior to any other, both for its scholarly approach in determining the place of evangelicalism in American social and religious history and for its portrayal of the overpowering impact of Moody's personality. It will be particularly fascinating to those interested in American social history and the history of evangelism, the man and the movement.

JAMES F. FINDLAY, JR. is an associate professor of history at DePauw University in Greencastle, Indiana. A Danforth Fellow, he received his Master of Arts degree from Washington University in 1954, and a Doctorate in 1961 from Northwestern University. He is editor of *Contemporary Civilization,* and has published essays in *Church History, Journal of Presbyterian History,* and the *New England Quarterly.*

D1449855

Dwight L. Moody
AMERICAN EVANGELIST

JAMES F. FINDLAY, JR.

Dwight L. Moody
AMERICAN EVANGELIST
1837-1899

With a Foreword by
Martin E. Marty

THE UNIVERSITY OF CHICAGO PRESS
CHICAGO & LONDON

Library of Congress Catalog Card Number 69–13200

The University of Chicago Press, Chicago 60637
The University of Chicago Press, Ltd., London W.C.1

To Doris and the Children

Acknowledgments

I have a number of personal obligations that must be acknowledged which were crucial in the development of this book. Three people took time from their own work to render important critical observations at a very early stage of the evolution of the manuscript. Professor Arthur Link taught me almost the first principals of grammatical construction and the art of precise yet imaginative word usage that is essential to any effective historical writing. Professors Bernard Weisberger and Warren Susman freely offered searching critical judgments of my early efforts to which I returned many times for suggestions and insights as I struggled to rework and rewrite my materials. Kindly but critical readings of portions of the manuscript by John K. Nelson, George Daniels, Walter Arnstein, Mrs. Ruth Kruppa, and especially the review of the entire final draft by Martin Marty, all provided the encouragement needed to persevere in my work. In the later stages of drafting a manuscript, long and illuminating conversations with two colleagues at DePauw, Drs. Robert Newton and Robert King, were indispensable to any understanding I may have of Moody's theological attitudes.

I wish to express my deepest gratitude to Mrs. Emma M. Powell of East Northfield, Massachusetts, and Mrs. Frank R. Smith of New York City for their willingness to share with me treasured personal papers that were essential in constructing this account of their grandfather's life. DePauw University, through its Faculty Improvement program and through research funds of the Grad-

Acknowledgements

uate Council, supported at crucial junctures both the research and the writing of this book. I appreciate also the help I received from library staffs at Northfield School for Girls, Mount Hermon School for Boys, the Y.M.C.A. Historical Library in New York City, Moody Bible Institute in Chicago, Northwestern University, Newberry Library, Garrett Biblical Institute, McCormick Theological Seminary, Chicago Theological Seminary, Yale Divinity School, DePauw University, Wisconsin State Historical Society, the Library of Congress, the National Archives, and the British Museum. Mrs. Marion Crandall and Mrs. Charlotte Swope removed from my shoulders the burden of typing a final draft and did so with efficiency and constant good cheer.

If paeans of praise are any guide, "sentimental" historians again and again have asserted how deeply influenced by and obligated to their wives they are, just as the sentimental self-made men of Moody's day asserted publicly the shaping influence of a mother over each of their lives. Unfortunately, I do not intend to break with the traditional assertions of historians. A sentimentalist I may be, but it seems simply true that more than anything else my wife's sustained encouragement and support over the years has made this book possible.

Contents

Foreword	1
Preface	5
1. Northfield and Boston, 1837–1856	25
2. Chicago in the 1850's: Earnest Christian	54
3. The 1860's: Apprentice Evangelist	92
4. Beginnings as a Revivalist	136
5. Climax Overseas: Revivals in England	164
6. Mass Revivalist in the United States: Preaching and Practice	192
7. The Theology of a Popular Preacher	227
8. Gauging the Fever of Spiritual Enthusiasm	262
9. New Approaches to Evangelism: Schools in the East and in the Midwest	303
10. The Evangelist at Home	339
11. Last Days	388
A Note on Sources	422
Index	427

Foreword

Critics of revivalism are almost inevitably critics of Dwight L. Moody. Defenders of revivalism almost automatically defend him. At a critical stage of American religious history, the Chicago-based evangelist could plausibly have been called Mr. Revivalist and perhaps even Mr. Protestant. Most people in the late twentieth century, however, are neither critics nor partisans of Protestant evangelism. They are free to ignore it or to notice it with mild interest only when an heir of Moody like Billy Graham shows up in headlines as he golfs with presidents.

To most people the subject of this biography would be merely quaint. The context in which he appeared seems now to belong to the world of cigar-store Indians, Mississippi River steamboats, Fourth of July orations, and Mrs. O'Leary's cow. Evangelism, Moody's chosen field for expressing his entrepreneurial and redemptive purposes, can be regarded along with everything that went with sawdust trails, anxious benches, camp meetings, gatherings at the river, or "getting saved." Collectors of antiques cannot be expected to evade the charm of the pages which follow: they represent authentic Americana.

Devotion to quaint archaic flourishes from what has been dismissed as Victorian America could distract potential readers from the larger context in which Mr. Moody must be seen. The evangelism which he cultivated has a world-historical significance. In its prime, before Madison Avenue domesticated it, revivalism represented threats or promises to community comparable to those effected in a later day by Black Power, the New Left, or the forces of urban backlash. The whole destiny of local and national communities was seen to be involved in the fateful decisions made by those people who were being confronted by revivalists. If Moody came upon that scene of confrontation a little late in the game, and if both the terrors and the rewards had by then been somewhat compromised, he was still a legitimate representative of a long movement.

After the Enlightenment, religious people in Western Europe, the British Isles, and America had to pick up the pieces of a shattered Christendom. Philosophes, Deists, and Founding Fathers regularly questioned historic religion; they had begun writing social charters which did not demand specific religious commitments from citizens and did not penalize those who made the wrong ones or, for that matter, none at all. In that epoch, reason and nature had been looked to at the expense of revelation and history. God would be found in the open and patent scheme of things or he would not be found at all. Certainly he could not be discovered in the domains of priestcraft and superstition. One could well have prophesied the impending end of Western religion to coincide with the end of the eighteenth century.

In the later decades of that century and throughout the first half of the nineteenth, however, various kinds of reaction and revival took form. Some turned out to be genteel and romantic movements of reasonable sophistication: the Oxford Movement in England, liturgical and doctrinal renewals on the Catholic and Protestant continent, and the Episcopal High Church movement in America. Public attention turned more to the statistically overwhelming and emotionally awesome movements of awakening and revival which rose with Wesleyan Methodism and Evangelicalism in England and with almost all Protestant groups in the young United States.

Revivalism there had precedent in one colonial event of (approximately) the 1730s, the First Great Awakening. That awakening was an inter-colonial and trans-creedal occurrence which began to provide people from Massachusetts to South Carolina with some common religious symbols and rhetoric. Jonathan Edwards and George Whitefield were the towering names of the era. But the preoccupations of colonial wars, the Revolution, nation-building, and a kind of American Enlightenment had led to the demise of the movement, distraction from religious appeals for conversion, and disaffection with the churches.

The evangelism, then, in whose tradition Dwight L. Moody stood, derived more from a Second Great Awakening in the early 1800's. This two-phased movement quickened the more settled Eastern churches and was involved with the winning of the West and the churching of the frontier. Yale president Timothy Dwight was a leader in the former, and Charles Grandison Finney or Peter Cartwright, agent of "muscular Christianity," typified the latter.

When Americans set a precedent by disestablishing religion and separating church and state (after fourteen centuries of the opposite practice in the Western world), they inaugurated a policy which has come to be called "voluntaryism." People voluntarily joined or refused to join churches. The revivalist sometimes represented one brand of religion against its competitors. More often he competed against infidelity or lackadaisicality as he tried to to awaken people from what one of them called Nothingarianism to Christian participation.

The British historian, E. J. Hobsbawm, points out that during the rise of industrialism most religious forces were quiescent or failing. But Anglo-American evangelicalism moved with imperial self-confidence into all the world.¹ Both the missionary movement and the later commercial and military empires were connected with this force. In the late nineteenth century domestic evangelism in England and America was to meet new problems and possibilities with the growth of cities. Dwight L. Moody more than any other man drew attention in America for his leadership in the time of urban transition.

Author Findlay, fortunately, does not pursue the cosmic implications of every turn in his biographical plot. He is not writing a philosophical essay on the world-historical significance of evangelism. But while he concentrates on the Moody microcosm, readers will acquire accidental benefits along the way. They will derive new understanding of the relations between religion and the American Business Creed, the urban-rural myths, the cult of success, and the individualist credos which came to be associated with evangelism. By the end of the book, much in Moody will still look quaint and antique, but it will also be clear that in his movement patterns and modes which still shape men and cultures were being born.

MARTIN E. MARTY
The University of Chicago

Preface

In the spring of 1894 an old friend asked D. L. Moody for permission to release a biography of the evangelist stamped with his approval. Moody declined, and in so doing expressed the hope that not until after his death would a serious account of his life be attempted, and then only by one who had known him intimately. He delegated this task to his son Will, reportedly remarking at the time, "There are many who think they know me better than anyone else, and would feel themselves best able to interpret my life. If you do not do this work there will be many inaccurate and conflicting 'Lives.'"[1] His fears of misinterpretation were not unfounded. Hardly had he died than a spate of sketches of his life began to appear, which in turn forced his son to publish rather hastily the first edition of his "official" biography to undercut the effect which the unauthorized versions of his career might have.

In part Moody based his comments in 1894 on previous experience. He had attracted the attention of amateur biographers since the 1870's. The first books appeared in 1875 as his fame as a popular religious hero in England and in the United States began to affect the public consciousness. Nearly all of the first efforts seemed

1. William R. Moody, *The Life of D. L. Moody* (New York: Fleming H. Revell Co., 1900), p. 1, hereinafter cited as *Moody* (1900). Even earlier the elder Moody had shown concern about possible misrepresentation in the works being published about him. Two decades before his death he was emphasizing the need for historical perspective before his life could be understood adequately. See *St. Louis Globe-Democrat,* January 7, 1880, p. 5.

Preface

designed primarily to capitalize financially on Moody's newly acquired significance, rather than to offer serious studies of his life. Brief eulogistic accounts of his life were usually mixed with narrative descriptions of the revivals in Great Britain, or perhaps added to a small selection of his sermons to produce enough pages for a marketable book. The most useful of these early publications probably was a sketch of Moody written by a Methodist minister in Chicago, W. H. Daniels, who had known and observed the young man from the time he arrived in the Windy City, and who mentioned in his book numerous incidents about these early days that are not available elsewhere. But as a biographical study Daniels' work cannot be considered a serious or successful effort by present scholarly standards.[2]

Uncritical admirers of Moody have continued to publish up to the present day. Although they often have paid the closest attention to the details of Moody's day-to-day activities, their portraits have remained flat and two-dimensional. Great stress was placed on the evangelist's personal piety, the importance of his "conversion" experiences in his earlier years, and his power to convert countless souls to an evangelical faith. Moody's relations with the rest of his family were never systematically explored. The precise nature of the very considerable influence his wife exerted over him, as well as the illuminating attitudes of the evangelist toward children and grandchildren, were usually ignored. Moody was left as a shadowy figure, only a thin imitation of the vigorous personality which he actually was.[3]

2. William H. Daniels, *D. L. Moody and His Work* (Hartford, Conn.: American Publishing Co., 1875); Rufus W. Clark, *The Work of God in Great Britain under Messrs. Moody and Sankey, 1873–1875, with Biographical Sketches* (New York: Harper and Bros., 1875); R. Grant Barnwell, *Life of Moody and Sankey, the American Evangelists, Together with Scenes and Incidents of the Revival in Great Britain* (Philadelphia, 1875); John Hall and George H. Stuart, *The American Evangelists, D. L. Moody and Ira D. Sankey, in Great Britain and Ireland* (New York: Dodd and Mead, 1875). A list of most of these early studies of Moody can be found in Wilbur M. Smith, *Dwight Lyman Moody: An Annotated Bibliography* (Chicago: Moody Press, 1948), chap. 1. Although there was no documentation in Daniels' biography, a year after the book was published the author listed some of his sources, including members of the evangelist's immediate family, in an article he wrote for *Advance*, 9 (April 20, 1876): 622.

3. The work of the eulogistic school has been continued recently in

6

Preface

Writers of Moody hagiography were motivated by reasons other than a desire to venerate the evangelist in their publications. Since the 1920's, at least, most people of this sort have found themselves influenced by the raging controversies that split American Protestantism early in the twentieth century into "liberals" and "conservatives," or, more precisely, "fundamentalists" and "modernists." Most of the apologists for Moody have been vociferous advocates of fundamentalism. Although in the writings on Moody they usually avoided making explicit references to the doctrinal divisions that plagued the church, their underlying biases were unmistakable. Moody was "one of them," one of the greatest of all conservative Protestants, and therefore a man almost without blemish.[4] Moreover, their assiduous efforts have not gone unrewarded, for it is their image of Moody as the successful revivalist, closely associated with the conservative Protestant groups of the twentieth century, that remains the widely accepted picture of the evangelist today.

Interestingly, Moody has also had a few champions in the so-called "liberal" wing of American Protestantism. His chief supporter in the liberal ranks was his own son, Paul, who sparked in the 1920's a controversy with the fundamentalists over the question of how the evangelist's religious views were to be interpreted. He argued that his father should not be classified arbitrarily as a fundamentalist. In 1938 Paul published a slim volume, *My Father: An Intimate Portrait of Dwight Moody*, in which he restated the views he had expressed a decade earlier and provided some documentation for his assertions.[5] His work was an antidote

Richard K. Curtis' biography, *They Called Him Mr. Moody* (Garden City, N. Y.: Doubleday & Co., 1962). Although Curtis does attempt an independent study of some of the available primary sources, he relies too much on the books cited above and others like them for his facts and interpretations. The end result perpetuates most of the weaknesses noted in these earlier works.

4. For typical assessments of this sort, see Charles R. Erdman, *D. L. Moody: His Message for To-Day* (Chicago: Fleming H. Revell Co., 1928), pp. 12–13; Richard E. Day, *Bush Aglow: The Life Story of Dwight Lyman Moody, Commoner of Northfield* (Philadelphia: Judson Press, 1936); W. M. Smith, *Annotated Bibliography*, p. xi; J. Wilbur Chapman, *The Life and Work of Dwight L. Moody* (New York: W. E. Scull, 1900).

5. Paul D. Moody, *My Father: An Intimate Portrait of Dwight Moody* (Boston: Little, Brown and Co., 1938), pp. 183–86, 190–94, 197–98.

Preface

to the prevailing interpretations and offered important observations about the personal and family life of the evangelist unobtainable elsewhere. Just as important, perhaps, was the way in which his arguments reflected the divisions which had plagued Protestants for several decades.

Divisions accentuated by theological differences further affected the Moody household and the memoirs members of the immediate family wrote after the death of the elder Moody. Paul's attitudes were perhaps most sharply at variance with those of his brother-in-law, A. P. Fitt. Fitt was an official at the Moody Bible Institute in Chicago and identified fully with the fundamentalism espoused at that school after 1900. He wrote two brief accounts of Moody's life which were not too unlike the traditional eulogies in emphasis. The older son, Will, although holding to a conservative evangelical faith, seemed to possess some of his father's irenic temperament, and his theological biases did not intrude noticeably into his work. He published two versions of the "official" biography of his father, the first hastily in 1900, the second after careful revisions in 1930.[6] All of these family accounts remain useful to the historian, but they were marred by the inevitable coloring of uncritical sympathy and devotion to a famous relative. Moreover, all of the books generally ignored the broader historical developments which had impinged upon the evangelist and shaped his life and career.

Amateurs and family writers were not the only people to pass judgment on Moody. Since the 1920's, at least, professional historians have mentioned the evangelist, although usually briefly, in their writings. Comments about him appeared especially as social and intellectual history achieved a vogue for the first time, making revivalism fair game as a subject for historical study. These early discussions did not produce flattering images of the evangelist. As inheritors of the progressive-liberal tradition, historians

6. A. P. Fitt, *The Shorter Life of D. L. Moody* (Chicago: Bible Institute Colportage Association, 1900), and *Moody Still Lives: Word Pictures of D. L. Moody* (New York: Fleming H. Revell Co., 1936); W. R. Moody, *Moody* (1900); and William R. Moody, *D. L. Moody* (New York: Macmillan Co., 1930), hereinafter cited as *Moody* (1930). The latter volume is especially significant for the space devoted to the evangelist's career outside revivalism. See chaps. 45–69.

of the thirties thought of Moody simply as the churchly manifestation of a time of unrelieved crassness and materialism. He
seemed little more than a robber-baron with a clerical collar.[7]

Vernon Louis Parrington, in his *Main Currents of American
Thought*, probably summed up the attitude of the historical
guild in the pre-World War II period toward the revivalist in
the vivid description he penned of Moody and Sankey. "There
was revivalist Moody, bearded and neckless, with his two hundred
and eighty pounds of Adam's flesh, every ounce of which 'belonged
to God.' There was the lyric Sankey, afflicted with two hundred
and twenty-five pounds of human frailty, yet looking as smug as
a banker and singing 'There were ninety and nine' divinely
through mutton chop whiskers." Almost in the same breath Parrington went on to lump Moody and his song leader with such
contemporaries as Boss Tweed, a man of "pugnacious rascality,"
John Fiske, a "philosophic hippopotamus," Ben Butler, who was
"oily, puffy, and wheezy," and Diamond Jim Fisk, the "prince of
vulgarians." [8]

Perhaps the most significant thing that can be said about the
attitude of professional historians toward Moody is that they all
but ignored him. Their lack of comment was in itself revealing.
Before and after World War II, students of social and intellectual

7. Allan Nevins, *Emergence of Modern America, 1865–1878* (New
York: Macmillan Co., 1927), p. 345; Arthur M. Schlesinger, Sr., *The
Rise of the City, 1878–1898* (New York: Macmillan Co., 1933), pp. 324–
25; Van Wyck Brooks, *New England: Indian Summer, 1865–1915* (New
York: E. P. Dutton & Co., 1940), p. 98. A curious though important exception to these statements was the study of Moody written by Gamaliel
Bradford in the 1920's entitled *D. L. Moody: A Worker in Souls* (Garden
City, N. Y.: Doubleday & Co., 1927). Bradford was not a trained historian and thus avoided much of the animus felt toward Moody by specialists. At the same time, his work was several cuts above that of the
eulogistic school. Influenced by the Freudian craze of the twenties, Bradford developed into a fine art the "psychograph," a combination of
psychological analysis and biographical data. Concentrating on an
explication of personality, however, Bradford all but ignored the general
historical milieu in which his subjects lived. Thus the weaknesses in his
work on Moody paralleled those of writers previously discussed, but his
unique methodology and rather sophisticated result deserve separate
comment.

8. V. L. Parrington, *The Beginnings of Critical Realism in America:
1860–1920*, vol. 3 of *Main Currents in American Thought*, 3 vols. (New
York: Harcourt, Brace & Co., 1927–1930), p. 13.

history by no means neglected American religious life and thought in the late nineteenth century. Until relatively recently, however, scholars tended to concentrate on the emergence of the "New Theology" and the Social Gospel, and on the rise of new and creative institutional responses within the church to the industrialization of America.[9] Revivalism, which Moody obviously represented, had long been present on the American scene. Yet precisely because of that fact the movement seemed to deserve less of an examination than these newer and more exciting forces. It may also be that historians' distaste for the anti-intellectualism that accompanied revivalism further militated against studying such historical movements. In any case, Moody and his followers were largely ignored, even though general religious trends in his time were analyzed extensively. Thus, in effect, social and intellectual historians left Moody as much in limbo as did his most aggressive defenders and eulogists among conservative groups in American Protestantism. Neither group of writers did much to give the reading public a balanced, reasonably accurate picture.

Church historians, too, contributed relatively little to an understanding of the revivalist and his work. Specialists in American religious history have always been limited in numbers, and until recently they have been prone to concentrate their efforts on the colonial era or the early national period, seemingly mesmerized by the obvious possibilities of research in the history of Puritan New England or frontier revivalism.[10] Indeed, until the time of

9. For example, see C. Howard Hopkins, *The Rise of the Social Gospel in American Protestantism, 1865–1915* (New Haven: Yale University Press, 1940); A. I. Abell, *The Urban Impact on American Protestantism, 1865–1900* (Cambridge: Harvard University Press, 1943); Henry F. May, *Protestant Churches and Industrial America* (New York: Harper and Bros., 1949); Frank H. Foster, *The Modern Movement in American Theology* (New York: Fleming H. Revell Co., 1939); Barbara M. Cross, *Horace Bushnell, Minister to a Changing America* (Chicago: University of Chicago Press, 1958); Ira V. Brown, *Lyman Abbott, Christian Evolutionist: A Study in Religious Liberalism* (Cambridge: Harvard University Press, 1953); Jacob H. Dorn, *Washington Gladden: Prophet of the Social Gospel* (Columbus, Ohio: Ohio State University Press, 1967).
10. Richard C. Wolfe, in "The Middle Period, 1800–1870: The Matrix of American Christianity," *Religion in Life: A Christian Quarterly of Opinion and Discussion*, 22 (winter, 1952–53): 72–73, underscores this bias of church historians, citing half a dozen surveys of American religious

Preface

William Warren Sweet, who towered over the field of American church history during the thirties and early forties, historians associated with the seminaries were seldom willing to devote much of their energy to studying the American religious scene.[11]

Sweet provides a good illustration of the singular lack of interest shown in Moody and his supporters. Despite the wide range of this historian's interests, his work was controlled by certain presuppositions which prevented him from analyzing Moody thoroughly and within an adequate conceptual framework. Sweet was strongly influenced by Frederick Jackson Turner and the frontier thesis. Thus in the collections of documents he published and in his personal research and writing, Sweet concentrated on the colonial and national periods when the frontier had its greatest and most obvious effect upon American institutions. His principal study of revivalism, for example, dealt chiefly with the pre–Civil War period when connections between religious excitement and the frontier were most prominent. In this work he did note that revivalism appeared in the urban centers of the country even before the Civil War, but he devoted only one chapter to the history of religious enthusiasm after 1865 and entitled it "Revivalism on the Wane." Likewise, Sweet's synthesis of American religious history, *The Story of Religions in America*, devoted all but the final three chapters to America before the Civil War. Moody

history to prove his point. Winfred E. Garrison, in *The March of Faith: The Story of Religions in America Since 1865* (New York: Harper & Bros., 1933), offered the first general survey of American religion devoted exclusively to the post–Civil War period. Garrison dismissed Moody and revivalism in one chapter of nine pages, quoting Parrington's views verbatim and with obvious approval. An exception to this generalization is Luther A. Weigle, former dean of the Yale Divinity School, who wrote a well balanced sketch of Moody for Allen Johnson and Dumas Malone, eds., *Dictionary of American Biography*, 22 vols. (New York, Charles Scribner's Sons, 1928–1944), 13:103–06.

11. As late as 1952 a leading church historian quoted with approval the comments of a professional colleague who had said that "the most significant work in the elucidation and interpretation of American Christianity . . . is being done not by Church historians but by professors of literature, of philosophy, and of history." (Sidney E. Mead, "Recent Studies in United States Church History," *Church History*, 21 [June, 1952]: 150.) See also Leonard J. Trinterud, "Some Notes on Recent Periodical Literature on Colonial American Church History," *ibid.*, 20 (December, 1951): 72–74.

and urban revivalism were dismissed in a single page of the narrative.[12]

Recently, however, significant alterations in perspective among historians have affected their understanding of revivalism and thus also their attitude toward Moody and his work. In part these changes manifest a general revival of interest in American religious history on the part of the historical guild. The reasons for this renascence are varied and need not detain us here, since they have been delineated well elsewhere by Henry F. May.[13] But one result of this "recovery of American religious history" has been the publication of studies in depth of the whole phenomenon of nineteenth century revivalism. One of the earliest and most exciting of these works was Whitney R. Cross's *The Burned-over District*, published in 1950. Cross studied intensively the patterns of religious excitement which swept over western New York in the first half of the nineteenth century. Perhaps his most significant contributions were his study of the social makeup of the supporters of the extremist movements which abounded in the area and his conclusion that small towns and urban centers were as much the source of revivalistic fervor as the traditional frontier. This discovery suggested connections between Moody's urban evangelism of the post–Civil War era and revivalism earlier in the century.

Timothy L. Smith's *Revivalism and Social Reform in Mid-Nineteenth Century America*, appearing in 1957, supplemented Cross's work. Concentrating particularly on the 1850's, Smith empha-

12. William Warren Sweet, *Revivalism in America: Its Origin, Growth and Decline* (New York: Charles Scribner's Sons, 1944), and *The Story of Religions in America* (New York: Harper and Bros., 1930), pp. 481–82. In his later years Professor Sweet was preparing a multi-volume history of American religion. None of the work on the post–Civil War period had been published at the time of his death. A fuller treatment of Moody probably would have been included here. For a critique of Sweet's contribution to American religious history, see Sidney E. Mead, "Prof. Sweet's *Religion and Culture in America*: A Review Article," *Church History*, 22 (March, 1953): 33–49.

13. Henry F. May, "The Recovery of American Religious History," *American Historical Review*, 70 (October, 1964): 79–92. See also William A. Clebsch, "A New Historiography of American Religion," *Historical Magazine of the Protestant Episcopal Church*, 32 (September, 1963): 225–57.

sized the importance of the shift of revivalism into the rapidly expanding industrial centers of the country. This movement culminated in the revival of 1857–58, which was a national phenomenon clearly emanating from such metropolitan centers as New York and Chicago. The emphases in this revival were on lay participation, interdenominational cooperation, and the espousal of an Arminian theology over against traditional Calvinistic doctrines. Moody also represented these tendencies. Thus Smith laid bare more clearly than ever before some of the antecedents to Moody's work in the 1870's.[14]

It seemed only a matter of time before a detailed general account of American revivalism would be published. The public has been rewarded with two such efforts in recent years: Bernard Weisberger's *They Gathered at the River* in 1958, and William G. McLoughlin's *Modern Revivalism* in 1959. Since both writers emphasized the historical development of revivalism in the nineteenth and twentieth centuries, their works dealt in some detail with Moody's career, placing him for the first time within a broad and meaningful historical context.[15]

Of the two writers McLoughlin did a more complete job of research and therefore described in much greater detail the institutional developments connected with Moody's revivals. Weis-

14. Whitney R. Cross, *The Burned-over District: The Social and Intellectual History of Enthusiastic Religion in Western New York, 1800–1850* (Ithaca, N. Y.: Cornell University Press, 1950), chaps. 4, 5; Timothy L. Smith, *Revivalism and Social Reform in Mid-Nineteenth Century America* (New York: Abingdon Press, 1957), chaps. 3–5. Both books have been republished recently in paperback editions. See also Smith's article, "Historic Waves of Religious Interest in America," *Annals of the American Academy of Political and Social Sciences*, 332 (November, 1960): 14.

15. Bernard Weisberger, *They Gathered at the River: The Story of the Great Revivalists and Their Impact upon Religion in America* (Boston: Little, Brown and Co., 1958), chap. 7; William G. McLoughlin, *Modern Revivalism: Charles Grandison Finney to Billy Graham* (New York: Ronald Press, 1959), chaps. 4, 5. Besides the previously cited work of Sweet, there have been several other attempts to write general accounts of revivalism in America. They were either written too early to take much account of Moody or were popularized works which have added little to our knowledge of his activities. Probably the best of the lot is Grover C. Loud, *Evangelized America* (New York: L. MacVeagh, The Dial Press, 1928). For further listings, see W. M. Smith, *Annotated Bibliography*, chap. 6.

berger wrote with greater verve and perhaps with more intuitive insight. His narrative also revolved more around personalities than did McLoughlin's account. Thus Weisberger's portrait of Moody the man and his description of the forces that motivated the revivalist were the most sympathetic and warmly appealing. The overall conclusions of the two historians, however, did not differ substantially. Their chief achievement was to reveal in some detail how Moody and the tradition-oriented groups in American Protestantism which he represented struggled in the 1870's to adjust to the near-revolutionary changes that came with the onrush of industrialism. McLoughlin and Weisberger filled a significant gap in our general knowledge of the post–Civil War era. More important for our purposes here, their work also seemed to signal the end of a preoccupation of historians with "liberal" Protestant movements in the late nineteenth century and a widening of concerns to embrace the activities of the entire Protestant community.

Perhaps, too, these new emphases reflect the more general reevaluation of the Gilded Age which has now been underway for some time. We noted earlier the preconceptions of an older generation of historians regarding post–Civil War America and how these attitudes affected their treatment of Moody and urban revivalism. The comments of these writers rested ultimately on a point of view that condemned almost without hesitation the politicians and businessmen of the time as reckless exploiters of the nation. In essence, a moral judgment against these dynamic individuals served as the first principle of this historical interpretation. Correspondingly, in their evaluations these historians tended to favor the "exploited," or those who opposed the rulers of this new age of machines. There appeared, then, throughout the works of these writers a seeming dichotomy of the "good" and the "bad," of the "exploited" and the "exploiters." [16]

16. Expressions of this attitude can be found in Matthew Josephson, *The Robber Barons: The Great American Capitalists, 1861–1901* (New York: Harcourt, Brace & Co., 1934), and *The Politicos, 1865–1896* (New York: Harcourt, Brace & Co., 1938): Chester M. Destler, *American Radicalism, 1865–1901* (New London, Conn.: Connecticut College Press, 1946); Charles and Mary Beard, *The Rise of American Civilization* (New York: Macmillan Co., 1930), chaps. 20, 23, 25; Parrington, *Critical Realism*.

Preface

Recently a different interpretive framework for the period has emerged alongside the older structure of ideas. Historians who embrace the newer viewpoint start out differently. They assume initially that the industrial revolution was the basic force which affected every phase of American life during the period, and that for many people this was an entirely new experience. The novelty of this new way of life, coupled with the far-reaching impact of the revolution, meant that this was a time of confusion, of extemely painful adjustment, of rough trial and error for everyone. What must be studied, these historians maintain, are the responses of *all* institutions and special interest groups to the driving force of industrialization. In so doing one can better understand the era.[17] Obviously, such an approach tends to dissolve the old "exploiter-exploited" dichotomy and suggests as fruitful possibilities for historical study individuals and movements which previously had been treated with a certain amount of disdain. Perhaps it is not surprising that serious historical studies of Moody appeared just as the climate of opinion among historians began to undergo this change.

There were inadequacies, however, even in the fine studies of McLoughlin and Weisberger. Since both books focused attention on the development of revivalism, sections devoted to Moody not unnaturally concentrated on his career as a revivalist and on those factors in his early life which eventually influenced his later work. But Moody's heyday as a revivalist lasted only a decade, beginning in the 1870's. His varied career in the last twenty years of his life is still largely ignored by historians.[18]

17. Samuel Hays, *The Response to Industrialism: 1885–1914* (Chicago: University of Chicago Press, 1957), was the first comprehensive attempt to apply the new interpretive framework. More recently Robert Wiebe has pursued similar themes in his *The Search for Order, 1877–1920* (New York: Hill & Wang, 1966). See also H. Wayne Morgan, ed., *The Gilded Age: A Reappraisal* (Syracuse, N. Y.: Syracuse University Press, 1963). There are a number of monographic works which reflect the shift in attitudes. The footnotes and bibliographies of the books just cited offer guides to much of this material.

18. In 1963 an Angelican clergyman, John C. Pollack, published the most recent biographical study, *Moody: A Biographical Portrait of the Pacesetter in Modern Mass Evangelism* (New York: Macmillan Co., 1963) Thoroughly grounded in the primary sources both in this country and

In addition Weisberger and McLoughlin both viewed revivalism, at least in Moody's time, as principally a *response* to stimuli generated by conditions and forces outside the religious community. Weisberger saw Moody's success based to a great degree on his identification with the business society of the 1870's, on his ability to echo the desires of Americans for the simpler agrarian world now being destroyed by industrialism, and on the fact that Moody had created unconsciously in himself "something of an ideal Victorian father image." McLoughlin's analytical structure was more complex, but ultimately he viewed Moody and revivalism generally as part of the process of "reexamination and redefinition of the nation's social and intellectual values which must take place from time to time in order to maintain a balance between tradition and change." [19] These judgments were in many respects correct, but for both writers, ultimate standards of interpretation rested above and beyond the specific movement which Moody represented.

Revivalism, however, possessed an inner dynamism, independent of external influences, welling up from the hidden sources of Christian faith and action. These internal drives were not sufficiently emphasized by those struggling to interpret Moody and his friends. The need in any further work on Moody is to pay particular attention to "the faith which is independent, which is aggressive rather than passive, and which molds culture instead of being molded by it." [20] Moody must be viewed not only as a part of the external structure of American culture and society, but also in relation to

in England, Pollack was the first writer to discuss systematically Moody's entire career. He did not, however, place the evangelist meaningfully in the context of his times. Lacking a fundamental understanding of historical developments, he was unable to evaluate his subject in a broad, critical framework. The result is a narrative that accepts Moody largely on his own terms, that is bogged down in the minutiae of the revivalist's day-to-day existence. Although providing us with a great deal of hitherto undetected data on Moody's life, Pollack's book is not a finished analysis.

19. Weisberger, *They Gathered at the River*, pp. 210, 213, 217; McLoughlin, *Modern Revivalism*, p. 7.

20. H. Richard Niebuhr, *The Kingdom of God in America* (New York: Harper and Bros., 1959), p. x. Niebuhr's book is an illuminating attempt at applying this principle to the whole sweep of American religious history.

this inner structure of religious ideas and forces which fundamentally shaped all of his actions during his adult years.

This special angle of vision forces a reexamination of the broad interpretive framework in which one views Moody's life and work. At this point one should stress in particular the significance of a powerful religious and cultural phenomenon called "evangelical Protestantism." Historians have tagged with this phrase a certain cluster of emotional, theological, and institutional forms which shaped American Protestantism, particularly at the popular level, during much of the nineteenth century. Evangelical Protestantism probably reached the apogee of its influence in the years just prior to 1870; thus Moody, along with every churchgoer of his day, was fundamentally affected by the movement.

Richard Wolfe, a church historian, was one of the first among present day scholars to point to the need for study of evangelical Protestantism. In 1957, John C. Greene, a specialist in intellectual history and the history of science, suggested that all students of nineteenth-century America should know more about "evangelical orthodoxy." He argues that this phenomenon could serve as a major clue in advancing the historians' understanding of our culture as it existed a century ago, since the evangelical faith undergirded the thought of all churchmen — and therefore a sizable percentage of Americans — in the mid-nineteenth century.[21]

In the last decade and a half, considerable work has been done to achieve the goals first suggested by Wolfe and later by Greene. Sidney Mead was a pioneer. In a series of articles published in the 1950's, he began to sketch the broad lineaments of evangelical Protestantism and suggested the general nature of its historical evolution throughout most of the nineteenth century. In a sense Mead prepared for these broadly interpretive essays by publishing in the early 1940's a detailed study of Nathaniel Taylor, a New England minister whose life spanned roughly the first half of the nineteenth century. In this book Mead described the disintegration of the orthodox Calvinist theology of New England in the early nineteenth century, its replacement by Arminian doctrines — a

21. Wolfe, "The Middle Period," pp. 78–84; John C. Greene, "Objectives and Methods in Intellectual History," *Mississippi Valley Historical Review*, 44 (June, 1957): 72.

dominant theological motif within evangelical Protestantism —
and the central role that Taylor played in inaugurating the break-
down and transition.[22]

Other historians have made contributions to an expanding body
of materials about evangelical Protestantism. Clifford Griffin has
described one of the principal institutions constructed by the
evangelical Protestants to facilitate their practical work — the vast
interdenominational "benevolent societies" of the pre–Civil War
era. Robert Handy has uncovered in the burning desire to "Christianize America" one of the most powerful of the inner forces
motivating the evangelical groups. Winthrop Hudson has studied
the voluntary principle, which was a central characteristic of the
evangelical churches. Timothy Smith's previously mentioned work
was a highly important contribution because of its detailed description of revivalism and the mind of the average evangelical
believer in the 1850's. Smith's findings tended to be prefigured in
the analysis presented by Whitney Cross of the thinking and practices of the new evangelical Protestants emerging in western New
York in the 1830's. Cross also pointed the way for Griffin's study
in his suggestive comments about "Yorker benevolence" in the days
of Jackson and Clay.[23] These interpretations and findings have

22. Sidney E. Mead, *Nathaniel William Taylor, 1786–1858: A Connecticut Liberal* (Chicago: University of Chicago Press, 1942). Mead's
articles have recently been gathered together and published as *The
Lively Experiment: The Shaping of Christianity in America* (New York:
Harper & Row, 1963). See especially chaps. 2, 3, 7–9. See also "The
Rise of the Evangelical Conception of the Ministry in America: 1607–
1850," chap. 7 in H. Richard Niebuhr and Daniel D. Williams, eds.,
The Ministry in Historical Perspectives (New York: Harper and Bros.,
1956). Important supplements to Mead's work are two articles published
recently by Earl A. Pope. See his "The Rise of the New Haven Theology,
Part I," *Journal of Presbyterian History*, 44 (March, 1966): 24–44, and
"Part II," *ibid.*, (June, 1966): 106–21.

23. Clifford S. Griffin, *Their Brothers' Keepers: Moral Stewardship in
the United States, 1800–1865* (New Brunswick, N. J.: Rutgers University
Press, 1960); Robert Handy, "The Protestant Quest for a Christian
America, 1830–1930," *Church History*, 22 (March, 1953): 8–20; Winthrop
Hudson, *The Great Tradition of the American Churches* (New York:
Harper & Row, 1963), especially chaps. 2–7; T. L. Smith, *Revivalism and
Social Reform*, chaps. 1–6, 8–10; Cross, *The Burned-over District*, chaps.
7, 10–12.

been incorporated into the newer surveys of American church history, considerably strengthening these volumes.[24]

Yet in spite of these advances, surprisingly little work has been done on evangelical Protestantism after 1870. Moreover, this was an important moment for the evangelical community. Precisely then evangelicalism in this country began to disintegrate under the hammer blows both of industrialization and a rapidly changing society from without and theological disputes within. The fact that Moody was probably the most widely hailed representative of evangelical Protestantism after 1870 suggests that a detailed study of his life would help to illuminate this now relatively unexplored period in the movement's history. The reverse is also true. To understand the nature of evangelical Protestantism is to illuminate more fully the life of Moody.

Within such an interpretive framework a number of problems immediately thrust themselves forward to be examined and explained. For example, in analyzing Moody's work as a revivalist in the British Isles, one cannot help but notice the many common assumptions shared by evangelical groups in Britain and America. Thus when Moody began his first major revival campaign in England in 1872, he did not speak in a vacuum but used phrases and words in his sermons which were understood immediately by his audiences. The presence of this shared structure of ideas helps immeasurably to explain the relative ease with which Moody and Sankey scored their successes as traveling evangelists in England and Scotland. Moreover, if we study Moody's work in America without some understanding of the inner drives of evangelical Protestantism, we will be unable to perceive adequately what motivated Moody in his religious work in Chicago and elsewhere in Illinois in the 1860's, what prompted him to found his schools in Massachusetts and Chicago in the 1880's, and how he was able to collect

24. For example, Winthrop Hudson, *Religion in America* (New York: Charles Scribner's Sons, 1965), especially chaps. 5–7; Edwin S. Gaustad, *A Religious History of America* (New York: Harper & Row, 1966). William G. McLoughlin, in *The American Evangelicals, 1800–1900* (New York: Harper and Row, 1968), has assembled a useful collection of source materials and has prefaced the work with an important interpretive essay of his own on the evangelicals.

the huge sums he did to finance the welter of activities which he organized and directed throughout his life.

Finally, one must reverse the perspective hoping thereby to see what light Moody's career casts on the dilemmas facing the evangelical groups in the late nineteenth century. If the talk is about the theological developments of the time, it is only a truism to remark that by 1900 American Protestantism was breaking up into contending factions, liberal and conservative. What has not been made so clear is the common evangelical heritage of both of these groups. Timothy Smith was one of the first to suggest the close connection that might exist between evangelical Protestants of the mid-nineteenth century and the supporters of the Social Gospel a quarter of a century later.[25] Surprisingly, relatively little has been done to uncover the roots of fundamentalism in the pre-1890 period, although the assumption has always been made that most of the evangelical groups joined this faction as positions polarized at the end of the century.[26]

Moody's significance in relation to these problems becomes immediately apparent. Despite a decidedly conservative theological outlook, he maintained friendships with men in both the liberal and conservative camps until his death. Therefore, the story of his life may be quite instructive both in revealing the beginning of the fundamentalist movement within evangelical Protestantism and in showing how pressures both internal and external began to tear the evangelical denominations apart in the last years of his life. Moreover, an intensive analysis of his career can give us

25. T. L. Smith, *Revivalism and Social Reform*, chap. 10, p. 235.
26. An early student of fundamentalism, Stewart G. Cole, *The History of Fundamentalism* (New York: R. R. Smith, 1931), stresses the period after 1900. Robert T. Handy, "Fundamentalism and Modernism in Perspective," *Religion in Life*, 24 (Summer, 1955): 381–94, sketches very briefly some of the background in the nineteenth century. Much more helpful are Lefferts A. Loetscher, *The Broadening Church: A Study of Theological Issues in the Presbyterian Church Since 1869* (Philadelphia: University of Pennsylvania Press, 1957); C. Norman Kraus, *Dispensationalism in America: Its Rise and Development* (Richmond, Va.: John Knox Press, 1958); Ernest R. Sandeen, "The Princeton Theology: One Source of Biblical Literalism in American Protestantism," *Church History*, 31 (September, 1962): 307–21; and especially Sandeen's "Towards a Historical Interpretation of the Origins of Fundamentalism," *Church History*, 36 (March, 1967): 66–83.

an inkling of the rich variety of movements through which conservative Protestantism manifested itself during the last twenty years of the nineteenth century. Through Moody one learns of premillennialism, dispensationalism, and the revival of "holiness," or schemes for sanctification within Protestant circles in America. These are themes still all but foreign to the average historian of the period.[27]

Fundamental guidelines for interpreting Moody's life and work now begin to appear. First, he must be placed within the "inner" context of evangelical Protestantism as he knew and experienced it up to 1870. As an elaboration on this theme, his actions in his mature years must be viewed as one man's participation in and response to the process by which the widely accepted religious attitudes and practices of his younger days were gradually eroded away and then slowly transformed into unfamiliar shapes by the time of his death. Second, we must remember that Moody was not only a man of faith but also a participant in the secular world of the late nineteenth century. He must continue to be viewed as historians have generally viewed him in the past. He must be examined within the context of this "outer" world of the Gilded Age, responding to, and perhaps shaping a bit, the institutions and the thoughts and actions of the people of that era. Finally, the earliest writers about Moody have left us a legacy to be called upon in any attempt at a reassessment of his life. They testified again and again to the overpowering impact of the man's personality on all those with whom he came in contact. Something similar to their appreciation of and fascination with this personality must be communicated, seasoned perhaps with a dash of critical aloofness that would be alien to their perceptions. It is with these concerns in mind that the following pages are written.

27. In one of his recent publications, Timothy Smith has extended his research into the post-Civil War period and given us the first scholarly analysis of the "holiness" movement and its development in the years just prior to the end of the century. See *Called Unto Holiness: The Story of the Nazarenes: The Formative Years* (Kansas City, Mo.: Nazarene Publishing House, 1962); "The Theology and Practices of Methodism, 1876–1919" in *The History of American Methodism*, 3 vols., ed. Emory Stevens Bucke (Nashville, Tenn.: Abingdon Press, 1964), 2:608–27.

Dwight L. Moody
AMERICAN EVANGELIST

1

Northfield and Boston, 1837–1856

In the middle of August, 1875, D. L. Moody landed in New York at the end of a two year visit to the British Isles. He had left America in 1873 in relative obscurity, but his astounding success as a popular preacher in England and Scotland had made him a national figure upon his return. Newspapermen vied for his attention at dockside, and as he stepped from the boat people waited expectantly for some announcement as to when assaults upon religious indifference in this country would begin. With the speed and promptness that were characteristic of him, Moody brushed aside questioners and well-wishers, gathered his baggage and his family, and left the city immediately for the sanctuary of his birthplace and family home in Northfield, Massachusetts.[1]

Moody's return to his birthplace was more than a symbolic act, for he would make the town his permanent home thereafter. This was the first step in reasserting physical and psychic ties which had been broken twenty years earlier when he had left home to be on his own. But the overt act of rushing to Northfield after his return from overseas did seem to illuminate certain fundamental influences and tendencies in the evangelist's life. In some ways Moody was a representative of a new America emerging after the Civil War, earthy and dynamic, centered in the great cities spawned by industrialism. Yet at the same time he was also profoundly a child of pre–Civil War America, a society of small towns,

1. *New York Herald*, August 13, 1875; *New York Tribune*, August 16, 1875; *New York Evangelist*, 47 (August 19, 1875): 4.

of closely knit communities, of simple yet deeply felt values and commitments. Northfield had served as the specific place in which this latter influence had shaped Moody's personality. Perhaps it is not surprising then that he sought out this environment that seemingly remained true and unchanging as his spirits flagged from the burden of duties in the rushing, pell-mell urban world of the 1870's.

To a visitor in the 1870's or 1880's, Northfield would appear largely unchanged from descriptions available of the town in Moody's earliest days. The following observations were made by one such traveler: The 1500 inhabitants live in "farm-houses dotted over the road for seven miles," lying "somewhat thicker at a spot where there is also a post-office, a store or two, a couple of churches, and a railway station, that may be regarded as the heart of the town." The single street, serving also as a portion of the post road from Bennington, Vermont, to Boston, is "about fifty yards wide, shadowed by double or quadruple rows of ancient elms, and grass-grown, save for a very sandy track . . . [which] affords a course for the light-wheeled buggies and waggons of the farmers." Wooden houses, "their white walls and green window-screens bright in the brilliant sunshine," nestle in the woods; "the broad Connecticut flows with a leisurely calm through its beautiful valley; and undulating mountain chains . . . close in on one of the most pleasing landscapes you can find in America." [2]

Throughout the nineteenth century Northfield remained largely an agricultural community. Residents scratched out a livelihood from the rocky hillsides or tilled the more fertile fields in the flat lowlands of the river valley in which the town was situated. [3] Until the 1830's the chief cash crops were staples such as corn, oats, and rye. Corn held first rank; production was sufficiently great to serve both local demands and the expanding urban market of the downriver towns, where exports were sent by boat. In the

2. *Catholic Presbyterian*, 4 (October, 1880): 305.
3. In Margaret R. Pabst's study, *Agricultural Trends in the Connecticut Valley Region of Massachusetts, 1800–1900* (Northampton, Mass.: Smith College Press, 1940), Northfield is properly denoted as a town including both rich lowland areas and hill country, although the categories used to describe the economic characteristics of the town are often distressingly vague and imprecise. See especially pp. 3–5.

thirties a new crop, hops, began to be cultivated. This too was a product grown chiefly for export and soon became a highly profitable investment for the farmers in the town. By 1840 Northfield was the center of hops production for the entire county. By the 1850's a nascent lumbering industry had also appeared, although this activity was always secondary to the essential agricultural pursuits.[4] Industrial statistics compiled by the state of Massachusetts during Moody's youth indicate the town possessed a few business enterprises — a small tannery, a chair and cabinet shops, a wagon repair shop, and a boot and shoe factory (450 pairs per year). But most of these businesses did little more than provide essential services for the people of the community. Not until the late 1840's and early 1850's, when a lumber mill, a small brick and charcoal industry, and a hat factory appeared, did Northfield begin to feel permanently the effects of non-agricultural activities then permeating the economic life of the state.[5]

Nevertheless, even in the 1850's the economic base of the community remained not very different from what it had been twenty or thirty years earlier. There was a sense of regularity and routine to daily life that emerged out of the rhythm of the seasons and the agricultural pursuits that so many in the community followed. One Northfield citizen asserted that *"just about so,* is the motto of our town. In the quiet village, where the principle occupation is farming, we do not expect to find much stir in the streets . . . as we would under opposite circumstances. As it is each day brings its own routines of quiet duties." Another resident put it a bit differently: "Few changes or times of interest occur, or are likely to occur in 'Old Northfield,' proverbial for its unchangeableness. The occupation of the producing class of its inhabitants being

4. *State of Massachusetts, Statistical Information, Branches of Industry, Year ending June 1, 1855* (Boston, 1856), pp. 196–97; Herbert C. Parsons, *A Puritan Outpost: A History of the Town and People of Northfield, Massachusetts* (New York: Macmillan Co., 1937), pp. 260–61, 282–83; *Greenfield* [Mass.] *Gazette and Courier*, June 17, 1867.

5. John P. Bigelow, comp., *Statistical Tables: Exhibiting the Condition and Products of Certain Branches of Industry in Mass. for the Year Ending April 1, 1837* (Boston: Dutton & Wentworth, 1838), p. 101; John G. Palfrey, comp., *Statistics of the Condition and Products of Certain Branches of Industry in Mass. for the Year Ending April 1, 1845* (Boston: Dutton & Wentworth, 1846), pp. 203–04; *Massachusetts, Statistical Information, 1855*, pp. 196–97.

mainly agricultural." [6] A way of life linked closely to the agricultural base of the community seemed obvious to all. Such a common perception or point of view was perhaps the most elemental influence that shaped the attitudes of young Moody as he grew to adulthood in Northfield.

By the time of Moody's birth in 1837, towns further downstream had begun to grow as they found themselves affected by the quickening spirit of a changing economic order. The community of Orange, the county seat Greenfield, and historic Deerfield, all smaller than Northfield in 1820, had surpassed the latter village in population by 1850.[7] The key was industrialization, made possible by water power easily available in the rushing streams tributary to the Connecticut River. Northfield's town fathers never devised a way to harness effectively the slow-moving waters of the wide stream that split their community in half. Even the coming of the railroads in 1848 failed to break down completely Northfield's isolation from the outside world.[8]

The Vermont and Massachusetts Railroad, which by 1850 spanned the Connecticut River at Northfield as it snaked southward from Brattleboro, Vermont, did symbolize one important connection with the outside world. Much of the financing of this railroad came from businessmen in Boston, and its terminus lay in the Hub City. The railroad reflected the growing influence that this great urban center was exerting throughout the state by the time of Moody's birth. Throughout the colonial period Northfield was principally a part of the society that had taken root up and down the Connecticut River valley. The economic orientation of the community, and even the movement of people in and out of the town, always seemed tied to places of settlement downstream. Movement was along a north-south axis rather than east to the coastal areas and Boston.

6. *Greenfield* [Mass.] *Gazette and Courier*, December 27, 1869, March 6, 1865.
7. Jesse Chickering, ed., *Statistical View of the Population of Massachusetts from 1765 to 1840* (Boston: Charles C. Little and James Brown, 1846), pp. 25–26; Parsons, *A Puritan Outpost*, pp. 280–82, 292.
8. For the effect of industrialization by 1850 on towns like Greenfield, Deerfield, and Orange, see the information compiled in Bigelow, *Statistical Tables, 1837*, pp. 98–99, 102, 97; *Statistics, 1845*, pp. 194, 197, 204–05; *Massachusetts, Statistical Information, 1855*, pp. 185–87, 198–200.

Almost from the beginning of the nineteenth century, however, conditions began to change as the economic and political power of Boston expanded into the interior.[9] The post road that served as Northfield's main street and eventually ended in Boston, and the rail connections later, were constant reminders of this expanding relationship. The state government also made itself felt increasingly in western Massachusetts. For two centuries local government had been the locus of political power. It yielded to the Commonwealth only those elements of jurisdiction necessary to serve the common interests of all the inhabitants of the state. But in the years just prior to Moody's birth the government in Boston began to assert its authority in matters that had always been home concerns. By the 1840's, town officials throughout Massachusetts were being asked for regular reports on the vital statistics of births, marriages, and deaths; the state governments sought to regulate more carefully local care of the poor and insane; and the state board of education, under the vigorous leadership of Horace Mann, made its impact felt on the public school system. Slowly yet permanently the ties of a small town deep in the interior to the outside world were being altered.[10] These shifts in power and influence, clearly established by the time Moody had reached adolescence, help to explain why the young man unhesitatingly chose to go to Boston, rather than to one of the nearby river towns, when he left home in 1854.

During Moody's formative years the social homogeneity in his hometown seemed undeniable. It had been so from the earliest days of the town in the seventeenth century. Most of the inhabitants in the 1830's were of English stock, representing the descendants of settlers who had moved out of Connecticut and then

9. General population trends in Massachusetts in the first half of the nineteenth century confirm these generalizations. See Chickering, *Statistical View 1765 to 1840*, pp. 9, 11.

10. Parsons, *Puritan Outpost*, pp. 209–10, 290–98; Oscar and Mary Handlin, *Commonwealth: A Study of the Role of Government in the American Economy: Massachusetts, 1774–1861* (New York: New York University Press, 1947), chap. 10; Richard Birdsall, *Berkshire County: A Cultural History* (New Haven: Yale University Press, 1959), pp. 238–39; Edward C. Kirkland, *Men, Cities, and Transportation: A Study in New England History, 1820–1900*, 2 vols. (Cambridge: Harvard University Press, 1948), vol. 1, chaps. 4–6.

gradually populated all of the fertile river valley of which North-field was a part. This movement of people into western Massachusetts via a water route continued throughout most of the eighteenth century. It was, indeed, the route by which Moody's own paternal ancestor came to reside in Northfield. By the 1840's the pattern of migration had shifted enough to include a number of former Bostonians in the population. Even more important was the arrival of the Irish. Immigrants from the Emerald Isle had helped to build the railroad that reached the town late in the decade, and they had labored on the heavy granite-piered bridge which made it possible for trains to cross the Connecticut River at Northfield. By 1850 a rising number of young Irish men and women were settling in the community. Many of the men were being hired as farmhands, and the girls were finding jobs as domestics in the homes of the more affluent people in the town. Some of the Irish came as families, including a few who felt sufficiently secure to house and care for elderly immigrant relatives as well as their own small children. In the census of 1850 the Irish represented just about five per cent of the total population of the town.[11]

It is easy to overstress the immediate social significance of this new migration. By the mid-fifties, when Moody left home at the age of seventeen, the "Irish problem" had clearly emerged in Boston, and perhaps in the larger towns close to the coast. But the foreign-born were still only a small percentage of the population in Northfield, and most of them had lived there only a few years. Established residents still were very much in control of the town, and the traditional social structure shaped by long-recognized historical patterns was not seriously challenged, nor would it be during Moody's lifetime. The few Bostonians who had filtered into the town did little more than reinforce prevailing cultural patterns. Usually professional people with good educations, they quickly took their places among the respected families of the community.[12] At mid-century the unskilled, largely illiterate Irish la-

11. Parsons, *Puritan Outpost*, pp. 209–26; U.S., Bureau of the Census, "Schedule I, Free Inhabitants in Northfield in the County of Franklin, State of Massachusetts," *Seventh Census of the United States, 1850*, (microfilm copy, National Archives), 10:327–49.

12. Oscar Handlin, *Boston's Immigrants: A Study in Acculturation, 1790–1880*, rev. ed. (Cambridge, Mass.: Belknap Press, 1959), especially

borers that clustered in Northfield were chiefly a portent of a new socially pluralistic America that was developing hand in hand with industrialization. Even the small, backcountry communities near the eastern seaboard could not fully escape these forces that were beginning to transform the nation.

In probing the family background of the evangelist, one uncovers a web of life deeply enmeshed with the history of Northfield. Chiefly through his mother his ancestry extended back to some of the founders of the town. The Holtons, the Wrights, the Alexanders — the ancestral matrix which eventually produced Moody's mother and paternal grandmother — were families which had lived and farmed in or near the village for generations. By the time of the Revolution the Alexander family had achieved a position of considerable prestige in the community. Thomas Alexander, Moody's great-great-grandfather, was a member of the first Committee of Correspondence formed in Northfield in 1775, and later served in Washington's army. Thomas's son, Medad, was one of the town's leading citizens at the turn of the century, a stout Federalist and a perennially successful candidate for town selectman.[13]

All of these families produced numerous progeny, many of whom grew up and settled in Northfield. The family of Betsey Holton, Moody's mother, illustrates the point. By the mid-nineteenth century the farms or homes of brothers, sisters, and close relatives guarded almost all of the approaches to the town.[14] In terms of sheer numbers it was inevitable that the Holtons would play an important role in the life of the community. With several generations of Holtons present at all times, the family demonstrated to everyone in the town, in a subtle but largely unconscious way, the web of interpersonal ties and relationships that helped connect the community's past with its present, or indicated to newcomers to whom deference and respect were to be paid.

Moody's paternal ancestors were less closely connected with

chaps. 5–7; Bureau of the Census, "Free Inhabitants of Northfield," *Seventh Census*, pp. 328, 334, 338, 339.

13. J. H. Temple and George Sheldon, *A History of the Town of Northfield, Massachusetts* (Albany, N. Y., 1875), pp. 324, 325–28, 386, 388; Elsie Scott, comp., "Geneology of Dwight L. Moody," (MS, Northfield, Mass.); Parsons, *Puritan Outpost*, pp. 221, 228.

14. Parsons, *Puritan Outpost*, pp. 337–38.

Northfield's past. His grandfather, Isaiah, came to the town from Hadley, Massachusetts, in 1796. The arrival of the first Moody illustrates the movement of people up the Connecticut River valley that characterized the area to the end of the eighteenth century. Like most of these migrants, the Moodys were of old English stock. The first members of the family had come to Massachusetts from England in the 1630's, settling eventually in Hadley. Thus the family was fully a part of the prevailing culture in New England, and Isaiah's move to Northfield probably did little to jar either his or the community's traditional way of operating.[15]

Moody's grandfather was a brick mason, an occupation which identified the family with the artisan class and the lower-middling orders of early nineteenth century American society. For several generations bricklaying seemed to be the family occupation. Both Moody's father and another son of Isaiah, Lucius, who remained in Northfield throughout his life, pursued the trade. The income of a bricklayer in a town like Northfield was not exceptionally large when compared with the real estate and personal property values of the most affluent farmers in the area. But at the same time, economic disparities were not really extreme. Size of income, so often a determinant of social status in American communities, did not vary too dramatically between the lower-middle and upper orders of Northfield society.[16] In a seemingly classless society there were lines to be drawn, however. Recently an historian has suggested the manner in which divisions appeared in small towns

15. Temple and Sheldon, *History of Northfield*, p. 499; Scott, "Genealogy of Dwight L. Moody."

16. Temple and Sheldon, *History of Northfield*, p. 499; Bureau of the Census "Free Inhabitants of Northfield," *Seventh Census*, pp. 328, 330, 332, 336, 339; U.S., Bureau of the Census, "Schedule I, Inhabitants in the town of Northfield in the County of Franklin, State of Massachusetts, *Ninth Census of the United States, 1870*, (microfilm copy, National Archives), 8:316. As late as 1867 only five people in Northfield paid the state income tax then being assessed on all income above $1000. On those taxed, incomes remained within a narrow set of extremes. The wealthiest person on the list assertedly possessed an annual income of a little over $3000. This is a less accurate indicator of economic differences than figures quoted on real and personal property holdings in the national censuses of 1850, 1860, and 1870, but there is a suggestion here of relatively moderate economic differences in the community. See *Greenfield* [Mass.] *Gazette and Courier*, May 27, 1867, April 20, 1868, May 3, 1869.

throughout America, communities that were not unlike North-field.

> Distinctions that would have eluded an outsider — the precise location of a house, the amount of hired help, the quality of a buggy or a dress — held great import in an otherwise un-differentiated society. . . . At the top stood the few who not only had greater wealth than their neighbors, but con-trolled access to it as well. . . . Except in rare circumstances, custodians of a genteel but explicit Protestantism with Anglo-Saxon names enjoyed a powerful advantage over all com-petitors.[17]

In the 1830's the Moodys were clearly not a part of the elite in Northfield. But this did not mean that they were social outcasts. The impeccable family credentials of Betsey Holton Moody (Dwight's mother) prevented that. Her marriage to a relative new-comer like Edwin Moody also suggests how easily young people ignored convention and married above or below their own social position in the town. Moreover, the fact that a community like Northfield ordered so much of its daily existence around duties associated with agriculture and the farm, produced in its inhabit-ants a certain loose cohesiveness of outlook. This common per-spective could not help but promote social homogeneity and perhaps effect some further blurring of social distinctions.[18] The rough sort of social levelling that Dwight's immediate relatives experienced in their marriages and in the community surely af-fected a boy growing up under their tutelage. Perhaps this early environment helps to explain the evangelist's pronounced dislike

17. Robert Wiebe, *The Search for Order, 1877–1930* (New York: Hill and Wang, 1967), p. 3. A recent study of the small town by Page Smith, *As a City Upon a Hill: The Town in American History* (New York: Alfred A. Knopf, 1966) is disappointing in its comments upon this gen-eral topic.

18. Generalizations of this sort are based in part on weekly accounts of activities in Northfield printed in the newspaper at the county seat in the late 1860's. These accounts describe the town after Moody had left, but agriculture was still very much at the heart of village life, and occa-sionally there are hints of the lack of sharply defined distinctions in the social activities being reported. See especially *Greenfield* [Mass.] *Gazette and Courier*, November 19, 1866, May 20, 1867, September 14, 1868, March 1, 1869, August 16, 1869.

later of sham and pretense, and his own constant efforts to deal freely and naturally with all kinds of people.

Beginning with a rather low station in the social order, neither Dwight's grandfather nor his father were prevented from achieving acceptance into the broad stream of Northfield society. Isaiah Moody married Phila Alexander, the daughter of Medad Alexander, in 1799, shortly after he arrived in the town. The marriage immediately tied the young brick mason's fortunes in with one of the most respected families of the locality. Artisan that he was, possible social differences between Isaiah and the Alexanders evidently were not deemed sufficient to preclude the union. Nine children were born of this marriage. The oldest, Edwin, born on November 1, 1800, eventually became the father of Dwight. He too married advantageously, taking Betsey Holton as his wife on January 3, 1828, thus assuring the Moodys of connections with another of the long-established familial groups that served as pillars of the community.[19]

Little is known about the life of Edwin Moody. He became a brick mason like his father and he sired a large family, but few other concrete facts about him have been unearthed. Sources vary in describing his personal qualities. None report him to be an exceptionally good provider for his family, though the explanations for this fact vary a great deal. The most reliable accounts suggest that he did influence his children in several ways. Dwight's quick wits, good-naturedness, unceasing activity amounting to restlessness, and perhaps even the stout, square-shouldered figure he became as an adult, were characteristics drawn from the father.[20] In the last analysis, however, any description of Edwin Moody and his relationships with his family must be imprecise. Certainly the effort is complicated by the fact that in later years neither his

19. Northfield Town Records, "Births, Marriages, Deaths, Intentions, Society Certificates, Book B," Northfield, Massachusetts, pp. 116, 205, 225, 236; "Family Register," MS in the Moody Museum, Northfield School for Girls; *Greenfield* [Mass.] *Gazette and Franklin Herald*, January 8, 1828.

20. Northfield Town Records, p. 171. Unfavorable views of Edwin Moody can be found in the *New York Herald*, August 19, 1875; and E. W. Powell, "Moody of Northfield" (unpublished MS, Crozer Theological Seminary), p. 42. More favorable comments are in Parsons, *Puritan Outpost*, p. 350; and William R. Moody, *The Life of D. L. Moody* (New York: Fleming R. Revell Co., 1900), p. 19.

son Dwight nor any other close relative made public comments that would help the historian.

Dwight's seeming reticence about his father is probably largely explained by the fact that Edwin died very suddenly during the youth's early childhood. The future evangelist was born February 5, 1837, the sixth child and fifth son in the family. The father died May 28, 1841, when Dwight was four years old. Thus Edwin Moody exerted only a limited influence on the life and personality of his most illustrious son.[21]

If there are uncertainties as to the force of character, the shape of personality, and the paternal influence of Edwin Moody, the historical record leaves no doubt about his wife. Forceful and assertive, following her husband's death she played by necessity a decisive role as the sole parental guide for her children. She lived a long life, dying only a few years before her most famous son. In later years Dwight often extolled publicly her womanly virtues and pointed with pride to the impact she had made on his character and personality.[22] This unabashed enthusiasm of the revivalist must be discounted in part as typical Victorian rhetoric venerating "mother" and her shaping influence on the successful son. Yet more objective descriptions of the woman agree basically with the sentiments of her son — she was willful, determined, a person of character.[23] These were all essential personality traits of her son Dwight as well.

Betsey Moody's grit was tested severely at the time of her husband's death. The mother was left with seven young children, and twins were born to her soon after. Neighbors advised against trying to hold the family together, but she was determined and with considerable sacrifices succeeded in doing so. Many accounts of

21. Northfield Town Records, p. 171; Temple and Sheldon, *History of Northfield*, p. 500.

22. *New York Evangelist*, 46 (July 29, 1875): 6; *The Independent*, 27 (December 23, 1875): 5; *St. Louis Globe Democrat* (December 24, 1879); undated clipping, Chicago, 1897, Nettie Fowler McCormick Papers, Wisconsin State Historical Society, Madison, Wis. See also D. L. Moody to Betsey Moody, February 14, 1893, Moody Papers, Mrs. E. M. Powell, East Northfield, Massachusetts.

23. A most vivid vignette of Betsey Moody is to be found in Paul Moody, *My Father: An Intimate Portrait of Dwight Moody* (Boston: Little, Brown and Co., 1938), pp. 73–76. The image of a thrifty, puritanical matriarch emerges very strongly here.

this trying period suggest that Betsey weathered the storm largely unaided by people outside the family.[24] This triumph of self-help over poverty and adversity seems highly unlikely, however. The ties of kinship in Northfield were too numerous and deeply held to permit the family to suffer unaided. A host of Holtons in the area would see to that. Significantly, accounts of this period written by members of the Moody family all contain hints of precisely such assistance being offered.[25] Thus for young Dwight, these early years of difficulty not only served as lessons in thrift, hard work, and self-help, but also underscored the significance of the unity of the family, the importance of close ties with nearby relatives, and the fundamental value of simple yet deeply held familial attachments. Certainly his mother stood as a symbol of all these cherished attitudes throughout his life.

It would be a mistake to depict Betsey Moody solely as a rather dour, doughty New Englander. Underneath a rather grim exterior lurked feelings of tenderheartedness seldom evident to the outside world, yet apparently projected frequently into the midst of that private world which was her family.[26] For those interested in her evangelist son, this attribute assumes special meaning. As an adult, Dwight Moody demonstrated a sensitivity toward others and a softness of heart that at times bubbled almost instinctively to the surface. If he knew that he had hurt someone, he would seek immediately to apologize, sometimes publicly humiliating himself in the process; in one recorded instance in the bosom of his own family he broke into tears upon realizing the hurt that had accompanied a severe reprimand he had given to one of his children.[27]

24. For example, see J. Wilbur Chapman, *The Life and Work of Dwight L. Moody* (New York: W. E. Scull, 1900), pp. 45–47; John C. Pollock, *Moody: A Biographical Portrait of the Pacesetter in Modern Evangelism* (New York: Macmillan Co., 1963), p. 4; Richard K. Curtis, *They Called Him Mister Moody* (Garden City, N. Y.: Doubleday & Co., 1962), pp. 36–38.
25. Paul Moody, *My Father*, p. 73; W. R. Moody, *Moody* (1900), pp. 20–21.
26. For hints of this characteristic, see W. R. Moody, *Moody* (1900), p. 23.
27. Paul Moody, *My Father*, pp. 82–83; D. L. Moody to Miss Annie Anderson, July 27, 1868, typewritten copy of original in Moody Papers,

These actions were at least partially explainable by the age in which Moody lived, when sentimentality was widespread and often openly expressed. Yet "sentimentality" is too superficial a term to describe this particular trait of the evangelist. His actions suggest a certain feline grace — a touch of femininity — that seemed to be a rudimentary part of his personality. At the inner core of his being he lacked the toughness of fibre and ruthlessness of attitude that seemingly ought to have accompanied his unquestioned ambition, drive, and determination. It may not be wrong to conclude that this softness of heart stemmed partly from the fact that he lacked a father in his formative years, and that his mother, stern and formidable though she was, transmitted to this particular son some of her most womanly instincts. By some strange alchemy, early family experiences and relationships were transformed eventually into one of the most intriguing and appealing aspects of the personality of the revivalist of the 1870's.

Moody's early years in Northfield belied his later consuming interest in evangelical Protestantism. When he was five years old, he and the rest of the children were baptized as Unitarians, and on January 1, 1843, Betsey Moody became a member of the local Unitarian church.[28] Circumstantial evidence suggests, however, that for the Moodys Unitarianism was more a matter of personal taste than concern for and interest in theological controversy. In part, such a point of view was a reflection of the general attitude of the town toward religion. The Unitarian fellowship in Northfield had begun in 1827 when fifty-six members of the local Congregational church withdrew and formed a new society. This schism developed largely out of personal differences with the minister of the "orthodox" church, Thomas Mason. Many people assumed that after Mason's departure the two groups would reunite. Not until 1836, when the new church received a substantial endowment from one of its members linking it irrevocably with the "doctrines as taught at the Theological College in Cambridge," was it certain that the break would be permanent. Prior to 1827 Northfield Congregationalists had always identified with the liberal

Moody Bible Institute, Chicago, Ill.; D. W. Whittle Diary, November 27, 1876, Moody Bible Institute, Chicago.
    28. Powell, "Moody of Northfield," pp. 29b, 53.

wing of their denomination. They had strongly defended an earlier minister in the town charged with Arminianism, and in 1807 they openly sympathized with liberals in nearby Deerfield when a church council there refused to install the appointee of the congregation because of his lack of orthodoxy.[29] Thus the Unitarianism that Betsey Moody and her family learned never carried with it the overtones of heated debate and deeply felt schism which characterized the movement in Boston and other parts of New England.

Personal associations probably played the decisive role in drawing the Moody family into the Unitarian group. The minister of the church at the time of Edwin's death was Rev. Oliver Everett. He remained in Northfield until 1848 and during that time took a deep personal interest in the widow and her children. Betsey Moody joined the church at the time when this relationship was first developing. Although the evidence is not conclusive, there is reason to assume that Cyrus Holton and his family were also members of the Unitarian fellowship. If this is so, Betsey's tendency to lean on this brother for support in the difficult years following her husband's death may have helped her in the decision to join the Unitarians.[30]

Will Moody asserted in 1900 that "three books constituted the home library" in his father's childhood home — "a large family Bible . . . a catechism, and a book of devotions, comprising contemplations and written prayers." [31] Religious instruction from these sources apparently was of a distinctly non-theological nature. The first recorded instance of Dwight's thoughts on religion came shortly after he left home and went to Boston. As a condition for membership in the Mount Vernon Congregational Church in Boston, the deacons of the church tested the young man's theological perception. Revealing complete ignorance of even rudimentary facts and theories, Moody flunked his examination and was temporarily denied admission to the church. Late in life, when caught once in a reminiscent mood, Moody recalled that "I was 17 years

29. Parsons, *Puritan Outpost*, pp. 263–66, 277.
30. *Ibid.*, p. 303; *Greenfield* [Mass.] *Gazette and Courier*, April 22, 1867.
31. W. R. Moody, *Moody* (1900), p. 26.

old before I knew how to use a Bible." In this instance he was not too far off the mark.[32]

These incidents illuminate a religious upbringing that may come as a surprise to the reader who is familiar only with Moody the evangelist. Although the residents of Northfield spoke often of spiritual matters, theology was of little concern to most of them. The churches played several roles in the small town. They served as vehicles for a great deal of the organized social life of Northfield; they also proclaimed, and thus established, the prevailing patterns of morality and public conduct.[33] Thus religious faith was more an expression of piousness and conformity to moral standards for the entire community than of strong commitments to specific theological positions. Even though vague and imprecise in outline, the influence of such an environment on Moody cannot be entirely dismissed. This milieu served as a hazy, though necessary, backdrop to the more specific events and personal decisions of later years which eventually attracted the young man to his career as a great popular religious leader.

The liberal religious sentiments of Congregationalists in Northfield were also one reflection of an intellectual and cultural liveliness that expressed itself in the town throughout much of the nineteenth century. These activities worked as a counterforce to the parochialism inherent in village life generally, and in Northfield's relative geographical isolation in particular. In the years just prior to Moody's birth, the town had manifested a special interest in cultural affairs. A town library, one of the first in western Massachusetts, was organized in 1813 and operated continuously thereafter. In 1829 an academy for boys was incorporated, and a year later interested people established a local lyceum which became an important stimulant to the social and intellectual affairs of the community. These activities reflected the influence of a small but steady influx of young "outsiders" into Northfield. Many of these men were well educated; not too surprisingly many came from Boston and thus emphasized once again Northfield's

32. *Springfield* [Mass.] *Republican*, July 26, 1886.
33. For confirmation of these attitudes and practices see the *Greenfield* [Mass.] *Gazette and Courier*, February 4, 1867, February 18, 1867, April 22, 1867, October 14, 1867, December 7, 1868, January 4, 1869.

growing orientation toward the hub of New England. The outspoken and stimulating minister, Thomas Mason, had been instrumental in establishing the public library early in the century. The Northfield Academy had been financed and built by young men, only one of whom represented a long-established family in the town. The first preceptor of the academy was a young graduate of Harvard who quickly married into the family of the village's leading merchant, William Pomeroy. The community doctor, Thomas Mason's successor in the pulpit of the Congregational church, the second preceptor of the academy, and several young lawyers who were to become distinguished citizens — all arrived in the early 1830's. Several were graduates of Harvard, one a student at Princeton, and one or two, by means of marriage or kinship ties, had been fully exposed to the sophisticated life of certain upper class Boston families. The impact of such people on the small farming community was undoubtedly quite substantial.[34]

It is possible, however, to emphasize too strongly the intellectual and cultural achievements of the town during Moody's early years. The impact of these men and their thoughts upon the children of the town is especially difficult to measure. Probably for youths like Moody, formal education and debates at the lyceum or the local literary club were matters to be resisted, or to be ignored, or at the least to be placed in a secondary position to the primary task of having a good time. This was certainly Dwight's response. His schooling, for example, was spotty and inadequate. It included several years spent in grammar school and at least some time in the Northfield Academy for boys.[35] This latter fact in itself raises questions concerning the quality of the curriculum at this so-called secondary school. Henry Cutler, longtime superintendent of Mount Hermon School and a close friend of the evangelist in his

34. Parsons, *Puritan Outpost*, pp. 254–55, 266–74. For examples of the continuation of these tendencies in the life of the town a decade after Dwight Moody's departure, see the *Greenfield* [Mass.] *Gazette and Courier*, January 1, 1866, February 26, 1866, April 2, 1866, April 30, 1866, January 14, 1867, January 6, 1868, November 30, 1868, March 8, 1869, March 22, 1869.

35. Temple and Sheldon, *History of Northfield*, pp. 353, 361; *Third Annual Catalogue* (Northfield Institute, February, 1853), W. R. Moody Papers, East Northfield, Mass.

later years, once estimated that the sum of Moody's formal academic training was about the equivalent of a fifth-grade education in the twentieth century. If one judges the revivalist's education by the spelling and grammatical construction evident in all of his later correspondence, Cutler may have been overly optimistic. A telling comment came in 1875 from a New York reporter who was in Northfield seeking information about Moody's childhood. The reporter asserted that former schoolmates remembered the evangelist as "rather more remarkable for mischief than for close application to study." [36] In his adult years Moody came to recognize these weaknesses and was quite sensitive about them, although he never seemed to possess the time to correct the oversights of youth.[37]

The foregoing discussion suggests that in some ways the small-town milieu of Northfield was a study in contrasts, with perspective dependent upon the personal viewpoint of the observer. But in Moody's early days there undoubtedly was an underlying sense of unity, a deeply felt homogeneity of spirit that ultimately knit the community together. Seldom articulated publicly, these unspoken feelings and attitudes could only be perceived fully by observers of a later day and age. In the 1930's a lifelong resident of the town caught the essence of this spirit:

> Northfield . . . was unified in every interest. Its people knew each other to the last item of personality. They understood each other. Their differences in civic affairs were settled on a common basis of thrift and caution. . . . There were none very rich and few abjectly poor. The moderate fortunes, the fruit of slow accumulation, shrewd bargaining and honest labor, were snugly held. . . . There was an active social life, running to public entertainments, dramatic and musical, in which every spark of native talent was made to glow if it did not blaze. . . . Religious differences were respected, taken for granted, made no note of. There was never a voice

36. *Record of Christian Work*, 45 (July, 1926): 540; *New York Herald*, August 19, 1875.
37. For hints of Moody's feelings of inadequacy about his educational deficiencies, see the *Record of Christian Work*, 48 (August 21, 1929): 595; W. R. Moody to A. P. Fitt, January 7, 1907, W. R. Moody Papers.

raised nor an effort made to change one's church allegiance. No difference in faith carried beyond the church door.[38]

Here was an organic way of life, simple and uncomplicated on the surface, deeply conservative at its core, yet in many respects democratic in outlook and emphasis. Northfield represented well small-town America of the mid-nineteenth century; and the impact it had upon D. L. Moody, who lived there in his most impressionable years, was of lasting importance.

Emphasis has been placed on the fact that Moody's Northfield was representative of small-town America, not rural America of a century ago. The distinction is important. In the 1840's Northfield seemed to be a mixture of values and images that reflected both rural and urban influences. Throughout the nineteenth century agriculture remained the village's chief industry. The community was dependent upon farming for its continued existence. Nearly all men practicing specialized trades or professions there owned or lived on farms or small plots and thus conformed to the dominant pattern of communal life. The values and practices associated with the farmer were at all times a powerful, indeed predominant, influence in the community. Yet Northfield was more than an assemblage of farmers. The men in Moody's own family, for example, were artisans, people with specialized training, business interests, and a general outlook that did not necessarily coincide always with agrarian attitudes. Other members of the community, including some of the most influential citizens, by means of higher education or specialized professional training, helped to raise the cultural level and orient the town more to the outside world where farm and rural ways were declining in importance. Finally, by numerous means Boston extended her web of influences into the interior and subtly reoriented small towns like Northfield away from dependence upon the surrounding countryside and toward a new relationship with the forces of industrialization and urbanization.

In other words, small-town life was not coterminous with the world of the farmer and rural America. Historians have tended too often to speak of the rural-urban dichotomy in American his-

38. Parsons, *Puritan Outpost*, p. 338.

tory, lumping all segments of American society into one or the other of these categories. The small town, with a distinct way of life of its own, has unfairly been viewed simply as a portion of rural America.[39] In reality the small town in which Moody was born and lived his formative years served as a mediator, a critical point of contact between the distinctive modes of life associated with large urban centers and the farm. Attributes of city and farm existed side by side and shaped simultaneously the thoughts and actions of the town's inhabitants. Such was the case with Moody. He was deeply attached to the simple, slow-paced atmosphere of Northfield, yet as he grew older the outside world, particularly the irresistible city of Boston, tugged at his sensibilities. Eventually he left Northfield, yet the tension between rural and urban worlds that his early experiences had embedded in him remained. This dual attraction explains in large part his return to his birthplace in 1875, his decision to live in the town thereafter, and his constant effort to carry on as a revivalist in the eighties and nineties away from Northfield in the great urban centers of the country. Few of his contemporaries were able to act as he did — to live, quite literally, in both worlds. Yet his feelings were undoubtedly sensed and shared by the millions moving from countryside and village to the city in those days. Surely this dual aspect of Moody's thought and action, shaped fundamentally by his early years in Northfield, was a crucial element in the mass appeal he generated as an evangelist in the years following the Civil War.

Sometime early in 1854 Moody left Northfield to go to Boston to live. Since colonial days the hub of New England had been one of the principal ports of the country, flourishing on the strength of its shipping interests and its trade with the outside world. In the first half of the nineteenth century, Boston's eminence as a commercial entrepôt had begun to wane as a result of the emergence of the nearby port of New York to predominance over the entire

39. Rural sociologists have long noted some of the distinctions in small-town life which historians have ignored. A pioneering sociological treatise is Harlan Paul Douglass' *The Little Town* (New York: Macmillan Co., 1921). More recently Anselm Strauss, in *Images of the American City* (Glencoe, Ill.: The Free Press, 1961), made suggestive comments on the subject, although in a much different interpretive framework than Douglass' work.

country. Yet almost simultaneously, New England, with its abundance of natural water power and ready access to the trade lanes of the world, became the chief manufacturing region of America. Boston businessmen played a central role in pushing forward these developments, providing the capital and technical know-how to bring textile mills and railroads into existence. Thus, in reponse to these new economic forces, the city flourished in the years just prior to the Civil War, consolidating and then extending its influence throughout the rural sections of New England.[40] The not inconsiderable effect the city had on the village of Northfield has already been suggested. Moody's plan, then, to break from his family and start life on his own in Boston was a natural and logical step to take.

Furthermore, the danger of economic deprivation and possible failure occasioned by this break from family and home was reduced by the presence of relatives in Boston who could be of great assistance. An uncle, Samuel Holton, owned a retail boot and shoe store in the city, and undoubtedly the youth knew that he could find succor there if he were otherwise unsuccessful in establishing himself. Fruitless in his initial search for a job, the young man swallowed his pride after a short time and joined forces with his uncle.

The boot and shoe industry had become one of the principal underpinnings of the business and manufacturing complex developing in and around Boston in the pre–Civil War years. The industry had been a part of the Massachusetts economy since colonial days, but was undergoing a major transformation at the precise moment that young Moody came to Boston and became a boot and shoe salesman. Much of the manufacturing process took place in towns adjacent to the metropolitan area; prior to 1840 brogans were produced principally by the "putting out system," harking back to an age of craftsmen and semi-industrial processes. By the 1850's this system had changed drastically. The invention and use of sewing machines, pegging machinery, and mechanical

40. Justin Winsor, ed., *The Memorial History of Boston*, 4 vols. (Boston: James R. Osgood & Co., 1881), 4, chaps. 3–6, 8; Samuel E. Morison, *The Maritime History of Massachusetts, 1783–1860* (Boston: Houghton Mifflin Co., 1921), chap. 15; Kirkland, *Men, Cities, and Transportation*, vol. 1, chap. 6.

leather strippers and cutters made it possible to produce footwear in greater quantities and in much more precise categories of size and shape. Consequently, the entire process of production was gathered under one roof. Instituting the factory system revolutionized the industry and made it possible for shoe manufacturers to meet the expanding demand for shoes developing in the urban centers of the United States.[41] Boston thus served the boot and shoe industry in several ways — as a financial prop, as a crucial point for distribution of the finished product to the outside world, and as a representative part of the expanding urban market that enabled the industry to flourish. It was in this latter aspect of the business that Moody now found himself engaged, his activities reflecting a larger economic order that was being transformed by the forces of industrialization.

In many ways the young man seemed representative of those who had come to Boston seeking their fortunes and a newer, more exciting manner of life. The uncertainty and loneliness of his first days left vivid memories frequently recounted in later years. He took a room at 75 Court Street, in an area near the Boston Common (and close to his uncle's shoe shop) which offered numerous boarding houses for the convenience of new arrivals in the city. Perhaps his uncertainty was reflected in the fact that he wrote home frequently. In any case, these early letters, a few of which have been preserved, reveal his involvement in the life of the city. He eyed the girls who lived in a boarding house near his own. He went down to the wharves and watched immigrants come ashore, to be met joyfully by friends and relatives. With mock seriousness he chided his sister for inquiring about the pickpockets that get "fat by picking my pockets." Yet simultaneously he inquired constantly about affairs at home, the condition of crops and animals, what relatives and friends were doing.[42]

41. Blanche E. Hazard, *The Organization of the Boot and Shoe Industry in Massachusetts Before 1875* (Cambridge: Harvard University Press, 1921), chaps. 3–5; Winsor, *Memorial History of Boston*, 4:99.
42. *Boston Directory for the Year 1854* (Boston: George Adams, July 1, 1854), pp. 160, 219, 339; D. L. Moody to "Sister Lizzie," May 4, 1854, D. L. Moody to George Moody, May 4, 1854, D. L. Moody to "brothers," April 9, 1854, typewritten copies of letters in Moody Papers, Powell; MS note by Henry Rankin, March, 1900, Henry M. Rankin Papers, Mount Hermon School Library, Mount Hermon, Mass.

In retrospect, the most important thing to be remembered about Moody's two years in Boston was that while there he took his first steps toward a permanent religious commitment. During his earliest days in the city he demonstrated no particular interest in things of the spirit, at least if one is to judge from the letters he dispatched to relatives in Northfield.[43] The vague religious influences of his childhood may have made him generally receptive to the idea of joining the Boston YMCA, but other motivations were also operative when he became a member of that Christian association in the late spring or summer of 1854. As he explained to his brothers, "I shall have a place to go to when I want to go anywhere. . . . I shall have all the books I want to read free from expense, only have to pay one dollar a year. They have a large room and the smart men of Boston lecter [*sic*] to them for nothing and they get up a question box." [44] Moody saw the YMCA as a place providing useful services for young men like himself and as a vehicle for broadening his social horizons a bit. At the moment its religious purposes apparently counted for very little.

Evangelical Protestantism faced in Boston and other cities a new challenge comparable in scope and complexity to the problems posed by the rapid advance of American society into unsettled areas in the early decades of the nineteenth century. It did not take long for church people who came to these urban centers to see that one crucial group that deserved their attention were the thousands of young native Americans drawn to the cities by opportunities for economic advancement. Many of these young people were the offspring of evangelical households, making them prime candidates for the evangelistic efforts of the denominations. Moreover, they faced fewer obstacles than the immigrants, who were also flocking to the cities, in making their way quickly up the social and economic ladder. Thus these young men were quite likely to become the principal community leaders a decade or so hence. If the evangelical churches were to retain a significant posi-

43. D. L. Moody to George, Samuel, and Warren Moody, April 4, 1854, D. L. Moody to "Lizzie," May 4, 1854, D. L. Moody to George Moody, May 4, 1854, D. L. Moody to Samuel Moody, May 4, 1854, Moody Papers, Powell.
44. D. L. Moody to George, Samuel and Warren Moody, April 4, 1854, *ibid.*

tion of influence in these urban centers, they would have to mount some sort of concerted effort to retain the allegiance of the younger generation.

The YMCA was ideally suited to meet the challenge thus posed. Organized by young businessmen, attached specifically to no single denomination or local church, dispensing even with the familiar institutional apparatus and physical plant of a church in favor of "meeting rooms" in the business district, the YMCA blended perfectly into the commercial milieu of the cities that was becoming such a powerful attractive force for American youth.

Moody represented precisely the kind of individual the Association members hoped to lure into their organization. The Boston YMCA had been founded only two years before Moody's arrival, the first such group to be organized in the United States. The charter members were all members of evangelical Protestant churches who sought to bring the influence of their religious faith into the midst of those young men who had recently come from the backcountry to the city. Although they may have used somewhat indirect means to gain the attention of these young men, such as a reading room stocked with regional newspapers, a library, public lectures, and "Literary classes," there could be no mistaking their ultimate intent. The first annual report of the Association, commenting that "Christians in Boston have long seen with sorrow, the allurements to evil that surround the young men of the city," indicated that the Association had decided to organize a "social organization" which "shall meet the young stranger as he enters our city, take him by the hand, direct him to a boarding house where he may find a quiet home pervaded with Christian influences, introduce him to the Church and Sabbath School, bring him to the Rooms of the Association, and in every way throw around him good influences, so that he may feel that he is not a stranger, but that noble and Christian spirits care for his soul." Full membership was awarded only to recognized communicants of the evangelical churches of the community.[45]

45. William B. Whiteside, *The Boston Y.M.C.A. and Community Need: A Century's Evolution, 1851–1951* (New York: Association Press, 1951), pp. 21, 30–33, 36. Since Moody was at least nominally a Unitarian, he probably never received full membership. However, any man of "good moral character" could be an associate member, and this was undoubtedly

The earliest records of the Boston YMCA give some indication of the success of this mission among newcomers to the city and also suggest that Moody may have liked to go there partly because he was among his own kind. In the spring of 1854, at the time the youth from Northfield first indicated an interest in the YMCA, the membership rolls contained slightly less than a thousand names. Over fifty per cent of these people were born outside of Boston, yet in New England. There were a few professional men among them, but the overwhelming majority were clerks, bookkeepers, banktellers, and salesmen — that is, middle-class, white-collar workers like Moody.[46] The Boston YMCA had obvious attractions for a young man of Moody's upbringing and training. Most significantly, its religious orientation was definite and was carefully injected by a variety of means into the daily program. Thus although Moody may have entered the Association rather breezily, essentially unconcerned about religious matters, his involvement placed him in a position where the manifold influences of the evangelical Protestants of Boston could begin in a direct way to shape and restructure his life.

Even more important than the YMCA as an influence on Moody were the direct contacts he established with one of the leading evangelical churches in Boston. His reasons for initiating these contacts were just as revealing of his earliest religious attitudes as were his explanations for joining the YMCA. There is some evidence to suggest that he "shopped around" for a time, but that eventually he agreed to fulfill a demand made of him by his uncle at the time of his employment that he must attend the services of one church regularly. Probably within a few weeks after his arrival in Boston, Moody began to attend services at the Mount Vernon Congregational Church.[47] It seems certain, however, that

his officially sanctioned position. (*Ibid.*, p. 19.) See also *Congregationalist*, 4 (January 9, 1852): 6.

46. Whiteside, *The Boston Y.M.C.A.*, pp. 28–29.

47. The scarcity of source materials prevents one from developing an exact understanding of when Moody began attending services at the Mount Vernon Church. All available materials, which are either reminiscences or secondary accounts, contain contradictions. See, for example, *Sunday School Times* (April 8, 1876): 225–26; Powell, "Moody of Northfield," p. 65; W. R. Moody, *Moody* (1900), p. 39.

the young man did not undertake these activities because of a strong religious commitment.

Nevertheless, the Mount Vernon Church immediately began to exert its influence on Moody. In some respects the church was uniquely qualified to introduce this small-town youth into the special world of evangelical Protestantism. At the time of Moody's arrival it was, by Boston's standards, a relatively new church, organized in the early 1840's. Since its first days the minister had been Rev. Edward N. Kirk, and his distinctive stamp had been placed on the congregation. Prior to his pastorate at Mount Vernon, Kirk had been a respected and widely-known evangelist who traveled throughout New England "preaching up" revivals. Revivalism was of central concern to all evangelicals, and it was certainly at the heart of the work and thought of Kirk's gathering of believers. In the 1870's one of his former parishioners asserted with great conviction that the church was organized "as a *revival church*," and, perhaps even more to the point, was conceived from the beginning as a way to retain in Boston "the fiery eloquence, the holy zeal, and the glowing fervor of Edward N. Kirk, which, wherever he preached, had melted hardened sinners to penitence and love." [48]

Attending Sunday school and church services regularly, the impressionable young man could not help being affected by the people with whom he was associating. Moody's Sunday school teacher, Edward Kimball, eventually effected the youth's conversion. Probably as a part of his regular efforts to press the concerns of the church on those inquirers who were interested, yet not within the circle of faith, Kimball came to Samuel Holton's shoe store on April 21, 1855. Finding Moody in the back of the store wrapping shoes, Kimball asked the boy if he were ready to commit himself to Christ and "simply told him of Christ's love for him and the love Christ wanted in return." To these disarming gestures Moody's response was positive. In later years he was to assert that the experience meant simply that the following day the "old sun shone

48. *Sunday School Times* (April 8, 1876): 226. See also David O. Mears, *The Life of Edward Norris Kirk, D. D.* (Boston: Lockwood, Brooks, & Co., 1877), chaps. 8–9; Edward N. Kirk, *Lectures on Revivals* (Boston: Congregational Publishing Society, 1875), *passim*.

a good deal brighter than it ever had before . . . I fell in love
with the birds. . . . It seemed to me I was in love with all creation." [49]

Judging from his own words, it is hard to believe that Moody's
conversion was deeply felt at the time. Instead, it seemed to be
merely a part of the rather generalized interest in religion which
the lad was now beginning to demonstrate. The spirit came perhaps, but assuredly it brought no knowledge. On May 16, 1855,
Moody presented himself for examination by the deacons at the
Mount Vernon Church as a prelude to his acceptance into the
membership of the church. He was so lacking in understanding
that his examiners flatly rejected his candidacy. Kimball, who was
present at the examination, revealed at a later date in almost em-
barrassingly straightforward language Moody's inadequacies. He
"could not tell what it was to be a Christian; had no idea of what
Christ had done for him; and with the utmost encouragement . . .
he could answer but haltingly, chiefly in monosyllables, and then
only when the question was of the simplest, and its answer was
obvious. . . . Nothing was elicited at this interview which any
pastor or church committee could have considered satisfactory
evidence of his conversion." [50]

Moody's disastrous performance may have been partly the result
of stage fright, for he did have to face a rather august and over-
bearing assemblage of men.[51] But he also lacked even the most
rudimentary religious knowledge. After the examination he was
taken under the wing of two individuals specifically assigned to
the task of teaching him and others like him "the way of God
more perfectly." Yet when he again stood before the examining
committee almost a year later, "little more light appeared" and

49. Kimball's recollection of the incident is in the *Sunday School
Times* (April 8, 1876): 226. For Moody's statement see W. R. Moody,
Moody (1900), p. 41. The precise dating of Moody's conversion has been
presented convincingly by Elmer W. Powell in data included in a folder
entitled "Powell, Dr. Elmer," in the Moody Papers, Moody Bible
Institute.

50. *Sunday School Times* (April 8, 1876): 226. Kimball's account is generally supported by statements of E. N. Kirk, reprinted in Mears, *The
Life of Edward Kirk*, p. 227, and especially in a statement of former officers of the Mount Vernon Church printed in *Advance*, 10 (October 5,
1876): 79.

51. In support of this statement, see *Advance*, 2 (December 10, 1868): 6.

"he was still unable to give any intelligent reason for hoping that he had given his heart to God." Probably unintentionally, these words presented a severe indictment of the particular evangelical church's efforts at education of the young. Yet Moody was a determined and intent young fellow, with or without effective support from the church. With all of his weaknesses, the examining committee admitted him to membership "in view of his evident sincerity and earnest determination to be a Christian." He signed the membership rolls on May 3, 1856.[52]

Placed in the proper historical context, Moody's conversion experience appears as part of a relatively placid sequence of developments. It simply gave some sort of overt confirmation to a general tendency of his to be interested in religious matters. It was, in the last analysis, a not too startling extension of aspects of his childhood training, sharpened by his recent experiences in Boston, chiefly those connected with the YMCA and the Mount Vernon Church. No dark doubts assailed him prior to his conversion; his sunny and optimistic disposition remained unchanged by the experience. In William James's apt phrase, Moody's conversion experience was a "healthy minded" response.[53]

Nevertheless, it would be unfair to assert that the young man was largely unaffected by his religious awakening in Boston. Despite the seeming superficiality of it all, Moody had set out upon a new path. His cumulative experience in Boston with evangelical Protestantism, in a variety of institutional and personal contacts, *had* produced a change in his attitudes. The earliest and clearest evidence of this shift in sentiment is to be found in the first letters that he wrote to his family after he had left Boston for Chicago. These

52. *Sunday School Times* (April 8, 1876): 226; Membership Book, Mount Vernon Church, (Mount Vernon Church, Boston, Mass.), p. 28; Pauline Holmes, *One Hundred Years of Mount Vernon Church, 1842–1942* (Brattleboro, Vermont: Mount Vernon Church of Boston, 1942), p. 192.

53. William James, *The Varieties of Religious Experience: A Study in Human Nature* (New York: Longmans, Green and Co., 1929), contains many illuminating insights into the general nature of the conversion experience as a religious phenomenon. A man who observed Moody during his association with Mount Vernon Church testified in 1867 that "its remarkable that he [Moody] should be looking so much [now] for immediate conversion[s] when he was brought so gradually himself." (*Revival* [London], 16 [July 11, 1867]: 386.)

sources show that his interest in spiritual affairs had grown considerably from his pre-conversion days two years earlier. In a letter to his mother he spoke of two ladies who helped him on the train coming to Chicago. Commenting on their kindness he asserted that "they were so good Christians I fairly love them." After visiting with the family of his uncle who lived near Chicago, he noted with approval that they were "all religious." He followed the practice he had begun in Boston of attending prayer meetings regularly. Three months after his arrival he, like any knowledgeable evangelical, was exhorting one of his brothers in Northfield to "tend meeting regular" as a step towards a more conscious Christian commitment. From this time forward such exhortations and explicit quests after the souls of his relatives became standard features of letters mailed to Massachusetts.[54]

Moody had decided to move to Chicago shortly after his admission to the Mount Vernon Church. There are several explanations for this act. In the letters the youth wrote after he left Boston, he suggested to some of his relatives that he had had disagreements with his uncle which made their relations tense and uncomfortable.[55] Almost a year before he left he had begun to consider a move westward, and the tensions with Samuel Holton probably helped to make Chicago even more attractive to him. Close relatives also lived in the area to which he eventually migrated. An older brother, Isaiah, lived in Detroit, and another uncle, Calvin Holton, lived on a farm close to Chicago, near what is now the town of Des Plaines.[56] Again he would be near friends who could help him if he found it impossible to sustain himself alone in the

54. D. L. Moody to Betsey Moody, September 25, 1856, D. L. Moody to "brother," December 16, 1855, Moody Papers, Powell. No effort has been made to correct the obvious misspellings and other illiteracies which occur frequently in Moody's correspondence. His poor grammar is left untouched in order to preserve the flavor of his writing.

55. The explanations Moody gave his mother for leaving played down his differences with her brother. In letters to other members of the family, however, he made this conflict clear. (D. L. Moody to Betsey Moody, September 25, 1856, October 6, 1856, October 7, 1856, December 16, 1856, D. L. Moody to "sister," October 6, 1856, D. L. Moody to Warren Moody, October 19, 1856, *ibid.*)

56. D. L. Moody to "family," October 11, 1855, D. L. Moody to Betsey Moody, September 25, 1856, D. L. Moody to George Moody, March 17, 1857, *ibid.*; Temple and Sheldon, *History of Northfield*, p. 464.

new environment. Finally, Chicago could be all but irresistible to a young man of Moody's makeup. Energetic and ambitious, he was eager to get ahead in the world. His brief experience as a boot and shoe salesman provided him with a marketable skill that could be the means of working his way quickly into the business world of the Windy City. The youthful metropolis of the West was the embodiment of an expansive urban culture that was rapidly enveloping the United States. Shortly after his arrival in the city Moody viewed Chicago as "very lively . . . much more so than Boston." The excitement and glitter of the metropolis, and especially the possibilities of economic advancement, seemed to be the basic reasons why Moody went west. Two decades later, former associates of his in Boston were correct when they asserted that Moody went to Chicago "as thousands of other young men have done, solely with reference to advantages for business." On September 11, 1856, he arrived in the booming city at the southern end of Lake Michigan, eager to throw himself into the mainstream of affairs there.[57]

57. D. L. Moody to Betsey Moody, September 25, 1856, October 6, 1856, Moody Papers, Powell; *Advance*, 10 (October 5, 1876): 79.

2

Chicago in the 1850's:
Earnest Christian

The lustry brawling giant of a city that leaps from the lines of
Carl Sandburg's famous poem eulogizing Chicago was only a
toddler at the time Moody arrived there. But a foretaste of the
future was already in the air. Though it had been a mere village
on America's frontier only twenty years earlier, in the mid-1850's
the city had a population of about 80,000. Participants in the
life of the city found it an exciting place to be. Any attempt at
description seemed always couched in superlatives. "Chicago is a
marvel of cities; her growth is marvelous; her prospects are marvelous; the conduct of her people are [*sic*] marvelous." The sense
of forward movement in such a place was pervasive. "Everybody
is in a hurry. The pedestrian of the sidewalk moves as if he was
walking for a wager. The sturdy drayman thunder[s] and blun-
der[s] along, vying in speed with the 'fast' horse, with his airy,
Queen Knab like, vehicle. Merchants and clerks are always on
their feet. . . . Chicago is not the place for loungers, or loafers." [1]

Two facts of overriding importance promoted the rapid development of the city. The first was Chicago's strategic location. Situated at a point where she could serve as the entrepôt for the
entire upper Mississippi Valley, she stood athwart a major north-
south axis of transportation, connected to the Mississippi River by

1. *Northwestern Christian Advocate*, 4 (August 6, 1857): 126.

the Illinois and Michigan Canal, and to eastern ports by the Great Lakes. With the coming of the railroad the city linked itself much more directly with the great centers of commerce on the East Coast. Future greatness was assured when railroads reached the city. Even before the Civil War, iron rails radiated out in all directions from the southern tip of Lake Michigan. Like the tentacles of a giant sea monster thrown up on the shore, the railroads snaked westward into the limitless grain fields, drawing to Chicago great quantities of wheat, corn, and livestock, to be processed and sent to consumers further east. In 1856, eleven major trunk lines centered their operations in Chicago. The first railroad had entered the town only eight years earlier, while traffic with the East had begun as recently as 1852. Yet by 1856, the Chicago railroads were already doing a business of over seventeen million dollars annually and were helping to create in the city a complex economy and a cosmopolitan urban society.[2]

Trains entering Chicago from the East were often coach and Pullman cars carrying human cargo. The mushrooming factories and business establishments needed workers, as did the rapidly expanding farming areas of the nearby prairies. Native Americans and immigrants from overseas arrived daily by the thousands on the Michigan Southern or the Michigan Central. Many pushed on to places elsewhere in the West, but a sizable portion came to Chicago to stay. Moody joined a large number of fellow Easterners in Chicago. In 1850 people from New England and the Middle Atlantic states made up 47 per cent of the native-born population. They brought with them their distinctive ways of living and patterns of thought, adding much to the cultural milieu of the city. Many became the principal businessmen — clerks, salesmen, small and large business owners.[3]

By mid-century foreign born persons made up over half the city's population. Thus early in its history Chicago was in some ways a more cosmopolitan center than New York. The largest groups of immigrants came from Ireland, Germany, the Scandinavian

2. William Bross, *History of Chicago* (Chicago: Jansen, McClurg, 1876), pp. 71, 126.
3. Bessie Pierce, *A History of Chicago*, 3 vols. (New York: Alfred A. Knopf, 1937–57), 2:10, 81.

countries, England, France, and Scotland.[4] The poorer elements among these people, especially the Irish and the Germans, tended to congregate in slumlike districts on the near north side. The immigrants, whom Moody first noticed in Boston and who swelled the population of Chicago in the 1850's, reflected social changes that were nationwide in their impact. These people brought to the cities problems of illiteracy, low economic standards, and over-crowding. Their strange customs and patterns of living made it difficult for native Americans to accept them easily.

Moody himself reflected some of these new tensions in American life. Shortly after his arrival in Chicago he wrote to his family in Massachusetts, commenting emphatically about the "wicked city" in which he lived, where "many of the folks keep the stores open on the holy Sabbath," a practice which was "enough to sicken anyone." [5] Probably the shocked young New Englander was observing the practices of the German immigrants who lived on the north side of Chicago and who kept shops and beer gardens open on Sunday. Moody's remarks also revealed a bit of his developing religious sympathies. Evangelical Protestants took strong stands on the question of preserving the holy Sabbath, and on maintaining a circumspect personal life. Drinking, dancing, and card playing were taboo. People with such attitudes were quick to frown upon, or at least to misunderstand, the practices of recent arrivals from the Old World. Not too surprisingly, in the 1850's nativism and evangelicalism often flourished in the same quarters.[6] It is not true, however, that Moody turned with disdain from these people. The immigrants and the poorer groups in Chicago were soon to become one of his chief concerns. Later in life he came to call these people

4. *Ibid.*, pp. 13–22.

5. D. L. Moody to Betsey Moody, September 25, 1856, D. L. Moody to Warren Moody, October 19, 1856, Moody Papers, Mrs. E. M. Powell, East Northfield, Massachusetts. See also D. L. Moody to "brother," December 16, 1856, *ibid.*; Bessie L. Pierce, ed., *As Others See Chicago: Impressions of Visitors, 1673–1933* (Chicago: University of Chicago Press, 1933), p. 168.

6. Clifford S. Griffin, *Their Brothers' Keepers: Moral Stewardship in the United States, 1800–1865* (New Brunswick, N. J.: Rutgers University Press, 1960), pp. 207–18; Ray A. Billington, *The Protestant Crusade, 1800–1860: A Study of the Origins of American Nativism* (New York: Rinehart & Co., 1938), chap. 13 and *passim*.

the "unsaved masses," and he worried a great deal over his seeming inability to reach them. In any case he was forced early in his career to experience the discords of a new way of life that was emerging out of the melting pot of great new urban centers like Chicago.

When he reached Chicago, Moody was quick to notice the sprawling, though orderly, organization of the town. In a letter home he commented: "You can stand and look as far as the eye can reach and try to walk out of the city but it is impossible. . . . The population of Chicago is not more than 100,000 but it is so scattered it covers over four times the ground that Boston does," although the streets are "all lade out strate and broad." He went on to note another interesting topographical characteristic — that "Lake Michigan is almost as high as Chicago itself." Buildings in the business area, originally built at lake level, were ordered elevated by successive city ordinances in the 1850's. The jacking up of these buildings without a corresponding regrading of the streets produced a crazy patchwork of streets and sidewalk elevations. Moody observed that because of the low-lying land, water stood in the streets all but "two or three months in the year." Thus much of the time thoroughfares were bottomless seas of mud. Nevertheless, despite the fact that the city was "very dirty," Moody felt that it was "healthy hear." [7]

Chicago was a study in contrasts. Along with hovels for the immigrants and a jerry-built downtown section, the city could also boast fine homes facing the lake along Michigan and Wabash Avenues where wealthy merchants and the leaders of Chicago society lived. Perhaps with an eye to his own future prospects, Moody was quick to discover this area of the city and to comment upon it in letters back home. He felt that the city had "about the nicest dwelling houses I ever see." [8] Well-to-do homeowners on the

7. D. L. Moody to George, Edwin, Warren, and Samuel Moody, January 6, 1857, Moody Papers, Powell. See also D. L. Moody to "Mother," October 6, 1856, *ibid.*; Pierce, *As Others See Chicago*, pp. 157–58; Caroline Kirkland, *Chicago Yesterdays: A Sheaf of Reminiscences* (Chicago: Daughaday, 1919), pp. 52–53.

8. D. L. Moody to George, Edwin, Warren, and Samuel Moody, January 6, 1857, Moody Papers, Powell.

north side lived a rather sedate life, residing in frame residences with many columns surrounded by spacious, wooded grounds. On the south side houses grew up in close proximity to their owners' businesses. These southside homes were characteristically faced on the front with white marble slabs cut from limestone deposits located near the Illinois Canal. The daughter of one of Moody's closest Chicago friends remembered much later how these house fronts "glistened in the sunshine, and in the moonlight shone resplendent in their pale glory," and were "enhanced further by the well-kept lawns and bright-colored flower gardens around them." [9] These extremes of wealth and slums, of beautiful homes and muddy unpaved streets, mirrored a turbulence associated with dynamic growth. Raw and not yet fully formed, the city and its optimistic citizens looked always to the future.

For nearly every Chicagoan it appeared that business was the overpowering concern, and the inhabitants of the city spoke of it with authority. One asserted in 1856 that "the main-spring of action in Chicago, is the desire for wealth, with the growing prospect of success, which is exemplified by the success of so many." Another spoke aptly of fellow Chicagoans and their "real-estate airs." A foreign visitor of the 1850's remarked that "it seemed as if, on all hands, people came here merely to trade, to make money, and not to live." [10] This was a milieu in which Moody thrived. Plunging into the whirl of affairs, he became a clerk for E. E. Wiswall, owner of a retail boot and shoe company.[11]

By the time Moody reached Chicago the boot and shoe industry was fast becoming one of the most important segments of the rapidly expanding economy of the city. The first wholesale boot and shoe houses had been established only a year or two before his arrival; a decade later sixteen such firms were in operation. By 1864 there were over two hundred retail dealers and total sales of the industry were estimated to be $14,000,000.[12] Whether he realized it

9. Abby Farwell Ferry, *Reminiscences of John V. Farwell by His Elder Daughter*, 2 vols. (Chicago: R. F. Seymour, 1928), 2:51, 52.
10. *Northwestern Christian Advocate*, 4 (August 6, 1856): 126; Pierce, *History of Chicago*, 2:474; Pierce, *As Others See Chicago*, p. 129.
11. *D. B. Cooke and Company's Chicago City Directory for the Year 1858* (Chicago, January 1, 1858), p. 202.
12. Pierce, *History of Chicago*, 2:110.

at the time or not, Moody was entering a business where the opportunities for rapid advancement were most propitious. From the outset he seemed well satisfied. He wrote to one of his brothers that he was "in the largest retail store in the city, get good pay, good man to work for." He boasted to his mother that "I hav me one of the best situations in the city." A few months after his arrival he wrote his family with typical optimism that "the men that come out here and settled ten years ago are worth from ten to fifty thousand dollars." With perhaps somewhat less accuracy, he went on to assert that "we seldom ever see a poor person hear and very little stealing goin on hear." [13]

Moody's letters contained numerous references to a steadily improving economic position. He was making about thirty dollars a week. This was sufficient to provide a little surplus capital, which he used to speculate modestly in real estate. Boom conditions and rising prices made real estate dealings highly remunerative. Barely five months after he had arrived, Moody was investing in land in the Des Plaines area near his uncle's farm. He hoped to receive double the original investment on the property near Des Plaines and a 25 per cent profit from all other transactions of this kind in the future. [14]

He was also lending money to people in small sums. In one letter he asserted that he "lent $100 the other day and got seventeen per cent a day." If such exorbitant rates of interest were actually in effect, it is understandable why he could now elaborate on an earlier comparison of Boston and Chicago by stating that "I can make more hear in one weak than I could in Boston in a month." The moneymaking fever so overcame him that in the spring of

13. D. L. Moody to Warren Moody, October 19, 1856, D. L. Moody to Betsey Moody, October 6, 1857, D. L. Moody to George, Edwin, Warren, and Samuel Moody, January 6, 1857, Moody Papers, Powell. The young salesman also reflected the political persuasion of many of Chicago's businessmen, for he wrote his brothers at the time of the national elections in 1856: "I suppose you see in the papers that it is good for Fremont 15 shure and I guess more. I want you to send me the Greenfield paper that will tell me how old Northfield is again." (D. L. Moody to George, Edwin, and Samuel Moody, October 6, 1856, *ibid.*)

14. D. L. Moody to Betsey Moody, October 6, 1856, D. L. Moody to George, Edwin, Warren and Samuel Moody, January 6, 1857, *ibid.*

1857 he turned down a request from one of his brothers in North-field for financial aid in favor of the dazzling profits which seemed to lie immediately before him in the Middle West.[15]

Sometime late in 1857 or early in 1858 Moody left Wiswall's employ and became a salesman for C. N. Henderson, another boot and shoe dealer.[16] Part of his new responsibility entailed the collection of debts owed to his employer by customers scattered throughout Illinois. The young man's new job reflected a change that was occurring in the Chicago consumer goods industries as the economy of the city evolved into more complex structures. Until about 1850 most merchants served only as retailers, ordering supplies from eastern wholesale houses. With the coming of the railroad, many of the retailers attempted also to develop a wholesale trade with the prairie hinterland. Traveling salesmen and collection agents representing these Chicago merchants fanned out over the plains. The influence of eastern wholesalers was all but destroyed; the fabled figure of the traveling salesman came to serve as the symbol of the dominance of Chicago over the wholesale trade of the Mississippi Valley.[17]

Moody was on the road much of the time, traveling all over the state of Illinois. He obviously enjoyed his new position. He said to his brother that he liked it "better than anything I have ever done." In part he was enthused by new experiences and travel to new places. He was able to compare southern and northern Illinois with a knowledgeable air to attentive listeners in New England; and he could toss off comments casually about people he had met in St. Louis, Centralia, and Cairo, and about travelers from Cincinnati. He exclaimed to his brother that "it is nothing but excitement all of the time." The new job also provided another boost to his personal affluence. He did most of his work in the towns strung out along the railroads. This fact enabled him to boast to his family that he was being put up in "the best Houses" and that he was able largely to avoid the backcountry. Only occasionally

15. D. L. Moody to George Moody, March 17, 1857, *ibid.*
16. *D. B. Cooke and Company's Chicago City Directory for the Year 1859–1860* (Chicago, 1859), p. 287.
17. Pierce, *A History of Chicago*, 2:106–07.

did he "have to cross the Praries with a horse" and if he did he always had "a good one." [18]

His collections for Henderson were at first sporadic, as the recent depression of 1857 had made times hard. "I started the first of this month with $10,000 worth of notes," he wrote early in 1858, "& have not collected on $1,000 yet." Because of the scarcity of money he was forced to barter in agricultural goods — "we have to take horses, cattle, wheat, corn, oats, barley, Reepers & more land morgages." Only a short time later, however, his letters showed that the country was moving out of this economic slump. In May, 1858, he had to put off a contemplated visit to New England because business was so good that he felt he could not leave. A year later, in the summer of 1859, on returning from a business trip which took him along the upper reaches of the Mississippi River he wrote to his family, "the western country has not looked so well for years as it does now. Wheat is ripe . . . grate fields of grain as far as the eye can reach. I tell you if wheat bring a good price this fall things will look different in the western country." [19]

In line with his boomer spirit, Moody was enormously energetic and hard-working. Even when he was in Chicago he labored incessantly at the job of attracting customers and pushing sales for his employer. He far exceeded the other clerks in his devotion to duty. When customers did not readily appear in the store he would stand outside, or even walk the streets, hoping to drum up trade. He adopted the practice of watching the depots and checking the hotel registers to locate possible out-of-town customers who might be steered to the jobbing department of his boot and shoe company. Privately he set a goal of $100,000 as the size of the fortune he hoped to accumulate eventually. By 1860 he already had saved $7,000.[20] The young man appeared to lux-

18. D. L. Moody to "brother," February 22, 1858, D. L. Moody to Betsey Moody, May 21, 1858, Moody Papers, Powell.

19. D. L. Moody to "brother," February 22, 1858, D. L. Moody to Betsey Moody, May 21, 1858, D. L. Moody to "brother" (Samuel), July 18, 1859, *ibid.*

20. William H. Daniels, *D. L. Moody and His Work* (Hartford, Conn.: American Publishing Co., 1876), pp. 79–80; William R. Moody, *The Life* of D. L. Moody (New York: Fleming H. Revell Co., 1900), p. 48.

uriate in the materialistic, intensely competitive world of business which captivated all Chicagoans in the 1850's.

Moody's drive and determination singled him out as a comer. His employer, Mr. Henderson, evidently took a special interest in him. When the older man died suddenly late in 1858, Moody wrote home that he would "miss him very much. He seemed to take as much interest in my welfare as he would in the welfare of his own son." But Henderson's death necessitated a change in employers, and Moody moved on to a position with Buel, Hill, and Granger, another boot and shoe company. Even so, his business abilities were not forgotten by the family of his former employer. After Henderson's death the widow asked the young salesman to assume responsibility for managing the estate, which included collecting bills amounting to about $150,000. Moody hesitated, but finally accepted the job. Feeling much honored that these friends had entrusted him with such duties, with a certain amount of pride he confided to his family that "I have never been put in so responsible a position in my life." [21]

By 1860, scarcely four years after his arrival, Moody had so acclimated himself to prevailing opinion that he seemed almost a prototype of the businessmen who were coming to dominate Chicago and the nation. Barely twenty-three years old, he epitomized the youthfulness of these empire builders. He mixed almost limitless physical energy with native shrewdness, bravado. self-confidence, and a near-euphoric optimism. It was a volatile and highly dynamic compound. Yet the young man's personality reflected quite well the general atmosphere which characterized Chicago and which helped to drive the community forward with almost explosive force. Conversely, for the first time, the young New Englander found release in the Windy City for his expansive personal hopes and ambitions. The environment was a tonic to his soul, which even the most superficial observer could not fail to notice.

In addition to business, religion continued to attract Moody. As has been noted, expressions of his religious interests cropped up frequently when he spoke to his relatives, both in the Chicago area

21. *D. B. Cooke and Company's Chicago City Directory for the Year 1860–1861* (Chicago, 1860), p. 253; D. L. Moody to Betsey Moody, February 10, 1860, D. L. Moody to "friends at home," January 2, 1859, Moody Papers, Powell.

and back in New England. But his expressions of faith were not restricted to his family. Almost as soon as he arrived in Illinois he began to get involved in the ongoing activities of the evangelical denominations. Early in 1857 he made mention in his letters of the "great revival of Religion in this city." Evidently the nationwide revival of that year was already beginning in Chicago; or what is more likely, the young man was caught up in a period of spiritual enthusiasm that at that moment especially affected the Congregational church he was soon to join. In any case Moody reported home about his frequent attendance at prayer meetings and commented enthusiastically about the religious stirring. "How I do enjoy it. It seems as if God was here himself." These activities helped to draw him quickly into the life of the church in his new home. On May 3, 1857, he transferred his membership from the Mount Vernon Church in Boston to the Plymouth Congregational Church in Chicago, which was located on the near north side of the city in close proximity to both work and living quarters. Equally important, in late 1858 or early 1859 Moody plunged into the activities of the Chicago YMCA, where he started work as chairman of the "Committee to Visit Sick Members of the Association and Strangers." [22]

These two affiliations drew the young man irresistibly and irrevocably into the mainstream of American evangelical Protestantism. By the 1850's evangelicalism encompassed the great majority of Protestants in this country. It cannot be designated as a sharply defined theological system, for evangelicals embraced both Arminians and those with beliefs that rested on at least a residue of Calvinistic presuppositions. Yet there were recognizable religious attitudes and distinct ecclesiastical principles associated with the movement which can be isolated and described, and which applied with considerable accuracy to Moody and nearly all of his associates.

Evangelicalism in America was rooted in the religious history

22. D. L. Moody to "Mother," January 6, 1857, Moody Papers, Powell; *Congregational Herald*, 5 (May 21, 1857): 2; 1 (October 21, 1853): 2; *Northwestern Christian Advocate*, 3 (June 13, 1855): 95; *Manual of Plymouth Congregational Church and Society of Chicago, Illinois* (Chicago, 1875), p. 17; *First Annual Report of the Chicago Y.M.C.A.* (Chicago, 1859), p. 6.

of the colonial period. Its primary sources were the pietistic sects whose members immigrated to this country during the late seventeenth century and throughout the eighteenth century. In the years immediately following the Revolution these sects shifted their allegiance at least twice. First they joined the Deists to fight the established churches in the former colonies, now states, over the issue of freedom of religion. When this freedom was assured by provisions written into the new state constitutions, and finally by the Bill of Rights in the Federal Constitution, the incompatible union of rationalists and nonrationalists soon dissolved. With the coming of the French Revolution, American Deists, generally sympathetic with the changes generated by the great European upheaval, were increasingly identified in America with the forces of infidelity and atheism, which were attitudes that seemed to be so clearly associated with the developments in Europe. Both pietists and members of the orthodox — formerly established — churches, viewed Deists and supporters of infidelity as groups that would, by definition, work to undermine the Christian belief in special divine revelation. Thus in the first years of the nineteenth century the pietistical groups rapidly realigned themselves with orthodox Christians. Although outwardly evangelicals retained much of the orthodox churches' theological framework, in reality pietism became the core of American evangelical Protestantism in the nineteenth century.

The denominations served as the ecclesiastical framework of evangelical Protestantism. These organizations sprang up after disestablishment at the end of the eighteenth century and the beginning of the nineteenth century, when the former state churches, like the dissenting sects in colonial times, became forced to rely solely on their memberships for continued existence. *Voluntary association* by individual members with the denominations and their constituent churches was perhaps the root principle of nineteenth-century American evangelicalism. This characteristic evolved by necessity as the United States dispensed with a formal state church. Needless to say, it made the American religious establishment unique within western Christendom.[23]

23. Much of what has been said in the last few paragraphs can be traced to the work of Sidney Mead, especially three essays of his, two of

Religious voluntaryism also ushered in a period of tremendous physical growth for the American denominations, which reshaped the structure of Protestantism in this country. In 1800 the largest American denomination was the Congregationalist; Presbyterians were second, followed by the Baptists, Episcopalians, and Lutherans, in that order. The Methodists were still quite small, being only the tenth largest group in the nation. By 1850 the Methodists, perhaps employing the techniques associated with evangelical Protestantism more successfully than any other denomination, had vaulted into first place with 1,324,000 members. The Baptists were second, followed by the Presbyterians, Congregationalists, and Lutherans. An entirely new group, the Disciples of Christ, emerging chiefly out of the revivalistic ferment of the West, had become the sixth largest denomination, ahead of the Episcopalians.[24]

Before the Civil War the denominations devoted a great deal of their energy to home missions. In part this was a natural response to the challenge of a highly mobile society, moving rapidly westward into areas largely untouched by civilization. The Protestant churches became one of the primary institutions seeking to bring

which now serve in somewhat revised form as chaps. 3 and 7 of *The Lively Experiment: The Shaping of Christianity in America* (New York: Harper & Row, 1963). The third essay is entitled "The Rise of the Evangelical Conception of the Ministry in America: 1607–1850," and is printed in H. Richard Niebuhr and Daniel D. Williams, eds., *The Ministry in Historical Perspectives* (New York: Harper and Bros., 1956), chap. 7. See also Gary B. Nash, "The American Clergy and the French Revolution," *William and Mary Quarterly*, 3rd ser., 22 (July, 1965): 392–412; Timothy L. Smith, "Congregation, State, and Denomination: The Forming of the American Religious Structure," *William and Mary Quarterly*, 3rd ser., 25 (April, 1968): 155–76; Winthrop Hudson, *The Great Tradition of the American Churches* (New York: Harper & Row, 1963), chaps. 1–7. William C. McLoughlin, "Isaac Backus and Separation of Church and State in America," *American Historical Review* 73 (June, 1968): 1392–1413, has raised important questions about Mead's formulations concerning the Deist-sectarian alliance against the established churches in the late eighteenth century.

24. William Warren Sweet, "The Protestant Churches," in *Organized Religion in the United States*, ed. Ray Abrams, *Annals of the American Academy*, 256 (March, 1948): 47. For a scholarly assessment of the Disciples of Christ during this period, see David E. Harrell, Jr., *Quest for a Christian America: The Disciples of Christ and American Society to 1866* (Nashville: Disciples of Christ Historical Society, 1966).

a modicum of discipline, order, and culture into the daily experience of the farmers and frontiersmen of new areas of the country. But even more important, the evangelicals focused attention on missions because it was a life-and-death matter to them. Voluntarism made it imperative that they go out in search of new members. As we shall see, many of the established procedures of the churches were directed toward this end. In addition, great interdenominational societies, stimulated largely by the missionary impulse, sprang up in the pre-Civil War years. The American Home Missionary Society, the American Sunday School Union, and the YMCA exemplified this important phase of evangelical activity.[25]

The revival, however, was evangelical Protestantism's primary instrument for conquest of the individual. Revival preachers utilized most effectively the emotionalism and emphasis on personal religion which pietism had made so crucial a part of evangelical attitudes. Moreover, the revival provided a sure means of growth for the denominations, since its primary purpose was to produce conversions, the first step taken voluntarily by an individual toward church affiliation. The stress placed on revivals by men like Lyman Beecher in New England before 1830, by circuit riders and farmer-preachers on the frontier, and by the founders of mass revivalism at mid-century in the urban centers of the country, all attest to the continuing vitality and importance of this institution in the eyes of evangelical Protestants. By the 1850's Methodists in Illinois could echo the feelings of most evangelicals when they asserted that revivals were as important "to the health and purity of the church, as is congenial air to the invalid, or salt and soap to the health and cleanliness of civilization. . . . Revivals are necessities of the church." [26]

Evangelicalism became a religious faith which expressed itself

25. L. C. Rudolph provides a fascinating analysis of the efforts of Presbyterians to extend the Christian faith into Indiana as it changed from wilderness to settled society in *Hoosier Zion* (New Haven: Yale University Press, 1963). The great interdenominational benevolent societies have been studied intensively by Griffin in *Their Brothers' Keepers*.

26. *Northwestern Christian Advocate*, 4 (February 13, 1856): 27. For similar sentiments see the *Congregational Herald* (July 30, 1857): 1; *Zion's Herald and Wesleyan Journal*, 28 (December 2, 1857): 189; *New York Christian Advocate*, 47 (February 15, 1872): 52.

in daily affairs in a never-ending concern for the "condition of souls." It was the evangelical's chief responsibility to seek out and to draw into the fold, primarily through the conversion experience, any person who was as yet uncommitted religiously. The tenaciousness of this evangelical concern reveals itself in these words from an evangelical journal in 1857:

> The means of grace and the attending influence of the Divine Spirit hold many a man at the stage of awakened interest, . . . Many stand thus, troubled in their sins, yet held back by evil influences and an alienated heart from the great decision. All seems ready, and yet the soul lingers irresolute, as if some other influence were yet needed, some touch of special virtue to stir it from this fatal inaction. . . . Some Christian shall now approach this lingering one . . . pointing the way, removing difficulties, prompting him to action, and bringing to bear on him the secret force of faith and prayer in his behalf. . . . That is the way men are won to God. . . . Instrumentally men are to be the Saviors of one another." [27]

Moody quickly accepted as his own this evangelical interest in the individual. The central worry affecting him whenever he wrote to members of his family in New England was the fact that all of them were outside the community of believers. His earliest letters from Chicago were filled with importunities that his mother, brothers, and sisters all realize their waywardness and "be brought into the fold of Christ." [28] This was a fundamental concern which animated Moody throughout his entire adult life. He was learning well his lessons as a member of the evangelical community. And in so doing he revealed once again how evangelical Protestants hoped to actualize one of their chief aims, which was to Christianize the nation.

27. *Congregational Herald*, 5 (April 30, 1857): 2.
28. D. L. Moody to "Mother," January 6, 1857, Moody Papers, Powell. See also D. L. Moody to "Mother," September 24, 1860, D. L. Moody to "brother," December 16, 1856, *ibid.*; D. L. Moody to sister (Lizzie), October 17, 1856, D. L. Moody to "Mother," October 13 (no year), Moody Papers, Moody Bible Institute, Chicago, Ill.

An activist temperament, arising out of the imperatives of faith operating in the everyday world, characterized the evangelical wherever he labored. When one combined such activism with moralistic sentiments, as did most evangelical Protestants, earnestness in individual endeavor was the result. "Earnestness" was a favorite word of the evangelicals, whether it applied to the approved manner in which a preacher delivered his sermon or to the actions of a successful businessman.[29] In 1853 an unknown Congregationalist caught the spirit of this attitude among evangelicals when he tried to describe how a Christian should "Be Earnest in Doing Good":

> Oh Christian! time, time is passing away! opportunities are going, will soon be gone! We shall soon be at the bar of God. The Christian who means to do all he can, will say — "what can I do this week — this day — this hour?" This is the genius of earnestness. Are there any sick to be visited? Are there any poor to be relieved? . . . Delay not to speak a word of encouragement — direct that soul to Christ. . . . "Whatsoever thy hand findeth to do, do it with thy might."[30]

The strong sense of the need to act, the practical manner in which one demonstrated one's faith, the ultimate hope that he who was helped would soon "see salvation," are all in evidence. It is easy to see how the movements for moral reform which evangelicals supported so frequently in the pre–Civil War years could find their sanctions in expressions like these. Nor is it hard to see why evangelical Protestants were some of the best practitioners of the boomer spirit that enveloped a city like Chicago, and eventually America as a whole. Certainly young Moody fit well into such a milieu, for he was, if anything, earnest in all that he did. At a later date this characteristic undoubtedly added to his nationwide appeal to evangelicals, and contributed to his success as a revivalist.[31]

29. *Northwestern Christian Advocate*, 3 (February 7, 1855): 21; 4 (August 13, 1856): 130; *Zion's Herald* (July 16, 1868): 339; *Advance*, 3 (October 21, 1869): 1.

30. *Congregational Herald*, 1 (April 23, 1853): 1.

31. See especially the *New York Evangelist*, 46 (March 2, 1875): 6, where the success of Moody and Sankey as revivalists is attributed not

Chicago in the 1850's: Earnest Christian

Armed with a religious world view in numerous ways uniquely suited to his personal interests and temperament, Moody embarked in earnest upon his spiritual work in the world when he joined the Chicago YMCA. The Chicago branch of the Young Men's Christian Association had come to life in the nationwide revival of 1857–58. The religious excitement in Chicago first developed in a series of noon prayer meetings which Moody attended regularly. The churches of the city had inaugurated these meetings jointly on a week-by-week basis in 1857, but as the movement gathered momentum and people flocked to the services, it became necessary to hold daily sessions, and to move these gatherings to a centrally located downtown building with more adequate seating facilities. Because of its accessibility, this downtown location was also convenient for the many businessmen who were attending.

Several young Chicagoans participating in the revival were members of a nearly defunct Young Men's Society for Religious Improvement, and they hoped to perpetuate by means of a new institution the good effects of the religious turmoil. Thus they issued a call for all interested young men to help in forming a Young Men's Christian Association in Chicago.[32] In a series of meetings beginning March 22, 1858, the charter members adopted a constitution and elected officers for the new organization. In his inaugural address, the first president, Cyrus Bentley, outlined the general purpose of the group. It was to provide "a common place of resort, to which to invite the idle and thoughtless young men of the city, where they may pass their time pleasantly and profitably

to "genius, mental endowment, or even education," but "earnestness of conviction, concern, and labor for others." See also *Advance*, 3 (September 9, 1869): 6; D. L. Moody to C. H. Ingram, December 5, 1892, C. H. Ingram Papers, Wisconsin State Historical Society, Madison, Wis.

32. *First Annual Report*, p. 6; *Chicago Tribune*, March 19, 1869; *Northwestern Christian Advocate*, 15 (October 9, 1857): 326; Edwin B. Smith, John C. Grant, and Horace Starkey, *The History of the Chicago Young Men's Christian Association, 1858–1898* (Chicago, 1898), pp. 14–15, quoted from *First Report of the Chicago Association*. A discussion of the background to the founding of the Chicago YMCA is in F. Roger Dunn, "Formative Years of the Chicago Y.M.C.A.: A Study in Urban History," *Journal of the Illinois State Historical Society*, 37 (December, 1944): 329–50. See also Emmett Dedmon, *Great Enterprises: 100 Years of the YMCA of Metropolitan Chicago* (Chicago: Rand McNally, 1957), pp. 20–26.

in reading and in intercourse with Christian young men, and thus be brought under religious influence." The original constitution demanded the "evangelical test" for all voting members. Thus "any male member of good standing in any evangelical church, which holds the doctrine of justification by faith in Christ alone, may become an active member." [33]

The statement of purpose and proposed structure of the Chicago organization was noticeably similar to that of the Boston YMCA. This was no accident. Almost as soon as the Boston YMCA was founded, the leaders of the group had printed ten thousand copies of their constitution and mailed them to evangelical ministers and lay leaders throughout the country. This tactic quickly aroused great interest in the new enterprise in Boston, and requests flowed in for suggestions on how to form similar groups in other cities. Thus many of the local associations formed in the 1850's consciously followed the pattern established by the original organization in Boston when it began in 1852. [34] The founders of the Chicago YMCA were copiers of this sort. Undoubtedly the Chicagoans were inspired by civic pride as well as religious zeal. Knowing that associations were springing up in other cities, to organize such a group would be one more way to enhance the prestige of their town and to demonstrate to people that Chicago was becoming a leader among the cities of the country.

In several ways the new organization commended itself to the Protestant community of Chicago. Some viewed it as a "most effectual means of destroying rank sectarianism," which was certainly not an unknown phenomenon in the life of the denominations. In particular it seemed a pleasing prospect that the more destructive aspects of competition between the churches might be avoided in such a sensitive area of religious concern as the evangelization of the youth of the city. The YMCA could also serve

33. Smith, Grant, and Starkey, *History of the Chicago Young Men's Christian Association*, p. 16.

34. By 1856, fifty-six local associations had been organized throughout the country. About half the groups set up during the fifties patterned themselves after the Boston example. (C. Howard Hopkins, *History of the Y.M.C.A. in North America* [New York: Association Press, 1951], p. 23; William B. Whiteside, *The Boston Y.M.C.A. and Community Need: A Century's Evolution, 1851–1951* [New York, 1951], pp. 19, 21–24.)

as a sort of clearinghouse for new methods and ideas to be used in all the local churches. Even more important was the fact that the YMCA served the general purposes for which all evangelicals worked — to seek converts and thus new members of the denominations, and to expand the moral influence of the churches throughout society.[35]

Perhaps the shrewdest supporters of the new organization saw it performing still other functions in the burgeoning city. For these people the YMCA seemed to be a group especially suited to maintaining and expanding evangelical influence within the most influential circles in Chicago. The YMCA's reading room and its program of popular literary entertainments forced Chicagoans "to rely so entirely upon this Association for these intellectual treats, that it becomes at once incorporated with the interests of the city, and extends its influence indefinitely." Even more explicity stated were the mutual benefits to be gained from close associations with the business community. "Christian merchants, true to their own interests in common with the interests of society, are perhaps more ready to aid it [the YMCA] than any other institution; for it does not require a very long calculation to find that one good clerk of strict religious integrity (which may always be found in such an association) will pay him a large[r] percentage on his small investment in its funds, than any stocks or real estate." [36] Evangelicals apparently believed that religious training provided personal discipline and stability, and for young men in a turbulent city like Chicago, such training seemed particularly desirable. If the YMCA became such a scarcely concealed vehicle for social control, this too was an important duty for it to perform.

There were many things about this Christian association that attracted Moody. Previous experience in the Boston YMCA established an initial basis of concern. His membership in one of the evangelical churches of the city meant he had the necessary credentials for active membership. Certainly he approved of the

35. *Congregational Herald*, 5 (July 23, 1857): 1. See also *Northwestern Christian Advocate*, 17 (June 30, 1869): 203.

36. *Congregational Herald*, 5 (July 23, 1857): 1. For a similar appeal for the support of businessmen, see T. Smyth, *Nature and Claims of the Y.M.C.A.*, pamphlet in the files of the YMCA Historical Library, New York City, pp. 55–57.

emphasis placed on lay leadership; the organization was made to order for a young businessman with the excess energies he possessed, eager to expand evangelical influence in the workaday world. Finally, there was no better place to establish his credentials as a leader, and to establish contacts of importance with rising young businessmen like himself. Henceforward he was to make the YMCA, both at the local and national level, one of the principal vehicles through which he expressed his interest in public affairs.[37]

Moody's religious interests were also manifested in another way. Sometime in the first months of 1859 the young man organized his own mission Sunday school on Chicago's north side. Sabbath schools, as they were frequently called by the evangelicals, had long been an accepted part of the institutional paraphernalia of evangelical Protestantism. They performed several functions in the eyes of those who staffed and supported them. In the first place the Sabbath school had an educational task to carry out with children of church members. Evangelicals thought that religious education was primarily a duty of the family, but that if properly used, Sabbath schools could be "valuable aids to Christian parents in the religious instruction of their children." Even more important, these schools were to serve "children whose parents are not Christians, and whose homes are not Christian always." For this portion of the population "Sabbath-schools are indispensable."[38] As an instrument to be used by the missionaries of the church, the ultimate purpose of the Sabbath school was the same as that of the revival — to produce conversions and thereby new members for the evangelical groups. As one evangelical witness put it in the 1850's: "The conversion of the soul should be the great object and end of all Sabbath-school instruction."[39]

37. Moody's membership in the Chicago YMCA is recorded officially only in 1862 when the Association elected him a life member. Board of Managers, *Minutes* (Archives, Chicago YMCA), April 14, 1862. No record has been found of earlier membership, but probably he fell into the active classification before the date mentioned.

38. *Interior*, 17 (May 27, 1886): 1. See also the *Northwestern Christian Advocate*, 3 (July 18, 1855): 113; *New York Observer*, 43 (January 5, 1865): 2.

39. *New York Observer*, 30 (May 6, 1852): 146. For similar expressions see *Northwestern Christian Advocate*, 3 (February 7, 1855): 22; (February 28, 1855): 34; 15 (June 5, 1867): 180; *Interior*, 6 (January 28, 1875): 4.

As the great urban centers connected with industrialism mushroomed in the years just prior to and after the Civil War, it became clear that the evangelical churches faced an almost overwhelming task in seeking to convert, or at least influence, the vast number of people coming to live in these metropolitan regions. Shrewdly perhaps, some evangelicals realized that the most promising place to begin the process of Christianization was with small children. The Sabbath school was a ready-made device for carrying out such a program. Evangelical leaders also realized that the Sabbath school could become one further avenue for the Americanization of the horde of immigrants who congregated in the cities, and in addition serve as a method of social control over the rowdy elements of a society caught up in turmoil. In Chicago in Moody's day, evangelical leaders expressed their feelings, a mixture of religious and secular purposes, quite openly. "We consider the Sabbath school as the only hope for city heathenism. The church has no other means by which she can enlighten its darkness, or penetrate its interior." When speaking of the Irish immigrants in the city, one Protestant journal asserted that their children "grow up in ignorance, and destitute of those moral checks which would restrain them from vice." The duty of evangelicals was clear. "Let Sunday schools be sustained, and let the children of foreigners be looked up and sent to school, if we wish well to our country." [40]

During the 1850's and 1860's many of the churches in Chicago sponsored mission Sunday schools in the rundown areas of the city. These mission schools gave evidence of the evangelical concern for the poor and for those outside the fold, yet they were also a way to keep these people somewhat at arm's length and apart from active participation in the established churches until they had been properly trained and educated. By 1865 there were thirty-one such mission Sunday schools listed in the Chicago city directory, of which twenty-seven were sponsored by the four major evangelical Protestant denominations. [41] A call in 1856 for laymen particu-

40. *Northwestern Christian Advocate*, 4 (August 27, 1856): 138; (August 20, 1856): 136. Similar attitudes are expressed in *ibid.*, 4 (April 9, 1856): 57; 7 (January 6, 1869): 6; *New York Observer*, 43 (January 5, 1865): 2.

41. T. M. Halpin, comp., *Halpin's Chicago City Directory, 1865–1866* (Chicago, 1865), p. xxxv; Pierce, *History of Chicago*, 2:511. The influence

larly, and others, "now comparatively asleep over this subject," to push forward the Sabbath school movement, had evidently been heeded.[42] Within this context it is easy to understand why Moody decided to set up his little mission school on the north side of Chicago in 1859.

Moody also had personal reasons for initiating his school, which did not necessarily coincide fully with the interests and desires of recognized church leaders. There are some indications that the young man's blunt ways did not make him very popular with the controlling elements in Plymouth Church. At a later date one of his friends recalled that sometimes in his prayers Moody "would express opinions to the Lord" concerning the church elders "which were by no means flattering." Apparently before long he "received the same fatherly advice which had been given him in Boston — . . . leave the speaking and praying to those who could do it better." Moody also discovered that the usual routine of churchly activities did not satisfy his craving for action. He began to associate with a group of young men from the First Methodist Church who dubbed themselves the Mission Band and visited downtown hotels and saloons on Sunday mornings, distributing tracts and extending personal invitations to people to come to the Methodist worship services. He also began to recruit vigorously pupils for a small mission Sunday school already operating on Wells Street on the near north side.[43]

Soon the young man struck out on his own. Frustrated by criticism from his Congregationalist brethren, perceiving an obvious need for missionary work in the downtown areas of Chicago, and blessed with all the personal enthusiasm and physical stamina necessary to the task, Moody organized his own mission Sunday school early in 1859.[44] In so acting, a crucial element in Moody's

of the revival of 1857–1858 on the establishment of Sabbath schools in Chicago is quite noticeable. Fourteen, or almost half of the total still functioning in 1865, were started during the years of the revival. The number of new mission schools declined as the effects of the religious excitement wore off, with only two appearing between 1860 and 1862.

42. *Northwestern Christian Advocate*, 4 (August 27, 1856): 138.

43. Daniels, *Moody and His Work*, pp. 31, 32.

44. W. H. Daniels, *Moody: His Words, Work, and Workers* (New York: Nelson & Phillips, 1877), p. 20; William R. Moody, *D. L. Moody* (New York: Macmillan Co., 1930), p. 48.

personality flashed to the surface. Throughout his life, whenever he found his way blocked or anxieties and difficulties piling up around him, his most characteristic response was to strike out along a new path. The way to resolve the tensions of life was to view these problems from a new perspective; in other words to *act* by making a sharp break with past efforts and attempting to by-pass the obstructions completely. Thus when the small-town atmosphere in Northfield began to imprison him, he sought out the greater freedom of Boston. When frustrations and disagreements with his relatives in Boston created tension, he left New England and migrated westward. Now as he experienced his first rebuffs in Chicago he sidestepped the difficulties again by setting up his own religious organization into which he could pour unhampered his almost limitless energy and enthusiasm. The fact that his school had no denominational affiliations underscored the founder's apparent desire to disassociate himself from previous church connections and operate more independently.

This event in Moody's life also suggests that a certain flexibility and open-endedness existed in the institutional structure of evangelical Protestantism. Allowing young enthusiasts like Moody, eager to advance the traditional purposes of evangelicalism, to work somewhat independently of standard church groups was a wise policy to follow. Indeed, it appears that one of the secrets of the continuing vitality of the denominations was that individuals or small groups within the larger community of faith were often free to adapt tactics of mission work and evangelism to the shifting reality of the external world. Moody took advantage of this flexibility several times during his life, and in so doing he did much to maintain, and perhaps even to expand, evangelical influence in the country at large.

The youthful Chicagoan chose to locate his mission school near the Sands, a notorious section of the city close to the lake and north of the Chicago River. This was the acknowledged red-light district of the community, infested with saloons, gambling establishments, and miserable wooden shanties.[45] Immigrants made up the bulk of

45. Pierce, *History of Chicago*, 2:433–34. A published report of the first year of Moody's school includes evidence which reveals the kind

the dense population of the area; in particular it was the center of the German and Scandinavian migrations. Closer to the lake and only a few blocks north stood the elegant mansions of wealthy businessmen like Cyrus McCormick. Some of these men became Moody's personal friends. The sharp juxtaposition of social and economic extremes in the Gold Coast and the slums that has characterized the social structure of the near north side of Chicago to the present day was already present in Moody's day and well reflected in his experience.

The usually accepted story of the founding of Moody's mission says that the enterprise began in an abandoned saloon. Eventually the pressure of expanding enrollments forced a move to the upstairs of the North Market, a combination public hall and market located just two blocks from the Chicago River.[46]

Moody served principally as organizer and recruiter of staff and students. Much of the task of instruction was left to a Presbyterian layman-friend, J. B. Stillson. Informal singing and group discussions filled the schedule in the earliest months. This was not a very demanding program, although probably about all that was feasible with the unruly ragamuffins put under Moody's command. When the school moved to the North Market Hall, however, conditions became a bit more stabilized. Moody and his supporters formed regular classes, obtained additional teachers, and set up

of children such conditions produced. Nine of the first-year students ended up in reform school, three went to the city Bridewell, and twelve eventually had to be placed in the city's Home for the Friendless. (*Chicago Press and Tribune*, October 16, 1860.)

46. Daniels, *Moody and His Work*, pp. 33–34. A contemporary newspaper account of the organization of the school does little to verify these details. However, since the newspaper report only vaguely describes the original location of the mission, Daniels' narrative may embody the essence of the truth. A fire heavily damaged the North Market Hall in April, 1859; since the newspaper report says nothing of dislocations of the school because of the fire, it is possible to assume that Moody moved his enterprise to the hall only after its restoration. At least implicitly Daniels' account is corroborated. (*Chicago Press and Tribune*, April 20, 1859, April 27, 1859, October 16, 1860.) The date of the founding of the school listed in the newspapers in 1860 is used in preference to the widely accepted, though less precise, date of 1858. For examples of use of the latter, see Halpin, *Chicago City Directory, 1865–66*, p. xxxv; W. R. Moody, *Moody* (1900), p. 56; W. R. Moody, *Moody* (1930), p. 48.

a permanent organization by writing, and then formally adopting, a constitution.[47]

The record of the school in its first year was a mixed one. Noisy children so distracted prayer meetings held on Thursday and Sunday evenings that some adults were heard to exclaim only half-jokingly that "the conduct of the children was more of a sin than the prayers offered in their behalf." [48] Unruly students, however, did not deter Moody from seeking additional recruits. Attendance steadily climbed, with the weekly average increasing 75 per cent from the beginning to the end of the first year. The youthful leader also established a small library of 700 volumes to make available religious books, tracts, and periodicals to parents and others who were interested and able to read them. An annual day-long picnic and outing away from the area for the children of the school became another enticing event on the calendar.[49]

Moody designed the educational and social functions of his school to appeal to both the young and old in his district. But he and his helpers never forgot their primary objective, which was to achieve conversions. From the outset, apparently, this quest after the heathen was effective. The earliest report on the activities of the school noted thirty-four conversions in the first year, twenty-five of these in the final three months.[50] Moody conceived his chief task to be that of recruiting new members for the school. He pursued this assignment with a zeal and determination which was almost frightening in its single-mindedness. He devoted all of his free time to the work, staying out on the streets at nights until ten or eleven o'clock. People throughout the slum area came to know him. He enticed children into his embrace by the promise of sweets drawn from an inexhaustible supply in an inside pocket. One friend called this his "missionary sugar." He also bought clothes for his young charges and purchased baskets of food for the needy families of which they were a part. These were both the natural gestures of a young man sensitive to the difficulties

47. *Manual, Illinois Street Church* (Chicago, April, 1867), p. 45; *Chicago Daily Journal*, October 16, 1860. The permanent organization apparently took place about the middle of October, 1859.
48. *Chicago Press and Tribune*, October 16, 1860.
49. *Chicago Daily Journal*, October 16, 1860.
50. *Ibid.*; *Chicago Press and Tribune*, October 16, 1860.

of others, and shrewd tactics to ensnare his charges and their families in the missionary net cast out by the evangelical churches. Already that practical, common-sense approach to evangelism which characterized much of his later work as a revivalist was exhibiting itself.

He was also given to more forceful methods of persuasion. He pursued urchins quite literally off the streets into their tumble-down homes. Sometimes he met opposition from parents to these dramatic acts, but he viewed his intrusions as a way to meet adults and draw them as well as their children into his mission program.[51] The vigorousness of Moody's methods did not make him unpopular, however. His obvious sincerity, the gusto which accompanied everything he did, his utter lack of pretense in ignoring possible distinctions between himself and those whom he served, made it difficult for people not to like him. Inhabitants of the area near the school revealed their feelings about Moody at the gathering held as a first anniversary celebration for the North Market Hall mission. At the end of this meeting Moody found himself surrounded by his students, who presented him with a beautifully embossed Bible which served to express their gratitude for the time, money, and prayers he had lavished upon them.[52]

Moody greatly enjoyed his adventures on the near north side. He indicated some of his sentiments in a letter he wrote to his brother Samuel in October, 1859. Away from Chicago on a business trip at the moment, he asserted that "I shall expect to have a good time next Sunday when I get home for I have been away some time now and the children are so glad to see me when I return. . . . I think," he said, in a burst of enthusiasm and pride, "I have the best school there is in the west, anyway it is the largest schools there is this side of N York."[53]

A local newspaper reporter visited the North Market Hall mission in 1867 and wrote afterwards a vivid description of Moody among his young charges. The short and stocky figure mounted a platform to sing and speak with a "quick nervous step that means business." Back of a "round, ruddy and good humored" face la-

51. Daniels, *Moody and His Work*, pp. 38, 43–45.
52. *Ibid.*
53. D. L. Moody to Samuel, October 18, 1859, Moody Papers, Powell, See also D. L. Moody to "brother," June 29, 1860, *ibid.*

bored a "busy brain." It was the intensity of Moody's actions that everyone noticed immediately. The young man's attempts to be a song leader served as a case in point. He was a monotone, unable to sing a note adequately by himself. This seemed hardly a handicap, however. He gave "a wonderful impetus to singing by an attempt to imitate the beating of time and appearing to sing, but really reciting the words in a low monotone . . . not heard . . . off from the platform." Later, when Moody spoke briefly to the school, his intense manner once again commanded attention.

> When Moody speaks, everybody listens. Even those who do not like him. His remarks are short, pithy and practical, and his exhortations impressive, and sometimes touching even to tears. . . . His remarks always have a martial ring. He wants "to wrest this State from the power of Satan and take and hold it for Christ." What he wants done he wants done NOW. . . . As a brother once said of him, "He acts as if he were going to convert the world off-hand." [54]

In other ways, too, Moody stamped his personality upon his congregation. There was an informality and heartiness in the atmosphere which was difficult to resist. Strangers were welcomed, all the teachers offered "a cordial grasp, a friendly nod or a pleasant word" as they met each other. The children were all known by name and were greeted by Moody at the door when they left. Spontaneity was embodied in an extraordinary way in the weekly "Sunday Evening Tea." Gathering around a long, bare, pine table, munching crackers and sipping steaming mugs of tea, the teachers and the superintendent exchanged notes on the work in the classes, recited favorite Scripture passages, and heard exhortations to rekindle lost enthusiasm. As one participant put it, "even the stammering tongue seemed touched with fire, and as we look down the long table, with its simple fare, we can see how . . . the disciples gathered with their Saviour . . . and we feel that we taste somewhat of the joy which they tasted, and that He who made their meal a happy one, also blesses this one with His presence." [55]

54. *Advance*, 1 (November 7, 1867): 4.
55. *Ibid.*

Although Moody may have been a bit unsophisticated in his tactics and though "there was not much attention paid to order and system," there was no doubt that "earnestness and directness, in great measure, made up" for these shortcomings. In short, the school in numerous ways reflected the temper of its founder. One could agree that "much of his [Moody's] success is due to the *personality* of his efforts." [56] Already he possessed elements of a personal charisma that were to be essential parts of his later success as a popular evangelist.

From the beginning the little mission was an independent effort, unconnected with any particular denomination. Logically enough, its chief support developed among individual members of the Chicago YMCA. With the departure of Stillson in June, 1859, a major vacancy in the staff had to be filled. Not long afterward John V. Farwell, a well-to-do Chicago dry-goods merchant, became the superintendent of the school. The historical record does not reveal where Moody and Farwell first became acquainted. Since both were active in the YMCA, the friendship may have begun and undoubtedly flourished there. Evidently Farwell was also a member of the young Methodist Mission Band which Moody joined in downtown Chicago in the months prior to the founding of his North Market Hall school. In any case, Moody was able to persuade Farwell to accept the superintendency. Apparently the latter's duties were primarily administrative and Moody continued to direct most of the concrete programs of the school. Farwell remained superintendent until January 1, 1867.[57]

Farwell's daughter once accurately observed that her father had a love for Moody similar to that which existed "only between David and Jonathan." [58] In the sixties the older man revealed clearly the high esteem in which he held his young friend by providing a great deal of personal financial support. This was exceedingly

56. *Ibid.*
57. Managers' *Minutes*, April 14, 1862; *Chicago Press and Tribune*, June 19, 1860; undated newspaper clipping from [Rochester, New York] *Post Express*, W. R. Moody Papers; *Manual, Illinois Street Church*, p. 45; J[ohn] V. Farwell, Jr., *Some Recollections of John V. Farwell* (Chicago: R. R. Donnelley & Sons, 1911), p. 102; Daniels, *Moody and His Work*, pp. 41–43.
58. Ferry, *Reminiscences of John V. Farwell*, 2:66.

important since by that time Moody no longer had a regular salary. Moreover, one of Farwell's chief functions at the mission school was to act as treasurer — that is, to make up any deficiency between annual income and expenses.[59] The young shoe salesman's association with this prominent Chicago merchant was a forecast of the many friendships he was to develop with other wealthy men in business. He understood these men, as he did Farwell, because in so many ways he and they thought and acted alike.

During Moody's day, and even earlier, there was a close link between the business elements in the emerging cities and evangelical Protestantism. In part this relationship grew out of the fact that most business leaders in industrial centers like Chicago were native-born. If they had religious inclinations, it was likely that they belonged to one of the evangelical denominations.[60] There are other more telling ways, however, to explore and explain the interconnections between evangelicals and businessmen. In particular there were attributes of evangelical thinking and acting which tended to confirm the importance of businessmen and their place in American society, and to make it easy for the average churchgoer to identify himself with this group.

Perhaps the place to begin in understanding this interrelationship is with the taproot of evangelical experience and practice, the oft-expressed necessity for conversion of the individual sinner. In order to participate in this all-embracing missionary endeavor of the denominations, church people had to be involved in the world, working and doing. In the narrowest sense this simply meant fulfilling effectively the demand placed upon all local

59. For evidence of Farwell's financial contributions, see *ibid.*, 2:64; Farwell, Jr., *Recollections of John V. Farwell*, pp. 114–15; D. B. Towner, "Special Subjects," undated notebook, Moody Papers, Powell.

60. One hint of this connection between religious and secular groups is suggested by the location of evangelical churches in Chicago. Of the twenty-nine Episcopalian, Presbyterian, and Congregational churches functioning in 1865, twenty were in sections of the city inhabited by wealthy or middle-class citizens. Only two were in areas where immigrants, usually among the poorest of the population, were likely to provide most of the church members. The Methodists and Baptists also possessed large and important congregations in the middle-class neighborhoods, although they were somewhat better represented in the poorer areas of the city than the first three denominations mentioned. (Pierce, *History of Chicago*, 2:355.)

churches to evangelize. " 'Working' churches," observed one evangelical writer, should be houses of God "filled with busy evangelists, going out two by two, and bringing back to its [sic] altars the prodigal children wandering in temptation." [61] This was an appeal that an evangelical easily understood and would try to follow.

Religious activism, combined with the demand for personal conversions, created within evangelicalism a heavy stress upon individualism. "Religion is of little value or power," exclaimed one of the evangelical journals in the 1860's, "except as it becomes personal. . . . It has proved to be one of the mightiest of forces because it appeals directly to the conscience, claims mastery over every soul, and inspires individuals to glory or shame. Whether, therefore, it be heathenism, or Christianity, Popery or Puritanism, religion has to do with men personally." [62] All issues, within or outside the churches, tended to be placed in a personal, individualized context. For evangelical Protestants the great reform movements of the pre–Civil War decades were deemed important because they dealt primarily with concrete problems of the individual — temperance, prison reform, rights for women. This individualist viewpoint also affected many abolitionists as they attacked the inhumanity of white masters to Negro slaves, but tended to ignore or were unable to come to grips effectively with the deep-seated institutional problems associated with slavery. Moral reform was attractive as a means of dealing with society, precisely because it brought together the religious enthusiasm and the bent toward individualism which were essential characteristics of evangelical Protestantism. In 1868 a writer expressed the sentiment of many evangelicals on this matter quite forcefully. "All Christians, without exception, are imperatively called to promote by every possible means every species of moral reform. . . . Temperance, social purity, political honesty — no member of Christ's church is excusable, who does not do all he or she can to promote

61. *New York Christian Advocate*, 47 (February 8, 1872): 44. See also *Zion's Herald*, 28 (May 14, 1868): 230; *New York Observer*, 31 (February 10, 1853): 42.

62. *Advance*, 3 (February 17, 1870): 4; *Northwestern Christian Advocate*, 3 (January 3, 1855): 1; *Congregationalist*, 18 (March 16, 1866): 42.

these." [63] Therefore, whether they were dealing with religious questions or with the church's relations with the outside world, evangelicals evinced their unshakable belief in individualism and the need for activism in the world at large.

From here it was only a short step to the point of identifying with those groups in American society that embodied most fully in the secular world the same ideals of individualism, activism, and practicality. For a young man in the 1850's and in the immediate post–Civil War era, the connections between the evangelical church and the business community were most obvious. "Shun speculative piety," urged one evangelical minister of his fellow believers in 1869. "Meditate, but meditate in order that you may *do.* . . . 'Be diligent in Business.' This will help you to be fervent in spirit and better to serve the lord." Perhaps it was a slip, this mixing of a cliché from the business world with evangelical exhortation, but it was a meaningful slip of the tongue, not at all unnatural. Any reader of the religious weeklies constantly found himself exposed to this intermingling of secular and religious attitudes. Indeed, sometimes the evangelical publications dropped their religious terminology entirely and unabashedly glorified the business community by means of printed brief biographies of successful businessmen, or abbreviated guides on "How to Begin in Business," all for the edification and guidance of their readers.[64]

Another point where secular and religious concepts overlapped was in the use of the word "work." In pleas to their constituencies, evangelical leaders often used this word. Only by means of hard "personal work," could souls be saved. The true church was the "working" church.[65] Belief in the discipline and correctness of hard work, but not necessarily for religious ends, was also a central article of faith in the secular ideal of self-help, a popular philosophy espoused by many of the businessmen of Moody's day.

63. *Zion's Herald*, 28 (May 14, 1868): 230.

64. *Advance*, 2 (November 11, 1869): 6; *Northwestern Christian Advocate*, 3 (July 18, 1855): 113; (October 17, 1855): 168; (November 14, 1855): 181; 4 (July 23, 1856): 120; *Congregational Herald*, 5 (April 30, 1857): 2; *New York Christian Advocate*, 47 (April 25, 1872): 134; *New York Evangelist*, 54 (November 29, 1883): 6.

65. *New York Evangelist*, 47 (January 6, 1876): 4; *New York Christian Advocate*, 47 (February 8, 1872): 44.

Not too surprisingly, popular evangelical thought eventually tended to fuse the two concepts, religious and secular. Moody himself provides some evidence of this development. Although as a revivalist Moody frequently spoke of "work" in the traditional religious context of the need for increased evangelistic efforts, from the time of his earliest public pronouncements he also showed that he believed strongly in hard work *generally*, unconnected in any specific way with the work of evangelization. Indeed, he believed that a sure sign of a Christian was the man who worked hard. The invidious obverse side of the coin — he who was lazy was suspect as a Christian — was an attitude Moody also accepted. At YMCA gatherings in Chicago in the 1860's, and later as a revivalist, he made plain his views. "There is no hope for a man's reformation who does not go to work. Laziness belongs to the old creation. I don't know what to do, and I don't see what God can do, with a lazy man." Or, "I want to say that I never knew a lazy man to become a Christian. I have known gamblers and drunkards and saloon-keepers to be converted, but never a lazy man." [66] In this instance the secular ideal of work, used uncritically within the evangelical moralistic framework, had become the dominant theme. The distinctions between religious and secular uses of the word had broken down and disappeared. In such a context it is easy to see why businessmen and evangelicals often found each other congenial and mutually supportive.

"Be diligent in business," whether in its religious or purely secular context, served as a guide for action for many evangelicals. But diligence increasingly produced, especially for members of the business community, an avalanche of money and worldly goods, the personal profits garnered from a blossoming industrial system. To the evangelical mind this newfound wealth was not necessarily to be thought of as a curse or as a corrupting influence. A deeply rooted faith in Christian stewardship, traceable to the influence of Puritan thought in colonial times, still held sway among evangelical Protestants in Moody's day. This concept of stewardship began with the assumption that all wealth ultimately is a creation of God, and thus in a strict sense is His

66. *Advance*, I (July 30, 1868): 6; 2 (June 10, 1869): 6; *Northwestern Christian Advocate*, 52 (January 17, 1877): 5.

possession and not man's. As one evangelical phrased it, "Power to get wealth, . . . time, opportunity, natural materials, are all the Creator's, loaned and withdrawn at his will. . . . In the Christian vocabulary ownership is nothing but stewardship." [67]

How one used his money, then, became a primary test of Christian character, or better yet, a crucial indicator of Christian witness, especially for those with large private sums to be disposed. "No man has the right to live in luxury and self-indulgence, using his powers only for his own enjoyment. Whatever he does he must do it in Christian service. [Philanthropy] must be the spontaneous outpouring of Christian love — not a substitute for that love, nor for Christian toil in saving men from sin." Evangelicals did not hesitate to go on from such general statements and assert what constituted effective stewardship for the rich laymen in their churches. Money given to evangelical institutions and programs was of primary significance, to be used for such things as the "conversion of the far-off heathen, the support of religious institutions at home, the prayers, exhortations, testimonies and songs of social meetings." Regular donations to public institutions were to be expected, and personal fortunes were to be kept at a minimum. Those who departed from such standards of public giving were suspect as Christians and sometimes even condemned publicly.[68]

The point which deserves emphasis here is that the philanthropic activities generated by the evangelical rationale — and they were considerable — not only financed many of the missionary efforts of the evangelical denominations, but ultimately made these groups dependent upon the business community for much of their economic support. In Moody's day, businessmen and the evangelicals saw eye to eye not only because they thought alike but also because their economic interests coincided. While much that they did to-

67. *Advance*, 8 (August 19, 1875): 860.
68. *New York Christian Advocate*, 47 (May 2, 1872): 137; *Zion's Herald*, 28 (May 14, 1868): 230. For an especially vivid condemnatory statement, with precise comments as to the ways evangelicals might have used the private fortune of a deceased wealthy Methodist layman, see *Northwestern Christian Advocate*, 4 (July 30, 1856): 121. See also *New York Observer*, 30 (August 26, 1852): 261; *Advance*, 3 (November 11, 1869): 8; (December 9, 1869): 4; *New York Christian Advocate*, 47 (May 23, 1872): 161; 51 (August 10, 1876): 252; 50 (April 29, 1875): 134; *New York Evangelist*, 54 (April 12, 1883): 4.

gether was constructive, economic dependency made it difficult for evangelical leaders to criticize the business community, even if they so desired, in any terms other than through judgments on personal morality and individual actions taken in the business world.[69]

Evangelical piety could also become rather easily a handmaiden of Christian stewardship and thereby promote the close identification of religion and the business community. For many evangelicals piety was perhaps the primary manifestation of faith in the workaday world. Piety bespoke an emotional state that grew out of the daily use of private prayer, diligent personal study of the Scriptures, and a certain feeling that the Holy Spirit dwelt within the individual believer. All this created a "right attitude of heart toward God," a phrase which some thought "synonymous with piety." As the *Congregational Herald* asserted feelingly in 1857, piety was "a personal thing," whose "chief duties can never be done by proxy." [70] In the purest sense, then, piety was an inner, near-mystical aspect of faith which might be hard to define in really precise terms. Over the years, however, rough yardsticks of measurement developed which might serve the unsophisticated evangelical laymen as practical tests of true piety. To these activist-minded people, a test of piety naturally became what a person *did* in the world, especially in seeking converts and promoting the varied causes officially supported by the church. Subtly and almost unknowingly piety became known "by its fruits" and was transferred in part into a practical doctrine of justification by works. In such a context the ground was prepared to make Christian stewardship a function, or external manifestation, of piety.

And who better exemplified to the church people of Moody's generation the best practices of Christian stewardship (and Chris-

---

69. Some evangelicals were fearful that traditional concepts of stewardship might disappear as business profits soared and personal financial restraints crumbled under such conditions. For an expression of this uneasiness, see the *New York Observer*, 43 (July 27, 1865): 234.

70. *Congregationalist*, 18 (February 23, 1866): 29; *Congregational Herald*, 5 (August 28, 1857): 2. See also *Congregational Herald*, 1 (April 30, 1853): 2; *Northwestern Christian Advocate*, 4 (June 18, 1856): 98; 17 (April 28, 1869): 132; *Congregationalist*, 25 (June 5, 1873): 177; *New York Evangelist*, 40 (October 14, 1869): 1; *New York Christian Advocate*, 51 (May 4, 1876): 140.

tian piety) than the Christian businessman? The interconnections were often made explicit for the evangelicals in their own denominational periodicals. In a Congregational publication of the 1850's, for example, a writer seeking to delineate his understanding of piety used the following revealing illustration:

> A Christian merchant . . . who is overwhelmed with his own business, surrounded by the din and clatter of gigantic enterprise, jostled in his patience and in his integrity by the tricks of the trade, . . . yet in all this maintaining the simplicity of his piety, keeping the flame of devotion alive in his closet, in his family and in the church, opening his heart and his hand to the worthy objects of benevolence and everywhere sustaining the deportment of a humble disciple, is developing a strength and beauty of piety which nothing but these very circumstances could have produced.[71]

It was in statements like this that the possibilities of intermingling the sacred and the secular became manifest, blurring the divisions between the two worlds in the popular mind until all seemed of a single piece.

Theological shortcomings were one final factor that made it easy for church people to embrace secular values. The anti-intellectualism of evangelical Protestantism, stemming from its pietistical biases, stood in the way of effective work by theologians. Churchmen needed to create theological positions that were based on Biblical authority, were relevant to the business-evangelical world, yet because of their Biblical grounding could be independent of, or even stand over against, the secular world of the nineteenth century. No such theological system, widely recognized and acceptable to large numbers within the churches, appeared in the years that Moody was shaping his religious perspective. Lacking an independent theological perspective, most evangelicals adopted with little question popularly expressed secular attitudes when dealing with social and economic questions.[72]

71. *Congregational Herald*, 5 (May 14, 1857): 2. See also *Northwestern Christian Advocate*, 4 (July 2, 1856): 106.
72. For indicative comments on this subject, see Mead, *Lively Experiment*, pp. 127–29.

A mixture of practical, economic, and ideological factors, therefore, enabled evangelical Protestants and businessmen to discover
mutual sympathies of considerable significance. Moody well represented this congruence of interests. His faith seemed fully compatible with the intensely competitive life he lived each day in
the world of business. Not too long after he arrived in Chicago,
the young shoe salesman wrote a lenghty letter to one of his
brothers in Massachusetts. Without any sense of unease or em-
barrassment, Moody boasted in one instant about lending money
at usurious rates and described his efforts at land speculation on
the outskirts of Chicago, and in the next moment pleaded for
his brother's conversion, hoping that he would "hold on to the
promise in the Bible" and not let "anything keep you from the
full enjoyment of God's love." [73] Perhaps it is easy to understand,
then, why after Moody left the market place for full-time religious
work, his social and economic values remained essentially those
of a conservative entrepreneur of the post–Civil War era. His interest in spreading the Gospel, a full-scale affair from the 1860's
on, can also be viewed as merely a more intense version of
the same concern professed by most of his business friends. Not
too surprisingly, in his later years the evangelist continued to consider business leaders across the country as some of his closest and
most helpful friends.

In June, 1860, Moody decided once again to steer a new course:
to abandon his career in the boot and shoe industry and to devote
his future entirely to religious work. Unfortunately the historical
remains are so scanty that we can only make a few educated guesses
as to why he followed the path he did. In some ways the reasons
for his decision are puzzling. The element of frustration present
when he chose to leave Boston, or when he established his little
school in the slums, did not appear to be a factor in this case. The
prospects for business success could not have been greater. As a
salesman on commission he had made $5,000 above his salary
in 1859. The growing demands of the mission school and the fact
that his job forced him to be outside of Chicago a great deal of the
time did create personal tensions. But seemingly he had resolved

73. D. L. Moody to George Moody, March 17, 1857, Moody Papers,
Powell.

these difficulties by securing a railroad pass from a friend, the superintendent of the Chicago, Burlington, and Quincy Railroad, which covered most of the territory he worked. At little expense to himself he was able to return every weekend to Chicago to carry out his duties at the North Market Hall.[74]

Moreover, if he gave up his business career, some of the immediate alternatives were not altogether pleasing. If he quit his job and thus relinquished a regular income, this would add uncertainty not only to his life but especially to the relationship developing between him and another young Chicagoan, Miss Emma C. Revell.[75] The two young people had announced their engagement, and lack of income would almost certainly delay plans for marriage. Finally, some people in the community had begun to wonder about his unorthodox tactics in scouting out sinners, which could very easily have raised doubts in his own mind about his ultimate effectiveness as a religious worker.[76]

Nevertheless, events were pushing him inexorably toward the point of decision. Bit by bit, almost undetected, his religious concerns were coming to dominate his life. These activities, at the outset only an after-hours pastime, now demanded a great deal of his thought and energies. When Moody believed in something deeply, his commitment was never halfhearted. Such was the case with the North Market Hall school. In addition, demands for his service in the YMCA might soon place additional burdens upon him. It was undeniable, too, that he thoroughly enjoyed his work with the poor people on the north side of Chicago. As he pushed deeper and deeper into evangelistic work, the claims on his energies from his two great passions — business and the Christian faith — were simply becoming too great even for his stout frame to bear. It became clear that he would have to decide to put one or the other first and end his dual role of businessman and Christian worker.

We can only surmise at all the reasons for his final decision. Assuredly, however, the break with the past was not as sharp as it

74. W. R. Moody, *Moody* (1900), p. 63; Daniels, *Moody and His Work*, pp. 80–81.
75. W. R. Moody, *Moody* (1930), p. 67.
76. *Northwestern Christian Advocate*, 18 (November 13, 1867): 36; W. R. Moody, *Moody* (1900), p. 75; *Advance*, 2 (March 19, 1868): 6.

seemed to be on the surface. In particular Moody was held in high esteem by many men in the Chicago business community. Working through and for the YMCA would do nothing to shatter that esteem. The views of all these men would remain quite similar, with Moody simply expressing his religious convictions a bit more professionally than the rest. Undoubtedly, too, these close connections with the business community enabled the young evangelist not to worry excessively about his future financial problems. John Farwell in particular had already demonstrated his willingness to draw on his rapidly expanding personal fortune to aid Moody's work. As long as Moody labored hard and produced in the realm of the spirit, why shouldn't his business friends reward him as a part of their benevolent activities? How better to implement their belief in stewardship than to support the spiritual endeavors of one who only recently was a full-time businessman and who obviously had a faith similar to their own!

Later in his life when Moody sought to explain why he had decided as he did in 1860, he always told a touching story about a young man teaching in his school who was leaving Chicago, dying of tuberculosis. Physically broken, he asked Moody to help him convert his class of young girls before he left, and by this devotion to the faith, he convinced Moody of his own duty.[77] The tale is highly sentimentalized and obviously too simple an explanation of Moody's motives. It does, however, point to perhaps the most obvious factor which influenced the young man as he struggled to make his decision. This was the growing realization that only by committing himself utterly and completely to the demands of his religious faith could he truly find happiness. Such a commitment meant taking huge gambles with his future, but it is only in such a context that the step Moody finally took makes sense. Another statement made by him in later years underscores this point more effectively than does the familiar tale about his Sunday school assistant in Chicago. In 1882 Moody asserted that "no man ought to give up his business & enter the ministry unless he feels

77. The story has been reprinted many times in later biographical studies. For example, see W. R. Moody, *Moody*, (1900), pp. 64–66; W. R. Moody, *Moody* (1930), pp. 65–67; John C. Pollack, *Moody: A Biographical Portrait of the Pacesetter in Modern Mass Evangelism* (New York: Macmillan Co., 1963), pp. 33–36.

that he can't help it." This meant that "a man should only enter the ministry when he is constrained to do so by love to God & love to man." Moody admitted that he had been sorely challenged by his vocational conflicts, but he finally decided as he did because "I was driven to it." [78]

Perhaps it is dangerous to accept too easily as correct the words of the person being scrutinized, but in this instance Moody's comments do seem to ring true. He had at last reached the point where he could throw himself on the mercies of Christ and believe that He would show the way, provide daily sustenance from some source, and assure ultimate success to this fledgling in the field of evangelism. The web of contacts Moody had established previously with influential people, the young man's innate shrewdness and willingness to act decisively to solve his problems, even mere circumstance and good fortune, would all play a part eventually in making him a figure of historical importance. But his religious faith had pressed upon him an imperative to evangelize, and had helped to harden his will in order to do so. All this caused him finally to take the path he did in 1860. In retrospect this appears to be one of the most decisive acts, if not *the* most decisive act, of Moody's life. Instinctively the young man sensed this, for later he stated that he wrestled with himself for three months or more before he finally made up his mind.[79] But for a man of Moody's temperament, after basic decisions were made, one acted immediately upon those decisions. Once turned in a new direction he never looked back, but began to apply all of his energies to the tasks which were thrust quickly into his hands.

78. *Evangelistic Record,* 1 (May, 1882): 5.
79. *Springfield* [Mass.] *Morning Union,* July 8, 1893. See also *Evangelistic Record,* 1 (May, 1882): 5.

3

The 1860's: Apprentice Evangelist

In the 1860's Moody matured considerably, as a wide range of new responsibilities pressed down upon his shoulders. The change can be noted by examining the few pictures of his countenance still available from that period. A daguerreotype printed in 1860 shows him still possessing a trim, lithe figure, and the familiar beard was as yet only side whiskers. He was still a youth. During the sixties and seventies his powerful, heavyset frame filled out. Gradually the lines under his eyes deepened, and the grave, unsmiling face seemed to add years rather rapidly with the appearance of a full beard.[1] A solid, bulky figure added to Moody's rather commanding presence, and he projected to the eye of anyone he met a sense of considerable physical energy and force.

Certainly he was a colorful figure, roughhewn and unorthodox in many ways. With part of his savings he purchased a pony to carry him about the north side of Chicago on his missionary endeavors. It was another method calculated to attract attention — and little heathens — to him. Contemporaries could recall later seeing the young man's pony literally covered with small-fry, with other children tagging along hoping for a ride. All of them were being led ever closer to Moody's mission school. In a rude, blundering sort of way, he accosted passersby on the street to inquire bluntly, "Are you a Christian?" As they sang or prayed, worship-

1. Many of these photographs have been reprinted in William R. Moody, *The Life of D. L. Moody* (New York: Fleming H. Revell Co., 1900), pp. 34, 69, 70, 88, 105, 142.

pers at the Illinois Street mission or at the noon prayer meetings of the YMCA nervously watched him striding up and down the aisles, seeking out those who seemingly lacked enthusiasm. Such people were to be cajoled, entreated, or even pushed immediately toward a decision for Christ.[2] Everyone respected his sincerity, but his indiscriminate and forceful accosting of strangers on the street and in his services to inquire after their souls undoubtedly irritated those who were used to more gentlemanly ways of dealing with people.[3]

Moody's excessive concern for everyone who walked the streets sometimes took on ludicrous overtones. One of his regular practices in the late sixties was to exhort the passersby in the evenings from the steps of the court house. Often these impromptu gatherings drew as many hecklers as supporters. Once as he strove to overcome the jeers of opponents, he discovered he was also shouting against the shrill voices of inmates of the city jail cells for women, which overlooked the scene.[4] Many Chicagoans probably viewed these rather crude efforts at evangelism as merely a reflection of Moody's naiveté and general lack of sophistication. Perhaps his questions were valid, but his manner of asking them upset people considerably. Some dismissed the queries and him with an irritated shrug of the shoulders, or even outright laughter.

2. Mention of Moody's pony is in D. L. Moody to "brother," January 13, 1862, Simeon King to A. P. Fitt, November 11, 1908, Thomas Stevens to W. R. Moody, February 20, 1923, Moody Papers, Moody Bible Institute, Chicago. The other incidents are cited in W. H. Daniels, *D. L. Moody and His Work* (Hartford, Conn.: American Publishing Co., 1875), pp. 83, 135–37.

3. Most of the accounts of Moody's forceful questioning came from the pens of his friends, who presented his tactics in a favorable light. Frederick F. Cook, however, in his reminiscence of *Bygone Days in Chicago: Recollections of the "Garden City" of the Sixties* (Chicago: A. C. McClurg, 1910), pp. 307–08, adopts the tongue-in-cheek attitude that some people undoubtedly maintained toward the young evangelist. See also the *Chicago Times*, October 28, 1867, clipping in the files of YMCA Historical Library, New York City.

4. See comments of Dr. J. N. Taylor, Crawfordsville, Indiana, in "Special Subjects" notebook, Moody Papers, Mrs. E. M. Powell, East Northfield, Massachusetts. Moody experienced open criticism of his ventures on the steps of the Court House. He did not hesitate to reply to his critics several times at the noon prayer meetings of the YMCA. (*Advance*, 2 [August 6, 1868]: 6; [September 3, 1868]: 6.)

Perhaps it was not surprising that although he was known all over the city for his distinctive tactics, in some circles he was called "crazy Moody."[5]

The young man's faith in the direct approach carried with it a brusque manner which annoyed people. He could deal summarily with those whom he disliked. The Unitarians, for example, sometimes used Farwell Hall, the YMCA building in downtown Chicago, for their activities. Once they hired it for a fair, and at a late hour tables were cleared away for dancing. Moody had come to clean up after the closing, and he registered strong objections. When the Unitarians ignored his protests, he ended the differences and the festivities for the evening by dousing the lights.[6]

There was also a certain officiousness about Moody's manner, at least in these younger days, which observers noted. Perhaps it was because he never seemed at a loss for words — was never hesitant to speak out, even when people did not solicit his opinions. In 1868 while in New York, he attended an examination of candidates for admission to the Plymouth Congregational Church of Brooklyn. During the proceedings he sought unabashedly to engage the nationally-known minister, Henry Ward Beecher, in dispute. "Suppose that I should come here," Moody asked, "a timid young man, scared nearly to death with the idea of being publicly examined before all these people, what would you do with me?" Beecher shot back the perfect squelch: "I cannot conceive that you could possibly come here under such circumstances."[7]

This incident also illuminated aspects of Moody's personality in ways which Beecher never realized. When one recalls the young man's painful experience many years earlier when he stood before a similar church examining committee in Boston, the question asked in Brooklyn assumes a special poignancy. The earlier event had been a moment when Moody's ignorance and religious

5. W. R. Moody, *Moody* (1900), p. 75. Much later his son asserted that Moody was able to tone down considerably this aspect of his personality as he grew older and mellowed somewhat. (Paul D. Moody, *My Father: An Intimate Portrait of Dwight Moody* [Boston: Little, Brown and Co., 1938], pp. 186–87.) The evangelist did eventually forego some of the more extreme manifestations of his proselytizing in Chicago, but he never abandoned fully the directness of approach noted here.

6. Daniels, *Moody and His Work*, pp. 150–51.

7. *Advance*, 2 (December 10, 1868): 6.

uncertainty stood nakedly revealed. Moreover, the church elders had rebuked him then for his inadequacies. The event remained a vivid memory for Moody fifteen years later. This fact suggests the evangelist's great sensitivity toward criticism, a personality trait he possessed throughout his life. One of his close associates once observed that in private Moody often wept "at the abuse heaped upon him by those who misunderstood and opposed him." In London in 1873, in the midst of a revival campaign, the evangelist discovered one of his Mount Vernon church examiners in the audience. Forcing him out of the shadows, Moody made him the object of laughter and made pointed comments about his failure at the hands of this man.[8] Seemingly Moody had constructed a tough exterior to help ward off life's blows, but in reality his sensitive nature lay very near the surface and he often reacted quickly and strongly to harsh words or the memory of earlier rebuffs.

The young man's touchiness and sensitive feelings sometimes were a detriment to him, but these traits were also a part of the more attractive side of his personality. This sensitivity especially revealed itself in his attitude toward children. Throughout his life young people in general, and his own children and grandchildren in particular, occupied a special place in Moody's affections. Perhaps it is no accident that his earliest private ventures in evangelism were among children, for whom he had an "intense and almost womanly love." There was a boyish, childlike element in Moody which also seemed to give him instant rapport with young people. He was unafraid to romp with boys and girls in the wildest fashion, beating them at their own games, and yet at the same time winning their fullest confidence. He was, as one writer has so well observed, "the biggest and jolliest boy of them all." [9]

Underneath his rough exterior there existed a man of simple warmth and affection. Gruff one minute, he could be reduced to tears the next. Coming from relatively humble beginnings, he never consciously allowed the affectations of social distinctions to stand between himself and less fortunate people. In his later years, as his individualist social ethic became increasingly irrelevant in the

8. D. W. Whittle Diary, November 27, 1876, Moody Bible Institute, Chicago, Ill.; Daniels, *Moody and His Work*, pp. 24–25.
9. Daniels, *Moody and His Work*, p. 37.

industrial society developing in this country, he was less able to maintain his affinity with all social groups. But during the almost two decades he lived in Chicago he was particularly successful in identifying with the poor, sharing their interests and problems, as well as those of the well-to-do segments of society.[10]

Moody also carried within him a streak of humility which saved him sometimes from difficulties created by his bluntness and impetuosity. His personal sensitivity caused him to realize, almost at the very moment he was hurting people, the damage to personal relationships that was occurring. Once this realization struck him he was quick to make apologies, even if it meant a public recantation which caused great pain to himself. Several dramatic incidents of this kind have been recorded, and there probably were others.[11]

As is so often the case, marriage helped considerably to mature the brash young man. He married Emma Charlotte Revell, a young girl of nineteen, on August 28, 1862. She quickly became a major influence in his life.[12] One of his sons once remarked that there seemed to be two things about which Moody never ceased to wonder. First was the use that God made of him in spite of his obvious handicaps; second was the miracle of having won the love of a young lady from a background so different from his and seemingly a person so superior to him in every respect.[13]

Emma Revell's father was a shipbuilder of Huguenot ancestry who emigrated to England and there met and married Moody's mother-in-law. Following business reverses and an accident in the shipyards that impaired his health, he emigrated with his family to America in 1849. His daughter Emma, who was born in London, was six years old when they finally settled in Chicago. Shortly after Moody arrived in the city the two young people met while both were teaching Sunday school. When Moody founded his own

10. *Advance*, 3 (September 2, 1869): 6.

11. *Association Men*, 40 (February 1915): 234, 246; *Advance*, 3 (September 2, 1869): 6; William R. Moody, *D. L. Moody* (New York: Macmillan Co., 1930), pp. 467–68; Paul Moody, *My Father*, pp. 82–83.

12. D. L. Moody to Betsey Moody, June 5, 1861, September 13, 1862, December 12, 1864, Moody Papers, Powell; Moody Family Bible, Moody Museum, Northfield School for Girls, East Northfield, Massachusetts.

13. Paul Moody, *My Father*, p. 52.

independent Sunday school, Emma Revell became one of the teachers. The two young people were engaged in 1859, shortly after Emma graduated from high school, and their marriage took place three years later.[14]

Pictures of Moody's wife while she was in her teens show her to have been quite beautiful. By the late seventies she had acquired maturity and a womanly charm that added to her attractiveness. She had a reserve which was the outward reflection of an unusual degree of self-control. Members of her family could never remember seeing her excited or flustered, even in the most trying moments. Frequently she communicated to her husband the poise he needed; we shall see this revealed most clearly in the crises that developed at the time of the founding of Moody Bible Institute in the 1880's. One evidence of Emma Moody's self-discipline came in the last two years of her life when she learned to write with her left hand after neuritis had crippled the right. At the time of Mrs. Moody's death, one of her husband's closest friends in his later years pointed out the special effects the evangelist's wife had had upon him. She had done much "in softening his asperities, . . . she polished his manners, she modified his brusqueness," and, perhaps to a degree, "taught him self-restraint." [15]

Moody and his wife differed in many personality traits. He was impulsive and outspoken, loved publicity, and possessed little formal education. She was retiring, intensely conventional and conservative, far better educated than he, fond of reading, and possessed a discriminating taste generally. She was averse to publicity, and her happiest hours were spent in her home, pursuing the daily tasks of housekeeping, writing letters, and entertaining her husband's innumerable friends.[16] Even in their physical makeup, husband and wife differed fundamentally. Emma was never

14. *Institute Tie*, n.s., 4 (November, 1903): 77–78.
15. *Ibid.*, p. 79.
16. Only in the writings of her sons and her granddaughter is the significance of Emma's influence on Moody made clear and biographical material made available. Much of what is said here comes from P. D. Moody, *My Father*, chap. 3. See also Emma M. Powell, *Heavenly Destiny: The Life Story of Mrs. D. L. Moody, by Her Granddaughter, Emma Moody Powell* (Chicago: Moody Press, 1943).

strong and suffered throughout her life from intense headaches.[17] In contrast were her husband's robust health and tireless energy.

Yet the two complemented each other perfectly. The evangelist always relied greatly upon her judgment, which in some respects was keener than his. In later years she acted as his personal secretary, caring for most of his correspondence. She took over entirely the financial affairs of the family, paying bills and taxes, and even putting money in the evangelist's pockets before he left on his many trips.[18] She did everything she could to free him from petty details so that he might engage in what he deemed to be the larger work of the moment.

She never allowed her influence to be evident on the surface. Seldom did she display herself at his public meetings. In the early revival campaigns, held after they left Chicago, she did help occasionally in the inquiry rooms, but she shunned even this public exhibition in her later years. Yet her son Paul rightly observed that when Moody died in 1899 his wife's "incentive was gone, the mainspring broken." She lived less than four years beyond her husband. So completely had her life been wrapped up in his that there was little left to live for when he passed away.

Throughout his life only a few of Moody's closest associates realized the extent to which he leaned on his wife, and she on him, for support. Even their correspondence, spanning several decades, fails to reveal the depths of the relationship. But one understands why Emma wrote to a close family friend from Edinburgh, Scotland, in 1881 that although Moody at first left his family in England when he went north to preach, he discovered

17. Emma C. Moody to W. R. Moody, January 14, 1886, February 16, 1889, Moody Papers, Powell; Whittle Diary, October 14, 1876; Emma C. Moody to "Mother," February 28, 1883, Emma C. Moody to W. R. Moody, May 7, 1888, February 4, 1889, February 11, 1889, Mrs. Frank R. Smith Collection, Library of Congress. Mrs. Moody's physical ailments probably possessed psychosomatic overtones; however, it may also be true, as her granddaughter has suggested, that her headaches were the product of allergies which were undetected at the time because of inadequate medical understanding. (Conversation of author with Mrs. Frank R. Smith, December 30, 1966.)

18. See especially Emma C. Moody to Betsey Moody, December 2, 1881, Emma C. Moody to Henry Rankin, May 17, 1882, Moody Papers, Powell; J. Mackinnon, *Recollections of Dwight L. Moody*, (Edinburgh, privately printed, 1905), p. 38; *Institute Tie*, n.s., 4 (November, 1903): 79.

that he "needed our care quite as much as we need him." Thus he had called for them to join him, and after the reunion his wife had observed, "we are very glad to be together again." In the same spirit Emma wrote to another friend on an earlier visit to England. "I know you will be pleased to know that . . . my husband . . . is going to spend Christmas here with us. I think I am more of a baby than either of the children, for I had really felt that I should have hard work on Christmas not to be homesick without him. It was always a *family* day . . . with us and we were always together then." [19]

Two of Moody's three children were born in the sixties. Emma arrived in 1863. This first child they named after Moody's wife, at his insistence. William Revell was born in 1869. Finally in April, 1879, during a long visit to Baltimore, the evangelist's second son, Paul, was born.[20] Moody's love for his children was almost as great as that he held for his wife. Letters written to relatives in New England provide glimpses of this deep personal affection. In a communication to his mother in 1864, for example, he spoke of the fact that his tiny daughter's little fingers were "as crooked as mine." This was a slight physical quirk that extended at least through three generations to Moody's grandchildren. The evangelist seemed not displeased that his daughter possessed the family trademark and thus perhaps was tied to him in a special way. Before he left Chicago, incidents from his experiences with little Emma and "Willie" found their way into his talks and sermons, which suggested his attachment to them and that they were never too far from the surface of his thoughts.[21] Thus the responsibilities of being a husband and then a father undoubtedly helped to round off some of the sharp corners of Moody's jagged personality.

19. Emma C. Moody to H. N. F. Marshall, December 22, 1881, Emma C. Moody to Mrs. J. Mackinnon, December 22, 1884, Moody Papers, Powell. See also earlier letters of Emma C. Moody to "Mother," December 1, 1862, September 2, 1874, Emma C. Moody to "brother," October 5, 1866, *ibid.*

20. Northfield Town Records, "Births," p. 35; Emma C. Moody to Betsey Moody, June 17, 1869, D. L. Moody to George Moody, April 19, 1879, Moody Papers, Powell.

21. D. L. Moody to Betsey Moody, December 12, 1864, Moody Papers, Powell; *Advance*, 2 (April 30, 1868): 6; (December 24, 1868): 6; 3 (February 4, 1869): 6.

The 1860's: Apprentice Evangelist

Changes in the evangelist's attitudes and personality were slow to occur, usually noticeable only in a cumulative way over a period of years. Moody's public career in the sixties, however, was much easier to trace and analyze. He began by working informally for the YMCA, spending most of his time encouraging people to attend the noon prayer meetings, which had fallen on declining days as the revival fervor of the late fifties faded. After he left the business world permanently, one of his biggest difficulties was his finances. Despite the lack of a regular salary, he could live cheaply since at that time he was a bachelor with relatively limited needs. But to cut expenses to the barest essentials, he lived for a time in the YMCA rooms downtown.[22] These actions seemingly contrasted sharply with Moody's previously mentioned interest in large financial gain and materialistic concerns. The shift in emphasis serves as one of the best indications of the seriousness of his decision to drop his business career, even if it meant foregoing some of the worldly pleasures that accompanied the work of a businessman. But he did have the prospect almost at the outset that most of his economic wants would be met satisfactorily. For a time Moody did have to scrimp. For a number of months he lived off his accumulated savings, but eventually he was able to rely on the steady financial backing of John Farwell and other businessmen who were connected with the YMCA. Although it is probable that he suffered some economic hardships in the first months after he left the business world, the widely repeated assertion that Moody remained in a state of semipoverty almost until he left Chicago seems overdrawn.[23]

22. Since Farwell was president of the Chicago YMCA at the time, he probably had a hand in working out these arrangements. See Emmett Dedmon, *Great Enterprises: 100 Years of the YMCA of Metropolitan Chicago* (Chicago: Rand McNally, 1957), p. 366; D. L. Moody to J. V. Farwell, May 7, 1874, Moody Papers, Moody Bible Institute.

23. One of the most recent statements emphasizing Moody's financial difficulties is in Bernard Weisberger, *They Gathered at the River: The Story of the Great Revivalists and Their Impact upon Religion in America* (Boston: Little, Brown and Co., 1958), p. 188. For contrary evidence, see Moody's own evaluation in *Boston Post*, April 26, 1877. See also Bessie Pierce, *A History of Chicago*, 3 vols. (New York: Alfred A. Knopf, 1937–57), 2:359, n. 19; D. L. Moody to J. V. Farwell, May 7, 1879, Moody Papers, Moody Bible Institute.

His efforts on behalf of the Association soon became more formalized. The YMCA hired him "as Librarian with the understanding that he shall act as an agent for the Association and City Missionary." This was in reality a grandiloquent honorary title, for Moody received no salary. But his new duties did make him the first full-time employee of the Chicago YMCA.[24]

Prior to 1861 the Chicago Association struggled to remain in existence. Frequently there was a lack of funds, more often the absence of concerted leadership. The lay leaders, burdened with other business and civic responsibilities, seemed to lack the time or the will to make the Association effective. Late in 1859 members had given serious thought to a suggestion that the group disband.[25] But meetings continued to be held, and by 1861 two new developments had changed the picture noticeably. The first event of significance was the coming of the Civil War, which made new demands upon the organization. The result was a burst of fresh enthusiasm and a renewed flow of money from the purses of members to finance the expanding operations of the YMCA. The second factor of importance was Moody himself. He was chiefly responsible for translating the new interest in the YMCA into concrete programs. Most important, he brought to the Association a consistency in daily planning and leadership that could weld it into a highly effective organization. "He more than any other man," it seemed, "provided the energy and leadership necessary to capitalize on these new opportunities and push the YMCA into the foreground." [26]

As soon as the Federal army began to take shape, a demand arose for religious workers to circulate among the troops. The Chicago YMCA set up an army committee to offer help, and in the autumn of 1861 Moody went to Kentucky and southern Illinois as the first representative of the Association to the soldiers. Evidently he was popular with the men, for one regiment asked him to remain as their chaplain; but eventually he had to return home

24. Board of Managers, *Minutes* (Archives, Chicago YMCA), May 13, 1861.

25. *Advance*, 2 (March 19, 1868): 6; F. Roger Dunn, "Formative Years of the Chicago Y.M.C.A.: A Study in Urban History," *Journal of the Illinois State Historical Society*, 37 (December 1944): 342–43.

26. Dunn, "Formative Years of the Chicago Y.M.C.A.," p. 345.

because of the press of duties in Chicago.[27] These early attempts of Moody and the Chicago YMCA to minister to men in the ranks were localized efforts, lacking any coordination with a nationally organized movement to evangelize the troops. As the war turned into a protracted conflict, the United States Christian Commission emerged as the organization providing the most direct link between the evangelical churches and the armies in the field. Organized in November, 1861, the Christian Commission was the principal institution through which YMCA members contributed to the war effort. The Chicago Association served as the headquarters for the northwestern branch of the Commission.[28]

The prewar interdenominational benevolent societies actually served as the foundation stones on which evangelicals built the Christian Commission. An historian of the prewar movement has aptly described the Commission as "the benevolent societies geared for war." Most of the national officers of the Commission were also leaders in one or more of the groups which overarched the evangelical denominations. George H. Stuart of Philadelphia, the president of the Commission, was an officer in the Sunday School and Temperance Unions; Joseph Patterson, a Philadelphia bank president, was treasurer of the Christian Commission and manager of the Sunday School Union. Other Commission leaders included William E. Dodge, a wealthy New Yorker and a member of the Bible Society and the Temperance Union, and nationally-known evangelical ministers Charles P. McIlvaine and Russell S. Cook, both high officials in the Tract Society. The Commission readily identified with northern war aims to preserve the Union and punish the treason of seceding southerners. But as might be expected, the greatest concern was for evangelism among the ranks of blue-coated army men. The volunteer agents of the Commission fanned out over the battlefield

27. *Advance*, 2 (March 19, 1868): 6; A. T. Andreas, *History of Chicago: From the Earliest Period to the Present Time*, 3 vols., (Chicago: A. T. Andreas, 1884–86), 2:182–83; Lemuel Moss, *Annals of the United States Christian Commission* (Philadelphia: J. B. Lippincott & Co., 1868), p. 309; Edward P. Smith, *Incidents of the United States Christian Commission* (Philadelphia, J. B. Lippincott & Co., 1869), p. 60; D. L. Moody to Betsey Moody, November 19, 1861, Moody Papers, Powell.
28. Moss, *Annals, Christian Commission*, p. 105.

areas seeking conversions and preaching the need for the continuance of those standards of personal morality long sanctioned
by evangelicals everywhere. The agents used the familiar propa-
gandistic procedures of the benevolent societies, distributing cheap
Bibles and religious tracts and holding temperance and revival
meetings.[29]

Serving as one of the volunteer agents for this national organization, Moody visited the battlefields at least four times during
the war. He happened to be one of the first representatives of
the Commission to enter the fallen Confederate capital of Richmond in 1865. During his terms of service he helped to care for
the wounded, and invariably sought to spread the Gospel, in his
own inimitable way, among the men in uniform.[30] These experiences in association with the Christian Commission formed an
important part of the background to his later career as a revivalist. He saw the war at first hand, building up in his memory
a reservoir of sights and sounds to be drawn upon in the seventies
and eighties for homely sermon illustrations common to the
experience of many men in his audiences. His work for the Commission also enabled him to meet people from many parts of
the country. Commission representatives were usually ministers
or YMCA members; thus Moody was already establishing personal contacts that eased his way as a revivalist in many localities
a decade later. For example, William E. Dodge, George Stuart,
and John Farwell were the key leaders of the Christian Commission in New York City, Philadelphia, and Chicago. Ten years
later each of them played important roles in organizing Moody's
revivals in their respective cities.

Moody did most of his war work, however, in the Chicago area.

29. Clifford S. Griffin, *Their Brothers' Keepers: Moral Stewardship in
the United States, 1800–1865* (New Brunswick, N. J.: Rutgers University
Press, 1960), chap. 13, especially pp. 242–54. The quotation in the paragraph is on p. 249 of Griffin's study.

30. Moss, *Annals, Christian Commission*, pp. 492, 122; E. P. Smith,
Incidents, Christian Commission, p. 63; "Annual Statistical Reports of
Branch Offices, 1864, Chicago Committee," "Register of Delegates, United
States Christian Commission," "Delegates' Register, No. 3, United States
Christian Commission, commencing January 1, 1865," "Names of Dele-
gates Commissioned by the United States Christian Commission," MSS
in the National Archives, Washington, D. C.

Camp Douglas, at the southern edge of the city, was a focal point for his activities. He conducted frequent prayer meetings at the camp, published and distributed soldiers' hymnbooks, and handed out innumerable religious tracts to the men. Soon after the war began the Federal army turned the camp into a prison for captured Confederate soldiers. Moody also sought converts among these southerners. The evangelist was not impartial in his political loyalties, however. He was always an unquestioning supporter of the northern cause. When the war started, for example, he was personally active in recruiting a battalion of volunteers for Lincoln's armies from the young members of the Chicago YMCA. And patriotic sentiments quickly obliterated thoughts of rebel conversions when he heard of a conspiracy among the prisoners at Camp Douglas to attempt a mass escape and then burn Chicago.[31]

During the war the YMCA also expanded its relief work among the civilian population of Chicago. Moody took a prominent role in developing these services for the community. Privately he had begun to distribute food and clothing to the poor in 1860, but during the winter of 1861 he merged these limited individual efforts with those of the YMCA. The Association set up a carefully devised system of distribution with Moody's Sabbath school as its base of operations. Moody and the mission school staff selected prospective families to be helped; people were sent goods only after they had been carefully screened by a committee composed of YMCA members and citizens at large.[32] This activity of the YMCA probably related more to the side effects of urbanization than to difficulties created by war. Ethnic and occupational groups, as well as the church, engaged in works of benevolence of this sort throughout the sixties. Moody's efforts were only part of a widespread attempt by both public and private organizations

31. Moss, *Annals, Christian Commission*, pp. 76, 308; *Fourth Annual Report, Chicago Y.M.C.A.* (Chicago, 1862), pp. 9–10; Managers, *Minutes*, September 8, 1862; *Advance*, 2 (March 19, 1868): 6; John V. Farwell, *Early Recollections of Dwight L. Moody* (Chicago: Winona Publishing Company, 1907), pp. 44–45.

32. *Fourth Annual Report, Chicago Y.M.C.A.*, p. 9. In the first year the Association disbursed almost $2300 worth of food, fuel, clothing, and medicine to over 550 families.

in Chicago to cope with the economic insecurities felt by many people in the city.[33]

Yet for evangelicals the YMCA's program of relief always carried with it aims and purposes that set it apart from the general public's attempts to provide support for the poor. The YMCA was engaging in a program of evangelism as well as public relief. This was made clear by the president of the Chicago Association in 1862. "Very many heads of families," he claimed, "have through this agency [of relief], been induced to attend Mission prayer meetings . . . thus bringing joy and gladness to hundreds of homes in our city, heretofore mortgaged to Satan." Church people understood this justification of the work of Moody and the YMCA perfectly, and approved it. The general community was not to be misled concerning the intent of the local Association. It was "not organized to be a Relief Society," emphatically asserted one Chicago-based evangelical journal, "but to do distinctive, religious work. The desire to save men explains the ground upon which this Association has stood with reference to the distribution of charity to the poor." But care for the soul could not be neatly compartmentalized and set apart from concern for the body. Thus evangelicalism instilled in its adherents a sensitivity toward the ills and disabilities of the unfortunate that was fully consistent with the ultimate spiritual goals of the faith. "Earnest working Christianity is apt to be comprehensive, and to care for both soul and body. No harm ordinarily comes from doing good in both simultaneously." Indeed, where better to look for an example to follow than to the Lord of faith? "It was the same Jesus who first preached the gospel all day to the multitudes, that then fed them miraculously." [34] Probably in some such way did Moody and the other members of the Chicago YMCA view their work as they expanded services to the poor in the early 1860's.

Under Moody's leadership the YMCA also developed a system for the city-wide distribution of religious tracts. He served on the Association's tract committee beginning in 1862, and as city missionary the practical execution of the program rested almost en-

33. Pierce, *History of Chicago*, 2:442–52.
34. *Fourth Annual Report, Chicago Y.M.C.A.*, p. 9; *Advance*, 1 (November 7, 1867): 4.

tirely in his hands. Not content with utilizing the membership of the YMCA, he cajoled churches and Sabbath schools throughout the city to cooperate in distributing this evangelistic literature. The scope of this effort at evangelism can be seen in a report printed in 1863 which announced that during the previous year and a half, in the course of thousands of visitations to individual homes and businesses, the YMCA had given away religious literature totaling well over half a million pages.[35]

Moody also continued to use the North Market Hall Mission as an outlet for evangelism. The school gradually found itself drawn under the sheltering wing of the YMCA, yet it also remained a very personal expression of Moody's religious work, since he remained the overall supervisor and spent a great deal of time involved in the school's activities. In April, 1862, the board of managers of the YMCA voted to bring the school "under the patronage of the Association." This seemed to be a natural step to take since the mission's nondenominational character paralleled that of the sponsoring organization, and because members of the YMCA were the school's principal supporters.[36]

By the middle of 1862 some 450 children were attending the North Market school regularly. Still believing that the school had responsibilities to the adults as well as to the children of the area, Moody also conducted prayer meetings for the parents. The congregation evidently attracted immigrant families, for one of the school's programs was designed to help such people adjust to their new environment. During the winter months a "school . . . was maintained gratuitously . . . three evenings in the week, for instruction in the common English branches."[37]

This evening educational program pointed implicitly to the very real inadequacies in the common school system in Chicago.

35. *Northwestern Christian Advocate*, 11 (November 18, 1863): 364; *Fourth Annual Report, Chicago Y.M.C.A.*, p. 13; Managers, *Minutes*, May 19, 1862, July 14, 1862, November 9, 1863. For a slightly different estimate on tract distribution, covering approximately the same period, see the *Chicago Tribune*, March 18, 1863.

36. Managers, *Minutes*, April 14, 1862. No information other than the statement of the board is available to explain Moody's role in effecting these arrangements.

37. *Chicago Tribune*, February 23, 1864; *Fourth Annual Report, Chicago Y.M.C.A.*, p. 8.

Between 1850 and 1870, even as new residents poured into the city, school enrollments showed a steady proportionate decline of children of alien parents. Thousands of youngsters in the city from both immigrant and native American backgrounds went to school only occasionally or not at all. It has been estimated that during the 1860's only thirty-five per cent of the school population was cared for in even a fairly satisfactory way.[38] It was understandable that a man like Moody, with his intimate contacts among the groups most directly affected by such conditions, should try to ameliorate the situation.

Attacking illiteracy was a primary and obvious goal of the mission school's educational efforts. But even more important, Moody's program played a part in the Americanization of the newcomers. Instruction in English helped to break down those social and cultural distinctions which tended to set the immigrants apart. It worked to eliminate the "strange" ways and seeming aloofness of these people from the rest of the population. Americanization was also to be viewed as another method of social control. Through the program of instruction at North Market Hall, native Americans could begin to suggest to the new arrivals in this country what constituted desirable social attitudes and norms of public behavior.[39]

By 1863 the Sabbath school had outgrown its facilities and Moody began to lay plans for the erection of a separate building for his mission. With expanded facilities, devotional work with the parents could be expanded. Such thoughts pointed in turn toward the eventual creation of a free church designed primarily to serve the poor on the north side of Chicago. With substantial gifts from John Farwell, who provided more than half the money to meet expenses, Moody's group purchased a lot on the corner of Illinois and Wells streets, and by February, 1864, workmen

38. Pierce, *History of Chicago*, 2:390–91.
39. Similar attitudes were present in the larger community. In the Chicago public schools in the 1860's, for example, courses designed to inculcate patriotic sentiments in the students were given special emphasis. This development reflects perhaps both the desire of native Americans to make the newcomers conform, and the recognition on the part of the immigrants that embracing the flag was one of the surest avenues to rapid amalgamation into their newly adopted society. (Pierce, *History of Chicago*, 2:393.)

had completed a large brick edifice. The building included an auditorium seating 1,500, numerous classrooms, and a chapel. The hopes of the directors of the school that improved facilities would enhance their prospects were soon fulfilled. Enrollment spurted upward in the months immediately following completion of the building. By the end of 1865 there was an average weekly attendance of 750 students, and Moody's work had become the second largest mission Sabbath school in Chicago.[40]

Almost as soon as the building was finished, Moody made a move to expand his operations there by founding what came to be known as the Illinois Street Church. This development partly reflected the problems facing a Sabbath school that lacked the sponsorship of a particular church or denomination. As time passed, members of the school grew up and thus technically were no longer eligible to attend. But the evangelical churches evidently had questions about accepting Moody's converts into their fellowships. This was in contrast to the YMCA, whose members could often point to previous connections with one of the denominations. The usual practice was for the churches or YMCA officials to inquire about these connections, and then assign individuals to an appropriate local church group for further nurture and care.

Moody's charges were different. Many had no formal religious antecedents and thus were looked upon with some suspicion. Moreover, the ties of friendship and emotion binding them to the school were often quite strong. As a contemporary observer commented, "they had come up together out of poverty and ignorance; they had learned their duty in the same school, and under the same teacher; and thus their fellowship of suffering, as well as their fellowship of faith, was something with which no stranger might intermeddle." [41] The Sunday school had been their only spiritual home and they did not want to go elsewhere to worship. They could rationalize this desire further by arguing that as the

40. *Chicago Tribune*, February 23, 1864; Emma R. Moody to Samuel Moody, December 26, 1863, Moody Papers, Powell; *Manual, Illinois Street Church*, pp. 45–47; *Halpin's Chicago City Directory, 1865–66*, p. xxxv; Pierce, *History of Chicago*, 2:370.
41. Daniels, *Moody and His Work*, p. 104.

school rapidly expanded, adult workers would be needed in increasing numbers, so that to leave might actually work a hardship on Moody.

Along with friends from the YMCA and his own mission school people, Moody invited representatives of all the evangelical churches to participate in discussions leading to the formation of the new organization. Some of the ministers who were asked to participate indicated a desire to integrate Moody's work into the programs of their particular denominations. Moody rejected these suggestions. Ultimately only the Congregationalists provided direct assistance. The young evangelist's practical emphasis on a "gathered" church and his distaste for ecclesiastical hierarchies blended well with Congregational sentiments. Unquestionably his personal connections with local groups in this denomination also counted.[42] In any case, the Congregationalists played an important role in helping Moody organize his church, especially in shaping the doctrinal statements of purpose and the bylaws which the new group sought to follow. With plans completed, the Illinois Street Church came into being officially on December 30, 1864. Moody headed the list of twelve charter members.[43]

The statement of objectives and the policy outlined in the first bylaws of the church may well serve as one of the earliest indications of Moody's religious preferences, for his concurrence was essential in any effort to explain and justify publicly the new

42. Moody was changing churches for the second time since his arrival in Chicago when he helped form the Illinois Street Church. On January 4, 1863, he had moved to the New England Congregational Church from the Plymouth Congregational Church on the near north side. His release from membership there came on December 28, 1864, pending organization of the Illinois Street Church. (Records, New England Church, Chicago Theological Seminary Library, pp. 139, 144, 175; Register of Church Members, New England Church, Chicago Theological Seminary Library, p. 10.)

43. Daniels, *Moody and His Work*, pp. 105–12; August F. Fry, Jr., "D. L. Moody: The Formative Years, 1856–1873" (unpublished B. D. thesis, Chicago Theological Seminary, 1955), pp. 12–17; *Manual, Illinois Street Church*, pp. 10–12. Whether there was conscious intent on the part of the charter members to pattern their actions after the number of Christ's original disciples is not known, but this identity in numbers is striking.

venture. These bylaws suggest that the young man's spiritual interests were clearly evangelical but not strictly denominational in character. This nondenominationalism in thought as well as institutional loyalties was particularly important in facilitating his eventual move into revivalism. Almost unknowingly his religious activities were creating for Moody a perspective that reached beyond that of the average church leader of his time. He espoused key aspects of evangelical doctrine which commended him to the faithful of all churches, yet at the same time he was easing himself out of some of the institutional constraints which affected other men of perhaps equal abilities, people burdened too much with denominational responsibilities and allegiances. Because he never really thought in terms of the sometimes constricting denominational framework, it would be relatively easy for him to slip into the role of the professional revivalist, who professed to be the representative of all denominations.

The founding of the Illionois Street Church also pointed to a weakness in the evangelical community which obstructed and frustrated the evangelist occasionally in his work, both in the 1860's and later. A powerful identification with middle class values sometimes made it difficult for the evangelical churches to implement fully and effectively the imperatives of their faith to evangelize *all* people, including the less advantaged groups in society. A man with large personal sympathies, Moody seemed able to work toward this all-inclusive goal more successfully than some. Occasionally he was even willing to devise somewhat independent institutional forms in order to reach people outside the church when conditions within militated against their ready acceptance. Thus the cultural bias of evangelical Protestants favoring middle-class social values produced mixed results for Moody. Although he readily embraced these values in many ways, at times during his life he came into conflict with them. Then his deepest passion, that of evangelizing the world, was rendered partially ineffective by insensitive churchgoers who ignored or deliberately avoided people whose status and habits clashed with their own standards of behavior.

In its daily operations the new independent church also sought to maintain the informality that was such an appealing aspect of the Sabbath school that preceded it. The Sunday evening tea meeting of the early sixties was continued, although now it convened for an hour and a half on Friday nights, a combination business meeting for the officers of the church, prayer meeting open to all, and social gathering for the congregation. The binding effect that these gatherings had upon the church continued to be as extraordinary as it had been earlier for participants in the Sabbath school.[44] In many ways these Friday evening tea meetings became the central institutional expression of the life of the church, even though regular church services were held at the traditional times on Sunday.

Another almost equally popular part of the church's program was the Sunday school, held regularly on Sunday afternoons. Although ostensibly set up for the education and religious nurture of the children of the parish, many adults also came because Moody taught a class regularly. The evangelist evidently had the knack of speaking quite effectively to a mixed audience of children and grown-ups. Starting out with the prescribed lesson plans of the National Sunday School Union, Moody added his distinct personal flourishes. He fashioned, for example, a huge blackboard, eight by ten feet in size, dragged it into the classroom, and used it to help dramatize his comments or applications of the lesson. Soon hundreds of adults crowded in to hear these lectures. Moody soon changed the title of his Sunday afternoon talks from "Sunday school lessons" to "Bible classes," to make his older hearers more comfortable.[45]

The church officers devised a system for the careful examination and admission of new members, exhibited constant concern for the sick, and developed a visiting system that applied to all members of the congregation and to the parish generally. By the end of the sixties, Moody's church seemed well established. At the same time, the pragmatic, freewheeling spirit of the leader of the congregation also expressed itself sufficiently in church programs to keep the fellowship alive and alert. Institutional order and freedom to change or innovate seemed blended together in a most effective manner. In the early 1870's membership was

44. *British Evangelist* (February 2, 1874), p. 91.
45. *Ibid.*

estimated to be near 800. While this figure may represent an inflated estimation, it is clear that under Moody's guidance the Illinois Street Church did not take long to become an effective religious organization that meant a great deal to those who participated in it.[46]

As the Civil War came to an end, Moody found his horizons still relatively limited. With the exception of the time spent with the Christian Commission, he had devoted nearly all of his energies during the war to work in the Chicago area. Soon, however, he was to take on new responsibilities which were to broaden greatly his contacts and experience. One event of importance occurred in 1866 when he was chosen president of the Chicago YMCA for the first time.[47] Since he was reelected three times thereafter, a four-year term in office enabled him to utilize considerably his organizational talents. In one of his early speeches given as president, Moody radiated the enthusiasm which sparked the Association in its new tasks. "It seems to me the Association has just commenced its work. There are those, indeed, who say we have reached the limit of our power. But we must rally round the Cross; we must attack and capture the whole city for Christ." [48]

By means of public pronouncements like this and through an expanding network of activities, the YMCA under Moody's leadership sought to push forward personal evangelism throughout the city. In Moody's eyes, probably the most important program designed to implement this purpose was the daily noon prayer meetings conducted in the downtown headquarters of the YMCA. Here the message of repentance and conversion to the Christian

46. *Ibid.*, pp. 91, 92.

47. Moody's rise to the presidency can be clearly traced in the minutes of the board of managers. The evidence shows that it was all but inevitable that Moody would eventually become president. In late 1862 the board first asked him to sit with them at all their regular meetings. The following year he became a member of the board with all but official approval. During the war he was a member of almost every important committee of the association. His election to the presidency first came on March 26, 1866. (Managers, *Minutes*, December 8, 1862, July 13, 1863, March 29, 1866, March 25, 1867, March 10, 1868, March 22, 1869.) See also Managers, *Minutes*, July 10, 1865, July 20, 1865, October 9, 1865.

48. Quoted in Daniels, *Moody and His Work*, p. 126.

faith was presented at a time and place designed to confront most directly the aspiring young businessmen of the Windy City. The idea for these meetings at the YMCA undoubtedly originated in the great noonday gatherings in downtown Chicago which were a primary manifestation of the revival of 1857–58. Moody had participated in these earlier meetings, and it was easy for him to borrow from earlier experiences.[49]

For many evangelicals, prayer meetings reflected more fully than perhaps any other activity the quality of day-to-day life in the churches and nondenominational evangelical organizations. "The prayer meeting," asserted a Presbyterian of Moody's time, "is a sort of thermometer to measure the religious temperature of the congregation." This writer went on to assay the specific functions of the prayer meeting. "It is the life of the church, the expression of its desire for the salvation of sinners, the united power it puts forth to bring down the blessing."[50] This meant, first, that the prayer meeting was the primary means by which groups of believers maintained a continuous process of spiritual renewal. Usually stressing private contemplation and individual and corporate public expressions of prayer, the prayer meeting was a highly effective way of carrying out corporate worship in a religious community as deeply committed to pietism as were the evangelicals. Thus prayer meetings often served as the heart of the ongoing life of many local congregations.

The prayer meeting also served two other not entirely unrelated purposes. As evangelicals searched for sinners outside the fold,

49. Managers, *Minutes*, November 9, 1863; *Fourth Annual Report, Chicago Y.M.C.A.*, pp. 11, 13. There were other services sponsored by the YMCA, all of them expanded during Moody's term as president, which were more secular in emphasis. Lyceum lectures attracted great interest, the program of tract distribution was continued, and the Association's library was expanded. All of these programs, however, were thought ultimately to serve religious purposes. The lectures usually stressed moral themes heavily, and Moody himself admitted privately that he wanted the "lending library of the northwest under control of the friends of Christ" whose principles of selection of books would differ noticeably from those governing other private lending libraries in Chicago. (Managers, *Minutes*, March 10, 1868; Dunn, "Formative Years of the Chicago Y.M.C.A.," pp. 345, 347–59; *Advance*, 2 [March 19, 1868]: 6; D. L. Moody to Cyrus H. McCormick, January 1, 1869, Cyrus H. McCormick Papers, Wisconsin State Historical Society, Madison, Wis.)

50. *New York Observer* (March 23, 1865), p. 89.

they came to recognize the importance of prayer in drawing the unconverted to God. It was a means of attracting the Lord's attention to specific individuals as yet spiritually untouched, and also a way, indirectly perhaps, of "softening the heart" of the person sought after, thereby easing the way to his eventual conversion. Intercessory and supplicatory prayers to fulfill this purpose thus became a common part of the life of worship within the evangelical churches. Finally, it was recognized that an essential precondition for the periodic showering-down of revival blessings upon the churches was fervent, insistent supplications for such blessings from the congregations which desired to be affected. For a religious community like the evangelicals, in which revivals were almost a condition of survival, prayer meetings were more than justified. These meetings, then, were important because their threefold purpose related directly to the innermost springs of action within evangelical Protestantism — the corporate life of daily worship, the search for the unconverted, and the drive to ignite revivals from time to time within the body of believers. Thus it is easy to see why Moody thought it important to maintain and expand the daily noon prayer meetings if the Chicago YMCA were to be a truly evangelical body, for "the promises of Christ are there to be pleaded, with combined confidence, and great is the good that comes from such union of heart and soul, in making known our requests to God." [51]

The format of the prayer meetings organized by Moody under the auspices of the YMCA possessed considerable flexibility. The techniques and procedures used deserve some attention, however, for they are reminders of many of the tactics utilized by Moody in his revivals in the 1870's. This was true even of the efforts used initially to attract eligible young men off the city streets into the YMCA meeting rooms for the services. Moody himself once described these attempts at aggressive salesmanship. YMCA members stood on all the bridges crossing the Chicago River and leading to the central sections of the city, there to extend personal invitations to meetings. Near the YMCA's rooms in the Loop, the "best looking, most attractive" young men, in Moody's words,

51. *Ibid.*

were stationed, prepared to guide inquiring strangers inside.[52] Shrewd methods of advertising were already in evidence in Moody's work.

The order of worship in the prayer service varied somwhat from day to day. Moody led personally most of these services. Sometimes he made rather extended remarks which served as a sermon; at other times he included opportunities for discussion and comments from the floor. These were the moments when Moody began to hammer together the structure of his personal religious beliefs. By the late 1860's he was even using illustrations in his talks that he used frequently in the sermons he preached later as a revivalist.[53] The evangelist also came to realize the value of music — to have variety in hymns and to use a song leader in the service. A brisk tempo in the pace of the service was important, for this made things "lively and interesting." Moody used a simple device to keep windy prayers and extended testimony from the floor within bounds. He had a large bell installed which struck like the sound of doom at the end of three minutes' comment. Members of the Chicago YMCA became famous for the amount of information and words they could spew out in a three-minute speech or prayer! Other parts of the service were more traditional — the reading of "requests for prayer" sent in by those fearing for the spiritual welfare of languishing relatives and friends, reports of successful revivals and evangelistic work being carried on outside Chicago. Nearly all these procedures became a part of the more elaborate prayer meetings held in conjunction with Moody's great urban revivals a decade or so later.[54]

Moody's evangelistic tactics for the YMCA were wedded almost

52. *Proceedings of the Fifteenth Annual Y.M.C.A. National Convention* (June, 1870), p. 49.

53. *Advance*, 2 (January 9, 1868): 7; (August 6, 1868): 6; 3 (January 28, 1869): 6; (December 12, 1869): 6; 4 (May 12, 1870): 6. For a sound recent analysis of Moody's early theology, reconstructed from reports of the noon prayer meetings in *Advance*, see Fry, "D. L. Moody: The Formative Years." See chap. 7 for a more complete consideration of Moody's theological views.

54. *Proceedings of the Fifteenth Annual Y.M.C.A. National Convention* (June, 1870), p. 71; *Proceedings of the Thirteenth Annual Y.M.C.A. National Convention* (June, 1868), pp. 107–08, 122, 123; *Advance*, 1 (January 30, 1867): 7; (November 21, 1867): 3; (December 12, 1867): 6; 2 (February 13, 1868): 6.

invariably to enthusiasm and fervor. The young evangelist once sought to explain his missionary efforts, particularly as he applied them in the noon prayer meetings, to some associates.

> We speak out plainly no mistake. Then, when all is at white heat, I jump for the first stranger, and ask him . . . "Are you a Christian?" "No, Sir!" "Well, don't you want to be one?" "Yes sir!" Then our young Christians "spot him!" They surround him and follow up the capture.

These words with military overtones reflect quite well Moody's zealousness in his everlasting pursuit of potential Christians. Although he became a bit more restrained in his methods later, he never fully lost his all but compulsive tendency to try to push prospective converts "headforemost into the Kingdom of Heaven." [55]

During the years that Moody was president, the Chicago Association also carried on an extensive building program. Under his leadership the members financed and built the first fully equipped YMCA building in the United States. In January 1868, scarcely three months after the dedication of the $200,000 structure, it was destroyed by fire. This was a crushing blow to the Association, but the membership immediately laid plans to rebuild. With surprising dispatch, in little more than a year a new hall was opened to the public.[56]

Moody played a prominent role in raising money needed to construct these buildings. The fund-raising techniques which he began to develop at this time were to be of inestimable value to him during the rest of his life, helping him to finance his large scale revivals in the 1870's and to underwrite much of the annual budgets of the three schools he founded in the 1880's.[57] The young

55. *Proceedings of the Fifteenth Annual Y.M.C.A. National Convention*, p. 49; Daniels, *Moody and His Work*, p. 137.

56. *Chicago Times*, October 1, 1867; *Ninth Annual Report, Chicago Y.M.C.A.* (Chicago, 1867), pp. 9–10; Managers, *Minutes*, January 7, 1868; *Chicago Tribune*, January 8, 1868, January 20, 1868, January 20, 1869.

57. By means of personal solicitation and royalties from the sale of hymn books written by him and his partner, Ira D. Sankey, Moody raised during his lifetime almost $2,500,000 for charitable enterprises. See pp. 318–19, for further comments about the evangelist's fund-raising activities in later years.

man's handling of Cyrus McCormick as a prospective donor to the YMCA in 1866 is instructive. He sought to use McCormick as the bait with which to hook gifts from other businessmen — gifts to be used in the Association's building program. As Moody shrewdly observed to the inventor and manufacturer, "The public will think, if you take hold of it, it must succeed." Moreover, once McCormick had agreed to help with $10,000, Moody made the first public announcement of the gift at the annual anniversary meeting of the Chicago YMCA, which he knew would be reported fully in the Chicago newspapers.[58]

Moody worked as a fund-raiser before the era when huge, impersonal community or nationwide drives for charitable agencies were conducted. In the less complicated world of the 1860's his work was limited to personal, individual contacts and solicitation. Based on common sense and a knack for handling people, his techniques worked quite well. Yet Moody's achievements as a fund-raiser, begun while in Chicago and sustained until his death at the end of the century, also pointed to and were products of the new industrial era. Vast sums, unknown even to the wealthiest men in pre–Civil War America, were falling into private hands. A great deal of this wealth was funnelled into a wide variety of philanthropic enterprises. The close connections between the captains of industry and evangelical Protestantism, and a widespread acceptance of the evangelical concept of stewardship, naturally led to large-scale giving to religious programs and institutions. Both general attitudes toward giving and the techniques used to solicit funds have changed considerably since the 1860's. Nevertheless, Moody's activities in raising money were

58. D. L. Moody to Cyrus H. McCormick, April 5, 1866, typewritten copy of original in Cyrus H. McCormick Papers; D. L. Moody to C. H. McCormick, April 17, 1866, February 9, 1881, March 15, 1881, McCormick Papers. In one of his attempts to solicit McCormick's interest, Moody also used a time-honored device of the fund-raising profession, enclosing with a personal letter to the industrialist attractively printed circulars and leaflets explaining past achievements of the YMCA as well as future projects for which money was needed. (D. L. Moody to C. H. McCormick, November 26, 1869, *ibid.*) For Moody's continued use of this device later, see mimeographed copies of letters of solicitation and lists of prospective donors in notebook entitled "Copies of Letters, Dwight L. Moody," YMCA Historical Library.

a foretaste of what was to occur when the new wealth associated with industrialism and the peculiar attitudes of the American people joined together to produce modern American philanthropy.[59]

As president of one of the most important local Associations of the YMCA, it became Moody's responsibility to travel much more than before. Each year he attended the national convention of the YMCA — at Detroit, Albany, Portland, Oregon, and Indianapolis. The business of the Chicago Association also occasionally took him away from home. By 1870, when he gave one of the principal addresses at the national convention in Indianapolis, Moody had become well-known throughout the national organization.[60]

The young evangelist also widened his contacts in other ways. One method he used was involvement in two interdenominational movements which were attracting many evangelical Protestants in the Midwest. Representatives of the Sunday schools of the evangelical churches were the spearheads of one of the movements. As early as 1859 the Sunday schools of Chicago had organized themselves into a city-wide "Sabbath School Union." After the Civil War similar groups began to organize on a state and regional basis throughout the Middle West. Activities came to be centered in a yearly series of county and state Sabbath school conventions.[61] Delegates came to these conventions to compare notes on Sunday school curricula and methods of training and to absorb from featured speakers a certain religious enthusiasm to be carried back to their local churches. Another interdenominational movement of so-called "Christian conventions" also emerged in the Midwest after the Civil War. The functions of this and the Sunday school movement seemed almost indistin-

59. A good brief introduction to the subject of philanthropy in America is Robert Bremner, *American Philanthropy* (Chicago: University of Chicago Press, 1960).

60. *Advance*, 3 (August 12, 1869): 6; 4 (November 24, 1870): 4; Managers, *Minutes*, May 7, 1866, December 10, 1866, January 14, 1867; *Indianapolis Journal*, June 24, 1870, June 25, 1870, June 27, 1870.

61. *Congregational Herald*, 7 (May 5, 1859): 3; *Advance*, 2 (November 5, 1868): 2. Apparently these activities had no connection with the American Sunday School Union, one of the large interdenominational organizations originating in the pre–Civil War era.

guishable. A similar system of annual state and county conventions was set up, and in both instances there was a strong emphasis on lay leadership.[62]

It was natural for Moody to play a prominent role in both movements. His position as president of an important lay-centered organization like the Chicago YMCA and his persistent deemphasis of denominational allegiances blended well with the purposes of the Sunday school and Christian convention movement.[63] Moreover, having achieved wide recognition as the founder of a highly successful mission Sunday school in Chicago, he was an obvious person to be invited to speak at these state and regional meetings. Finally, he had played an active role in the development of the state Sunday school movement in Illinois both before and during the Civil War.[64] By the time he had become president of the Chicago YMCA he was marked as a leader of the Sabbath school movement. In 1865 he accepted an appointment to the executive committee of the Illinois Sabbath School Union. By then he was spending several weeks each year traveling about the state attending local or county-wide conventions. Soon he began to fill speaking engagements in other states. In 1868, for example, he attended meetings in Iowa, Wisconsin, Kansas, Massachusetts, and Minnesota.[65] Thus because of his growing reputation as an attractive, aggressive religious leader, Moody was drawn into an ever-widening circle of responsibilities.

These activities cast into relief once again the extensive interdenominational efforts that characterized evangelical Protestantism. Feelings of amity and the need to cooperate were strongly felt sentiments at the grass roots in Illinois and elsewhere in the

62. *Advance*, 3 (July 22, 1869): 2; *Institute Tie*, n.s., 2 (March, 1902): 252.

63. For Moody's statements about nondenominationalism, see the *Peoria* [Ill.] *Daily Transcript*, October 31, 1867; *Bloomington* [Ill.] *Daily Pantagraph*, October 2, 1868.

64. D. L. Moody to Betsey Moody, June 5, 1861, Moody Papers, Powell; *Northwestern Christian Advocate*, 10 (June 11, 1862): 185; *Bloomington* [Ill.] *Daily Pantagraph*, June 11, 1869.

65. *Northwestern Sunday School Teachers' Quarterly*, 1 (March, 1865): 120; *Alton* [Ill.] *Telegraph*, September 11, 1868; *Advance*, 2 (February 2, 1868): 6; (April 9, 1868): 6; (April 16, 1868): 6; (June 25, 1868): 2; (July 2, 1868): 5; (August 27, 1868): 5; *The National Sunday School Teacher*, 4 (April, 1869): 111; *The Sunday School Teacher*, 2 (February, 1867): 60.

Midwest. Perhaps better than the great national benevolent societies, these local or regionally-oriented Sabbath school unions and Christian conventions confirmed that there were common attitudes and a certain identity of outlook among the major evangelical denominations. Significantly, too, in Illinois these convention movements flourished noticeably in the small towns and rural areas. Evangelicalism had always been particularly strong in these regions. Support was not lacking, however, from large urban centers like Chicago and St. Louis. Many of the people moving to the cities from farms or small towns continued established religious practices in the new environment. Moody was not unlike these people in transition. Now he lived in the big city,[66] but he had grown up in a small town and was used to the ways of small town inhabitants. This coincidence of views may help to explain further his appeal to the many evangelical convention-goers of the Midwest.

The county and state Sabbath school and Christian conventions which Moody attended in the late sixties served as another testing ground for many of the tactics of evangelism he used later in his revivals. Here, as in his talks in the noon prayer meetings in Chicago, certain of the themes of his later sermons appeared.[67] Newspaper accounts of the conventions also give us some inkling of the revival techniques he was developing.

The Christian convention, lasting several days and discussing practical methods for improving the life of the churches, was an idea Moody incorporated bodily into his revivals in the seventies. At the Illinois State Sunday School Convention held in Bloomington in 1869, Moody revealed another technique that he used

66. Moody's "citified airs" and the prestige associated with them were recognized in DuQuoin, Illinois, in 1868. He and other Chicagoans had chartered a Pullman Palace Car for their trip to the state Sunday School convention in DuQuoin. They used the car throughout the convention as their headquarters as well as a place to sleep. The local newspaper took due note of the car and spoke somewhat enviously of the accommodations therein, especially the "luxuriant beds" and interior appointments. (*DuQuoin* [Ill.] *Weekly Tribune*, June 18, 1868.)

67. *Peoria* [Ill.] *Daily Transcript*, October 31, 1867; *Jacksonville* [Ill.] *Daily Journal*, November 4, 1869, November 6, 1869; *DuQuoin* [Ill.] *Weekly Tribune*, June 8, 1868; *Alton* [Ill.] *Daily Telegraph*, September 9, 1868.

later. On the final night of the convention the young evangelist gave the closing address in a packed auditorium. At the end of his talk he asked all those who desired to "reconsecrate" themselves to God to rise. One newspaper reporter, watching with fascination, recorded the results. "The whole assembly rose. . . . Everything was as still as death, not a motion, not a word was spoken, not a whisper heard." After a prolonged period of quiet, Moody broke the "solemn silence" and with characteristic fervor "poured out his soul in prayer to God." Perhaps it was not surprising that when he asked that the meeting be closed with a recital in unison of the Lord's Prayer, everyone uttered the words "almost involuntarily." [68] Moody repeated this dramatic act of "reconsecration" in nearly all of his later revival campaigns. His procedure never differed substantially from that used in Bloomington.

Because of the confusion and swirl of events that accompanied any mass revival, the director of the revival had to be cool and levelheaded, able to cope with any unforeseen difficulties which might arise. Moody demonstrated such capabilities at a convention held in Quincy, Illinois, in 1870. Unexpectedly, a controversy erupted among the delegates on the convention floor, bursting, as one observer put it, "like a bombshell upon the assembly." Charge and countercharge, shouts, and tumult filled the air. Moody was directing the meeting. He leaped to his feet and attemped to still the disorder. Failing at first, he called on the organist and convention song leader to help. The music that poured forth turned out to be "Blessed Be the Tie That Binds"! Ironic, perhaps, but the effort proved effective. Moody then proceeded to offer one of his best and most fervent prayers and this further calmed the crowd. With the meeting finally back under his control, Moody led a question and answer period until the meeting was adjourned. [69]

The evangelist's musical assistant at this moment, Phillip Phillips, evidently was also a man of quick reactions. Phillips played the organ and led the singing in a number of the Illinois

---

68. *Bloomington* [Ill.] *Daily Pantagraph*, June 11, 1869.
69. *Quincy* [Ill.] *Whig and Republican*, June 10, 1870; *Advance*, 4 (June 23, 1870): 5.

conventions. He possessed considerable talent in making the music an integral part of the proceedings. He could, for example, add a great deal to the enthusiasm and excitement of the crowd by leading the people in singing hymns which fitted in well, both in content and tempo, with the themes of speeches and comments being made on the convention floor. Most of this congregational singing was improvised on the spot, to fit the prevailing mood of the delegates.[70] Partly because of Phillips's achievements, the song leader had become a real asset.

About this time Moody began to look for a man who would work full time with him as a musical director in Chicago. In the noon prayer meetings, and even earlier in his mission Sunday school, Moody had recognized the value of vigorous singing as well as vivid preaching as a means of stirring the spirit. D. W. Whittle, a close friend in Chicago, had conducted sidewalk meetings in the 1860's, aided by a young Pennsylvanian, P. P. Bliss, who composed and then sang in these meetings some of the best-known popular religious ballads of the time. Bliss and Phillips provided solo singing in evangelistic meetings which Moody found highly attractive and useful.[71] Although tone deaf and unable to sing a note properly himself, Moody realized the effect a capable song leader could have upon an audience, and thus the idea of a "co-worker in song" began to take shape in his mind. When he finally was ready to establish such a partnership, he turned first to Phillip Phillips, but the latter was not available at the moment.[72] Events had now brought him to the threshold of his famous acquaintanceship with Ira D. Sankey.

Prior to his association with Moody, Sankey's life had been of quite ordinary dimensions. He was born on August 28, 1840, in the village of Edinburgh, in western Pennsylvania. While in his teens the family moved to New Castle, Pennsylvania, where his father became president of the local bank. The young man got interested in church affairs, chiefly because the choir provided

70. *Daily Quincy* [Ill.] *Herald*, June 10, 1870; *DuQuoin* [Ill.] *Weekly Tribune*, June 18, 1868.
71. Weisberger, *They Gathered at the River*, pp. 198–99; *Sunday School Teacher*, 3 (January, 1868): 30; *Advance*, 8 (May 6, 1875): 625.
72. W. R. Moody, *Moody* (1930), p. 141.

an outlet for his musical interests. During the Civil War he twice served in the Union army. His service proved unexceptional. From 1862 on he remained in New Castle, content to assist his father in his business and to serve as the local internal revenue collector. He had an easy way about him and this made for popularity. His likeableness probably brought about his election as head of the town's YMCA when it was organized in 1867. Still holding this position three years later, he thereby qualified as a delegate to the national convention in Indianapolis, where Moody met him.[73] 1870

Sankey was a typical petit bourgeois American, unambitious and not overly enterprising, content to live a moderate, unexciting life in one of the small towns that formed the backbone of mid-nineteenth century society in this country. In this sense he could be sharply distinguished from his aggressive partner in evangelism. Moody clearly dominated the relationship that developed between the two men. Yet both of them had an ability to get along with people relatively easily, and this fact undoubtedly enabled their personalities to mesh successfully. Nor was there any doubt that Sankey was as deeply committed an evangelical Protestant as was Moody — his early identification with the YMCA and his lifelong support of the Methodist Church indicate that fact.[74] Although in the last years of Moody's life the two grew apart somewhat, the close personal ties established at the beginning were never completely severed.

The preacher first heard the singer in one of the smaller sessions of the YMCA convention they were attending in Indianapolis in 1870. When the proceedings dragged, Sankey volunteered to lead in some hymn singing. This unrehearsed performance struck Moody so forcibly that he approached Sankey afterwards, and in his usual blunt manner asserted that the song leader was to join him soon in Chicago. Sankey was at first surprised and weakly protested. But after a short visit to Chicago where he tried out

73. Ira D. Sankey, *My Life and the Story of the Gospel Hymns* (New York: Bigelow & Main, 1906), pp. 13–19; Samuel P. Bates, *History of the Pennsylvania Volunteers, 1861–5*, prepared in compliance with acts of the legislature, 5 vols. (Harrisburg: B. Singerly, state printer, 1869–71), 1:117–18, 123; 5:1147–48.

74. Sankey, *My Life*, p. 14.

as Moody's assistant, the future singing evangelist cast aside his doubts and moved west early in 1871.[75] Sankey was beginning an association which would bring him national recognition in less than a decade. At the same time he was to become a key to Moody's success as a revivalist. There is no doubt that without Sankey's assistance, Moody's triumphs in England from 1873 to 1875, and in the great revivals in America which followed, might never have occurred.

The late sixties and early seventies were critical years in Moody's life. Even as he built a successful career as a religious leader in Chicago, he was unconsciously beginning to sever the ties that bound him to the Midwest and was engaging in activities which would lead him eventually onto the national stage. The creation of his partnership with Sankey led in the new direction. In the spring of 1867 he also made his first trip to England. He remained there four months, traveling widely, observing and exchanging ideas with English evangelicals concerning mutual problems such as prayer meetings, Sunday schools, and young men's associations. He maintained particularly close contact with officials of the YMCA in Great Britain, speaking frequently at local association meetings about the work of his group in Chicago, and of developments in the national movement in America.[76] He did manage to leave behind him one tangible trace, a noon prayer meeting, founded in London with his guidance and in connection with the central YMCA. Obviously patterned after the work in Chicago, this prayer group achieved a certain notoriety because of its origins. The emphasis was on "free, voluntary, earnest, heartfelt testimony," in contrast to the more restrained procedures of ordinary English meetings.[77]

75. *Ibid.*, pp. 18–22.
76. *Chicago Tribune*, July 25, 1867; *Advance*, 3 (August 12, 1869): 6; *Revival* [London] (April 11, 1867): 199; (May 16, 1867): 271; (May 30, 1867): 300; (June 6, 1867): 320; (June 13, 1867): 332; (July 4, 1867): 366. There are some interesting bits of information about this first visit to England in a letter written by Moody's wife to his mother from Edinburgh, Scotland, May 28, 1867, Mrs. Frank R. Smith Collection, Library of Congress.
77. *Chicago Tribune*, July 25, 1867; *Revival* [London] (April 18, 1867): 221; (May 7, 1867): 263; (May 16, 1867): 278. Moody hoped that the idea of these meetings would spread to other cities in England, but evidently

Moody's public achievements on this trip were rather minimal. The most lasting results were personal, developing out of the informal contacts he established with different evangelical groups and individuals in England. For example, he became interested in the activities of a lay, pietistic sect known as the Plymouth Brethren, whose members were scattered throughout the country. Originally his specific concern had been the work of George Müller, a member of the Brethren who was setting up orphan schools in Bristol. Moody's work in Chicago prompted a natural interest in Müller's schools.[78] Out of this and other contacts, the Brethren eventually exerted a lasting influence on the evangelist.

This small, "primitive Christian" sect began in the 1820's as a protest against certain developments within the established church in Britain. Although at first the group did not seek separation from the Anglicans, their radical doctrines eventually brought this to pass. From the beginning they advocated a lay ministry and sought to dispense with all the ecclesiastical and liturgical trappings maintained by the Church of England. They hoped to return to the pristine simplicity of the early church, and they found no scriptural authority for either an ordained clergy or the apparent excesses in existing organization and worship procedures in the established church. There were parallels between these attitudes and Moody's feelings about ecclesiastical organizations, so it is easy to see why he became interested in the Brethren. Later in the century, as Anglicans fought over acceptance of higher criticism, and as some of their leaders moved toward a rapprochement with Roman Catholicism, the Brethren adopted an uncompromising stand against these tendencies. Under the vigorous leadership of John N. Darby, they preached the absolute inerrancy of the Scriptures and conversion through a heartwarming "experience." They were also premillennialists, advocating the imminent bodily return of

this desire never materialized. (D. L. Moody to Betsey Moody, [no date] 1867, from England, Moody Papers, Powell.)

78. D. L. Moody to Betsey Moody, (no date) 1867, from England, Moody Papers, Powell; Managers' Minutes, May (no date), 1867; *Advance*, 2 (February 13, 1868): 6.

Christ, who would bring destruction and the final judgment of God upon the world.[79] Both scriptural inerrancy and premillennialism became central tenets of Moody's mature religious faith. How far he had progressed toward these views in the late sixties is not precisely known, but probably this early association with the Brethren had something to do with his eventual acceptance of these doctrines.

The Brethren specifically influenced the evangelist in two ways. First, Moody learned a great deal from their writings. He probably studied a series of commentaries or "Notes" on the *Bible*, written by C. H. MacIntosh and widely distributed among evangelical Protestants in America.[80] Second, through his personal contacts with the Brethren he came to a further appreciation of their point of view. Possessed of great evangelical zeal, the Brethren traveled widely to propagate their beliefs. Many of them came to America both before and after the Civil War. Moody himself spoke often of the influence that one of the Brethren, Henry Moorhouse, had on his thinking following Moorhouse's visit to Chicago in 1868. Even John Darby visited this country several times in the sixties and early seventies and probably even spoke under Moody's auspices at Farwell Hall in Chicago.[81]

79. Henry A. Ironside, *A Historical Sketch of the Brethren Movement* (Grand Rapids, Mich.: Zondervan Publishing House, 1942), *passim*; Horton Davies, *Worship and Theology in England: From Newman to Martineau, 1850–1900* (Princeton: Princeton University Press, 1962), pp. 150–53.

80. Ironside, *A Historical Sketch*, pp. 71, 82.

81. *Ibid.*, p. 81; Clyde Norman Kraus, *Dispensationalism in America: Its Rise and Development* (Richmond, Va.: John Knox Press, 1958), p. 46; Napoleon Noel, *The History of the Brethren*, 2 vols. (Denver, W. F. Knapp, 1936), 1:120–21. Moody frequently told the story of Moorhouse's visit to Chicago and the power of the latter's message (*The Great Redemption*, [Chicago: Century Book & Paper Co., 1889], pp. 262–66; George C. Needham, *Recollections of Henry Moorhouse, Evangelist* [Chicago: Fleming H. Revell, 1881], pp. 108–11; *Cleveland Leader*, October 18, 1879). Brief accounts of Moody's comments before and after Moorhouse's visit are in print. These reports reveal little that would confirm or deny the later assertions of the evangelist. If Moorhouse did influence Moody, the results were not immediately apparent. (*Advance*, 1 [December 5, 1867]: 6; [January 9, 1868]: 7; [March 19, 1868]: 6; [April 30, 1868]: 6; [June 4, 1868]: 6.)

The American evangelist, however, never swallowed Brethren-ism whole. In Chicago Darby and he strongly disagreed over theological issues. Evidently Moody's acceptance of Arminian views concerning freedom of the will clashed with Darby's strong belief in predestination and the doctine of election. Darby, writing in 1872 from Illinois to friends in England about the difficulties of teaching Americans "the first principles of grace," asserted that only "old school Presbyterians, or some of them, have the most of it. It is otherwise resisted or unknown." He then went on to say, in an apparent reference to Moody, that "the active man at Chicago, lately in England, is deep in the mud of this [lack of understanding]." In later years Moody sharply criticized the schismatic effect the Brethren movement had on evangelical-ism in the British Isles. While preaching in England in the eighties, for example, he and the Brethren were frequently at odds.[82] In summary, it is true that members of the sect influenced Moody's thought at a number of points. But when it came to the practical application of doctrine, Moody and the Brethren frequently parted company. In 1867, however, most of the disagreements lay in the future.

Moody's first trip overseas was also important for his future because of the personal contacts he established in England. Most of the important evangelicals he met lived and worked in London, which in many ways served as the center of activities for all the English evangelicals. In the great metropolis the major evangelical newspapers and periodicals were published, and many of the leading evangelical ministers, both Low Church Anglican and Nonconformist, administered to their flocks there. At Mildmay in north London was the conference center where huge, annual religious conventions were held which sought to achieve, however briefly, a sense of unity within the sprawling evangelical movement.

82. *Letters of John Darby*, 3 vols. (Oak Park, Ill.: Bible Truth Publishers, n.d.), 2:193; Ironside, *Historical Sketch*, pp. 81–82; Mackinnon, *Recollections of Moody*, p. 65; Whittle Diary, February 4, 1884, February 23, 1884. See also Elmer W. Powell, "Plymouth Brethrenism," *Crozer Quarterly* 16 (January, 1939): 32–40, for further comments on Moody's connections with this group.

It is little short of amazing how quickly Moody met and became friends with many of the leading evangelical figures in the London area. His mode of entry was the London YMCA. The young American had established his headquarters there, and had organized the noon prayer meetings with the assistance of members of the London group. He soon came to know George Williams, the founder of the YMCA, Reverend Newman Hall, a leading evangelical minister, Henry Varley, one of the best-known Nonconformist laymen, and T. B. Smithies, editor of the *British Workman*, an important evangelical periodical. Charles Spurgeon, probably the most famous evangelical preacher in the London area, supported Moody's noon prayer meetings and even presided personally for a week over the proceedings. Perhaps most important was the close friendship Moody developed with Robert C. Morgan. The latter was editor of a widely read weekly, *The Revival*, soon to be renamed *The Christian*. In the mid-seventies Morgan and his journal were to become major instruments of support when Moody initiated his great revival campaign in England.[83]

Moody seemed to affect these people just as he had Chicagoans. An indication of his impact after only four months in the English capital comes from the farewell meeting held for him as he was about to depart for home. He and his friends gathered at the YMCA in Aldersgate Street in London for a meal and testimonials. His wife, who had been with him throughout the trip, received a gold watch and Moody was handed a substantial honorarium "as a token of the affection and esteem" felt towards him. Several speakers testified to the new ties of solidarity established between evangelical groups in England and America as a result of Moody's visit.[84] All this seemed a remarkable demonstration of the young American's ability to marshall support quickly and to make friends easily wherever he went. That he had penetrated into important circles within the English evangelical community was also important for the future. Close contacts with people of in-

---

83. George E. Morgan, *Mighty Days of Revival: R. C. Morgan, His Life and Times* (London: Morgan & Scott, 1922), pp. 170–71; *Revival* (May 16, 1867): 278. Morgan visited Moody in Chicago in 1869 and attended noon prayer meetings there. (*Advance*, 3 [August 12, 1869]: 6.)
84. *Revival* (July 11, 1867): 386–88.

fluence and power in Britain made it easier a few years later to consider leaving Chicago for a new career in revivalism, and to think of starting that career in England instead of in America.

Upon his return to the United States, Moody plunged quickly into a new round of activities. His engagements outside Illinois continued to grow in number. In 1868 officials of the national YMCA movement appointed him to a committee which was to work out the details of a new national organization of Sunday schools. Later that same year he attended a national Christian convention in New York City, and reports filtered back to Chicago that with the exception of Henry Ward Beecher, Moody was "the most popular man in the convention." Eventually he had to send out a general plea to convention planning committees to stop placing his name on the list of those present without first conferring with him for verification.[85] His name had become a valuable drawing card, whether he attended or not. In 1870 his service as president of the Chicago YMCA came to an end. He remained active in the organization,[86] but now he was freer to look about for new opportunities. The list of speaking engagements expanded, and he became a veteran convention-goer, following the itinerant's path for two months each winter in the early seventies.[87] His personal contacts and friendships outside Chicago now began to grow rapidly, and this in turn generated further invitations.

By 1870 perceptive observers in Chicago seemed to realize that Moody was outgrowing even that expansive metropolis in his interests, and that it would be only a matter of time before he left. Some expressed their feelings openly. One writer asserted that "Mr. Moody is too valuable as an awakener to be shut up in one city. . . . His gifts . . . are enough to put him in the very front rank. If he devotes himself to stimulating Christian laymen to work, and if he gives himself to the whole country, we doubt not he will work a revolution." [88] Between 1870 and 1873 several

85. *Advance*, 2 (November 25, 1868): 4; (August 31, 1871): 6.

86. *Independent*, 22 (March 17, 1870): 6. See also the *Chicago Tribune*, March 22, 1870.

87. Managers, *Minutes*, March 21, 1870, November 28, 1870, December 12, 1870, March 20, 1871, May 24, 1873.

88. *Advance*, 4 (November 24, 1870): 4; 5 (June 29, 1871): 5; 6 (March 14, 1872): 5; (March 28, 1872): 5.

seemingly unrelated events coalesced to push that prediction closer to reality.

One of these events was the Chicago fire of October, 1871. This conflagration struck a devastating blow at Moody's fortunes. His home with his family's personal belongings, the YMCA's downtown building, and the church that had grown out of his mission Sunday school were all reduced to ashes. The problems of rebuilding were awesome. Others would provide leadership in rebuilding the YMCA, but he was expected to play an important role in the fund-raising efforts, and he did so.[89] The Illinois Street venture rested upon Moody alone. Bravely he shouldered this responsibility. Less than four months after the fire he had managed to erect a temporary structure to house his church. He sought aid on the East Coast and appealed to Sunday school children throughout the country to send their nickels to help him build the permanent edifice. Yet at the time he left for his lengthy stay in England in 1873, construction had not yet begun and nearly $30,000 of the eventual expenses remained to be raised.[90] These mountainous responsibilities undoubtedly acted like a heavy weight upon even Moody's seemingly tireless energies and bouyant spirit. He asserted later that the great fire was *the* event which caused him to decide to leave Chicago.[91]

Perhaps the future concerns of the evangelist were most directly

89. He was appointed immediately after the fire to two committees which were to secure funds for the association. (Managers, *Minutes*, October 25, 1871, October 30, 1871.) Moody continued to give financial aid to the Chicago YMCA until 1877 to help pay off its indebtedness. (See Farwell, *Recollections of Moody*, pp. 135, 170–71, 172.)

90. *Advance*, 5 (October 26, 1871): 3; 6 (May 16, 1872): 5; *Chicago Tribune*, September 5, 1875. In 1876 the new church was finally dedicated, debt free, built on newly acquired property on Chicago Avenue. Thereafter it became known as the Chicago Avenue Church. Moody had collected most of the remaining sums needed for the church from his friends and from the sale in England of the tremendously popular Moody and Sankey hymnbooks. (*Northwestern Christian Advocate*, 24 [July 9, 1876]: 5; *New York Evangelist*, 47 [July 27, 1876]; Whittle Diary, June 1, 1876; D. L. Moody to James Hitchcock, July 12, 1875, D. L. Moody to unknown, March 20, 1872, list of contributors, unsigned note dated March 20, 1872, Moody Papers, Moody Bible Institute.)

91. Whittle Diary, October 2, 1876. See also "The Church Reporter," *Chicago Pulpit*, 1 (February 17, 1872).

revealed when he made a short trip to England in the summer of 1872. He spent nearly all of his time in London participating actively in the noon prayer meetings still functioning at the YMCA, preaching in Nonconformist chapels throughout the area, and renewing his acquaintances. There is considerable evidence to suggest that his future work in England was already in his mind, and that this visit was literally a testing period for that contemplated large-scale evangelistic assault on the island. In late July, 1872, he gave a major address at the annual Mildmay Conference which exposed him to hundreds of evangelicals from all over England. Evidently his preaching was a considerable success.[92] R. C. Morgan and his widely-read publication, *The Christian*, reported Moody's activities in minute detail, and by the time he was ready to sail back to America, Morgan had strongly suggested that Moody would return shortly to England to conduct an extended revival campaign.[93]

In the late sixties and early seventies, Moody, usually sunny and untroubled in disposition, entered a period of emotional stress and spiritual uncertainty. General overwork, the result of his heavy schedule of speaking engagements and his struggle to rebuild the YMCA after its first building burned, was partly responsible. At the same time his growing recognition in religious circles outside Chicago, and his success both as president of the Chicago YMCA and in his Sunday school work, caused him to become rather conceited.[94] These strong feelings came into con-

92. The talk was reprinted in its entirety in *The Christian*, and it was reported that when Moody finished his speech, spontaneous applause broke out in the audience. (*Christian*, 3 [August 11, 1872]: 8–9.)

93. See especially these editorial comments, probably written by Morgan, in *The Christian*. "We . . . trust that he [Moody] may soon be led to recross the Atlantic, and pay us another visit. We think that if the way were made plain for him to come here for a year or more, accompanied by Mrs. Moody and their two children . . . that he would gladly respond to such an invitation, so soon as he could effect the necessary arrangements at home." (*Christian*, 3 [August 22, 1872]: 12.) For evidence that Moody's plans for a return to England were fully matured by the early part of 1873, see Emma Dryer, "Reminiscences of the Founding of Moody Bible Institute" (unpublished typewritten MS, January, 1916), in the possession of Mr. Gene Getz, Moody Bible Institute, p. 9.

94. *Advance*, 6 (September 9, 1869): 6; *Proceedings of the Fifteenth Annual National Convention of the Y.M.C.A.* (June, 1870), pp. 62–63.

flict with the dictum of his faith that "the first shall be last and the last first." At a later time his close friend, D. W. Whittle, described Moody's difficulties:

> He had become mixed up with building Farwell Hall [the YMCA structure] and was on committees for every kind of work and in his ambition to make his enterprises succeed because they were his had taken his eyes off the Lord and had been burdened in Soul and unfruitful in his work for months. He longed for deliverance.[95]

The evangelist's most powerful motivations seemed at war with each other — his deep-seated ambition, his desire for success and his pride when success was achieved, his search for humility, his need to be utterly obedient to the will of his Lord and God.

During the winter of 1871 in New York City, he eventually achieved inner harmony once again through a second "conversion experience," one evidently much more profound than his original experience seventeen years earlier in Boston. Whittle goes on to describe what happened:

> God blessed him with the *conscious* incoming to his Soul of a presence and power of His Spirit such as he had never known before. His heart was broken by it. He spent much time in just weeping before God so overpowering was the sense of His goodness and love.[96]

Moody's feeling of helplessness, his prolonged weeping, and his sense of the overwhelming presence of some unseen force suggest that he indeed went through a deep religious experience. This moment both stilled his clashing inner impulses and provided him with a new resolve to pursue his course beyond Chicago. As Whittle expressed it, "he lost interest in everything except the preaching of Christ and working for souls. He determined to go to England that he might be free from all entanglements in the

95. Whittle Diary, October 2, 1876. Other sources attest to this time of spiritual unrest in Moody's life. See *Advance*, 2 (January 9, 1868): 7; 3 (October 21, 1869): 6; (October 28, 1869): 6.
96. Whittle Diary, October 2, 1876. See also *ibid.*, May 22, 1876.

rebuilding of his Church and the [Farwell] Hall." [97] Moody had simply decided to start life anew. He would begin again, this time as a traveling evangelist, which was apparently the best way he knew to "preach Christ and work for souls." In an effort to make the break with his past complete, he would initiate this move overseas.

It was a bold decision, one of the boldest Moody ever made. The gamble paid off handsomely, for within a relatively short time he was being publicly hailed internationally as a popular religious leader. Yet it is clear that this act of moving overseas to begin a new phase of his career emerged naturally and logically out of his previous experience. He could not have picked a better time to embark on this new venture. Psychologically he was fortified with renewed zeal and determination. The return of self-confidence released by his conversion experience had accomplished that.[98] His preparation for his work as a revivalist had also been thorough. It was fortunate for urban revivalism that much of Moody's preparation stemmed from his experiences in Chicago, one of the great new urban centers in this country. But Moody's work in Sunday school and Christian conventions in the Midwest and elsewhere was also important, for it gave him additional insight into, and feeling for, evangelical Christianity, surrounded as it usually was in these conventions by the more traditional social setting of small-town America. Finally and more immediately, his well-secured contacts in England made it reasonably certain that evangelistic work there would receive strong support at least initially, thereby reducing appreciably the possibilities of failure.

The decision to go overseas also revealed again facets of Moody's personality mentioned earlier. When problems began to pile up

97. *Ibid.*, October 2, 1876.
98. Whittle observed in 1875, after Moody returned from England, that "for a year or more before Moody left Chicago he was continually burdened and crying to God for more power. . . . He did not seem to be in the state now. . . . He was one . . . who had just put himself *wholly* in God's hands and had *received* the baptism of the Holy Ghost and was being led in all things by Him." (Whittle Diary, September 4, 1875.) This passage shows clearly the importance of the second conversion experience in giving Moody the confidence he needed to undertake the new work in Britain.

that were too much for him, he "solved" these difficulties by getting out and starting anew. Although this was a recurrent theme in Moody's life, his flight from the Midwest also seemed to typify a more general pattern of American behavior — an aspect of the frontier spirit only occasionally remarked upon by historians. This was the feeling that it was easier to pull up stakes and try things in a new environment than to continue to work in the old and be content with less spectacular yields for the same effort.

In a way, too, the young man's flight reflected the changing world in which he lived. The new life to which he was committing himself, first in England and then later in America, was to be an integral part of a powerful, urban, industrial world which differed in many ways from the relatively unsophisticated, rural society in which Moody and previous generations of Americans had grown up. Already in Boston and Chicago this new world of industry and urbanization had deeply affected him. For Moody the city was the new frontier, a place of opportunity. The new world beckoned, but the old world of his youth also clung to him and shaped his responses, even as he moved away.

All of these various aspects of the evangelist's life were refracted ultimately through the prism of his religious faith. During the years in Chicago he had gradually sloughed off his other interests and focused all of his attention on the demand of the evangelical faith to bring all souls unto Christ. He had utilized a variety of means in this endeavor, but the underlying end always remained the same. His willingness to experiment with methods and techniques to meet the changing conditions of the external world blended with an unwavering fidelity to the ultimate goals of his faith. These principles characterized Moody's work as a revivalist throughout the seventies, as it had his work for the YMCA and the religious establishment of Chicago in the 1860's.

In June, 1873, Moody made the final break with Chicago. With financial backing from his friend John Farwell and with Sankey accompanying him, he left the city, bound for England. With characteristic regard for the need to convert the world at large, one Chicago evangelical journal marked his leave-taking by proclaiming that "he looks across the sea, and spying the heathen on the other side, straightway plans for their conversion and sets himself about it." [99] What neither Moody nor the citizens of Illinois realized at the moment was that two years later he would return to his native land, a religious figure of international repute ready to bring revivalism up to date for the masses living in American cities. The years of apprenticeship were ripening into the full fruit of Moody's spectacular career as revivalist and popular religious hero.

99. "The Church Reporter," *Chicago Pulpit* 2 (June 10, 1873). See also *Interior*, 4 (June 5, 1873): 8; Farwell, *Recollections of Moody*, pp. 53–54.

4

Beginnings as a Revivalist

Revivalism was the hallmark of American evangelical Protestantism. Perry Miller reminded us again of that point in the fragment of his comprehensive study of the American mind published shortly after his death. "For the mass of the American democracy," Miller said, "the decades after 1800 were a continuing, even though intermittent, revival." [1] The massive weight of the revival tradition in American culture, both prior to and immediately after the Civil War, makes it easy to explain the direction Moody's career took as he moved into the mainstream of American Protestantism after 1870. To speak of Moody as a revivalist — more precisely a *professional* revivalist — suggests that he was part of a self-conscious, institutionalized, historical movement. Nineteenth-century American revivalism became such a movement, but if we trace the revival tradition back to its origins in the colonial period, the image alters a bit.

Revivals were important in the life of the colonial churches, but they were not yet viewed as the single most powerful influence affecting the faithful. Church members in New England and in the settled parishes in the middle and southern colonies would never have uttered as unequivocally as did Charles Finney in the 1840's the assertion that "almost all the religion in the world has

1. Perry Miller, *The Life of the Mind in America: From Revolution to the Civil War* (New York: Harcourt, Brace, & World, 1965), p. 7.

been produced by revivals." [2] Throughout much of the eighteenth century, traditional patterns of procedure in worship and day-to-day activities held sway within the colonial churches. This meant settled congregations, emphasis upon a regular, recognized pattern of church activity, and leadership exerted by a resident minister, usually thoroughly trained in theological and biblical matters to assure his flock proper guidance in spiritual affairs. In this carefully structured context, revivals could only be viewed as exceptional, unusual occurrences, welcomed as "showers of bless-ing from on high," but not a part of the regular order of things. Revivals were primarily works of the Holy Spirit, welling up unexpectedly within a congregation or a group of churches, and not commonplace tools in the hands of men.

In 1735 Jonathan Edwards vividly described the Great Awak-ening in Northampton, Massachusetts:

> This work of God . . . soon made a glorious alteration in the town; so that in the spring and summer . . . the town seemed to be full of the presence of God: it never was so full of love, nor so full of joy, and yet so full of distress as it was then. There were remarkable tokens of God's presence in almost every home. . . . Our public assemblies were then beautiful; the congregation was alive in God's service, every one earnestly intent on the public wor-ship. . . . In all companies, on other days, on whatever occasions persons met together, Christ was to be heard of and seen in the midst of them. Our young people when they met were wont to spend the time in talking of the excellency and dying love of Jesus Christ . . . the wonderful, free, and sovereign grace of God, his glorious work in the con-version of the soul. . . . And even at weddings, which formerly were occasions of mirth and jollity, there was now no discourse of anything but the things of religion, and no appearance of any but spiritual mirth.[3]

2. Charles G. Finney, *Lectures on Revivals of Religion* (Boston: Charles H. Peirce, 1848), p. 9.

3. Jonathan Edwards, *A Narrative of the Surprising Work of God* (New York: American Tract Society, n.d.), pp. 16, 17, 18.

The formal expressions of church life continued along accustomed paths, yet at the same instant the community seemed all but overwhelmed by the sudden inrush of the "surprising work" of God. The Holy Spirit breathtakingly revealed itself in the guise of revival fervor and enthusiasm in the midst of a familiar round of activities.

In these revivals the primacy of God's action was clear. With God serving as the initiator of these spiritual irruptions, there had to be an element of uncertainty — of indeterminacy — accompanying the revival procedures. By common agreement there seemed to be no universally recognized, man-made principles around which a revival could be organized. Indeed, to institutionalize the revival would be to destroy that spontaneity which pointed to the movement's principal motive power, the Holy Spirit. This emphasis on the centrality of God's action also inevitably circumscribed the role of the revival leader. Since revivals emerged out of the day-to-day flow of the life of the churches, local ministers, attuned to the peculiar spiritual needs of those affected, were best suited to provide whatever guidance was necessary.

Itinerant revivalists were important figures in the Great Awakening, but up to the 1730's, and probably afterward, such men were atypical as revival leaders in the colonial churches. Indeed, one of the most shocking things about the Great Awakening to religious conservatives was the spread of the pernicious influence of these itinerants. Charles Chauncy, in biting sermons and a famous letter addressed to one of the most prominent of the revival preachers, James Davenport, has made clear for posterity how upsetting this new breed of men was. "What is the Tendency of the Practice, but Confusion and Disorder?" complained Chauncy. "If one Pastor may neglect his own People to take Care of others, who are already taken care of; . . . why not another, and another still, and so on, 'till there is no such Thing as Social Order in the Land?" For Chauncy and many church people of his time, the effect of revivalists without a parish could be summed up neatly. "This Itinerant Preaching . . . and the Principles, upon which it is supported, will disband all the Churches in the World; and make the Relation, between Pastors and People, a meer Nothing, a Sound without meaning." [4]

Assuredly Chauncy overstated his case, but the presence of itinerant preachers like George Whitefield, Gilbert Tennent, and James Davenport in the midst of a settled religious community did presage changes that were to transform both revivalism and the Protestant groups generally in America as the country moved beyond the colonial era. With disestablishment and the emergence of the denominations at the end of the eighteenth century, revivalism advanced further along lines sketched out by the itinerant ministers who participated in the Great Awakening. A certain institutionalization of procedures occurred; in the process revivals came to be led increasingly by men who devoted all their time to such activities and who moved about with no settled ministry of their own. For these people revivalism was becoming a profession, a branch of the ministry to be developed and promoted like any other occupation.

The Methodist circuit rider of the West undoubtedly contributed much to the acceptance of an itinerant revivalist ministry among evangelical Protestants, although his work embraced the other ministerial duties as well as that of conducting revivals. Tendencies leading toward the professional revivalist also appeared in the activities of men like Asahel Nettleton, a Congregational minister in Connecticut. He followed the itinerant's path in the western areas of his state in the second and third decades of the nineteenth century. Nettleton made no sharp break with the past, however. He strongly supported the idea of a settled ministry, and he was extremely sensitive to possible charges of intrusion as an outsider. Contemporaries asserted that if in conducting a revival, Nettleton found a congregation placing undue reliance on him for guidance, he would sometimes disappear suddenly for a time to discount the human agency in generating spiritual enthusiasm. His preaching and methods of persuasion,

---

4. Charles Chauncy, *Seasonable Thoughts on the State of Religion in New England* (Boston: Rogers & Fowle, 1743), p. 51. For comments from a British historian that parallel the judgments made here, see John H. Kent, "American Revivalism and England in the 19th Century," unpublished mimeographed paper presented to *Past and Present* Conference on Popular Religion, July 7, 1966, p. 8.

when compared with the tactics of later men, were subdued and restrained. One observer felt that Nettleton's efforts signified "no 'getting up' " of a revival, "no agitation . . . no noise." Rather, his work had "awed and subdued" the congregation. Probably this was because Nettleton denied that churches "could have a revival anytime. . . . He always maintained that a revival of religion, depends on the sovereign interposition of God." [5]

In spite of these traditional attitudes, the fact that Nettleton was a traveling evangelist meant he tended to break the hold of the established, settled minister on his flock. Called in as a specialist in revivalism, his presence tended to relegate the local minister to a secondary role in a vital area of religious activity. The prestige of the minister declined accordingly. Viewed with suspicion by the regular clergy, men like Nettleton inevitably created dissension in the churches; yet they were important in creating the climate of opinion in which professional revivalism could flourish.[6]

As the revivalist began to specialize in his trade, he also cast off the formal trappings of the minister. Increasingly he appeared as a layman, possessing little or no formal theological training. Once again the semi-illiterate backwoods circuit rider or Baptist farmer-preacher served as a model. This development was also in tune with the broad democratizing tendencies of the Jacksonian era. But perhaps most important as a causal factor was the voluntary nature of American Protestantism in the nineteenth century. Leadership in the evangelical denominations could develop only if it were acceptable to all the constituents therein. Thus lay leadership, reflecting the makeup of the existing religious bodies, came into increasing prominence. The revivalists of the new era would have to be men close to the people, preachers who could

5. Philemon H. Fowler, *Historical Sketch of Presbyterianism Within the Bounds of the Synod of Central New York* (Utica, N. Y.: Curtiss & Childs, 1877), p. 295; Bennett Tyler, *Memoir of the Life and Character of Rev. Asahel Nettleton, D.D.* (Hartford, Conn.: Robins and Smith, 1844), pp. 210, 208.

6. Brief, though helpful, comments on these historical tendencies are in Bernard Weisberger, *They Gathered at the River: The Story of the Great Revivalists and Their Impact upon Religion in America* (Boston: Little, Brown and Co., 1958), pp. 62–82.

arouse emotions and in a simplified, near-demagogic way proclaim the gospel to the common run of churchgoers.

Charles G. Finney was the first man fully to fit the specifications of the professional revivalist.[7] He began his career as an itinerant preacher in the early 1820's in western New York, shortly after he underwent a particularly traumatic conversion experience. With the aid of a forceful and dynamic personality, Finney forged the tools with which revivalism thereafter operated. A lawyer by profession, he refused formal ministerial training — even though he was ordained eventually by the Presbyterian Church. At this point revivalism broke permanently with the formally educated ministry. No popular evangelist after Finney considered it necessary to obtain a degree from one of the major seminaries.

Finney also brought into sharp focus changes in theological emphasis which nineteenth-century revivalism encouraged. He helped to thrust aside certain key Calvinistic concepts which had given shape to revivalism earlier. Primarily this involved modification in the belief that man must depend absolutely upon God for the ability to repent and achieve salvation. Finney asserted instead that man's free will played a decisive role in the act of repentance. As he once expressed it, "When an individual actually *chooses* to obey God, he is a Christian."[8] Such a point of view broke down the exclusiveness of the Calvinist doctrine of election and replaced it with the inclusiveness of Arminianism. Salvation was open to all men, each able to make his decision for Christ, unaided and alone. The passive role of man vis-à-vis the active, initiatory role of God in revivals, prominent in the time of Edwards, was now to disappear very rapidly.[9] By implication,

7. For summaries of his life, see Charles G. Finney, *Memoirs of Rev. Charles G. Finney: Written by Himself* (New York: A. S. Barnes, 1876); George Frederick Wright, *Charles Grandison Finney* (Boston: Houghton, Mifflin, 1891).

8. Finney, *Lectures on Revivals*, p. 358.

9. Important evidence suggesting that there was an effort to preserve Edwardsian views among revivalists on the frontier in Finney's day is in John Opie, Jr., "James McGready: Theologian of Frontier Revivalism," *Church History*, 34 (December, 1965): 445–56. Sidney Mead discusses the manner in which the ground was prepared for Finney's bald assertions of Arminianism in the 1840's in *Nathaniel William Taylor*,

such an attitude opened the way for a considerable expansion of the power and prestige of the leader of any revival. With the decision to turn to the Christian faith placed more fully in the hands of the individual, the proper choice of "means" to be used in revivals, hopefully designed to lead the individual sinner to a decision, became all-important. Those possessing experience — and therefore authority — in such endeavors were assured of expanded influence.

The peculiar needs of the Protestant denominations also facilitated the spread of the theological principles that Finney found so acceptable. The denominations were voluntary associations. A continued emphasis on the doctrine of election, with its restrictive implications when applied to membership, clearly threatened the evangelical organizations with stagnation and deterioration. When men became free to make a decision regarding salvation, and when the possibility of salvation was thrown open to all, a solution to the problem of maintaining membership was at hand. The spread of Arminianism widened the market for souls — and new church members! Now nothing more than a simple affirmation of faith in "Jesus Christ as Savior" qualified one to enter the portals of the evangelical churches.

Revivalism became the chief means by which evangelical Protestants exploited the shift that occurred in the realm of theology. With its exclusive concern for the conversion of the individual, the revival was an ideal instrument to apply intense pressure on the seemingly unlimited multitudes now deemed proper subjects for persuasion. Thus when Finney and his contemporaries warmly supported Arminianism in theology and the use of frequent revivals to quicken the life of the church, they were merely advocating that which seemed necessary and inescapable.

As stress was placed upon conversion, church people increasingly justified any and all means used to produce this end. Even Jonathan Edwards had defended the preaching of terrifying hell-

1786–1858: A Connecticut Liberal (Chicago: University of Chicago Press, 1942). See also Sydney Ahlstrom, "The Scottish Philosophy and American Theology," *Church History*, 24 (September, 1955): 257–72, and the same author's essay on "Theology in America," in *The Shaping of American Religion*, ed. J. W. Smith and A. L. Jamison, 3 vols. (Princeton: Princeton University Press, 1961), 1:254–60.

fire-and-brimstone sermons with the comment that it was quite proper to try to frighten men out of hell.[10] The machinations of backwoods preachers in the great western revivals at the beginning of the nineteenth century are well known in this respect. Everywhere evangelical Protestants sought to emphasize practical results. The churches correspondingly rationalized, systematized, and refined revival techniques to produce these results.

Finney well represented these tendencies. He was a strong advocate of certain "new measures," which elevated the emotions of the communities he visited to unprecedented heights. These measures included daily meetings, prolonged into the early morning hours, prayer for individual sinners by name, and the use of the famous "anxious bench," reserved at the front of the hall for those newly penitent and convicted of sin. Finney's vigorous exhortations of the damned, his piercing eyes with their hypnotic effect on the audience, and his vivid re-creations of the terrors of hell all added to his effectiveness.[11]

With the coming of professional revivalism the revival gradually lost its spontaneity, and above all its sense of the miraculous at work. While many people continued to speak about the "outpouring of the Holy Spirit" experienced in the revivals after 1840, in reality man's role became increasingly the more important one. Once again Finney epitomized this tendency when he claimed that a revival "is not a miracle, or dependent on a miracle, in any sense. It is a purely philosophical result of the right use of the constituted means."[12]

Those who followed Finney, however, were less exacting than he in defining what was right in promoting revivals and less precise about what should serve as properly constituted means. Because revivalism fed on excitement, there was constant pressure to provide a program that could entertain as well as convert the crowd. It was natural, therefore, for revivalists to turn to the secular world for aid. This tendency, which Moody eagerly em-

10. Sidney Mead, *The Lively Experiment: The Shaping of Christianity in America* (New York: Harper & Row, 1963), p. 124. Chapter 7 of this book has much bearing on the topics discussed here.

11. Finney later wrote out a rough codification of his techniques in his *Lectures on Revivals,* chap. 14.

12. Finney, *Lectures on Revivals,* pp. 12, 18–19.

braced, inevitably weakened further the religious meaning of revivalism and the techniques associated with that movement.[13]

For followers of evangelical religion in England, revivalism was also a matter of great importance. Because English evangelicals of the Victorian age traced their origins back to the pietistic sects of the left wing of the Reformation, and more particularly to the Wesleyan revival in England in the eighteenth century, they had always placed matters of the heart at the center of their religious life. The conversion experience was the starting point for the man of faith. Therefore revivals were to be expected — a part of the order of things in the religious realm.

There were differences, however, in the nineteenth-century English and American revival traditions, these differences being chiefly the product of different historical settings. As we have noted, the American version developed in large part as a means of meeting the unique challenges of disestablishment and of a population expanding rapidly into an almost limitless interior where society was raw and largely unformed. Revivalism occupied a position at the center of the daily life of the churches, yet it had lost a great deal of its earlier spontaneity and lack of institutionalization. By contrast, revivalism in England in the Victorian era existed in a milieu where tradition and order regarding worship and daily religious practice had rarely been challenged as fully as they had in the loosely-knit society of the New World. The major dissenting groups — the Methodists, Baptists, and Congregationalists — all possessed long-established institutional practices and procedures. It should also be remembered that English evangelicalism embraced Low Church Anglicans as well as members of the free churches. Thus the weight of the traditions and historical precedents of the established church, extending back in theory to the apostolic age, exerted its influence in subtle and unnumbered ways on the daily religious practices of people inclined toward a heartfelt religion.

Because of these influences, revivalism in England in the Vic-

13. Weisberger, *They Gathered at the River*, chaps. 1–5, and William G. McLoughlin, *Modern Revivalism: Charles Grandison Finney to Billy Graham* (New York: Ronald Press, 1959), chaps. 1–3, complement each other in their survey of revivalism before the Civil War. I have drawn heavily on both works in preparing this analysis.

torian era operated in a framework more nearly like that familiar to colonial Americans. Even in Moody's time the revival still appeared as an unusual occurrence in the life of the church. It was to be awaited wth hopefulness and anticipation, yet it was essentially a "gift from on high," not a movement manipulated by men, something to be "worked up" by preachers and revivalists. Not too surprisingly, leading evangelicals in England initially expressed some reservations concerning Moody and his importation of American tactics. The relationship, for example, between the young American and Charles Haddon Spurgeon, probably the greatest popular evangelical preacher in England at the time, was a bit strained. A decade before Moody's arrival Spurgeon stated publicly that he had "at all times been peculiarly jealous and suspicious of revivals." Anyone called a revivalist should be "set down . . . as a cipher." He went on to assert emphatically that "I would scorn the taking of such a title as that to myself." When Moody reached London, Spurgeon did attend one or two of his meetings and eventually invited the revivalist to speak at his famous tabernacle, but the ties between the two men were never strong.[14] Another major figure among the evangelicals, R. W. Dale, a preacher in Birmingham and national spokesman for the Congregationalists, was suspicious of Moody until he made a personal appearance in Dale's home city. As his biographer tells it, Dale "recognized their [Moody's and Sankey's] spiritual force, but declined to stand forward as an apologist for their methods in detail." [15] Later the famous Congregationalist was completely won over to the two Americans, but these early reservations were symptomatic of the caution that was characteristic of English attitudes toward American revivalism.

There were other forces at work in Britain, however, that seemed to be preparing the way for the acceptance of Moody and his

14. Charles H. Spurgeon, *Sermons Preached and Revised by the Rev. C. H. Spurgeon, Fifth Series* (New York: Sheldon and Co., 1859), p. 337; John C. Pollock, *Moody: A Biographical Portrait of the Pacesetter in Modern Mass Evangelism* (New York: Macmillan, 1963), p. 153; C. H. Spurgeon, *Autobiography*, 4 vols. (Chicago: Fleming H. Revell, 1898–1900), 4:167, 168; *Methodist* [London] (April 2, 1875): 5.

15. Alfred W. W. Dale, *The Life of R. W. Dale of Birmingham* (London: Hodder and Stoughton, 1898), p. 317. See also Dale's comments in *Congregationalist*, 4 (March, 1875): 130.

particular brand of religious activity. Recent commentators on Victorian life have noted in particular that it was an age of great preachers, both in the established and in the free churches.[16] As might be expected, the greatest of these preachers possessed styles of delivery and of presentation that were highly individualized. Style as well as message made them sufficiently arresting to attract large audiences and national recognition. Such preachers "loosened up" services of worship, particularly in the Church of England, from the formalism which had characterized much of the preaching in the early Victorian era. Moreover, these men developed large personal followings that tended to blur the lines between the established religious groups. Spurgeon was probably the best illustration of this tendency. His preaching was simple, direct, and full of vivid imagery, in many ways paralleling Moody's peculiar abilities as a popular preacher. Although Spurgeon was a Baptist in his formal connections, his Metropolitan Tabernacle in the heart of London drew thousands of worshippers each Sunday rather indiscriminantly from a variety of sources and religious backgrounds.[17] An element of irony exists in the fact that Spurgeon kept somewhat aloof from Moody, yet through his own work he had created attitudes among Englishmen which made them sympathetic toward the American when the latter arrived in 1873.

In the years just prior to Moody's arrival, the theological climate among evangelicals in England began to incline increasingly toward Arminianism. Belief in the possibility of universal salvation had, of course, always been a powerful current of thought among the evangelicals, for it had been a fundamental tenet of John Wesley and remained so for the thousands who were members of the Methodist connection in the nineteenth century. What was especially significant was that Arminianism also was becoming the dominant mode of thought within those Nonconformist bodies whose attachments historically had been with Calvinism. This transformation was a gradual process, taking almost a hun-

16. George Kitson Clark, *The Making of Victorian England* (Cambridge: Harvard University Press, 1962), pp. 180–81; Horton Davies, *Worship and Theology in England: From Newman to Martineau, 1850–1900* (Princeton, N. J.: Princeton University Press, 1962), chap. 10.

17. Spurgeon, *Autobiography*, 3, chaps. 60–62.

dred years to complete. It was marked by no great doctrinal controversies and is therefore rather difficult to identify and follow in the lush undergrowth that characterized nineteenth-century British theological activity.

The two most important influences which forced a revision in thought emerged in the first half of the nineteenth century. These influences reflected the broad shifts in theological perspective then occurring; they are distinctive because they originated on opposite sides of the Atlantic Ocean. One, emanating from England, was the evangelical movement, sweeping over both the established church and the dissenting sects in the earliest decades of the century. Imbued with great missionary and evangelistic zeal, these early evangelicals emphasized the theme of universal salvation strongly in their preaching. If challenged individually, Congregationalists, Baptists, and Presbyterians among them would say they "believed Calvinism still, but the living element of their creed, that which fired their passions, inspired their eloquence and sustained their work was something very different — and gradually . . . the dead articles of the creed dropped away, men hardly knew when or how."

The second influence which wrought changes in attitude came from America. The theological fight which revised orthodoxy in this country in the 1830's was closely observed in England. Articles reflecting the controversy — published originally in such leading American journals as the *Princeton Review* and the *Biblical Repository* — were collected, republished in England, and widely read. Charles Finney's books and the multivolume commentaries or *Notes* on the Old and New Testaments by Albert Barnes, a leading New Light Presbyterian minister, also achieved wide circulation. Certain of the writings of Moses Stuart, the great biblical scholar at Andover Theological Seminary who introduced American readers to the unsettling views of critical German scholarship in the pre–Civil War period, also were circulated. All of these men represented the shift to Arminianism. Thus developments in the United States had a share in "melting down the hard lines of our [English] Calvinism."

The victory in England was not total even on the eve of Moody's great revival campaigns. Baptists more than Congregationalists had retained the older views, and many of the evangelical clergy of the establishment remained attached to the idea of limited salvation. But the inroads were undeniably great. By 1870 one leader of the free churches had come to feel, with a noticeable tinge of regret, that "among Non-conformists" Calvinism "is practically gone." [18] Given such a state of affairs in the churches most directly in the path of the young and ambitious American revivalist, it is not surprising that Moody's revivals, grounded implicitly in an Arminian theology, found in Britain a congenial atmosphere in which to develop.

Religious developments in America smoothed the path for Moody and Sankey in England in other ways, too. As the nineteenth century wore on, the persistent tendency toward revivalism in evangelical circles in England flowed into ever more institutionalized channels. American practices were copied frequently. Hugh Bourne, for example, one of the two founders of the Primitive Methodists, seems to have borrowed ideas from the early nineteenth-century American evangelist Lorenzo Dow in shaping the first "camp meetings" held in England in the early 1800's.[19] By Moody's time the idea of itinerant evangelists moving about the country whipping up religious enthusiasm was not totally foreign to England, although not nearly as widely practiced as in the United States. There was even some interchange among evangelists in Britain and America. Charles Finney made several trips to England, preaching there as an itinerant; Moody's previous two visits to Britain might easily be viewed in a similar

18. The factual information and the quotations in the preceding paragraphs are drawn from an illuminating historical analysis written in 1869 by Robert W. Dale, serving then as a contributing editor to *The Advance*, a leading American religious periodical. See *Advance*, 3 (December 16, 1869): 1. For briefer suggestions on the same topic, see R. W. Dale's *History of English Congregationalism* (New York: A. C. Armstrong & Son, 1907), pp. 587–88; Kent, "American Revivalism and England," pp. 18, 30. The role of Albert Barnes in the great theological conflict that split the Presbyterian Church in the late 1830's has been carefully analyzed recently in Earl A. Pope, "New England Calvinism and the Disruption of the Presbyterian Church," (unpublished Ph.D. dissertation, Brown University, 1962).

19. William J. Townsend, Herbert B. Workman, George Eayrs, eds., *A New History of Methodism*, 4 vols. (London: Hodder and Stoughton, 1909), 1:563–65; Kitson Clark, *Making of Victorian England*, p. 182.

light. At the moment that Moody started to build his career overseas, one of England's best-known evangelists, Henry Varley,
was traveling through Canada and the United States, attracting
large crowds to his meetings. Finally, one great national upsurge
of revivalistic sentiment, the "awakening" of 1859, drew directly
on a similar impulse in America which occurred in 1857 and
1858.[20]

The English revival of 1859 provided part of the immediate
setting for Moody's work. This movement affected all of the evangelical groups in Great Britain and released spiritual energies
that had not yet dissipated themselves by 1870. For many people
the religious enthusiasm of the late fifties was still a vivid impression; to renew that enthusiasm and thereby the life of the
church seemed desirable. The immediacy of recollections of this
revival created a special milieu, one in which hope of spiritual
renewal by means of the peculiar device of the revival would
flourish.[21] The revival of 1859 also produced a sizable number of
itinerant evangelists who were still working when the Americans
arrived over a decade later. Lay-centered and not bound exclusively to a single sect or church, they provided one more means
by which English audiences were being familiarized with American techniques and attitudes.[22]

The situation thus augured well for Moody. Yet at the outset
a combination of circumstances almost nullified his efforts to
launch his career as an evangelist. Moody and Sankey went to
England on the strength of an invitation from Cuthbert Bain-

20. Finney, *Memoirs*, chaps. 28, 29, 34; Henry Varley, Jr., *Henry Varley's Life Story* (London: Alfred Holness, n.d.), pp. 113–19; J. Edwin Orr,
The Second Evangelical Awakening in Britain (London: Marshall, Morgan and Scott, 1959), chap. 1; Kent, "American Revivalism and England," pp. 14, 28. Kent is sceptical about the broad effects of the English
awakening of 1859.

21. See, for example, *Christian*, 4 (Jan. 9, 1873): 5; (Jan. 30, 1873): 3;
(April 10, 1873): 4; (June 12, 1873): 3. The editor of *The Congregationalist* asserted early in 1873 that "in every part of the country, men
are coming to feel that what we want most of all is a fresh baptism of
the Holy Ghost and of fire." (*Congregationalist*, 2 [Jan., 1873]: 1.) See
also *ibid.*, (February, 1873): 65–71; (March, 1873): 129–35; (April, 1873):
193–201.

22. McLoughlin, *Modern Revivalism*, pp. 183–85.

bridge, a wealthy layman of Newcastle, and the famous evangelical leader in London, William Pennefather. In 1872 these men promised Moody financial support for any revival work he might undertake.[23] When the American arrived in England he discovered that during the intervening months both of his expected benefactors had died. He had guaranteed Ira Sankey a salary of $1,200 for the trip, and both he and Sankey had brought their families with them. Now he could see no clear prospects for evangelistic work. As Sankey recalled later, "We had only one vague idea of starting [−] that was to go northward. The utmost of our hopes was to spend three months in Northern England and Scotland preaching [,] then return to America." [24]

Sankey's words suggest what was actually the case, that Moody did have one possible opportunity − an invitation from the lay director of the YMCA in York to conduct meetings there. It appears that this invitation had been tendered to Moody well before his departure from America, but looking for more dazzling prospects, the young American had failed initially to respond. When his plans collapsed at the time of his arrival in England, the invitation from York took on fresh significance. Although the letter of invitation was vague regarding specific commitments and proposals, Moody was not worried. In his usual dramatic yet direct manner he descended upon York all but unannounced, ready to begin work. The man who invited him recalled to Moody's son much later that the American evangelist had compared, perhaps only half-jestingly, the impact of his arrival on his host to that of a man "who got a white elephant and didn't know what to do with him." [25]

Lack of preparation hurt his efforts in York noticeably. Reports published in *The Christian* tried to keep up a brave front, but

23. Cuthbert Bainbridge renewed the invitation personally to Moody early in 1873 when he came to Chicago during a visit to the United States. (*New York Christian Advocate*, 50 [March 25, 1875]: 93.)

24. Cited in *Chicago Tribune*, August 13, 1875; John V. Farwell, *Early Recollections of Dwight L. Moody* (Chicago: Winona Publishing Co., 1907), p. 55.

25. Pollock, *Moody*, pp. 103–03; *Association Men*, 40 (February, 1915): 237; *Christian*, 4 (July 10, 1873): 392; "Bennett of York" to W. R. Moody, undated letter in Moody Papers, Mrs. E. M. Powell, East Northfield, Massachusetts.

local people admitted publicly that "we . . . were unprepared for the visit." After three weeks in York, Moody moved on to the town of Sunderland, but not before he had juggled his itinerary so that conflicting reports of his future whereabouts were printed, revealing for all to see his uncertainty and lack of direction.[26] The two Americans stayed in Sunderland four weeks, and after a short visit to the town of Jarrow, they moved on quickly to Newcastle where their fortunes began to improve. Attendance began to pick up; enthusiasm seemed genuine and widespread; even the nearly official reports in *The Christian* reflected the changed attitudes and outlook.[27] Moody and Sankey were on the eve of their first great successes as revivalist and gospel singer.

All accounts of Moody's first weeks in England have stressed the handicaps under which he worked.[28] Too often, however, these difficulties have become almost the whole story. A lackluster beginning contrasted sharply with resounding success a few months later in Scotland. The natural tendency of writers has been to seize on this contrast and to emphasize it. In light of all the evidence, however, the picture must be retouched somewhat. First, it should be stressed that at the time of his arrival Moody was not totally unknown within evangelical circles in England. Although certainly not a public figure as yet, he did have friends who could help a great deal if he found himself in distress. R. C. Morgan, the publisher of *The Christian*, was an indispensable supporter from the outset. Indeed, well before Moody arrived, Morgan sought to prepare the way. Throughout the last weeks of 1872 and the early part of 1873 he kept up a drumfire of statements designed to keep the young American in the eye of the reading public. *The Christian* announced Moody's arrival in the summer of 1873, served as an informal employment agency for the evangelist while he was in York, and eventually spread

26. *Christian*, 4 (July 10, 1873): 28; (July 17, 1873): 8; (August 7, 1873): 11.

27. *Sunderland* [Eng.] *Times*, August 5, 1873; *Christian*, 4 (August 7, 1873): 11; (August 28, 1873): 10; (September 25, 1873): 11; (October 30, 1873): 5; (November 20, 1873): 5; 5 (February 19, 1874): 9.

28. McLoughlin, *Modern Revivalism*, pp. 181–82; Pollock, *Moody*, pp. 101–12; William R. Moody, *D. L. Moody* (New York: Macmillan Co., 1930), pp. 141–51.

the good news of the coming of the American revivalist to Scotland in complimentary copies mailed to hundreds of ministers in the north country.[29]

Partly because of his network of acquaintances, Moody was also able to introduce imaginative flourishes into his procedures as soon as he sensed his efforts were flagging. At Sunderland, for example, he arranged for Henry Moorhouse, an experienced and widely-traveled evangelist living in Manchester, to join his entourage. Moorhouse was an undoubted attraction and provided a touch of English speech and practice to the proceedings. It was a deft stroke and Moody followed this practice throughout the remainder of his campaigns in Britain.[30] But Moorhouse could be contacted only because Moody had known him for some time. Indeed, the English preacher had visited Chicago and Moody's church there in the 1860's.

With the simple passage of time Moody began to develop a consistent pattern in his procedures that meant fewer errors each time he moved to a new location. As word of his presence spread and invitations to speak accumulated, he was able to plan his itinerary more carefully, projecting it further and further into the future. This in turn enabled evangelical groups along the way to prepare more thoroughly for his visit.[31] By the time Moody reached Newcastle in September, 1873, the rudimentary format of all his subsequent campaigns was established. This meant one or two large meetings each day coupled with after-meetings in the "inquiry room," and a growing number of specialized gatherings such as quick visits to outlying areas, services exclusively for women, for children, or for laborers. These special meetings could be improvised as the need arose.[32]

29. *Christian* (September 5, 1872): 6; (September 12, 1872): 9; (October 3, 1872): 10; (October 24, 1872): 14; 4 (March 6, 1873): 11, 12; (June 26, 1873): 17; 5 (January 1, 1874): 8.

30. *Ibid.*, 4 (August 21, 1873): 11; (September 11, 1873): 11; (October 23, 1873): 8.

31. See especially accounts of the preparations which were made prior to Moody's visit to Stockton-on-Tees at the end of his work in Newcastle. (*Ibid.*, 4 [November 20, 1873]: 4.)

32. *Ibid.*, 4 (October 23, 1873): 7; (November 6, 1873): 7; special edition included in bound volume 5 in the British Museum; *Congregational Advance*, 2 (January 1, 1874): 6.

In Newcastle Moody experienced the first really substantial response to his efforts. Contemporary observers who viewed these developments favorably thought his success to be sudden and little short of amazing. "Moody and Sankey entered Newcastle a few weeks ago almost as strangers in a strange land. . . . the general public knew no more about them than could be gathered from the bills on walls, which simply stated that Mr. Moody would 'preach' the gospel, and Mr. Sankey would 'sing' the gospel. . . . As the work approved itself day by day to be of God and not of men . . . now there is not a Christian body in the town but has its labourers, both ministers and laymen, engaged in the glorious work." [33] In reality success emerged out of a gradual and rather complex process. Moody's imagination and ability to improvise effectively when faced with novel situations, his friendships with people in the evangelical community who were in a position to help him, and his optimistic spirit which carried him through the initial period of frustration all played a part. Given time to learn through trial and error, he was able to move from the edge of disaster to eventual success and fame. By the time the mission in Newcastle was completed he had become, legitimately, a professional revivalist.

Events were now conspiring to carry him further north into Scotland. A minister of the Scottish Free Church in Leith, the port city of Edinburgh, was the first to advocate publicly extending an invitation to Moody and Sankey to come northward. Assured of widespread support from ministers of both the established and free churches in Edinburgh, Reverend Kelman went to Newcastle and approached Moody concerning a campaign in Scotland. Convinced that he would receive adequate backing, the young evangelist agreed. He opened his work in Edinburgh in the last week of November, 1873.[34]

The two Americans spent more than five months in Scotland. Almost until the end of January, 1874, they preached and sang in churches and secular auditoriums in Edinburgh. About the first

33. *Christian*, 4 (November 6, 1873): 7.
34. *Church of Scotland Home and Foreign Missionary Record*, n. s., 9 (April 1, 1874): 17; *The Free Church of Scotland Monthly Record* (March 2, 1874): 56.

of February they moved on to Glasgow and remained there until the end of April. Although they centered their attention on these two principal cities of the northland, interest and enthusiasm were great enough to warrant frequent trips of one to several days into the outlying districts of the country — to smaller towns like Berwick, Dundee, and Aberdeen. Wherever they went they attracted huge crowds. At the first meeting in Edinburgh, held in one of the largest meeting places in the city, crowds "densely packed . . . every corner," as well as "the lobbies, stairs, and entrance." Hundreds seeking admission were turned away. By the first week of January Moody and Sankey were being all but overwhelmed by the demands of their work. On the first Sunday of the New Year they conducted six meetings in as many hours, splitting their forces so that as many people as possible could see and hear them perform. Finally they rented on a regular basis the Corn Exchange, the largest public hall in Edinburgh, with a seating capacity of close to six thousand. Frequently they filled the exchange to overflowing.[35]

In Glasgow the response was equally great. The two Americans subjected themselves to man-killing schedules. Scarcely a week after the campaign opened there, meetings were being conducted in both churches and secular buildings, including the famous Crystal Palace, equal to Edinburgh's Corn Exchange in seating capacity. Special services "for children, for Sabbath-school teachers, ladies, and also for gentlemen," had been set up; Moody was so ebullient that he added to his burdens a series of lectures beamed at the academic community and given in the church connected with the Free Church college in Glasgow. The widespread support Moody and Sankey generated for themselves is revealed in the list of ministers reported to be attending the final Christian convention held at the close of the Glasgow campaign. Hundreds of clergy from small towns throughout Scotland in addition to those from Glasgow and Edinburgh were actively participating in the movement.[36]

35. *Christian*, 5 (January 8, 1874): 5; (February 19, 1874): 9; 4 (December 18, 1873): 4; *Edinburgh Courant*, December 18, 1873, December 29, 1873, January 5, 1874; *Glasgow Herald*, April 9, 1874.

36. *Glasgow Herald*, February 21, 1874; *Glasgow News*, February 7, 1874, February 21, 1874, April 2, 1874, April 17, 1874. A leading Scottish

There is more evidence available than the superficial enthusiasm created by large crowds, however, to suggest that Moody and his partner had touched sensitive nerves. Particularly revealing were the comments, official and unofficial, of ministers and leaders of the principal Scottish churches concerning the depth and extent of the revival. As the campaign neared its close in the spring of 1874, these analyses blossomed in newspapers, church periodicals, and in the speeches of speakers at the annual meetings of the national church bodies which followed on the heels of the revival. A common theme running through many of the assessments was a feeling of surprise that two *Americans* had become the instruments of a religious movement as powerful as this one seemed to be. A. H. Charteris, conservative theologian of the Church of Scotland and professor at Edinburgh University, articulated these feelings when he exclaimed to readers of a journal of the established church that "if anyone had told us six months ago that our still and decorous city [Edinburgh] would be stirred to its depths by two strangers, we would not have believed the tale." [37]

A scarcely suppressed sense of excitement and enthusiasm for what Moody and Sankey had done underlay all the attempts to estimate the effects of the revival. When the moderator of the Scottish Free Church spoke of the revival generally and of the specific contributions of the two visitors from overseas in his address to the general assembly of the church in 1874, the delegates spontaneously broke into applause. Special studies of the revival, carried out by officials of both the established church and the dissenting Free Church, documented for everyone to read the influence of the movement. The Free Church report demonstrated that the revival spirit had spread to areas of the country which

church historian has asserted that only "high-and-dry churchmen held aloof." The "outstanding evangelical personalities of the time" were all active participants in the revival. (J. R. Fleming, *The Church in Scotland, 1843–1874* [Edinburgh: T. and T. Clark, 1927], p. 235.)

37. *Church of Scotland Home and Foreign Missionary Record*, n.s., 9 (April 1, 1874): 15. See also *ibid.* (August 1, 1874): 137–38, for testimony of numerous ministers and *Glasgow Herald*, May 22, 1874, for the remarks of the moderator of the Free Church of Scotland which emphasize this theme.

Moody and Sankey never visited — "in a large number of the congregations in the Synods of Fife, and of Perth and Stirling, in Hawick, in Lockerbie, in Moffat, in Aberdeenshire, and in many other places." Others testified to the healing effect the revival had had on cleavages within and between the contending sects of Scotland. A spokesman of the United Presbyterian Church asserted solemnly that when Moody came to Edinburgh "in a brief space of time the city was moved, we may say, to its very centre." [38]

Scoffers and cynics could easily charge that most of the efforts to justify the revival came from officials of the churches, and that the revival was embraced with enthusiasm by churchgoers because it smoothed over or caused people to forget deep-seated difficulties which existed both within the churches and in Scottish society generally.[39] There is considerable truth in such charges. Yet one cannot survey the records of Moody's work in Scotland without being impressed by the legitimacy of his spiritual impact on these people. From this time on, Moody began his revivals with the initial advantage of being a well-known public figure. General public curiosity probably caused as many people to attend his meetings as did honest religious enthusiasm. He could not have begun with the same advantage in Scotland since he was largely unknown at the outset. Yet religious enthusiasm of unusual intensity did break out among the Scottish people under his leadership.[40] In Scotland Moody probably came closer than at any other

38. *Glasgow Herald*, May 22, 1874, May 27, 1874; *Glasgow News*, May 23, 1874, May 27, 1874; *Church of Scotland Home and Foreign Missionary Record*, n.s., 9 (April 1, 1874): 14–16; *Free Church of Scotland Monthly Record* (May 1, 1847): 96; *Missionary Record of the United Presbyterian Church*, n.s., 5 (February 2, 1874): 25.

39. McLoughlin, *Modern Revivalism*, pp. 190–94, offers, in a carefully documented and effective way, such an interpretation of Moody's efforts.

40. One of the most interesting manifestations of the enthusiasm Moody and Sankey generated can be found in the letters to the editors' columns of the major Glasgow and Edinburgh papers. During and after the revivals these columns were filled with dozens of epistles commenting — favorably and critically — on various aspects of the religious work. At no other time in Moody's career did his efforts evoke a comparable public response. The letter writing may say something about peculiar traits of the Scots — their sensitivity to and knowledge about theological issues seems especially acute — yet it may also be indicative of the intensity of the response that Moody provoked.

time in his career to igniting a revival in the classic sense in which Christians had viewed that phenomenon up to the nineteenth century.

In spite of widespread support for the spiritual awakening, the Scottish population possessed in their religious faith and practice enough structure and form to prevent them from swallowing American revivalism whole. Even while Moody's work was in progress, strong criticism was being levelled against it. In essence the misgivings were the same as those held by Charles Chauncy toward the Great Awakening in America in the eighteenth century and held by nearly all critics of revivals since that time. It was the "republican indifference to forms" displayed so prominently in this movement which worried many Scotsmen. A clergyman argued that a roving evangelist like Moody undermined the long-established authority of the minister in the local parish, and prophesied that because of Moody's success there might soon develop a "band of unordained and unauthorized preachers going forth on their evangelistic crusade without the slightest misgiving in regard to their calling, and without any pastoral or presbyterial supervision." The excitement of the revival also became a force that disrupted the established patterns of activity in the local parish. "How are we to be let down from the fever heat of these meetings to the quiet, old-fashioned manifestations of the Christian life," asked the ministerial letter writer. "The life born of such excitement will have great difficulty in surviving in the cold atmosphere of our work-a-day world." [41]

In the same vein but more specific in intent were the comments aimed at Sankey's "singing the gospel." Until recently, Puritan forms of worship had prevailed throughout the Scottish churches. Music was an unneeded adornment and was used only sparingly in the form of congregational singing and the use of the psalter. Organs were all but unknown in churches until the early 1860's and aroused heated opposition when first used. Sankey's gospel tunes, informal singing, and use of the harmonium startled and

41. *Glasgow Herald*, February 27, 1874. In a reply to these criticisms, *Ibid.*, February 28, 1874, one finds the phrase "republican indifference to forms."

intrigued many Scots, yet outraged the traditionalists. One writer made clear his dislike of these tactics when he described Sankey as "so new, so peculiar," that "careful inquiry" into the legitimacy of his efforts was necessary. The idea that the gospel "may be spiritually conveyed to the minds of men through the medium of music" seemed to this writer "to be nothing less than playing with the most sacred of all things . . . the Word of Truth — the Gospel of our Salvation." [42]

Attacks like these made the conservative critics vulnerable to the charge that their words only revealed the coldness of the church and its increasing irrelevance to a changing world.[43] Nevertheless, there was considerable substance in the charges brought by the traditionalists, and Moody's more thoughtful supporters remained uneasy in their allegiance to him. The report submitted to the general assembly of the Free Church shortly after the revival ended probably summed up the attitude of many churchmen as they reflected on what they had witnessed and experienced.

> Men will form their own judgment regarding it [the revival] as a whole, and also regarding each and all the modes of proceeding in connection with it. . . . That everything about it has been as it should be is not to be expected. But it has broken in on the coldness, carelessness, indifference, and formality so generally prevalent. It has aroused attention and awakened deep and widespread interest in spiritual things; and to obtain and secure that interest, one would tolerate a number of things that one cannot wholly approve. . . . Let us ask grace to enable us to discriminate in judgment, and be careful not to fight against God, because of things that man's ignorance or unskillfulness may add to God's work.[44]

42. *Glasgow News*, April 22, 1874; W. D. Maxwell, *Worship in the Church of Scotland* (Oxford: Oxford University Press, 1955), p. 167. For additional criticisms of the revival, see *Christian*, 5 (March 12, 1874): 7; *Glasgow Herald*, March 27, 1874, April 9, 1874; *Glasgow News*, April 20, 1874.
43. *Glasgow Herald*, February 28, 1874.
44. *Glasgow News*, May 23, 1874.

One additional fact puzzled many of those who had observed or participated in the awakening. The two leaders from abroad had almost no prior understanding of Scottish ways of thinking and acting. This made it doubly difficult to explain their success. In particular, ministers who had labored long in the same fields wondered, with a touch of envy and dismay, why their daily efforts could not somehow create the kind of response that Moody seemed to enjoy when he preached in the Corn Exchange, the Crystal Palace, or a Free Church chapel. A minister of the established church finally raised in public the question that many of the clergy were undoubtedly putting privately to themselves. "Why . . . with the same message to deliver and the same promise of blessing, should my success be in any respect less than that of the Chicago evangelist? Why, in other words, should Scotland be indebted to two strangers from North America for any measure of either spiritual light or life?" [45]

Answering the Scottish interrogator requires first a brief look at some previously mentioned historical developments. Arminian doctrines, now widely accepted among evangelicals in England, had also spread further north. In contrast to English divines, Scottish theologians had debated more openly the advisability of the shift away from Calvinist presuppositions, but the end result was much the same. By Moody's time, rank-and-file attitudes in Scotland had been noticeably altered. A contemporary English observer asserted that "a very large number of Scottish Presbyterians came to believe that in some sense Christ died for all men," a belief which in the long run was "certain to ruin the harmony and strength of systematic Calvinism." [46] Surely such feelings aided in preparing the way for Moody and Sankey.

Some people even suggested that the idea of universal salvation was a function of the culture of the Lowlands of Scotland, and of a "Lowland theology" flourishing in the cities and those areas where industrialism had had its greatest impact. By contrast, "a

45. *Church of Scotland Home and Foreign Missionary Record*, n. s., 9 (September 1, 1874): 156.

46. Statement of Robert W. Dale, printed in *Advance*, 3 (December 16, 1869): 1. See also Fleming, *Church in Scotland*, p. 235; John H. S. Burleigh, *A Church History of Scotland* (London: Oxford University Press, 1960), pp. 309–33.

Highlander yet believes, what was the common faith of Scotland after the Reformation, 'Christ died for his own.' " [47] Although geographical determinism probably oversimplified actuality, Moody did concentrate his efforts in the Lowlands where the largest towns were located. And some Scotsmen involved in the revival felt that the Highlands, somewhat isolated and rural in orientation, were less affected by Moody's work than other parts of Scotland.[48]

From the moment he began to preach in England Moody made special efforts to insure cooperation from all the contending sects interested in his revivals. He continued this practice when he moved north. In Scotland the church had been deeply split for thirty years prior to his arrival. The sudden appearance of the ecumenical spirit undoubtedly seemed a mighty pillar of support to those who sought to end these divisions.[49] Before 1843 Scotland was dominated by a single, established church. The great disruption of that year, the product chiefly of politico-ecclesiastical issues, led to a forked road in the religious experience of the Scots. After a ten year struggle, about a third of the ministers with their congregations left the established church and formed the Free Church of Scotland. Possessed of great evangelical zeal, the Free Church quickly built a nationwide network of congregations that eventually rivalled the Church of Scotland in power and influence. In 1847 two smaller groups, Calvinist in theology but outside the state-supported framework for some time, joined together and became the United Presbyterian Church, the third largest religious body in Scotland.

In the fifteen years prior to the arrival of Moody, attempts

47. *Glasgow Herald*, March 7, 1874. Included in this account is the assertion that if every minister in Scotland were "permitted to speak his mind without reference to the Standards he signed in his youth . . . a majority would affirm the truth of this Lowland theology." (*Ibid.*) See also *Church of Scotland Home and Foreign Missionary Record*, n. s., 9 (April, 1875): 19.
48. *Glasgow News*, May 27, 1874.
49. For expressions of this sort, see *Dundee* [Scotland] *Advertiser*, January 27, 1874; *Free Church of Scotland Monthly Record* (February 2, 1874): 26; *Church of Scotland Home and Foreign Missionary Record*, n.s., 9 (April, 1874): 15; *Glasgow Herald*, May 22, 1874; *Glasgow News*, May 16, 1874.

were made to end the divisions among the churches. The Free Church and the United Presbyterians were the first to make the effort. Negotiations, begun in the early 1860's, continued for ten years, but eventually foundered on the rock of theoretical differences over the nature of church-state relations. Much of the heat and passion engendered by this controversy remained when Moody arrived in 1874.[50] In that same year the English Parliament abolished formally the practice of lay patronage — the method used in the Church of Scotland for appointing ministers in local parishes — a long-standing source of tension between the free and established churches. Many people hoped this action by Parliament would open the door to the reuniting of the two largest religious groups in Scotland. But thirty years of practical experience as a voluntaristic body caused the Free Church to view this move as an implied threat to its existence outside the establishment. Instead of healing old wounds, the parliamentary effort produced violent agitation for the complete disestablishment of the Church of Scotland.[51] Almost at the very moment that this controversy burst upon the public, Moody began his preaching in Edinburgh and Glasgow.

Scottish churchmen in the 1870's were also upset about certain issues in the field of education. Until then, Scotland had no national system of primary education. Schools built and sponsored by the state, by various church groups, and by individual philanthropists made a hodgepodge of the educational system. The Scottish Education Act of 1872, seeking to bring some order out of chaos, produced extensive state intervention and, correspondingly, reduced the power and control of the churches over the schools. Men of faith evinced distaste and concern about their

50. Burleigh, *Church History of Scotland*, chap. 4; Alec R. Vidler, *The Church in an Age of Revolution* (Baltimore: Penguin Books, 1961), chap. 5; Peter B. Morgan, "A Study of the Work of Four American Evangelists in Britain from 1873–1905 and of the Effect Upon Organized Christianity of Their Work There" (unpublished B. Litt. thesis, Oxford University, 1958).

51. P. B. Morgan, "Study of the Work of Four Evangelists." For strong expressions of sentiment concerning the debate over disestablishment and patronage in the contemporary Scottish press, see the *Glasgow News*, May 21, 1874, May 30, 1874; *Glasgow Herald*, April 2, 1874; *Manchester Guardian*, November 20, 1874.

loss of influence over one of the basic institutions of Scottish society. The Education Act appeared to be an example of the steady advance of secular forces in Scottish life, and the unrest stirred up by the act had not entirely disappeared when Moody arrived.[52]

All of these controversies suggested that powerful movements for social change were stirring in Scottish society. The demand of Free Churchmen for the suppression of lay patronage hinted at the spread of democracy. Church people wanted to control religious affairs more at the grass roots, and this was one way to achieve that end. The disruption beginning in 1843 brought into the open previously expressed criticism of the Church of Scotland for its failure to provide adequate facilities for the rapidly expanding urban population. Disestablishment and a state controlled system of education reflected the tendency toward secularization that seemed so often to accompany the spread of democracy and the rise of an industrial economy.

Such developments had a profoundly unsettling effect upon the tradition-oriented people who comprised the constituencies of both the established and free churches in Scotland. In order to solve their many problems, perhaps it would be wise to cooperate rather than to bicker among themselves, as had been the case all too often in the past. Moody's stress on the spirit of unity, therefore, struck fire in many hearts. Perhaps, too, the tensions of the time caused his hearers to respond with special delight to his preaching, which it was said, "abounded with nothing so much as with Scripture."[53] For a *Bible*-centered people like the Scots, these words pointed to the simplicity and intensity of his message, striking close to the essentials of the faith. All this could be a powerful support for religious people unnerved by rapid social change.

52. For comments on the historical connections between education and the churches, see Stewart Mechie, *The Church and Scottish Social Development, 1780–1870* (London: Oxford University Press, 1960), chap. 9. Criticisms by Moody's contemporaries of the Education Act, expressing concern about the effect of the law on the churches, are in the *Edinburgh Courant*, September 20, 1873, September 26, 1873, November 14, 1873; *Glasgow News*, April 20, 1874.

53. *Missionary Record of the United Presbyterian Church*, n.s., 5 (February 2, 1874): 26.

Just as the Americans arrived in Scotland a letter writer to one of the major religious journals asserted the great need for "a revival of earnest, simple preaching of Christ in our pulpit. . . . The truth is, *that* is what the people *desire*, as well as *need*: simple loving words from the heart are far more popular than the most learned thesis on obscure passages." Evidently Moody's preaching was an answer to this need. Groping for words to explain his success among them, the friends of the evangelist only half-sensed what he was achieving. Simply put, his words and manner provoked a sense of assurance in a time of uncertainty.[54] For thousands of Scottish churchmen in 1874 there was no doubt about the effectiveness of the fascinating preacher from America. Forced to struggle with a bewildering array of complex issues related to the massive forces of democratization, industrialism, and urbanization sweeping over the western world in the nineteenth century, facing tensions within the churches created by long-standing ecclesiastical and theological disputes, Moody's simple message and call for unity among churchmen seemed irresistible. Precisely because he was unheralded at the outset and strictly an outsider, Moody seemed to convey a sense of authority. Temporarily at least, the American revivalist had made his mark upon the Scots. Because of these Scottish revival campaigns, Moody's future as a professional evangelist also seemed assured. It was only natural for him, then, to turn his thoughts and talents southward once again, to help the industrial centers of England feel the refreshing touch of the spiritual awakening now manifesting itself in provinces further north.

54. The quotation is from *Christian* (January 8, 1874): 7. Similar statements can be found in *Church of Scotland Home and Foreign Missionary Record*, n.s., 8 (December 1, 1873): 545; 9 (April 1, 1874): 18; *Free Church of Scotland Monthly Record* (February 2, 1874): 27; (May 1, 1874): 96; Fleming, *Church in Scotland*, p. 236; *Glasgow Herald*, May 27, 1874.

5

Climax Overseas:
Revivals in England

Throughout the late spring and summer of 1874 Moody moved
slowly through Scotland, visiting smaller towns and cities, spending
several days at each place he stopped. His fame had spread widely
and he found frequent opportunities to preach. Paisley, Kil-
marnock, Stirling, Perth, Arbroath, Nairn, Elgin, Inverness —
in all these towns people flocked to hear him and his singing partner. Early in the fall he moved on into Ireland, first to Belfast,
then to Dublin for a longer campaign.[1] Success in Scotland made
it easy to move into these new areas as a celebrity of sorts, with
curiosity already well developed in the general populace, and
with the strong backing of many Protestants all but assured.

The evangelist and his friends left nothing to chance, however.
During the weeks he was in Edinburgh and Glasgow, some of
his supporters mounted a campaign to make certain that news of
the Scottish revival would be broadcast throughout the British
Isles. R. C. Morgan expanded a plan for sending complimentary
copies of *The Christian* containing accounts of the Edinburgh
campaign to ministers in Scotland until it included England,
Wales, and Ireland. Contributions to underwrite this grandiose
venture were received; immediately religious leaders and churches
in almost two hundred communities throughout the islands be-

1. There is a convenient outline of Moody's itinerary, vague at several points as to exact dates, printed in Wilbur M. Smith, *An Annotated
Bibliography of D. L. Moody* (Chicago: Moody Press, 1948), pp. xxi–xxii.

gan to receive detailed information about the revival in Scotland. In February, 1874, Morgan began to mail *The Christian* regularly to all ministers in London. Another nondenominational evangelical periodical widely disseminated in Britain, *The British Evangelist*, changed from a monthly to a weekly publication during the period that Moody and Sankey were in Edinburgh and Glasgow. The obvious intent was to report events in Scotland in the fullest detail for the journal's readers, and special efforts were also made to expand circulation during this period.[2]

All this activity helped to prepare the way for Moody after he left Scotland. In Dublin, where he spent part of October and most of November, 1874, he faced a new obstacle — a population the great majority of whom were Roman Catholic. Nevertheless, the crowds that turned out to hear him seemed surprisingly large and his work lost little momentum. Ninety per cent of the Dublin Protestants were adherents of the Church of Ireland, but most Irish Anglicans were Low Church, in part because of the overwhelming presence of Catholicism. These Low Church sentiments probably explain the considerable support Moody and Sankey received from the Church of Ireland. The Catholics officially maintained silence or a studied neutrality in the face of the Protestant campaign. Moody's lack of emphasis on doctrinal issues and his reluctance to stress denominational ties perhaps affected the attitude of the Church of Rome. The net result was that many Catholics attended the revival meetings unencumbered by official restraint and spurred on by natural curiosity.[3]

2. *Christian* (January 22, 1874): 25; *British Evangelist*, 6 (January 15, 1874): 48. Copies of volumes 1–6 of the latter periodical, covering the years 1869–74, will reveal the changing format noted above. For comments on the effect these evangelical journals had in assuring Moody's success upon his return to England, see *Congregationalist*, 4 (March, 1875): 134.

3. *Christian* (October 22, 1874): 10. *Dublin Evening News*, November 6, 1874; *Freeman's Journal*, October 26, 1874; *Nation* [Dublin], November 7, 1874; Peter B. Morgan, "A Study of the Work of Four American Evangelists in Britain from 1873–1905 and of the Effect Upon Organized Christianity of Their Work There" (unpublished B. Litt. thesis, Oxford University, 1958), pp. 449, 452–53, 454, 459. Because of Presbyterian dominance in Scotland, Anglicanism there was high church; correspondingly, this explains the limited support Moody received in Scotland from the Anglicans.

Climax Overseas: Revivals in England

The two Americans left Ireland with their reputations still relatively intact, moving on into England and the best-known industrial centers of the north and midlands. In December, 1874, they were in Manchester; the following month they divided between Sheffield and Birmingham. Throughout February, 1875, they preached and sang in Liverpool. By springtime Moody was busily preparing for the final stage of his work in Britain, a four month campaign in London, beginning late in March and continuing until the first days of July.[4]

These months of itinerancy were the time when the techniques of mass revivalism were being hammered out by Moody and his associates. A full description of this machinery will be reserved for later, but some mention should be made here of several of the devices Moody was developing that were essential to his work thereafter. As his campaigns grew in size and complexity, the revivalist could not deal personally with all the myriad details that pressed for immediate attention. Thus in Edinburgh, and again in his later campaigns, he selected some local person, usually a well-known evangelical layman, to serve as a general administrator or coordinator. Working behind the scenes and largely unknown to the general public, these men became essential parts of the institution Moody was creating.[5] There was also a struggle to learn the best way to house mass revivals. Increasing popularity meant that hearers regularly overflowed the facilities. Issuing tickets for admission to the services was a way to establish some control, but to do so often cut down the size of audiences, and

4. *Manchester Guardian*, November 30, 1874, December 2, 1874, December 4, 1874; *Birmingham Daily Mail*, January 18, 1875; *Christian* (January 14, 1875): 13; (January 21, 1875): 6; (February 11, 1875): 12; [Liverpool] *Evening Express*, February 8, 1875, February 15, 1875.

5. In Edinburgh, a Presbyterian layman, James Scott, served as executive director. There devolved on Scott "correspondence with ministers and associations; the drawing up of the weekly programme for the noon-prayer meetings; . . . the serving of the free breakfast in the tent on Sabbath morning, as well as [providing the] supply of speakers in the evening." Scott also arranged Moody's speaking schedule throughout the Edinburgh area. (Andrew A. Bonar, *James Scott: A Labourer for God* [London: Morgan & Scott, 1885], pp. 35–36). Mr. Robert Paton, a London businessman, assumed the duties of behind-the-scenes coordinator there. (George E. Morgan, *Mighty Days of Revival: R. C. Morgan, His Life and Times* [London: Morgan & Scott, 1922], p. 183.)

this Moody wished to avoid.[6] In Dublin he was able to rent for the first time a public hall of truly immense proportions which seated almost 20,000 people. In Liverpool another variation was introduced. The evangelist deemed none of the buildings in the city large enough, so he had a huge temporary tabernacle constructed out of iron sheeting. It was dubbed Victoria Hall. Seating capacity was about 7,000 people; special features were incorporated into the building, designed to promote the smooth functioning of the revival. There was a single inquirers' room which effectively preserved the feeling of small quarters. The builders made special efforts to improve acoustics, inevitably a problem in the pre-electronics age. The cost of the tabernacle — about $17,000 — also suggests how rapidly Moody's work was expanding in size and complexity.[7] Only three times in later campaigns did Moody require such special structures. After the experience in Liverpool, however, it was clear that he commanded sufficient prestige that buildings to meet his desires would be built if such facilities were not immediately available.

Moody also worked to perfect his methods of advance preparations and to apply these methods systematically in each city he visited in order to raise public expectations and curiosity to a peak just as his campaign began. A newspaper reporter, observing the American's operations as he swept into Birmingham, described part of the system. "Local committees hold preliminary prayer meetings. Congregations are invited to use their influence in stimulating the movement. 'A great outpouring of the Spirit,' to use the evangelical phrase, is pleaded for." First in Glasgow, then again in Manchester and Liverpool, a house-to-house canvass of the residential districts was launched to advertise the revival then in progress. In London the same device became part of the preparatory efforts. The tactic of scattering circulars systematically throughout the huge metropolitan area prior to the revival

6. *Christian* (September 24, 1874): 616; (October 8, 1874): 644; *Interior*, 4 (December 4, 1873): 5; *London Globe and Traveler*, March 10, 1875.

7. *Christian* (March 5, 1874): 135; (October 15, 1874): 663; (November 19, 1874): 745; (February 11, 1875): 12; (January 14, 1875): 13; *Manchester Guardian*, January 5, 1875.

seemed useful, and Moody incorporated the idea into his procedures thereafter.[8]

Securing the cooperation of the local churches and clergy before beginning a campaign had always been a cardinal doctrine for Moody. As he gathered his forces late in 1874 and early in 1875 for the eventual assault on London, church divisions loomed as a real threat to his plans. In particular, High Church Anglicans, with their developed sense of church traditions and their emphasis upon ecclesiastical practice in the daily life of the Christian community, viewed Moody as an interloper who disrupted established patterns of community life. Other tendencies also caused these people to hold back. The High Church influence was expanding into many English parishes, primarily in the guise of a liturgical movement known as Ritualism. A late offshoot of the Oxford movement, Ritualism flourished more at the popular level of church life; but like its more intellectual forebear, it exacerbated the natural divisions existing between Low and High Church elements in the Church of England. Moody as an evangelical was a natural ally of the Low Church groups and the Nonconformist church bodies. Thus Ritualists and High Churchmen hesitated to support him, if for no other reason than that converts coming out of his revivals would probably be directed to local congregations controlled by their ecclesiastical opponents.

In Sheffield some of these uncertainties had affected the sizable group of local Anglican clergy who initially supported Moody's visit. As disagreements increased, these ministers withdrew from the local planning committee. Faced with a sizable defection of his forces, his principle of unity within the churches shattered, Moody prepared to cancel his entire campaign. Plans for a house to house visitation, which the Anglicans asserted interfered with legally defined operations of the church within parish boundaries, had caused the difficulty. When Moody ordered the visitation program abandoned, the dispute disappeared.[9] Despite the amicable

8. *Birmingham Daily Mail*, January 18, 1875; *Manchester Examiner and Times*, December 16, 1874; *London Times*, March 10, 1875; *Congregationalist*, 4 (March, 1875): 132–33.

9. *Manchester Guardian*, December 31, 1874; *Christian* (January 7, 1875): 10.

settlement of differences, the tension in Sheffield pointed to difficulties Moody would experience frequently in preserving his principle of unity and cooperation among local church groups.

Even before the incident in Sheffield occurred, clergymen in London were worrying over how to achieve the unity necessary to assure Moody's appearance in their city. Evidently the revivalist worried, too. With encouragement from the Americans, Londoners arranged a meeting in February, 1875, to which they invited leaders of all church groups, representing all parts of the city and the suburbs. Moody came to the meeting to expose himself and his views to the scrutiny of the clergy. He sought to explain and justify his methods, then allowed his hearers to question him in detail. Moody's concern was to play down differences, both doctrinal and practical. Ritualists were assured that converts professing an interest in a High Church parish would be encouraged to follow these inclinations. The tone of the evangelist's words expressed itself in his concluding sentence. "Our one object in coming here is to *preach Christ* . . . and [we hope] that, with God's blessing, we shall see many brought into the fold of Christ."

Hostility appeared openly in the question and answer session, but Moody kept his head and ended up making a good impression, even on many not inclined to sympathize with his work. One observer asserted later that the evangelist's "power of dealing with men" was never "more conspicuously shown" than at this moment.[10] In this meeting Moody's flair for effective preparation and promotion of his revivals, and his delicately tuned sense of timing revealed themselves. Once again his native shrewdness in turning a potentially volatile and unpleasant situation to his advantage came to the fore. But perhaps most important, this gathering with the London clergy drove home the idea that Moody was a leader of all the churches, and anything less than this would have caused the revivalist to hesitate in launching a revival cam-

10. *Dublin Evening Mail,* November 9, 1874; *Christian* (February 11, 1875): 8; *Church Times,* 12 (February 12, 1875): 82; (March 12, 1875): 128; (April 9, 1875): 180; unknown writer to W. R. Moody, March 10, 1900, folder entitled "Letters to W. R. Moody," Moody Papers, Moody Bible Institute, Chicago.

paign. This was a powerful and effective image to conjure up. Whether the image conformed to reality or not, Moody always used it as the cornerstone of his plans and procedures in Great Britain and throughout his later career.

As the American evangelist moved from the smaller campaigns of the early stages of his overseas visit to the larger efforts of 1874 and early 1875, and finally to the massive London revival, a corresponding decline in the spontaneity and freshness of his work occurred. In Scotland a frequent theme of commentators had been expressions of surprise at what Moody had achieved. It was all unexpected and built up so quickly, apparently from nothing or at least from unknown sources. As the machinery of mass revivalism developed, to be applied again and again in much the same way in different cities, carefully calculated anticipation replaced the feeling of experiencing the unexpected. As the revivals became increasingly man-made, they seemed to lose some of their legitimacy and integrity as agents of the spirit.

To illustrate this point one need only consider the amount of work necessary, prior to Moody's arrival, to arrange a revival like that conducted in London. Interested clergy in the city issued a formal invitation to the evangelist in September, 1874, and he accepted immediately. Actual preparations began during the first week of December. At that time a body of people in London formed the Central Committee, which operated continuously thereafter. Keeping in close contact with the two Americans, the committee laid plans to raise $50,000 to finance the campaign, drew up a list of workers and speakers — men of "distinguished evangelical gifts" from three continents — to be invited to participate, and reserved a giant exhibition building, Agricultural Hall, in central London for the opening phases of the revival. By January, 1875, committees of clergy and laymen in each of the major sections of the city had been formed. They helped, for instance, in organizing a large choir to be used in the revival services. By the end of February the house-to-house visitations, designed to reach "the whole population in their homes," had begun to function, directed by the man who had performed the same duties in Manchester and Liverpool earlier. Eventually financing became a problem. The Liverpool revival, representative of the earlier efforts, cost about $22,000. In contrast, expenses in London eventually soared to $160,000. Preparations to collect such sums had to start before the revival began. James Mathieson, a prominent London banker, took charge of collections, and his committee issued circulars both before and during the revival to raise funds from "well known Christian men of means." Eventually money "sufficient for all their needs" flowed in.[11]

All this paraphernalia of organization may have inhibited spontaneity, but it served another purpose admirably. It helped to arouse curiosity and steadily raised the general level of expectations concerning the inauguration of the religious crusade. "The result of all this high pressure," said the *London Times*, "was a very crowded attendance last night [March 9, 1875]." Over 12,000 people gathered in Agricultural Hall for the first meeting to hear Moody and Sankey.[12]

The two Americans spent the next four months seeking to cope with irreligion and spiritual inertia throughout the sprawling metropolitan area. London's great size prevented the revival from operating from a single headquarters. Moody divided the city into four sections and rented or constructed large buildings as the central gathering places for each of the sections. He and his organizers rented the Agricultural Hall in Islington and the Royal Opera House in the fashionable West End, then constructed two temporary structures in Camberwell Green and on the Bow Road, both in working-class areas of the city.

On July 12, 1875, Moody and Sankey held their closing service in the conference hall at Mildmay Park. This was a most felicitous setting for farewells — the center that embodied the evangelical movement throughout the islands. Moody's showmanship and unfailing sense of appropriate context carried through to the end. The audience, 2,500 strong, composed of friends and sup-

11. *Christian* (December 3, 1874): 772; (December 17, 1874): 185; (February 25, 1875): 141; *New York Christian Advocate*, 50 (January 28, 1875): 29; (September 16, 1875): 293; *London Daily News*, March 8, 1875; *Manchester Guardian*, January 5, 1875; *London Daily Telegraph*, June 24, 1875, July 9, 1875; *Chicago Tribune*, September 14, 1875.
12. *London Times*, March 10, 1875. For detailed descriptions of the opening of the London campaign, see the *London Evening Standard*, March 10, 1875, and the *London Daily News*, March 10, 1875.

porters including six hundred ministers from all the major religious bodies of England, seemed to provide dramatic testimony that unity had emerged from diversity, and that the revival had been a success.[13]

It is next to impossible to assert with full assurance that Moody's work in England had succeeded — or failed. Any careful observer faces primary evidence that projects a maze of conflicting views. Personal prejudice, usually strongly felt in one direction or another, seemed to determine most of the calculations. In both Scotland and in England estimates of converts varied a great deal and were often vague as to categorization.[14] Statistics on membership in the churches over the years were either nonexistent or too imprecise to be depended upon.[15]

In both Scotland and England a principal hope among church people was that the common touch of the two Americans would enable them to reach the "lapsed masses" — the working classes of the great industrial towns who were by now often outside the daily influence of the church.[16] Although Moody was no stranger

13. *London Evening Standard,* July 13, 1875; *London Daily News,* July 13, 1875; *Methodist* (July 16, 1875): 4.

14. For examples of rough estimates made in Scotland see *Missionary Record of the United Presbyterian Church,* n.s., 5 (February 2, 1874): 26; *Christian,* 4 (February 26, 1874): 8; (May 21, 1874): 7; (July 16, 1874): 7. In Liverpool it was noted that "one good authority believed there were under 1,000 [converts], another knew that there were at least 1,500, and a third, equally well informed, was sure that over 2,000 tickets [to the converts' meeting] had been given [out]." (*Christian World* [April 2, 1875]: 219.) For additional evidence of this sort, see *ibid.,* (June 4, 1875): 374; *London Daily News,* March 30, 1875; *Birmingham Daily Mail,* February 6, 1875; *Methodist* (February 12, 1875): 3.

15. Surveys of opinion concerning the impact of the revivals in England are in William G. McLoughlin, *Modern Revivalism: Charles Grandison Finney to Billy Graham* (New York: Ronald Press, 1959), pp. 196–200, and James F. Findlay, "Dwight L. Moody, Evangelist of the Gilded Age: 1837–99" (unpublished Ph.D. dissertation, Northwestern University, 1961), pp. 112–15, 116–18. McLoughlin has also surveyed the most reliable statistics on church membership in Scotland and has concluded that the revivals did not measurably affect membership in a favorable sense over the long run. (McLoughlin, *Modern Revivalism,* pp. 200–01.)

16. *Church of Scotland Home and Foreign Missionary Record* (February 2, 1874): 579; *Glasgow News,* May 15, 1874. Moody also made it clear that he hoped his revivals would reach the urban poor and minister

to life as it was lived in urban slums, the industrial centers of England revealed poverty and privation on a scale he had never previously experienced. He recoiled in shock and horror, expressing publicly his deep sense of urgency that the problem of the urban poor be dealt with in a substantive way by the church. After visiting Sheffield, a thoroughly industrialized city, he spoke of "this dark and terrible problem," accentuated by the fact that the chapels in town were so few in number that pews were unavailable for about two-thirds of the population — even if they desired to attend services. "Talk of being sickened at the sight of the world's degradation!" he exclaimed. "Rather let those of us who are Christians hide our faces because of our own, and pray God to deliver us from the guilt of the world's blood." [17]

Even before he reached the major cities of England, however, questions had been raised about Moody's success with this crucial segment of the population. In Scotland some of his supporters had tried valiantly to suggest that he appealed to "all ranks and conditions of men," yet it seems clear that lower class groups did not appear at the revivals regularly or in large numbers. In Scotland the soberest assessments, prepared by officials of churches generally sympathetic with Moody's work, spelled out clearly his failure to reach the unchurched. Especially revealing was a detailed analysis prepared for the Free Church. Surveying the work of the Americans in the north, the authors of the report admitted that "little effect has been produced on the masses among whom ignorance and open wickedness abound and abide. From large towns especially it is reported that . . . the masses have not been reached, and there is no perceptible change in their moral condition." [18] The same conclusions also appear to be valid for England.

Assuming Moody was sincere in the words he uttered after visit-

effectively to them. (See his statements, reported in the *Glasgow News,* [April 17, 1874].)

17. *Christian,* 5 (January 25, 1875): 5.

18. *Free Church of Scotland Monthly Record* (July 1, 1874): 135. An all but verbatim version was reprinted in *Glasgow News,* May 23, 1874. For expressions of a similar nature see *Church of Scotland Home and Foreign Missionary Record,* n.s., 9 (April 1, 1874): 15; *Glasgow Herald,* May 23, 1874; *Glasgow News,* February 21, 1874, May 16, 1874; *Christian,* 3 (December 24, 1873): 3; 4 (February 5, 1874): 8.

ing Sheffield, the fact that his mission did not reach the urban poor in any lasting or effective way in either England or Scotland must have been galling to him indeed. These negative results could also be interpreted as something of a rebuke to his efforts generally as an evangelist. A friendly critic noted at the end of Moody's London campaign that "I have always regarded the special mission of the evangelist that of reaching the masses who are outside of all our churches, and on whom the ordinary ministry can make no impression. Accordingly, I had high anticipations . . . as to the work that was to be effected amongst the thousands who crowd the courts and alleys of this city." [19] The American may well have harbored similar feelings. Yet everywhere he went it was middle and upper-class groups which responded to him. People who were already church members were those most likely to pour into his meetings. This had been true in Scotland and the experience was repeated in England.[20]

Because of these facts, perhaps, Moody had to admit the partial ineffectiveness of the revival of 1875 in London. To an English friend he confided that "he and Sankey should have stayed in London . . . at least a year, because of the vastness of the population." [21] The failure in both England and Scotland to reach those who stood outside the church may also explain Moody's search at a later time for means other than revivalism to cope with the problem of the "unchurched masses." His city evangelist training school in Chicago, and even the academies he founded in Northfield in the early 1880's, had as a basic purpose the preparation of young people for work among the urban poor. Thus the experience in England, the disappointments and the failures as well as the successes, shaped his career a decade later.

19. *Christian World* (July 23, 1875): 488.
20. *Ibid.* (April 23, 1875): 278; (May 7, 1875): 315; (May 21, 1875): 346; (June 11, 1875): 390; *Christian* (January 7, 1875): 13; *Methodist* (March 5, 1875): 10; *London Morning Post*, March 10, 1875; *London Daily News*, March 15, 1875; *Church Review* (March 20, 1875): 152; *Porcupine*, 16 (February 13, 1875): 72; *Glasgow News*, May 23, 1874.
21. G. E. Morgan, *Mighty Days of Revival*, p. 178. Other essentially negative conclusions concerning the results of the London campaign from sources generally friendly to Moody are in *Christian World* (May 21, 1875): 344; (July 23, 1875): 488; *Christian Monthly and Family Treasury* (August, 1881): 477–78; (November, 1881): 654, 656, 658.

For thousands of Englishmen, however, Moody's efforts seemed constructive and highly successful. The mere size of the crowds which he and Sankey attracted caused some of his supporters to jump to such conclusions. But even more thoughtful people believed strongly in the success of the revivals. For example, R. W. Dale, probably the leading spokesman for English Congregationalism, had stood aloof from the revival movement until Moody reached Birmingham, Dale's home. Observing the revivalist closely, Dale thereafter committed himself wholeheartedly to the cause. After the revival in Birmingham ended, Dale put into print the gist of his reflections and feelings. He concluded that the chief effect of the revival had been upon those who had "long been members of the Christian Church." People of this sort demonstrated a new "joyousness and elasticity of spirit" which had "transformed them" and which explained the "unostentatious eagerness with which they are taking up Christian work." [22] Dale's observations tallied generally with those of many others. The chief impact of the revival was upon those actually working within the church or on people at least sympathetic to the church and its work.

Although highly enthusiastic about Moody, in his more reflective moments Dale remained puzzled because of the evangelist's ordinariness — his seeming lack of any distinctive power. Yet the reality of the evangelist's influence seemed indisputable. For as Dale noted, to "impress an audience varying from three thousand to six thousand people for half an hour in the morning and for three-quarters of an hour in the afternoon," and to interest "a third audience of thirteen or fifteen thousand people for three-quarters of an hour again in the evening," Moody "must have power of some kind." Once in the heat of the revival in Birmingham the pastor had remarked rather bluntly to Moody that "the work was most plainly of God, for I could see no real relation between him and what he had done." [23]

For a Christian this was a perfectly proper, even complimen-

22. Alfred W. W. Dale, *The Life of R. W. Dale of Birmingham* (London: Hodder and Stoughton, 1898), pp. 317–20; *Congregationalist*, 4 (March, 1875): 146.

23. *Congregationalist*, 4 (March, 1875): 138, 139.

tary, comment to make. But it was not necessarily the only way to explain the religious upheaval which Moody had helped fashion. Outside the circle of faith other explanations could be added that worked to resolve the problem of causation. Perhaps most superficially Moody attracted attention simply because he was a Yankee and possessed habits or characteristics that struck the English as fresh or surprising. The public fascination for the revivalist and his singing partner was reflected in the numerous detailed descriptions and assessments of the two Americans that were a part of almost every newspaper report recording the opening of each of the major revivals in Britain. Englishmen read with delight about Moody's pungent and vivid phraseology, his quaint western-Massachusetts metaphors, his use of language, his ability as a storyteller, and his capacity to weave his sermon themes around jagged nuggets of life mined from the *Bible* and his own experience. They recognized his sense of humor and his aplomb in handling his vast audiences.[24] Undoubtedly Moody was injecting a freshness and directness into the somewhat formalized methods of English preaching that many of these commentators, and apparently thousands of his hearers, welcomed.

The popularity of Sankey's music also contributed substantially to the attractiveness of the Americans. In Scotland, as we have noted, Sankey commanded attention simply because solo singing and the use of the harmonium had been all but unheard of. In England, there was a notable tradition of hymnody and congregational singing connected with the evangelical movement, but this tradition had been declining at the time the two Americans came overseas. Consciously or unconsciously, Sankey did something to revive that tradition. Participants in the revival meetings noted that the singing evangelist often did not really sing his songs but instead "spoke" them in a tuneful way. He put primary emphasis on precise enunciation, to make clear the words and their meaning. He made music the servant of the

24. A sample of such analyses should include: *Christian* (February 12, 1874): 6; *Dublin Evening Mail*, November 28, 1874; *Manchester Examiner and Times*, November 30, 1874; *London Daily News*, March 10, 1875; *Christian World* (March 5, 1875): 161; (March 12, 1875): 170: *Methodist* (March 19, 1875): 5; *Birmingham Daily Mail*, February 6, 1875; *Nonconformist* (July 21, 1875): 744.

lyrics rather than the reverse.[25] This seemed roughly analogous to the "reciting" of hymns and the psalter that had occurred in an earlier day.

The melodies Sankey used were simple, yet when he performed them they often produced a noticeable emotional effect, since he was careful to utilize modulations in tempo and volume both in his voice and in the musical accompaniment. These songs caused a good deal of comment from Sankey's contemporaries. One of the most astute critics noted that the revival tunes were like those sung in Nonconformist chapels thirty years earlier, "often vulgar, but they were real tunes, easily learnt, easily remembered; they haunted people during the week." In contrast, hymns of more recent times had been composed or adapted by organists who wanted to dramatize the solemn effects they could get out of their instruments. These musicians, however, forgot how "to give the people something to sing." The writer concluded that "people want to sing, not what they *think*, but what they *feel*; and if they are asked to sing hymns in which there is no glow of feeling . . . they will not sing at all." [26] Because Sankey's tunes and method of singing approximated this desire or feeling, he and his melodies evoked the powerful response they did in the mass revival meetings. And indirectly, perhaps, this popular response served as a criticism of the hymnody then practiced in the churches of England.

A later historian has suggested that William Booth and the Salvation Army, emerging a few years after Moody and Sankey, revived in English evangelicalism the deeply felt national love of sound and color, extending back in time to medieval England with its constant emphasis on ritual and ceremonial.[27] Perhaps Sankey with his massed choirs and congregational singing, and his

25. One of the most perceptive contemporary judgments of Sankey's techniques is in *Christian World* (April 16, 1875): 255. See also *Church of Scotland Home and Foreign Missionary Record*, n.s., 60 (April 1, 1874): 17–18; *Missionary Record of the United Presbyterian Church*, n.s., 6 (February 2, 1874): 27; *Glasgow News*, February 21, 1874; *Church Times* (April 9, 1875): 181; *Methodist* (March 19, 1875): 5; (April 30, 1875): 5.

26. *Congregationalist* 4 (March, 1875): 136–37. See also the *Birmingham Daily Mail*, January 18, 1875.

27. Horton Davies, *Worship and Theology in England: From Newman to Martineau, 1850–1900* (Princeton: Princeton University Press,

creation of emotion and strong feeling in his solo performances, anticipated Booth and his army in touching this sensitive nerve in Englishmen, usually overlaid by outward reserve and decorum.

Dressed conservatively, exhibiting an acceptable portliness of build, sporting a carefully trimmed beard, Moody seemed the epitome of middle-class England. "If you had seen him behind a bank counter or in the office at a warehouse," commented one of his hearers in Manchester, "you would have been sensible of no incongruity between the man and his surroundings." Sankey, in turn, with his long whiskers and shaven chin, "might easily be taken for a middle-aged merchant or professional man." People spoke of Moody's "business tact" and his frequent use of "commerical phrases." [28] The Victorian era seemed the great age of the businessman and his middle-class friends. Samuel Smiles's manuals of self-help, in many ways important guides to popular thought in the 1850's and 1860's and excellent reflections of the thinking of the professional and business classes, embodied social and economic assumptions that Moody could accept almost without reservation. Although self-help, thrift, and sobriety were applied in different ways in the vastly different social systems of the United States and England, the parallels in thought and intent of these doctrines in the two countries were close enough to provide Moody one avenue of access to friendships and contacts among the comfortable merchants that dominated the middle sector of English society. His well-known early career in business and his general identification in Chicago with prominent businessmen also smoothed the way for him overseas. The fact that evangelical Christianity's great fortress of strength in England was the middle classes also promoted the easy identification of Moody with these groups.

Thus when one reads of Moody outside the revival hall, he was invariably in the company of, or in some way associated with, these businessmen-laymen and their families. Days of rest were

1962), p. 169. A contemporary recognition of the special appeal of the color and sound of the revivals to audiences ordinarily steeped in drabness may be found in *London Daily Telegraph*, April 18, 1884.

28. *Manchester Guardian*, December 4, 1874; *Sheffeld Christian Messenger* (January, 1875): 4; *Christian* (September 11, 1873): 12; (February 11, 1875): 9; *Church Times* (February 12, 1875): 82.

spent often at the country homes of these people. There are interesting accounts recorded of Moody's impish efforts to poke fun at the straitlaced attitudes of his pious companions with practical jokes. His eagerness to indulge with the youngsters in a fast game of rounders or a boisterous hour of croquet also seemed something of a contrast to his serious adult hosts.[29]

Only once did Moody's middle-class outlook negatively affect his relations with important people in English society. Partly at the urging of Quintin Hogg, a young well-to-do evangelical leader in London, the American agreed early in June, 1875, to conduct a meeting soon after at Eton, the famous public school and educational center for the young sons of the upper class. A great hue and cry erupted in Parliament. Members of the House of Lords especially opposed Moody's plans. As long as Moody spoke of saving "the masses," obviously by the traditional means of personal evangelization or through support of charitable organizations that in turn reflected upper and middle-class values, as long as his revivals seemed designed especially to appeal to the great body of evangelical churchgoers, the aristocracy could look on with a certain indulgence. But going to Eton meant that the revivalist was invading one of the sacred precincts of the upper classes, an upstart American preaching undesirable doctrines to young innocents being groomed carefully by the Church in religious tradition and faith. It could not be. Following remonstrances in Parliament and in the press, the formal invitation to Moody was withdrawn, and he held his service in the private garden of a home near the campus. Despite the short-lived nature of the incident, it revealed clearly the sharp social distinctions that existed in England at the time, divisions which relegated even a popular figure like Moody to his "proper place." Perhaps, too, it suggested the rather high repute that Moody had achieved in England, that a move such as this was considered seriously by

29. Emily Kinnaird, *Reminiscences* (London: John Murray, 1925), pp. 39, 74–75; Ethel M. Wood, *The Polytechnic and Its Founder, Quintin Hogg* (London: Nisbet and Co., 1932), pp. 138–41; Kathleen Heasman, *Evangelicals in Action: An Appraisal of Their Social Work in the Victorian Era* (London: Geoffrey Bles, 1962), p. 108; unknown writer to W. R. Moody, March 10, 1900, "Letters to W. R. Moody" folder, Moody Papers, Moody Bible Institute.

his evangelical friends and as seriously entertained by the officials in Eton, before the final rebuff was administered and the affair brought to an end.[30]

On the whole, however, Moody's identification with the leaders of the middling groups in English society served to swell his popularity rather than to diminish it. For one section of Moody's audiences this particular image was especially important as an avenue of communication. People in this group were a "forgotten class" of individuals from middle and lower-middle-class family backgrounds. They had grown up within the church and thus had received deep religious impressions, but these experiences had not issued in a "clear decision to serve Christ"; such people were left instead with "a dull aching of heart for God." What these words of an astute observer depicted were semi-believers, people existing in a twilight zone of faith–non-faith created largely by the powerful forces of secularism that were eroding away the foundations of personal religious belief throughout the Victorian years. The language used to describe these persons probably would apply to thousands of Englishmen in the last half of the nineteenth century.

> The sense of dissatisfaction with their condition never wholly leaves them; it sometimes makes them very restless. But when they listen to the preaching of most of us [ministers], they feel as if we were moving in regions which are inaccessible to them. If they come to our places of worship, they come without any hope of receiving help. Many of them, having found that we do not help them, never come at all.[31]

It is easy to see why Moody had a special appeal for these people. Lacking clerical garb and the refined accents of the minister, Moody substituted for these a business suit and the vernacular of

30. *London Times*, June 22, 1875, June 23, 1875; *London Daily News*, June 22, 1875, June 23, 1875; *London Standard*, June 22, 1875, June 23, 1875; *London Morning Post*, June 22, 1875, June 23, 1875; *Christian World* (June 25, 1875): 421.

31. *Congregationalist*, 4 (March, 1875): 134. In recent years Victorian scholars have placed especially strong emphasis on this tendency in the thought of nineteenth century England. For the fullest exposition of the theme, see Walter E. Houghton, *The Victorian Frame of Mind, 1830–1870* (New Haven: Yale University Press, 1963).

the business world and common, everyday life. Here was a man shaped in their milieu speaking to them about religious matters. Any mental blocks that might come simply from hearing a minister speak were not present in the revival meetings. Moreover there was Moody's message, simple and uncomplicated as to theology, made extremely vivid by his artful and compelling use of storytelling and the illuminating anecdote, driven into the consciousness of his audience by one obviously possessed of the certainty and reality of his own faith. This was a combination of circumstances which seemed bound to revive the flagging spiritual life of these hearers and to impart new hope or expectations into their lives. "When such people," asserted a friend of the revivalist, "heard that within a few months thousands of men and women had declared that while listening to Mr. Moody and Mr. Sankey, they had passed from religious indifference or despondency into the clear light of God, they began to think that for them too there might be hope." [32] Out of such a matrix of social identification, religious despair, and expectation, probably emerged many of those who became "converts" in the Moody meetings. Since the evangelist's appeal was essentially to the status-quo, in regard to both theological and socioeconomic issues, it is quite possible that for many of those affected initially by his revival, his message and impact did not permanently remove doubt and uncertainty. But for the moment it is easy to understand how his presence could electrify and move many in his audience.

Moody's success must also be viewed in the context of the general history of the Nonconformist groups in the last third of the nineteenth century. Between 1860 and 1900 Nonconformity fought successfully to reach a position of equality with the establishment in civil and legal matters. The effort to dispose of legal and social discrimination had begun early in the century, and important battles had been won earlier. Yet not until after 1860 did the final barriers begin to fall. This movement in religious circles roughly paralleled the rise of political liberalism in England. As they struggled for religious equality, the Nonconformists tended to join forces with the Liberal Party in the common fight against the status quo. Recognizing the political potential

32. *Congregationalist*, 4 (March, 1875): 134.

in their adherents from the dissenting chapels, the Liberals inserted items into their program designed to appeal exclusively to these groups. Many of these items passed into law shortly before and during the years Moody was in Great Britain. Church rates had been abolished in 1868; non-Anglicans were admitted to Oxford and Cambridge on equal terms for the first time in 1871; and the Burials Act of 1880 removed a long-standing grievance of dissenters. The incorporation of Free Church schools into the national education system that emerged from the Education Act of 1870 also illustrates the changing relationships between established church and dissenting sects.[33] In several ways Moody fitted in with these developments. The popular outburst of enthusiasm in his favor could be viewed as one more reflection of the power and strength that evangelicalism and the Nonconformists in particular were exhibiting in the 1870's. In shattering the legal shackles that bound them, Free Churchmen were participating in the effort to democratize English society and to end social practices that now appeared irrelevant or unjust. As a representative of democracy overseas, Moody seemed to emphasize the existence of this worldwide movement and implicitly reminded his hearers of their involvement in that movement.

In other ways the 1870's were a time of turmoil and distress for the church groups attracted to Moody. Scarcely a decade earlier Darwin had posed his fundamental challenge to traditional theology. Biblical criticism had won a solid footing in the work of German scholars early in the nineteenth century, but these efforts had been largely ignored in Britain. Until the 1850's traditional theological formulations still held sway among many church leaders as well as for the rank-and-file churchgoer. The biblical literalism of the evangelicals undoubtedly helped to promote this conservative outlook. Thus when Darwin's work appeared, with its overwhelming evidence that cast doubt on the literal truth of Genesis, the controversy that followed was doubly unsettling because it

33. Horton Davies, *The English Free Churches* (London: Oxford University Press, 1952), chap. 7; P. B. Morgan, "Study of the Work of Four Evangelists," pp. 9–10; Alec R. Vidler, *The Church in an Age of Revolution* (Baltimore: Penguin Books, 1961), chap. 12; *New York Christian Advocate* (April 18, 1872): 124.

had been so long delayed. Popularizers of liberal attitudes toward religious faith — such as Thomas Huxley outside the church, Matthew Arnold within the church, and the clerical authors of the famous *Essays and Reviews* published in 1860 — commanded widespread attention and created consternation in church circles. Most of Moody's friends, conservative theologically, viewed these developments with great suspicion and antagonism.[34]

By the time Moody arrived, cleavages of all sorts were rending the churches of England. In addition to the theological controversies, within the Anglican community the Ritualists, representing High-Church, Anglo-Catholic sentiment, had stirred great fears and resentments by their rapid advance into the local parishes. Low Church evangelicals opposed Ritualism, as did liberal or Broad Church Anglicans. We have already intimated how these disagreements over ecclesiastical practices affected Moody and his work. The struggle of free churchmen to achieve equality with the Anglicans produced frequent attacks upon the established church and even demands for the dissolution of the ties between church and state. All this made it seem unlikely that cooperation could occur between these groups, even though each possessed a large body of people animated by the common sentiments of the evangelical tradition. The differences generated by changed theological attitudes were merely fuel to be added to these fires of controversy.[35]

The previously mentioned problem of how to deal with the masses of unchurched urban workers and their families also plagued Moody everywhere he went. Recent research has made it plain that the churches were not losing their hold on thousands in the working classes. In reality these people had never been active

34. Vidler, *Church in an Age of Revolution*, chaps. 10, 11. *The Christian*, in particular, reflected the fears of Moody's friends concerning the rapidly altering theological climate. See, for example, *Christian* (January 1, 1873): 11, 13; (February 6, 1873): 7; (May 19, 1873): 19; (June 5, 1873): 13; (August 28, 1873): 12; (October 2, 1873): 9. For a carefully reasoned expression of concern, see *Congregationalist*, 2 (April, 1873): 194.

35. Davies, *Worship and Theology in England*, pp. 7–8, 115–16, 117, 139; *Advance*, 1 (October 10, 1867): 1; *New York Christian Advocate* (August 5, 1875): 241.

in the life of the church. Perhaps the first generation of workers, drawn from countryside to town, had a remembrance of religious practices in the local village, but these practices were not continued once the move to an industrial center had occurred. By Moody's time a generation of the urban population had grown up without any contact with or knowledge of the church and its ministrations. The great religious census of 1851 revealed this fact clearly. In a score of the largest towns in England, fewer than one person in ten attended any place of worship on the Sunday the census was taken. Attendance was lowest in London and the great manufacturing centers.[36] These trends continued with declining percentages to Moody's day twenty years later.

By the 1870's the churches, fearing the possibilities of social upheaval and a decline in their prestige and power because of the widening gulf between "classes" and "masses," had made this problem a central concern. The evangelicals, because of their intensely activist spirit, were especially prominent among those seeking a solution. Charitable agencies of all sorts and kinds blossomed in the urban areas. Ragged schools, soup kitchens, children's homes and orphanages, homes for prostitutes and wayward girls, even the temperance movement, were all reflections of this aroused interest. Thus the working class in the industrial towns had become very much a subject for public discussion.[37]

Into this complicated situation strode the American evange-

36. For a discussion of the census and the implications of its findings, see Kenneth S. Inglis, "Patterns of Worship in 1851," *Journal of Ecclesiastical History*, 11, 1960): 74–86; and David M. Thompson, "The 1851 Religious Census: Problems and Possibilities," *Victorian Studies*, 11 (September, 1967): 87–97; Edward R. Wickham's *Church and People in an Industrial City* (London: Lutterworth Press, 1957), a detailed examination of religious activities in Sheffield in the mid-nineteenth century, tends to confirm Inglis' generalizations about the working classes and the church. See also Standish Meacham, "The Church in the Victorian City," *Victorian Studies*, 11 (March, 1968): 359–78.

37. Kathleen Heasman provides a sympathetic account of the work of the churches in the cities of Moody's day in her *Evangelicals in Action*. A much more critical report, covering roughly the same time period, is Kenneth S. Inglis's *Churches and the Working Classes in Victorian England* (London: Routledge and Kegan Paul, 1963). For a different approach, see Trygve R. Tholfsen, "The Transition to Democracy in Victorian England," *International Review of Social History*, 6, pt. 2 (1961): 226–48.

list proclaiming doctrines that on the surface seemed to bring relief from all the conflict and tension. Moody was theologically
conservative, yet at the same time undogmatic and personally
able to get along with those with whom he might disagree on
questions of scripture or doctrine. Thus he provided reassurance
for those upset by the rapidly shifting currents of theological dis-
putation, yet his message was dressed up in such vivid anecdotes
and preached so energetically that his opponents were often dis-
armed or at least neutralized. His frequently reiterated interest
in the "unsaved masses" caused him to draw to his side those
churchmen concerned about this problem. Finally his constant
emphasis upon the need for unity among all groups within Christendom struck a responsive chord among those wearying of many
seemingly petty differences that fragmented the churches in England as they had in Scotland.

Before and during the time that the revivalist and his singing
partner were in England, an unusual mood manifested itself within
portions of the evangelical community. It was a spirit of expectation, a feeling which seemed to say that out of the welter of conflict perhaps there would emerge a new wave of religious enthusiasm that would bring an end to internal tensions.[38] The
Americans sometimes seemed to provide the rather surprising answer to these expectations. In Liverpool, just prior to Moody's
arrival, a speaker at one of the preparatory meetings for the
revival there expressed such feelings. The churches, he asserted,
had been for some time in a state of spiritual degeneracy. "Here-
sies were rife, and false doctrines on every side — Rationalism,
Ritualism, Romanism . . . had reared their heads amongst
them. . . . The drunkenness of their town was a disgrace and
a scandal, not to the world, but to the Church. There were from
two to three hundred thousand persons in Liverpool who never
attended a place of worship, and this, too, was a scandal to the
Church of Christ." Here all the uncertainties and fears of church
people stood out, explicitly revealed to the world. But now, hap-

38. See especially articles by Robert W. Dale in the *Congregationalist*,
2 (January, 1873): 1–7; (February, 1873): 65–71; (March, 1873): 129–135;
(April, 1873): 193–201; and *Christian World Magazine*, 2 (January,
1875): 5–8.

pily, "two foreigners were coming amongst them whom God had blessed wherever they had gone . . . [with] manifestations of divine grace and divine power." Although actually a compound of good timing and appropriate technique, as well as spiritual fervor, the appeal of Moody and Sankey seemed no less real to their supporters. Understandably, then, the people of Liverpool were admonished to let the Americans "be heartily welcomed." [39]

In essence what has been said is that Moody was effective because he appealed to the traditional and familiar in the religious realm. He was a respectable conservative in an age of flux and change. The timing of his appearance in England underscores further the validity of this observation. The 1870's have for some time been recognized as a fundamental dividing point in the history of Victorian England. In the last quarter of the nineteenth century Britain's industrial preeminence began to be challenged by Germany and by England's giant offspring in North America. The "Great Depression" of 1873–96 with its agricultural decline, falling prices and profit margins, and intermittently high rates of unemployment, tended to spread a sense of uncertainty among many late Victorians. Christianity, the moral cement of Victorian society, suffered attacks from numerous quarters. A mass labor movement, increasingly articulate and well-organized, began to suggest the stirrings of lower-class groups for public recognition that would characterize more fully an England of a later day. The rudiments of government planning and the welfare state have also been traced back to these same years.[40] In a variety of ways the forces of science, democracy, and technology were altering the confident, optimistic, bourgeois "workshop of the world" that had been England at mid-century. Even though he was an outsider, as a representative of middle-class evangelicalism Moody stood for these traditions that were now beginning to disintegrate.

39. [Liverpool] *Evening Express*, February 5, 1875.
40. R. C. K. Ensor, *England, 1870–1914* (London: Oxford University Press, 1952), p. 136 and *passim*; David Roberts, *Victorian Origins of the British Welfare State* (New Haven: Yale University Press, 1960); Herman Ausubel, *In Hard Times: Reformers Among the Late Victorians* (New York: Columbia University Press, 1960); Kathleen Woodroofe, "The Making of the Welfare State in England: A Summary of Its Origin and Development," *Journal of Social History*, 1 (Summer, 1968): 308–17.

His work reaffirmed, for all to see, the values and assumptions of a passing order.

Yet at the same time Moody might well be viewed as a harbinger of the newer order of things stealing into English society. A clue to this interpretation of the revivalist comes indirectly from comments made by Moody's contemporaries about Ritualism. More than one person had observed that the Ritualists seemed to represent a democratic movement of sorts welling up within the Anglican Church. Unlike their fathers the Tractarians, who had been men of culture and refinement, these priests arrayed "in Amice and Alb, in Girdle and Stole," bowing before the altar "in embroidered Chasubles resplendent with gold," were much more men of the local parish and more representative of the common run of churchgoer. Their democratic tendencies caused the Ritualists to attack their opponents recklessly and to be less scrupulous than their forebears in their use of invective and extremely harsh language. There was an element of the demagogic about them which upset churchmen accustomed to order and a sense of responsibility in the registering of protest and the desire for change.[41] But perhaps these characteristics bespoke nothing more than democracy attaching itself to the innermost citadel of respectability within English society, the Church of England.

Moody's revivals can also be viewed within this democratic context. The preaching, praying, and singing of the missionaries from America served to dramatize the fustiness and crabbed nature of the traditional service in the evangelical chapels. Moody and Sankey spoke and sang from a secular auditorium and invited the entire population to attend their services. There were overtones, in a restrained way, of the demagogic about them, too, which undoubtedly spurred the popular response to their work. The Moody revivals and Ritualism, then, should be viewed as two sides of the same coin. This coin was the tendency toward democratization which was affecting all of English society.[42] When the

41. *Advance*, 1 (October 10, 1867): 1.
42. Suggestive comments concerning similarities between Ritualism and Moody's revivals are to be found in the *London Daily Telegraph*, April 18, 1884.

revivalist is viewed in this context he becomes, Januslike, a foretaste of England's future as well as a reflection of her past. Perhaps this too helps to explain his extraordinary appeal to Englishmen.

If Moody produced a measurable effect upon the people of England, the reverse was no less the case. We have mentioned several times the importance of these English experiences in serving as the crucible in which mass revivalism first took shape. But these years spent outside the United States were also influential in laying the groundwork for the evangelist's activities in his later years, when he in part turned away from his exclusive concern with revivalism. The journey overseas caused him to realize more fully than at any time previously the immense social problems facing countries caught up in the industrial revolution. Perhaps specific institutions would have to be devised by the church to deal with these problems effectively. Moody's attitudes at this point departed considerably from the thinking of most evangelicals in the United States concerning urban problems and industrialization. Too often obsessed with the intellectual challenge that Darwinism and biblical criticism were posing to their literalistic biblical world view, the evangelical bodies in America were much less inclined to grapple in a serious and practical way with the problems of city life than were their compatriots in England. Moreover, because of the pronounced individualism that had always been so powerful a force in American evangelicalism, the ability or desire to construct institutions to deal with these urban difficulties was much less manifest in the United States than in England. In theory English evangelicals emphasized the central importance of the personal conversion experience, as did the Americans, and this could and did serve as a powerful stimulus to individualist attitudes in Great Britain. Yet Englishmen found such thinking strongly tempered, and sometimes overruled, by attitudes that grew out of their participation in a heavily textured structure of church life that was the result of long historical experience and practice. The weight of religious traditions and institutional practices that had taken shape over generations severely limited English evangelicals in expressing in their religious life the unfettered individualism that was so characteristic of American evangelicalism.

In part Moody's work in Chicago enabled him to perceive and embrace the English attitudes toward social concerns. In the 1860's he had channeled much of his religious enthusiasm into the YMCA, specifically organized to work with people in urban areas, and he had created institutions of his own when he saw a need and nothing present to fill the void. But he was further influenced by his associations with English evangelicals and the many social agencies they were devising to bring uplift to the urban masses.[43] He continued his support of the YMCA in Scotland and England. Chiefly this took the form of fund-raising requests connected with his revivals. Buildings in London, Liverpool, Manchester, Dundee, and Glasgow were all in part made possible by his appeals.[44] Yet Moody also found himself reaching out for some way beyond these established means to touch those portions of the urban population that were ignorant of religion. Even before he reached London he spoke publicly of the need for workers "apart from the regular pastor" — lay workers who would become city missionaries without the full training of ordained ministers. He could cite specific efforts in London and elsewhere which served as examples.[45] The parallels with the purposes which underlay his schools founded in the 1880's in Masssachusetts and Chicago are

43. Mrs. Heasman, in *Evangelicals in Action*, pp. 21, 40, 57, 59, 95, 107–08, 125, 131, 146, 179, documents in detail the number of specific charitable organizations with which Moody had connections. She credits him with providing the incentive for the evangelicals in setting up a number of their projects to aid the urban poor. See also *Christian Monthly and Family Treasury* (November, 1881): 658.

44. *Glasgow Herald*, March 23, 1874; *Manchester Examiner and Times*, December 31, 1874; "Thirtieth Report of the Young Men's Christian Association, 1875," *London Central Y.M.C.A. Reports, 1863–1879* (n.p., n.d.), p. 39; unknown writer to W. R. Moody, March 10, 1900, "Letters to W. R. Moody," folder in Moody Papers, Moody Bible Institute.

45. See especially *Christian* (June 11, 1874): 6, for illuminating comments by the evangelist on this subject. For descriptions of English evangelical institutions which might have influenced Moody's thinking, see *ibid.*, p. 7; *Christian World* (June 18, 1875): 412. The connections between the institutions at Mildmay and some of Moody's later work at Northfield are suggested in William Y. Fullerton, *F. B. Meyer: A Biography* (London: Marshall, Morgan, and Scott, 1929), p. 41; Emma Dryer, "Reminiscences of the Founding of Moody Bible Institute," (unpublished typewritten MS, January, 1916), in the possession of Mr. Gene Getz, Moody Bible Institute, p. 7.

almost exact. Thus his overseas experiences shaped his future in ways not planned or even realized at the moment, drawing him beyond the limited tasks he had set for himself when he left America in 1873.

As Moody prepared to leave England in the summer of 1875, it became obvious that he was to reap one other benefit from his crusade in the island. Success in Great Britain had created a platform of notoriety from which he could easily spring into his career as a revivalist in his own country. By the time he arrived back in the United States, newspapers and religious periodicals had created enough public interest that a large audience was eagerly awaiting his call for a spiritual reawakening. Beginning in 1874, the religious journals in America commenced to print regular reports of his meetings. As enthusiasm built up in England, the variety and length of the accounts increased, and by the time the evangelist reached London he was already being approached informally about conducting revivals in New York, Chicago, and Philadelphia.[46] Secular newspapers in America were much slower to evince an interest in Moody's activities. Eventually convinced of the legitimacy of his success, these journals finally joined the chorus of praise. From the moment Moody and Sankey docked in New York in August, 1875, eastern newspapers reported their activities in the minutest detail, and the two men were compared with the "apostles of old," who had "turned the world upside down."[47]

The young Chicagoan had left the United States in 1873, largely unknown. He returned from Britain less than three years later, a public figure of considerable importance. Effective publicity, capitalizing on his successful revivals overseas, had largely created the image of Moody now in the public mind. To the average citi-

46. *Northwestern Christian Advocate*, 22 (June 10, 1874): 4; *Interior*, 5 (August 13, 1874): 4; *New York Christian Advocate*, 4 (November 5, 1874): 357; 45 (August 12, 1875): 253; *Western Christian Advocate*, 42 (January 13, 1875): 13; *New York Evangelist*, 46 (January 4, 1875): 1; (February 11, 1875): 2; (February 18, 1875): 1, 6; (May 27, 1875): 8; *Chicago Tribune*, October 5, 1875; *New York Tribune*, November 18, 1875.

47. *New York Times*, June 22, 1875; *New York Herald*, August 16, 1875, as quoted in William R. Moody, *D. L. Moody* (New York: Macmillan Co., 1930), p. 244.

zen, however, this man assuredly served as another example of the sudden climb from obscurity to fame. The image fitted the "rags to riches" theme, which suited public sentiment of the time perfectly. With all the exhilarating and manifold experiences of his sojourn to England to draw upon, with public interest and concern in his work already at a high level in this country, Moody was now prepared to assume the role of one of America's great popular religious heroes.

6

Mass Revivalist in the United States:
Preaching and Practice

Moody needed to rest after his exhausting labors in England, and
he looked forward to a few weeks of relaxation with family and
friends in Northfield following his arrival in this country. In New
York City he and Sankey parted company briefly as the singing
evangelist traveled to Pennsylvania for a reunion with his relatives there. Moody rushed on to Northfield by train, with short
stopovers in Hartford, Connecticut, and Springfield, Massachusetts. Although proud of the success of the young evangelist, the
people of his hometown seemed much less outwardly moved than
those in New York City where the ballyhoo for popular heroes
was most intense. A newspaperman trailing him to his birthplace
noted that Moody "arrived at the depot the same as any ordinary
passenger," welcomed by one of his brothers, who "quietly
drove him to the old homestead in a rickety buggy, scarcely
less honored by time and service than the careful and gentle steed
which hauled them." As the two men drove the mile or two from
the station through the town to the Moody homestead, they
confronted now and again old-time residents who recognized the
evangelist. Invariably there was a "short and cordial greeting,
but beyond this there was nothing to signify the presence here
of one of the most distinguished men of the period." [1] This absence
of public excitement, which surprised the city newspaperman a

1. *New York Herald,* August 19, 1875.

bit, was precisely attuned to Moody's senses at the moment and seemed quite in character with the rather slow-moving pace of activities in the small town. Eager to shun crowds and public tumult since his arrival in New York, the evangelist undoubtedly felt at home very soon.

Life centered around the family farm, located about a mile from the center of Northfield on an eminence known locally as "Moody's Hill." From this vantage point one commanded a sweeping view of the surrounding hills and the silver thread of the Connecticut River winding through the valley below. It was a spot where it seemed natural to be rather leisurely. Moody sought to refurbish his skills as a horseman with regular morning rides along the nearby roads. Our curious newspaperman noted this activity, and "the skill and speed displayed" seemed to suggest "an experienced jockey rather than the Christian hero whom [sic] he really was." Shortly after he arrived, the evangelist also displayed proudly the blooded sheep he had purchased in England to augment the family stock owned by his brothers living in Northfield. In showing off these animals, "he seemed to take no less interest than in spiritual matters." [2]

Gradually friends from other parts of the country began to visit and, in some cases, to stay and help begin the difficult process of laying plans for the promised revival campaigns in America's largest cities later in the fall. At first, even as the circle of friends expanded, daily activities remained informal. There were long buggy rides, with the evangelist as host, up and down the dirt roads of the Connecticut River Valley. One day early in September the entire group at the Moody house packed lunch baskets and drove a few miles out of town to the highest of the nearby hills for a picnic. One participant recorded in his diary how discussion flowed freely, and, under the spell of the natural beauty all about them, individuals found themselves so moved by visual and verbal senses that the gathering ended in an impromptu prayer meeting. At another moment, crossing the river on the local ferry from an excursion into the hills, Moody indulged his whimsy for practical jokes on his friends. Ira Sankey, who had rejoined his partner,

2. *Ibid.*; *Chicago Tribune*, October 5, 1875.

sang as the party crossed the river. Even as Sankey warbled his tunes, someone noticed that the boat moved more slowly than usual toward the far shore. Moody turned out to be the hindrance, pulling against the ferryman on the wire that propelled the ferry across the river, in order to extend the concert time of his singing associate.[3]

Rustic simplicity and innocent horseplay offered Moody the diversions he needed at the moment, but he could not shake off the fact that he was now a popular and widely acclaimed religious figure. Within a week after his arrival at home he had begun to preach to the people of Northfield and the surrounding countryside. By early September the crowds coming to hear him on Sunday were too large to be accommodated in the small Congregational church in the town. Some even drove from Springfield, Massachusetts, fifty miles away, and stayed overnight in nearby hamlets, driving on to Northfield by carriage early Sunday morning. The church lawn was spacious, and even the wide main road of the town which ran along in front could be encroached upon as the crowds grew. It was a picturesque scene, "very much like baccalaureate Sunday in some country college town" pencilled one participant, as Moody stood on the steps of the church with Sankey at his side, his audience of a thousand or more standing in groups or seated in carriages drawn up under the stately elms that lined the main street and shaded the church property. The evangelist spoke twice each Sunday, and other meetings were organized when out-of-town churchmen who had come to visit expressed an interest. Moody's work as a revivalist in the United States was already beginning.[4]

More important than preaching to curious New Englanders, however, was the need for a decision on the location of his first major revival in America. The choice was difficult to make. Every city in the country, it seemed, hoped to have the honor and prestige of being host to the first campaign. The two evan-

3. *Greenfield* [Mass.] *Gazette and Courier*, August 16, 1875; D. W. Whittle Diary, September 4, 1875, Moody Bible Institute, Chicago, Ill.
4. *Greenfield* [Mass.] *Gazette and Courier*, August 16, 1875, September 13, 1875, September 27, 1875; *Christian Register*, 44 (September 25, 1875): 1; *New York Christian Advocate*, 50 (September 16, 1875): 293; *New York Evangelist*, 46 (September 16, 1875): 4.

gelists had no concrete plans for the future at the time of their arrival from England, and their vagueness only served to increase the jockeying for position among the rival claimants.[5] By the first week of September, prominent evangelical leaders from New York and Philadelphia were appearing in Northfield to press their attentions upon Moody and Sankey. In addition the evangelical churches in Chicago and New York were holding organizational meetings and by mid-September had extended formal invitations to the evangelists. Philadelphia's boosters applied pressure by reminding Moody that official preparations would soon begin leading to the opening of the great Centennial Exposition in the middle of 1876. Once the City of Brotherly Love focused attention on these activities, a revival would be difficult to inaugurate. Moody should come immediately or postpone his visit for at least a year.[6] All these maneuverings were extraordinary indications of the degree to which mass revivals in the urban world of Moody's day were slipping into a context of purely human manipulation and planning, eliminating more and more the feelings of spontaneity and surprised reawakening that had so frequently been present in revivals a century earlier.

On September 14, 1875, Moody held a conference at Northfield, inviting two representatives each from four cities — Chicago, Philadelphia, New York City, and Brooklyn — to help him answer the vexing question of where to begin his American revivals.[7] Even this gathering did not cause him to make up his mind fully. He continued to vacillate for almost another month. Criteria that had developed in England ultimately became the basis for his decisions. Throughout the rest of his career as a revivalist

5. In response to queries in New York as he disembarked from overseas, Moody had thought that he would probably visit Chicago first after a short rest in Northfield. Almost simultaneously Sankey was declaring rather vaguely that they would very likely begin work in the East — in New York, Brooklyn, or perhaps Boston. Another published report asserted positively that the two men would hold their first meetings in Springfield, Massachusetts. (*New York Tribune*, August 16, 1875; *New York Herald*, August 19, 1875.)

6. Whittle Diary, September 4, 1875; *Chicago Tribune*, August 17, 1875, September 14, 1875; *New York Tribune*, September 15, 1875.

7. *Greenfield* [Mass.] *Gazette and Courier*, September 13, 1875; *New York Times*, September 15, 1875.

these criteria served as the ground rules which determined whether or not he would enter a community to conduct a revival campaign. There were two indispensable conditions: first, the promise of united support from the evangelical denominations in a city, and second, a guarantee of adequate physical facilities. These requirements temporarily eliminated Chicago and New York City from consideration in 1875. There had been criticism of the revivalist within evangelical circles in both cities and neither could provide adequate housing immediately.[8]

Later in 1875 Moody added another requirement to his considerations. Supplementing his request for united backing from the evangelical denominations, he asked that no competing activities be held by the churches while the revival was in progress. This did not mean that he was trying consciously to vie with established church programs. By "competing activities" he meant any program which would interfere with the immediate pursuit of evangelization. At this particular moment his puritanical mind balked at "church fairs and festivals." The Philadelphia YMCA, whose members would certainly play a vital role in any campaign in that city, was planning such an event. This fact helped the evangelist to decide to hold his first revival in Brooklyn. A large public building was immediately available in the latter city, and everything reportedly was "ripe for earnest religious work." [9]

Building on his experience in England, Moody advanced one final requirement, the assurance of adequate financing for his campaign. In every city the principal item of expense was the preparation of a building of sufficient size to house the religious services.

8. *New York Tribune,* September 15, 1875; *Chicago Tribune,* October 5, 1875; *New York Times,* October 5, 1875; *New York Herald,* October 8, 1875.

9. *Brooklyn Eagle,* October 9, 1875. Moody remained in Brooklyn only a month, for he still wanted to hold meetings in Philadelphia before the spirit of the centennial took over. Led by John Wanamaker, Philadelphians almost persuaded him to change his mind after he had decided to go to Brooklyn. A series of conferences was held in mid-October in which Moody first cancelled his Brooklyn campaign, stated he was to start in Philadelphia, then finally reinstituted his original plans. This "backing and filling" indicated the intense pressure being brought to bear for his initial favor. (*Philadelphia Inquirer,* October 12, 1875; *Brooklyn Eagle,* October 12, 1875, October 13, 1875; *New York Times,* October 12, 1875, October 13, 1875.)

The edifice in Brooklyn required almost no alterations and could be rented cheaply, which eased the problem of finance there. By contrast, the lack of a permanent building of suitable size and the inability to raise funds immediately to construct one diminished Chicago's chances. A reported guarantee of $100,000 to underwrite the Philadelphia campaign considerably enhanced the offer of the committee from that city.[10]

By the middle of October, 1875, the basic decisions had been made concerning the launching of large-scale American revivals. Moody would begin in Brooklyn, then move on to Philadelphia, New York City, Chicago, and Boston. This would occupy him fully for the rest of 1875 and much of 1876 and 1877. Then he would move into some of the smaller industrial centers of New England, such as Providence, Springfield, Hartford, and New Haven. It took most of 1878 to complete this itinerary. In the large cities the revivals lasted from two to three months; in the smaller towns he stayed three or four weeks. Throughout this three-year period, Moody conducted his campaigns from a single meeting place, invariably located in the downtown section of the cities involved. After 1878 the evangelist changed his tactics somewhat, but the procedures he followed between 1875 and 1878 serve as a guide for most professional revivalists who came after him. The work of these years provided a rudimentary expression of the institutional procedures that have since characterized mass urban revivalism, despite constant tinkering and efforts at refinement on the part of Moody and his successors.

Once Moody made a decision to conduct a revival in a particular locality, preparations for the event began in earnest. Here again

10. *Chicago Tribune*, September 28, 1875, October 5, 1875; *Brooklyn Eagle*, October 10, 1875; *New York Times*, October 9, 1875. John Farwell, preparing for Moody's campaign in Chicago late in 1876, wrote to a business friend that "the raising of the money necessary to secure an appropriate building, was the only condition upon which Mr. Moody would consent to come, on the ground that this would indicate more than anything else the earnestness of the invitation." (J. V. Farwell to E. W. Blatchford, September 6, 1876, quoted in John V. Farwell, *Early Recollections of Dwight L. Moody* [Chicago: The Winona Publishing Co., 1907], p. 163.) See also Moody to John Wanamaker, October 9, (no year), letter in files of John Wanamaker Store, Philadelphia, Pennsylvania.

the evangelist drew principally upon his experiences in Britain for guidance. In order to make an impression upon a city of hundreds of thousands of people, the preparatory work was of considerable importance. In a calculated way Moody's supporters in each locale created a crescendo of activity which was timed to reach its peak precisely as Moody and Sankey arrived to launch formally their spiritual reawakening.

Unlike Billy Sunday, with his rather sizable staff of advance agents, and the tight direction of Billy Graham's revivals by professionals, Moody's work possessed a homegrown quality about it that signified that mass revivalism was still only in its formative stages.[11] As in England, the revivalist kept close watch over general developments, but volunteers, chiefly local ministers and businessmen, worked out most of the grubby details of organization. Often at the same meeting where they drafted the formal invitation proffered to the evangelist, these people set up committees to carry out duties similar to those of the central committee that did most of the legwork connected with the London revival.[12] Yet even amidst this informality, the complexity of his campaigns forced Moody inexorably toward systematization and standardization of procedures. In a fumbling, trial-and-error manner he sought to develop increasing administrative efficiency. When subordinates performed well for him, he did not hesitate to use them again in other cities. After the campaign in Philadelphia he took his choir director, William F. Fisher, with him to New York. Thomas K. Cree, the secretary of the executive

11. William G. McLoughlin, *Modern Revivalism: Charles Grandison Finney to Billy Graham* (New York: Ronald Press, 1959) contains considerable data suggesting the steady institutionalization of procedures in mass revivalism which occurred over the years. See especially pp. 32–33, 422–23, 495. An excellent summary of Moody and Sankey's techniques, perhaps too heavily influenced by psychological assumptions and phraseology, is Robert B. Huber, "Dwight L. Moody," in Marie K. Hochmuth, ed., *A History and Criticism of American Public Address*, 3 vols. (New York: Longmans, Green and Co., 1955), vol. 3, chap. 7. Huber's article approximates an abstract of his earlier dissertation, "Dwight L. Moody: Salesman of Salvation," (unpublished Ph.D. dissertation, University of Wisconsin, 1942).

12. *Chicago Tribune*, September 14, 1875; *Philadelphia Inquirer*, October 8, 1875; *New York Times*, October 12, 1875; *New York Tribune*, November 18, 1875; *Boston Evening Journal*, January 26, 1877.

committee in charge of arrangements in Philadelpha, also undertook similar duties in Chicago a year later.[13]

In Philadelphia, Cree, along with certain key businessmen, shouldered much of the responsibility for making certain that the revival moved along smoothly from day to day. From his office flowed a steady stream of circulars and printed instructions. These bulletins defined the duties of ushers and the choir, provided information to ministers about seats available to them on the platform, solicited money from evangelical groups throughout the city, and pleaded with out-of-town newspapers to advertise the revival in their columns more often. These handbills remain the clearest evidence available of the vast amount of painstaking work that had to be done behind the scenes in order to make possible the surface excitement of mass revivalism. Cree's efforts possessed more than a touch of modern publicity techniques and represented another facet of the large-scale organizational procedures that Moody and his friends were struggling to incorporate into urban revivalism.[14]

Cree had been a traveling secretary for the YMCA and he symblized the key role the Association often played in Moody's revivals in this country. Because of their nondenominationalism, local associations served as a neutral point from which the revivalist could direct his forces, and they fitted perfectly into his scheme for emphasizing evangelical, but not denominational, concerns in his revivals. Supporters of the evangelist often used the rooms of the Association as a meeting place for planning sessions and for the preliminary services which led up to the revival. Members of the YMCA also participated in house-to-house vis-

13. *Philadelphia Evening Bulletin,* November 20, 1875; *New York Times,* February 6, 1876; *New York Evangelist,* 47 (October 5, 1876): 4; *Interior,* 7 (November 9, 1876): 4.

14. The Moody Papers, Mount Hermon Library, and the files of the Presbyterian Historical Society in Philadelphia contain numerous samples of these handbills. Thomas K. Cree estimated at a later date that over 50,000 copies of these circulars were distributed to the public each week. His detailed report of the Philadelphia campaign, filled with statistics, is in an unpublished manuscript he wrote entitled "Mr. Moody as an Evangelist," (no date) in the files of the YMCA Historical Library, New York City.

itations and the other preparatory activities connected with the time of spiritual renewal.[15]

Communities used a variety of expedients to house the American revivals. Brooklynites quickly converted a skating rink into an auditorium seating 6,000 people. Moody's supporters in Philadelphia refurbished an abandoned railroad depot in the downtown section of the city, owned and donated by John Wanamaker. In the main auditorium workmen bolted into place seats for over 10,000 people. The depot also included three large inquiry rooms and a vestibule thirty feet wide which ran around three sides of the building. In New York the evangelist used the Hippodrome. It was a mammoth structure at Madison Avenue and Twenty-Seventh Street, which at one time had housed P. T. Barnum's menagerie and circus. In Chicago and Boston the planning committees decided to construct permanent brick buldings. Each structure had a large auditorium surrounded by smaller offices and conference rooms. The Chicago hall seated 8,000 people, the Boston tabernacle, 6,000.[16]

In some cases the businessmen who financed the construction used the buildings later for their own purposes. At the close of the Philadelphia revival, John Wanamaker converted the depot into his principal downtown department store, shrewdly capitalizing on the fact that the revival had familiarized most Philadelphians with the location of his new enterprise. Promoters of the revival in Chicago garnered financial support by assuring businessmen

15. *New York Christian Advocate*, 51 (October 5, 1876): 317; *New York Evangelist*, 47 (October 7, 1876): 6; *New York Times*, October 13, 1875; *Chicago Tribune*, September 17, 1876. Moody did not forget the help his friends in the YMCA gave him. At the closing meetings in all his major campaigns he asked that offerings be taken to underwrite the indebtedness of the local Association. Chicagoans pledged $7,000; New Yorkers, $150,000. In Philadelphia the YMCA received over $100,000 in pledges and money. Often pledges were not honored, but the financial aid was undoubtedly substantial in most instances. (*Chicago Tribune*, December 29, 1876; *Brooklyn Eagle*, November 18, 1875; *New York World*, April 20, 1876; *Philadelphia Inquirer*, January 25, 1876; *New York Herald*, April 20, 1876; John Wanamaker to John B. Devins, March 8, 1900, William R. Moody Papers, Northfield, Massachusetts.)

16. *Brooklyn Eagle*, October 15, 1875; *North American and United States Gazette*, November 20, 1875; *Chicago Tribune*, September 24, 1876; *New York Times*, February 4, 1876; *Boston Post*, January 26, 1877.

that they would eventually convert the basement and first story of the tabernacle into a row of business establishments.[17]

Mass revivalism as Moody conceived it was a rather expensive undertaking. This had become clear to the evangelist while he was in England as the scope of his operations there steadily expanded. Actually the London campaign was the most costly of his entire career, primarily because of its length in time and because he used four separate buildings. Expenses in America were considerable, however. In his larger revivals the bulk of the money collected was used to create a suitable house of worship. Moody never spent more than $10,000 for operating expenses. Ultimately the Philadelphia and Chicago revivals cost about $30,000 each, the campaign expenses in New York City were $45,000, those in Boston were $41,000. In Brooklyn, where the evangelist stayed just a month, expenses dropped to a less costly level of $8,000.[18]

Moody experienced little real difficulty in financing his work, however, for wherever he went prominent businessmen and men of wealth supported him. In Philadelphia, John Wanamaker, who was building a fortune as a pioneer department store merchant, and George H. Stuart and John Whitney, wealthy local bankers, served on major committees and contributed their money. The cashier for one of the city's leading banks served as receiving agent for donations. William E. Dodge, one of the leading copper manufacturers in the country, was in charge of arrangements

17. Henry Gibbons, *John Wanamaker*, 2 vols. (New York: Harper & Bros., 1926), 1:139–40; *Northwestern Christian Advocate*, 24 (September 27, 1876): 1; Farwell, *Recollections of Moody*, p. 40. Plans to convert the building built for the revival in Boston into a permanent religious center failed when funds to maintain the center were unobtainable. (*Boston Evening Journal*, April 26, 1877.)

18. *Philadelphia Inquirer*, January 15, 1876, January 18, 1876; *Northwestern Christian Advocate*, 24 (September 27, 1876): 1; *Chicago Tribune*, January 17, 1877; *New York Evening Post*, April 19, 1876; *Brooklyn Eagle*, October 25, 1876; *Boston Post*, April 27, 1877; *Boston Herald*, April 27, 1877. Moody's revivals in the smaller cities were much less expensive. In 1878 the campaign in Springfield, Massachusetts, which lasted a month, cost only $2,000. A decade later a revival in Louisville, Kentucky, which ran for several weeks, cost $4,000. (*Springfield* [Mass.] *Republican*, March 10, 1878; *Louisville Courier-Journal*, January 31, 1888.)

for the New York revival, while J. P. Morgan served as treasurer there. A published list of contributors to the campaign in Chicago included John V. Farwell, Henry Field, George and J. F. Armour, Cyrus H. McCormick, John Crerar, and Solomon Thatcher, who pledged amounts varying from $500 to $5,000.[19] Nor was the "little man" forgotten in the search for funds. Supporters of the revival made public appeals for money through the newspapers, and ministers mentioned the need for funds from their pulpits on Sundays.[20] If all these resources were still not sufficient, Moody usually had the assurance of his closest business friends that they would cover any deficit.[21]

Because of this strong financial position, Moody did not ordinarily take collections to defray expenses during the scheduled meetings in his revivals. Some of his better-known successors, including Sam Jones, B. Fay Mills, and Billy Sunday, relied much more willingly on the collection plate to meet expenses. But if the need arose, Moody did not hesitate to pass the hat. In Boston, for example, after efforts to gather money before he and Sankey arrived had fallen well below expectations, a freewill offering was taken at the dedicatory services for the newly constructed tabernacle.[22]

Moody also differed from those who followed him in his attitude toward personal finances. When professional revivalists began to take regular offerings, they deemed it their right to pocket a certain percentage of the proceeds. Sam Jones boasted that he was the best-paid preacher on the continent at the turn of the century, his income averaging $30,000 a year. Billy Sunday sanctioned the taking of offerings in his revivals that were specifically designated to cover his personal expenses.[23] Moody's backers paid

19. *Philadelphia Inquirer*, January 11, 1876; *New York World*, March 1, 1875; *Chicago Tribune*, January 17, 1877.

20. *Philadelphia Inquirer*, January 15, 1876; *Northwestern Christian Advocate*, 24 (October 18, 1876): 4; circular, December 4, 1875, Moody Papers, Mount Hermon Library.

21. *Chicago Tribune*, September 28, 1875.

22. McLoughlin, *Modern Revivalism*, pp. 302, 332–33, 423; *Boston Post*, January 26, 1877, January 27, 1877. For another instance when Moody resorted to the collection plate to help defray expenses, see the *Louisville Commercial*, February 13, 1888.

23. McLoughlin, *Modern Revivalism*, p. 327; *idem, Billy Sunday was His Real Name*, (Chicago: University of Chicago Press, 1955), pp. 110–16.

him for his services in a more informal manner. In each locality, well-to-do supporters contributed to an honorarium that the evangelist received at the close of a revival, usually in a private gathering instead of in the public eye at one of the revival meetings.[24]

There is no evidence that Moody ever put pressure on local committees for these sums, although undoubtedly after the pattern was established, an element of expectation of gift-giving existed which could not be entirely ignored as his revivals came to an end. Nevertheless, there was a circumspectness about Moody's handling of these somewhat delicate matters that spoke well of him. Roughhewn though he was in many ways, he often respected many of the niceties of established social intercourse. The ballyhoo that accompanied mass revivalism eventually affected even the manner in which the revival leader was paid for his services, but Moody was never a party to this crass aspect of the new approach to spiritual uplift. This set him distinctly apart from his more brazen successors, whose public calls for money for themselves fitted more neatly into the materialistic urges of the age. Ironically, Moody's reticence about personal finances in some way made the general public suspicious, for questions often were raised at his meetings about the nature and extent of his income. Both he and Sankey had to state repeatedly that they were not profiting privately from the large sums collected during the revivals.[25]

Embarrassing questions about monetary returns underlined how deeply revivalism in post–Civil War America had been affected by secular, materialistic processes. The new institutional procedures which Moody and others were forced to create in order to make mass revivalism effective promoted similar tendencies. The manmade elements of a revival came increasingly to dominate the thoughts and concerns of all participants, and spirituality often lost out as a result. For example, the element of purely human

24. J. V. Farwell to W. E. Dodge, March 6, 1876, quoted in Farwell, *Recollections of Moody*; F. G. Ensign to unknown, May 6, 1887, Robert Scott to C. H. McCormick, Jr., May 10, 1887, Nettie Fowler McCormick Papers, State Historical Society, University of Wisconsin; *Louisville Commercial*, January 18, 1888.

25. *Chicago Tribune*, September 14, 1875; *New York Evening Post*, April 19, 1876; *Boston Herald*, February 4, 1877.

calculation noticeably increased as Moody and his evangelical followers picked a precise time and place for a revival to begin, and then worked diligently to build public interest to a high point of enthusiasm just as the evangelist and his singing partner began their work officially. Here was perhaps the clearest evidence of men seeking to "work up" rather than "pray down" a revival, as had been the case in earlier times.

Moody, however, did not have, or rather did not take, the time to reflect fully on the possible consequences of his actions. There were pressing demands for his services and preparations had to be made. For the evangelist, planning for a revival had to be comprehensive in scope and carefully executed. Tactics first tested in England reappeared in America. In 1876 his supporters in Chicago conducted house-to-house visitations, carrying with them handbills advertising the coming revival campaign — an idea first used in Liverpool and then again in London.[26] As in the British Isles, in each city a huge choir and a large corps of ushers were organized. Usually the choir held several rehearsals before the opening of the revival, which was another way of generating interest. Calls went out to the local evangelical churches for lists of names of those who might serve as ushers. "Representative Christian men," whose presence would "add weight to the meetings," were most desirable. In Philadelphia, the clerks at Wanamaker's store, encouraged by their employer to volunteer, made up a sizable percentage of the three hundred odd ushers there. In New York the young men were divided with military precision into "companies" to handle the crowd in various parts of the building. Instructions used in the Philadelphia meetings specified seven categories of ushers, to be identified by colored badges worn on the lapel. The "Rules for the Ushers" also gave explicit instructions on how to handle seating, possible disorders, and sickness in the crowd.[27]

26. *Chicago Tribune*, September 30, 1876.
27. *Brooklyn Eagle*, October 25, 1875; *New York Times*, February 6, 1876; *New York World*, January 29, 1876, February 6, 1876; *Chicago Tribune*, September 29, 1876; Gibbon, *Wanamaker*, 1:133; "Rules for Ushers of the Religious Meetings," pamphlet in Moody Papers, Mount Hermon Library.

The local churches also did a great deal to create the proper climate of expectation among their parishioners. First they held weekly union "revival prayer meetings," starting several months before the formal opening of the revival; then as the beginning date neared, the churches added more services to their regular schedules. One popular device was a special day of "fasting and prayer," celebrated city wide just before the revival began. This meant holding day-long union services in numerous churches where the spiritually inclined offered prayers for the success of the revival. At the regular Sunday services, preachers chose sermon topics which fitted the spirit of the hour and expounded on the necessity for a spiritual reawakening.[28] In New York a final boost to the campaign occurred the night before Moody's arrival. The staff for the revival — ushers, choir members, inquiry room workers — joined together at the Hippodrome for a special meeting, presided over by William E. Dodge. Over a thousand persons attended.[29]

Although Moody took no active part in the completion of the details of a campaign, he made certain before the revival began that what had been done met his standards. He and Sankey usually arrived a day or so before the first scheduled meeting in order to inspect the physical arrangements and to give Sankey an opportunity to hold at least one rehearsal with the choir. Moody tested the acoustical properties of the hall, made sure inquiry rooms were easily accessible, and arranged seats in the main auditorium to his personal satisfaction. These seemingly trivial activities were an important part of the last-minute preparations. The actions of the two evangelists enabled them to es-

28. Two Sundays before Moody began his campaign in Brooklyn, six of the borough's prominent clergymen preached on the forthcoming revival. Henry Ward Beecher, for example, chose Psalm 85:6, "Wilt Thou not revive us again that Thy people may rejoice in Thee?" as his text. (*Brooklyn Eagle*, October 11, 1875.) See also *New York Times*, November 20, 1875; *New York Christian Advocate*, 51 (January 13, 1876): 13; circular issued by Executive Committee, Philadelphia meetings, November 5, 1875, in files of Presbyterian Historical Society, Philadelphia; Diary of Edwin Post, Methodist Archives, DePauw University, Greencastle, Ind., November 15, 1875.
29. *New York World*, February 7, 1876.

tablish rapport with the local workers and to make absolutely certain that all would proceed smoothly during the meetings.[30]

Services held in the central meeting place on Sundays and each weekday evening were always the chief attraction in one of Moody's revivals. The evangelist tried to emphasize that he was not competing with the local churches. Thus he held the main services of the revival at a relatively early morning hour and in the evening on Sundays to avoid conflict with regularly scheduled church services. In Boston he held a series of smaller afternoon meetings at a time that avoided the hours when Sunday schools were in session in many churches. These efforts were another indication of the revivalist's desire to preserve interdenominational harmony.[31]

Moody conducted the services in the central tabernacle from a platform at the front of the auditorium. This platform usually seated several hundred dignitaries and the choir. Prominent clergymen and leading businessmen usually found places there. Special invitations issued by the central planning committee entitled a person to one of these seats. The ministers who sat there were visible evidence of the united support given the revival by the local churches. "Bring in the ministers," Moody said, "and they will bring in their congregations."[32] The people on the platform also provided a focus of interest for the crowd below, who craned their necks to see just what dignitaries were present for the day.[33] Finally, these reserved seats gave Moody and his com-

30. In Boston Moody objected to the location of the reporters' desks because they were placed so as to draw attention from the speakers' platform. (*Boston Post*, January 27, 1877.) See also *Brooklyn Eagle*, October 25, 1875.

31. *New York Evangelist*, 46 (March 4, 1875): 6; *New York Christian Advocate*, 50 (June 24, 1875): 196; *Brooklyn Eagle*, October 9, 1875; William H. Daniels, *Moody: His Words, Work, Workers* (New York, 1877), p. 61. Some observers questioned whether Moody's policy for the scheduling of meetings really achieved its purpose. In Philadelphia, for example, one reporter noted that Sunday schools and regular Sunday morning church services were "conspicuous for an unprecedented absenteeism" during the revival. (*Philadelphia Evening Bulletin*, November 20, 1875.)

32. *Chicago Tribune*, October 3, 1876.

33. Probably the most distinguished set of platform visitors Moody ever entertained was at Philadelphia on December 19, 1875. President

mittee something akin to patronage in the hands of the politician. They gave out tickets as favors for services rendered or hoped for, in lieu of recognition of individuals from the floor during the service, or simply to satisfy the requests of their personal friends and acquaintances.

The preacher ordinarily spoke from a railed dais either raised a foot or so above the rest of the platform or thrust out in front of it. Sankey always placed himself and his melodeon close by. The arrangement gave the revival leaders and the audience unobstructed views of each other. Newspaper reporters found desks conveniently placed for them just beneath the platform. Decoration of the barn-like structures was practically impossible, although occasionally someone attempted to string the words of familiar Bible passages along the walls.[34] These were rather pathetic efforts to create a church-like atmosphere. "Is it a religious service we are come to?" exclaimed one first-time visitor to a Moody service. "All around the hats are on; gossip is lively. . . . These heads of households, followed by their 'all' [children]; of what are they talking? To tell the truth, there is chiefly recognition of friends, hand-waving from arena to platform and box."[35] The physical surroundings and the general attitude of the crowds usually contributed very little to feelings of spirituality as the services began. Such feelings would have to be created, if at all, by other means, chiefly by those who led and partly by the other participants in the service of singing, worship, preaching, and praise.

Whenever Moody was asked at Christian Conventions held in conjunction with his revivals how church services could be improved — it was a stock question — his reply was simple and

Grant visited the city that day to inspect the preparations being made for the Centennial Exposition to be held the following year. He and his entourage of politicians and officials attended the revival services. They filled the platform and helped to draw a curious, capacity audience to the meeting. (*Philadelphia Inquirer*, December 20, 1875; *Philadelphia Evening Telegraph*, December 20, 1875.)

34. *Brooklyn Eagle*, October 15, 1875; *Philadelphia Inquirer*, November 20, 1875; *Philadelphia Evening Telegraph*, November 18, 1875; *Northwestern Christian Advocate*, 24 (September 27, 1876): 1; *Boston Evening Journal*, January 26, 1877.

35. *Methodist* [London] (April 30, 1875): 4.

unvarying — "make the meetings interesting." [36] For the evangelist, technique was of great concern. The ultimate purpose of his
revivals, it seemed, was clear enough — to preach the gospel and
to reach out for converts to the evangelical faith. But in order
to achieve this purpose effectively, given the largely secular milieu
in which he and Sankey had to operate, the traditional patterns
of worship had to be altered. Moody believed even the churches
themselves deserved a good shaking up in liturgical and preaching procedures, but his sentiments were peculiarly applicable to
the special environment in which he worked as a revivalist. A
close look at the worship services conducted in the brick tabernacle
in Chicago, or the Hippodrome in New York, or the Brooklyn
skating rink suggests the vague outlines of a traditional Protestant
church service. A typical program included hymns, several
prayers, music of some sort, a scripture reading, and Moody's sermon. But there was a certain informality — a liveliness about
which the evangelist often spoke, and which he never neglected
in the services he directed — which set these proceedings apart
from the ordinary Sunday morning service.

A half hour of congregational singing inaugurated every large
revival meeting. This in itself was something of an innovation,
especially when one considered the size of the audience engaged
in the singing. Congregational singing was less of a new idea in
Protestant circles in the United States than it was among evangelicals in England, where Moody and Sankey first began the
practice. Britishers were suspicious at first, but like Sankey's solo
singing, it soon caught on.[37] Usually the huge choir recruited for
the revival led off the singing, but the congregation often was
asked to join in on the chorus of songs or the last lines of a hymn.
Sankey or the choirmaster also used this period to teach new
tunes to the crowd, even though the more familiar gospel songs
were requested and sung repeatedly as well. All this was a way
of warming up in an impersonal atmosphere. The informality
and good spirits generated by audience participation helped to

36. *New York Evangelist*, 47 (April 6, 1876): 2.
37. The Anglicans, with their powerful liturgical traditions, were the
most hesitant to accept the American practices. See *Christian*, 4 (August 14, 1873): 463.

unify the crowd and to focus the attention of all the participants on the service that followed. In a yet more practical manner the musical preliminaries helped to muffle noise and confusion as latecomers searched for seats.[38]

"Those who place Mr. Sankey's singing before Mr. Moody's preaching as a cause of the revival are probably mistaken; but it goes hand in hand with the preaching in its influence upon the people." An English critic of the two Americans offered this observation, but it applied at home as well as overseas. The singing evangelist helped mightily in weaving a spell over the vast revival audiences. "His black hair is worn so as to expose fully a prominent brow; and his eye, capable of a language of its own, aids him in giving effect to his songs. He is rather a 'smart' looking man, and his trimmed whisker and shaven chin give him a more 'civilized' look than his colleague." [39] Suave, better looking than Moody, always impeccably dressed, Sankey brought to the proceedings a requisite glamor — or masculine sex appeal, if one cares to use more recent terminology — which the rugged Moody could never provide.[40]

Sankey never had formal vocal training. His baritone voice, although observed to be "full, round and resonant," was not exceptional. Long years of overwork and straining eventually ruined what natural talents he possessed.[41] He made his impact primarily

38. *London Globe and Traveler*, March 10, 1875; *London Daily Telegraph*, March 23, 1875; *Brooklyn Eagle*, November 9, 1875; *New York World*, February 14, 1876.

39. *Christian World* (April 16, 1875): 255; *Birmingham* [Eng.] *Daily Mail*, November 18, 1875.

40. An incident which occurred in Brooklyn illuminates this point. Once, when leaving a heavily attended evening meeting, Sankey found himself surrounded by a fluttering group of female admirers, all of whom sought eagerly to talk with him. Laughingly he "pushed them to one side, saying in a loud voice, 'Any who wish to speak with me concerning their souls will please step into the chapel. I have got no time for anything else now.'" In Philadelphia the singing, not the preaching, evangelist was sought out by autograph fans. (*New York Times*, November 14, 1875; *Philadelphia Evening Telegraph*, November 22, 1875.) See also Post Diary, December 30, 1875.

41. *Boston Post*, January 29, 1877; Paul D. Moody, *My Father: An Intimate Portrait of Dwight Moody* (Boston: Little, Brown and Co., 1938), p. 125. A qualified music critic in England noted forthrightly that Sankey "uses nothing but the chest register and is sometimes pain-

through the intensity of conviction with which he sang. English-men, who observed him especially closely because he was some-thing new to their experience, noted "the strong passion that stirs his frame," so much so that sometimes he is "so affected at the con-clusion of his songs as to weep like a child." Sankey himself recognized this element of deep feeling that affected his per-formance, for he once asserted that "I never sing the second verse of a tune as I sang the first verse, nor do I sing the third as I sang the second. Why should I? The words are different, the mean-ing is different and so the rendering must be different." [42]

This basic attitude of Sankey inevitably affected his techniques in other ways. In an effort to convey the full meaning of each song to his hearers, he went to extra efforts to project his words precisely and exactly. Clear enunciation was essential. Indeed, Sankey was "more of a musical reciter than a singer; the time is altogether sacrificed to the words, and much of the natural ring of the voice is necessarily lost in the effort to articulate clearly." He also had a way of rolling the ends of phrases and of pausing frequently for a moment between the lines of a song, which served further to rivet an audience's attention upon the singer. Prior to Sankey's time, this technique had never really had a vogue in churches. As some of his contemporaries noted, this was a musical device akin to those used by vaudeville performers and comic singers in the music halls of the day.[43]

The gospel songs which Sankey sang — simple, catchy tunes that were easy to learn, and a number of which he had com-posed — fitted neatly into his purposes. Nearly all of these songs

fully flat on the higher notes. He touches F with difficulty, and E flat evidently strains his voice. His manner of gliding from note to note, and of pushing his voice upwards to a higher note, is very objectionable." The critic concluded, however, that "these are all faults which training would remove." (*Christian World* [April 16, 1875]: 255.)

42. *Christian World* (April 16, 1875): 255; clipping from *Pittsburgh Leader*, December 23, 1894, in Ira D. Sankey Collection, Public Library, New Castle, Pennsylvania. See also *Boston Post*, January 29, 1877; Wil-liam Lyon Phelps to Frederick B. Sankey, June 24, 1940, Sankey Collection.

43. *Christian World* (April 16, 1875): 255; *Christian* (December 6, 1883): 9; William Lyon Phelps to Frederick B. Sankey, June 24, 1940, Sankey Collection.

contained a refrain or chorus which the congregation picked up by ear after a round or two. Soon the singer was playing off an audience of thousands against a choir of hundreds, then both of these against the voice of the soloist. The new result was to unite "soloist or choir with the congregation in inter-reacting sympathy, drawing all into the circle." Sankey also displayed the ability to manipulate volumes of sound in such a manner as to intensify the dramatic effects of his work still further. This procedure was peculiarly appropriate for use with the vast gatherings associated with urban revivalism. Once, after choosing to sing the gospel hymn,

> We shall meet beyond the river
> By-and-bye; by-and-bye,

Sankey announced that he would sing the first line himself, the choir was to sing the first "by-and-bye," and all the people in a distant end gallery the second. A participant sitting on the speaker's platform asserted later that "almost as if, indeed, from another world, the words at last floated to them, touching most powerfully the feelings of the congregation below." [44]

The simplicity of the gospel tunes enabled the average person, even if musically untutored, to grasp and appreciate their intent almost instantly. Stately and complicated chorales or church anthems seemed dull and unrewarding by comparison. Many people left the revival services humming the tunes under their breath; the melodies became household commodities in every city that Moody and Sankey visited. *The Nation* perceived the net effect of these revival hymns. "Determine the pleasure that you get from a circus quick-step, a negro-minstrel sentimental ballad, a college chorus, and a hymn all in one, and you have some gauge of the variety and contrast that may be perceived in one of these songs." [45]

The words of the gospel hymns fitted well with the music. Often the verses contained statements of theological principle, but the intent of these passages was invariably exhortative, not educa-

44. *Christian* (December 6, 1883): 9.
45. *Springfield* [Mass.] *Republican*, February 14, 1878; clipping from *Pittsburgh Leader*, December 23, 1894, Sankey Collection; *Philadelphia Evening Bulletin*, November 29, 1875; *Nation*, 22 (March 9, 1876): 157.

tive. The words, like the music, were designed primarily to create a mood or feeling. The unvarying evangelical concern with salvation of the individual found expression again and again. In pathetic terms connected with approaching death and the dangers of failing to find the Savior in time, a verse called "Watching and Waiting" asked the question:

> When softly the watcher shall say, "He is dead,"
> And fold my pale hands over my breast;
> And when with my glorified vision at last
> The walls of "that City" I see,
> Will anyone then at the Beautiful Gate
> Be waiting and watching for me?

The words accompanying another of Sankey's tunes, entitled "The Open Door," expressed the same theme somewhat differently, but in a more immediate context:

> I know I am weak and sinful
> It comes to me more and more
> But when the dear Saviour shall bid me come in,
> I'll enter the open door.

Sankey's ability to utilize pianissimos and double fortes with skill found an echo in some of the verses of the tunes he and his audiences sang. One of the most popular of the gospel hymns, "Jesus of Nazareth Passeth By," indicated clearly by the words how the first two choruses should be sung:

> What means this eager, anxious throng, which moves with
> haste along –
> These wondrous gatherings day by day? What means this
> strange commotion pray?
> In accents hush'd the throng reply: "Jesus of Nazareth passeth
> by."
> In accents hush'd the throng reply: "Jesus of Nazareth
> passeth by."
> Who is this Jesus: Why should He the city move so mightily?
> A passing stranger, has He skill to move the multitude at
> will?

> Again the stirring notes reply: "Jesus of Nazareth passeth
> by."
> Again the stirring notes reply: "Jesus of Nazareth passeth
> by."

Not all of the songs were designed to wring tears from the audience or induce a state of melancholy. Some were bright, almost martial airs, expressing the heartiness which pervaded the revival meetings and which also was so characteristic of the personalities of the two revival leaders. Suitable words of gusto were devised to fit the tempo of these robust hymns. One which combined enthusiasm with traditional evangelism went something as follows:

> "Whosoever heareth." Shout, shout the sound!
> Send the blessed tidings all the world around;
> Spread the joyful news wherever man is found;
>   "Whosoever will, may come."
> Chorus: —
> Whosoever will, whosoever will,
> Send the proclamation over vale and hill;
> 'Tis a loving Father calls the Wand'rer home —
>   "Whosoever will, may come."

Probably the most popular tune of this sort was "Hold the Fort," based on an incident which reportedly occurred in the Civil War. A blood and thunder rescue of beleaguered warriors was transposed easily into a perhaps more religious context.

> Ho! my comrades, see the signal waving in the sky!
> Reinforcements now appearing, Victory is nigh!
> "Hold the fort, for I am coming," Jesus signals still,
> Wave the answer back to Heaven — "By Thy grace we will."
> Fierce and long the battle rages, but our Help is near;
> Onward comes our Great Commander, Cheer, my comrades,
>   cheer!
> (Chorus repeated) [46]

46. *Hartford Courant*, January 9, 1878, January 10, 1878, January 12, 1878; P. P. Bliss and Ira D. Sankey, *Gospel Hymns and Sacred Songs* (New York: Biglow and Main, 1875), pp. 10, 12, 16. The latter volume

Through his words and musical gimmicks, Moody's partner hoped to grasp mightily the imaginations and hearts of everyone in his audience. Music, words, audience response, and the special talents of the singer fused into a single process that could become very meaningful to participants in the revival. Sankey himself once described this process and its results. "You can't do it with music alone; you've got to make them hear every word and see every picture of the part. Then you'll get that silence of death, that quiet before God." [47] He sought to express musically the feelings of joy, expectation, and even an occasional sense of failure and inadequacy, which had always been at the center of the devotional life of the Christian community. Given the secular surroundings in which he usually worked, this was an immensely difficult task to perform. In such a context, Sankey's undeniable vulgarity was probably essential to his success, for it enabled him to represent accurately a musical vernacular shot through with strong religious sentiment, attuned to the interests of an emerging mass society, yet couched in terms that even the commonest sort in his audience could understand and appreciate.[48]

As an evangelical Christian, Sankey conceived of his music serving yet another purpose that was distinct but not completely separate from the general intentions just mentioned. Like his preacher-partner, Sankey hoped his work would lead eventually to conversions among individuals in his audience. This sentiment soon affected his work in the revivals. Rather early in the tour through Great Britain he adopted the practice of introducing each of his solos with little sermonettes. This usually meant offering brief observations on how men had been saved or awakened by his rendering of a particular gospel hymn. This same hope of achieving conversions probably motivated him eventually to hold

is one of the chief precursors to Sankey's more famous compilation of gospel hymns, *Sacred Songs and Solos* (London: Morgan and Scott, 188?).

47. Clipping from *Pittsburgh Leader*, December 23, 1894, Sankey Collection. See also *London Daily News*, March 10, 1875.

48. For a perceptive discussion of the special contribution of Sankey's music to the revivifying of evangelical psalmody in England, see *Congregationalist* [London], 4 (March, 1875): 136–38.

separate services in each revival devoted exclusively to "song and praise." In such gatherings he could exercise his peculiar abilities to the fullest in awakening unbelievers to the need for salvation.[49] In his own mind and probably in the thoughts of many who heard him, Sankey was not a musical performer but a preacher through music. Moody aptly called his partner's efforts "the singing gospel." This perspective, shared both by the singer and his audience, could impart a special urgency and meaningfulness to Sankey's work that it might not otherwise possess.

Sankey's solo singing, and particularly the songs he and his audiences enjoyed so much, represented the fusion of several related tendencies in mid–nineteenth century American hymnody. The earliest of these developments originated in the Sabbath school movement. The need for light, attractive airs to make youth services more attractive resulted in the creation of an extended series of Sunday school song books. The first of these popular music manuals appeared in the 1840's. By the time of the Civil War the contagious melodies in these little books were widely recognized among evangelical groups. The vogue for these bits of word and music soon spread to the YMCA and eventually into the work of the agents of the Christian Commission among the soldiers of the Federal armies in the Civil War. This was not surprising, since supporters of all three movements were often identical. The form and content of all these songs differed little from what were known by 1870 as gospel hymns.

"Praise services" organized as early as 1851 by members of the Boston YMCA, solo singing at Association conventions in the 1860's by H. Thane Miller and W. H. Doane, and the "Services of Song" of Philip Phillips in Sunday school conventions in the midwest, enabled the repertoire of tunes to be expanded steadily, and ever larger numbers of the rank and file in the churches became familiar with the new modes of worship. Even before Moody and Sankey returned from England, P. P. Bliss, working in tandem with D. W. Whittle in this country, had published a small collec-

49. *Boston Herald*, February 27, 1877; *Philadelphia Evening Telegraph*, December 8, 1875; George E. Morgan, *Mighty Days of Revival: R. C. Morgan, His Life and Times* (London: Morgan & Scott, 1922), p. 175.

tion of gospel songs, including about fifty he himself had composed. This volume, combined with the tunes Sankey had gathered as a consequence of his efforts in the revival in Great Britain, became the basis of the famous *Gospel Hymns and Sacred Songs,* used in all subsequent Moody revivals. It is clear, then, that Sankey did not create entirely new musical forms; instead he popularized on a vast scale procedures with which many evangelicals were already familiar. His work was a culmination, not a beginning.[50]

Whatever the quality and extent of his success as a musical innovator and as an evangelist, Sankey set a spectacular example for those that followed him. Every professional revivalist from Moody's time on felt it a necessity to have a partner who could sing the gospel. Sankey had shown the way in devising techniques to adapt church music to mass tastes on a scale never before achieved. Yet not all was commendable about some of the tendencies in Sankey's work. Adapting church music to the lowest level of popular feeling and understanding led to the blurring of any clear distinction between the sacred and the profane. In a society rapidly turning secular, this might well mean a greater loss to evangelicals than to those outside the church. Indeed, the music of the revival embraced so many elements from the popular milieu it served that without too much effort it could be adapted to purely secular uses. In the national political campaign of 1876 the Republicans transformed one of the most familiar gospel songs into "Hold the Fort for Hayes and Wheeler," and in Chicago, couples at a fashionable wedding party waltzed to jazzed-up versions of "What shall the harvest be?" and "Almost persuaded." Moody and Sankey would have been horrified at such goings-on, but these were some of the effects possible with the popularization of church music.[51]

Moreover, in less skilled or less scrupulous hands than Sankey's, his techniques could easily degenerate into mere gimmickry which did little to create legitimate and honest religious sentiments.

50. Louis F. Benson, *The English Hymn: Its Development and Use in Worship* (New York: Hodder and Stoughton, 1915), pp. 482–92. See also Henry W. Foote, *Three Centuries of American Hymnody* (Cambridge: Harvard University Press, 1940), pp. 263–71.

51. *Christian Register,* 15 (December 30, 1876): 2.

The words of a contemporary of the singing evangelist strike to the heart of this issue:

> The defenders of this popular hymnody . . . very gravely under-estimate the capacity of the popular mind to rise above vulgar embodiments of truth and to shake itself free from perverted sentimentality, and they constantly mistake the zest of animal enjoyment in a rub-a-dub rhythm or the shout of childish pleasure in a 'catchy' refrain for real religious enthusiasm.

Some people found Sankey vulnerable to such criticism. The careers of Charles Alexander and trombone-playing Homer Rodeheaver, Billy Sunday's musical man Friday, two men who followed on the heels of Sankey in the late nineteenth and early twentieth centuries, bear out the charges more fully.[52]

Moody's physical appearance seemed in contrast with that of Sankey. Compared to the urbane, carefully groomed singer, the preacher's physical bulk and uncultured manner presented a surface impression of roughness and the commonplace. The evangelist had put on weight since leaving Chicago in 1873, but his physique, though ample, had not yet loosened into the paunchiness of later years. He still was a compact, solidly-built man. His large head and short, bullish neck rested on somewhat rounded shoulders that would have served a present-day football tackle well. Those who spoke to him personally, or caught him in more informal moments, noted his large expressive eyes, "bright, kindly, and pleasant," a firm, clear-cut mouth, and a laugh which was contagious. The beard he had begun to grow before leaving for England now lay thick and heavy on his face. This made him seem even more neckless than in his youthful days in Illinois. He had a somewhat swarthy complexion and his dark hair drooped "over his forehead like the famous lock of 'the little Corporal.' "[53]

---

52. Waldo S. Pratt, *Musical Ministries in the Church*, p. 62, quoted in Benson, *The English Hymn*, p. 489; McLoughlin, *Modern Revivalism*, pp. 374–77, 421–22.

53. *Advance*, 8 (June 24, 1875): 730; *Birmingham* [Eng.] *Daily Mail*, January 18, 1875; *Brooklyn Eagle*, October 26, 1875. See also *Independ-*

In spite of the seeming contrast with the clean-shaven Sankey's impeccable habits, in his own way Moody was very careful about his personal appearance. He never left his whiskers unkempt in public, and he was careful to buy clothes that fitted well and that conformed to the best standards of grooming and good taste. Despite his unostentatious manner, he deeply disliked anything that spoke of cheapness or the shoddy. Not surprisingly, people in America as in England saw in him the clear-cut image of a businessman going about the Lord's work. One reporter at the revival meetings graphically asserted that "there is a breadth of beam in his whole appearance . . . suggestive of business stability. He looks, as he stands there . . . more like an English merchant than an American preacher." [54]

Neither of the two evangelists seemed overly prepossessing when people confronted them for the first time. Some noted an "absence of starch" in both men that went along with their naturalness and easygoing personalities. Yet in an age when solidness of character and physical frame often suggested leadership abilities, Moody and Sankey fitted the stereotype rather well. In the case of Moody in particular, the quality of earnestness was unmistakable. In part this personality trait reflected his inexhaustible physical energy. In the seventies his work schedule was of man-killing proportions. In most revivals he held three to five large meetings daily, supervised the inquiry meetings, and attended continuously to numerous minor details of organization. He was on the move from eight in the morning until midnight or later five or six days a week. Yet year after year he bore this burden of work cheerfully, even enthusiastically, and seemed equal to every demand levied against his physical and emotional resources. This great physical vitality was an almost indispensable asset, given the large tasks he set for himself. Although seldom referred to openly as an element of his success, his robust physique actually made possible much of what he achieved as a revivalist.

There were other manifestations of this single-minded will to

ent, 27 (November 11, 1875): 14; *Philadelphia Evening Telegram*, November 22, 1875.

54. Paul Moody, *My Father*, pp. 18–19; *Chicago Tribune*, August 17, 1875.

218

do the Master's bidding in the world. An observant Englishman stated once that Moody had a "terrier-like aspect — a sort of look which, if he had been given to fighting wild beasts at Ephesus or anywhere else, would have boded ill for the wild beasts. They would not make a martyr out of Moody without a struggle." The evangelist was a "muscular Christian." This meant vigorous religion, heartfelt and expressed day to day in deadly seriousness. It was a phrase applied to many evangelicals in the Victorian era. Yet seriousness without good humor could be irritating and terribly boring. This, too, has been a criticism levied at the Victorians. Such a charge could not be sustained in Moody and Sankey's case. People noted with pleasure that for both of them "religion is a joyous matter, and not a thing to pull long faces about," as was true of too many of the ministers who graced the speaker's platform at the revivals. Because the evangelists were "cheerful, good-natured men," they were "just the sort of men to inspire confidence." [55]

Hearty self-confidence characterized Moody's work as a revivalist, but for him it was not superficially achieved or felt. His self-assurance seemed very much the outgrowth of the unforgettable second conversion experience which he had passed through in 1871. In intimate conversations with one of his closest friends in 1875, he admitted to an occasional uncertainty about his work in England and America when he stopped to think about the magnitude of the tasks that confronted him. "But as he looked back," his friend recorded, "all he could think of was Jeremiah's experience that God gave him a forehead of brass to go before the people. He had that consciousness of the presence of God in His meetings in London that the people, Lords, Bishops, Ministers or whoever they were, were as Grasshoppers." Spending relatively little time in secret prayer during the demanding final stages of his English campaign, Moody remained spiritually unburdened and anxiety-free. Paraphrasing the evangelist's words, his friend asserted that "his work kept him in the spirit of prayer and dependence upon God, and he just gave himself wholly to

55. *Advance*, 8 (March 4, 1875): 481, quoting the *Sheffield* [Eng.] *Post*; *Birmingham* [Eng.] *Daily Mail*, January 18, 1875; *British Evangelist* (January 8, 1874): 19.

the work." This was the attitude of a secure and happy man, and his inner serenity revealed itself to many who watched him in the great revivals. To those who had known him since the Chicago days, a qualitative difference in tactics expressed itself as a result. An acquaintance of the 1860's said in 1875 that Moody now possessed "an unwonted tenderness which impressed many at once." Comparing earlier days with the present, this man went on: "His manner of old was of one who would seize men by the collar and drag them out of danger. Now he puts his arm around them, and pleadingly draws them away." [56] Moody had a sensitiveness of feeling even in the 1860's. Nevertheless, his later experiences evidently touched the emotional springs of his being sufficiently to provoke the full flowering of a rather appealing personal trait that in turn noticeably affected the revival meetings.

On the platform Moody's actions were quick and vigorous, adding further to the picture of a man of decisiveness. In comparison with the hellfire-and-brimstone preachers of the frontier, however, Moody was rather sedate. Instead of delivering highly emotional sermons, he kept himself under control and spoke relatively unobtrusively. To one observer he seemed "utterly devoid of elocutionary effort"; another described his opening remarks to be even "offensively harsh and unpleasant," made by a voice in which there was "absolutely no music." [57] But all this was in line with both his and Sankey's oft-expressed desire to avoid the emotional excesses which too often had characterized revivalism before them.

As the evangelist proceeded through the service he became more absorbed in his work and gradually captured the attention of his audience. Moody had demonstrated in Illinois that as a leader of public meetings he possessed some sixth sense which enabled him to improvise and to rearrange the order of worship as he proceeded in order to bend the will of his audience to *his* desires. After much practice in the intervening years, he had refined this power of improvisation into a high art of subtle persuasion which

56. Whittle Diary, September 4, 1875; *Advance*, 8 (June 24, 1875): 731. See also *British Evangelist* (January 8, 1874): 19.
57. *Brooklyn Eagle*, October 26, 1875; *Boston Post*, January 29, 1877.

cast its spell over almost every one of his giant revival gatherings.[58] Since no programs listing the order of worship were distributed, the possible combinations of personal prayer, songs, solo-singing by Sankey, hymn singing by the audience, Scripture reading, and preaching proved almost limitless.

Sankey and he always worked closely together, but this was especially true in bringing each service to an end. The closing moments were the climax of all the large public meetings. The sense of solemnity generated was designed to encourage backsliders and unbelievers to move on to the after-meetings where their sins and misgivings could receive individual attention. Moody was particularly careful that the closing hymn fitted the mood that he had created with his sermon. "Jesus of Nazareth Passeth By" was especially effective when the evangelist had just warned of the dangers of foregoing the gift of salvation. "Almost Persuaded,' or "Lord, Here am I, Send Me," represented variations on the same theme. Once Moody ended his sermon with a retelling of one of his familiar anecdotes about a dying child, an inconsolable father, and hopes of eventual reunion in heaven. After a "moment or two of silent prayer," one could hear soft strains from the harmonium and Sankey singing softly:

> Come home, come home;
> You are weary at heart.
> For the way has been dark.
> And so lonely and wild;
> O, prodigal child!
> Come home, O, come home!

Not unexpectedly, "some thousands remained to the after-meeting." [59]

58. One reporter, after attending Moody meetings over a number of years, claimed that a special mood always settled on the crowd at these large gatherings, and Moody invariably was able to use it to good advantage. (*Chicago Tribune*, September 27, 1889.) For similar remarks, see *Congregationalist* [England], 4 (March, 1875): 138; comments of C. I. Scofield, undated, in "Special Subjects" Notebook, Moody Papers, Mrs. E. M. Powell, East Northfield, Massachusetts.

59. *New York Christian Advocate*, 50 (April 8, 1875): 105; *Christian*, 5 (January 8, 1875): 17; 4 (March 5, 1874): 136; *"To All People": Comprising Sermons, Bible Readings, Temperance Addresses, and Prayer-*

Occasionally unforeseen incidents occurred which, if not controlled, could distract the crowd from the primary business at hand. Usually Moody nullified the disruptive effects by interjecting the incidents into his talks as illustrations.[60] Sometimes the revivalist prepared little dramatic acts of his own to please as well as instruct his hearers. Often he spoke familiarly to those on the platform, weaving the dialogue into his sermon. In Brooklyn, to the delight of the crowd, he compared several of the most noted local clergy present to the Israelite priests circling the walls of Jericho and blowing on rams' horns to break down the walls. Soon after he queried the same platform guests as to their state of readiness for ascent into heaven. Their replies served to emphasize his point of the need for immediate preparations. Sometimes he directed his words at a particular person, either asleep or inattentive, an act which invariably had an electrifying effect on both the individual and the entire audience.[61] This informality in the service was another means of creating a sense of individual involvement and contradicted the impersonality inevitably associated with such large gatherings.

When reading Scripture the evangelist spoke slowly, as though repeating a difficult matter to a small child. Frequently particular passages evoked digressions for exposition and explanation. When he began the sermon the tempo picked up considerably. Even the speed of his delivery increased. Moody had never lost the flavor of rural New England in his speech; thus contractions of many words tumbled out in his discourse. When he referred to biblical figures, for example, they emerged as "Sam'l" and "Dan'l," or "Gidjon and his army of three hundred." Combining vernacular with rapid-fire delivery, the revivalist became the bane of reporters struggling to copy his words precisely for newspaper readers. One writer asserted that the last of his sermon "was

Meeting Talks Delivered in the Boston Tabernacle by D. L. Moody (New York: E. B. Treat, 1877), p. 107; *Philadelphia Inquirer*, October 22, 1875.

60. *Brooklyn Eagle*, October 20, 1875; *Boston Post*, April 20, 1877; *Chicago Tribune*, June 12, 1893.

61. *New York Times*, October 25, 1876; *Brooklyn Eagle*, October 26, 1875; *The Great Redemption; or, Gospel Lights, Under the Labors of Moody and Sankey* (Chicago: Century Book and Paper Co., 1889), p. 304; Whittle Diary, April 23, 1876.

like a cavalry charge. You had either to go with it or get out of the way." Using equally vivid metaphors, another reporter noted that in the "scuffle among the words for suitable places in his hasty sentences, they become chipped and mutilated. Final letters disappear, middle syllables are elided and the outer ones run together." [62] Although it was probably unintentional Moody's peculiar style of speaking forced listeners to strain for words and meaning — to listen more carefully than might be the case with a preacher who spoke more easily and slowly. It was one way in which the attention of a vast crowd was forced to focus on the stoop-shouldered figure who earnestly confronted them with matters religious.

The real heart of Moody's elocution consisted of other techniques, however. His success lay primarily in his ability to tell a story, to recite a piquant anecdote, to inject pathos and humor into the biblical accounts he used repeatedly in his sermons. In a simple, almost childlike manner, as he retold the ancient stories which made up the biblical narrative, these accounts came alive for him and in some inexplicable way he transmitted his excitement and enthusiasm to his hearers. D. W. Whittle described the process once as the revivalist read aloud to a few friends the familiar tale of the Good Samaritan. "His eyes would fill and his voice tremble as he read over the description to me of the wounded man and glisten with joy as he came to the account of the Kind Samaritan. . . . His power is in its [the story's] *reality* to him." [63]

Even in his later years Moody remained the peerless storyteller. In 1937, Henry Sloane Coffin, then president of Union Theological Seminary in New York City, recalled a moment when the evangelist spoke to a group of college students in the 1890's about "Dan'l."

> Mr. Moody, speaking in the name of the King, leaned over [the side of the pulpit] and said: "Oh, Dan'l, servant of the living God, is thy God whom thou servest continually able

62. Paul Moody, *My Father*, pp. 113–14; *Boston Post*, January 29, 1877; *New York Evangelist*, 46 (October 28, 1875): 8; *Springfield* [Mass.] *Republican*, February 11, 1878; *New York World*, February 8, 1876.
63. Whittle Diary, April 24, 1876.

to deliver thee from the lions?" Then from this profound pit came the voice: "Oh, King, live forever. My God has sent his Angel and has stopped the lions' mouths."

Coffin added:

> There was nothing bizarre, nothing spectacular, nothing theatrical, nothing irreverent. This was the word of God, but it was so vivid to him that he made us feel that we were right on the spot.[64]

It is clear that when Moody told these stories he was not merely describing a scene or reciting a narrative. Possessing instinctively the talents of shrewd observer and popular dramatist, he could etch a personality as well as trace the bare outlines of the story. Perceptive hearers noted that he puts "smart speeches into the mouths of those of whom he discourses," and he is "not afraid even to make them give forth Yankee phrases." In England especially this practice offended a well-developed sense of propriety in many people, but the result even there was "to realize the Scripture more vividly than before," and to impart "freshness, reality, and power to the preaching of Mr. Moody." [65]

Moody's preaching carried conviction because vivid storytelling was also a mode of discourse often found in the narratives of the Old and New Testaments. To a generation steeped in the *Bible*, with its rich lode of stories about vigorous and very human men and women, Moody could easily appeal. The revivalist himself fully recognized this fact. In 1882 he asserted that "we must imitate the mode of teaching of Jesus Christ. He taught in parables; and travelers say that there is hardly a natural object in Palestine that He did not make use of to illustrate some truth." As was the case with Moody's Lord, so also with the evangelist; "stories and object lessons help to fix truths in the mind. . . .

64. Unpublished mimeographed address of Henry Sloane Coffin in folder entitled "Moody Mass Meeting, Carnegie Hall, New York," October 27, 1937, John R. Mott Papers, Yale Divinity School.

65. *Nonconformist* (July 21, 1875): 744. For similar comments from the English press, who were fascinated with Moody's platform performance, see *London Daily News*, March 10, 1875; *Christian* (February 25, 1875): 14, quoting the *Liverpool Mercury*; *Christian World* (March 5, 1875): 161; (March 12, 1875): 170; *London Times*, March 16, 1875.

What is addressed to both the eye and the ear, make more impression than what is addressed to the ear alone." [66] Moody had grasped fully the concreteness of illustration and argument of the book he studied and loved so much. In a most striking way he was biblical in his preaching, and this fact was not lost on his audiences.

Supplementing his sketches of biblical characters and their activities, the revivalist also sprinkled his sermons with word pictures drawn from personal observations and experience. When he recalled effecting incidents of spiritual awakening in the midst of war, when he remembered the loneliness of the first days he spent in the cities, or when he spoke of vice and evils in the new urban centers, his listeners knowingly nodded. He talked of backsliders as good church people when they were surrounded by friends in a small rural church, but who had grown cold in the more impersonal atmosphere of a big city.[67] Out of his commonplace experience he drew facts and events which all could understand. For the average person, facts and events remain the bedrock of experience; finespun theories about the nature of existence carry little conviction. To be effective, then, popular preaching has always had to be primarily illustrative and factual. Thus it is not really surprising that Moody's preaching took the form it did. Indeed, he would not have made his mark as a revivalist if he had lacked the gift of citing details from the *Bible* and from life itself. Fortunately he possessed this gift in abundance, and that fact explains a great deal about his success.

But for some of his hearers his meaning went deeper, conveying what it was like to be grasped personally by the Christian gospel. As Henry Coffin expressed it long after Moody's death, "The Gospel was never, to him, something to be discussed. . . . The Gospel was to him the power of God, and as he talked about it we knew that he had seen it work again and again, and to us it became something not to be talked about, but to be tried and passed on." For Moody, the division between the sacred and the profane was

66. *Evangelistic Record*, 1 (May, 1882): 5.
67. *The Great Redemption*, pp. 276–77; *Great Joy: Comprising Sermons and Prayer-Meeting Talks Delivered at the Chicago Tabernacle* (New York: E. B. Treat, 1877), p. 65.

obliterated, but in this instance it was the spiritual which engulfed and controlled the secular aspects of life. He could never be anything but an earthy, largely uneducated man of the people, but he was unusual in that his earthiness and his commonness were lifted up and transformed in some way by a power or powers beyond himself. Nearly all of his close associates and many others of his contemporaries sensed this fact, but few were able to articulate their feelings very effectively. One who did, put the matter this way: "He has humour, and he uses it; he has passion, and he uses it; he can tell racy anecdotes, and he tells them; he can make people cry as well as laugh and he does it. [Yet] to him nothing is common or unclean. He has given himself to God, all that he has, all that he is, and he uses every faculty and resource of his nature to prevail upon men to hate sin and to trust and love Christ." [68] Here, ultimately, was the source of Moody's power as a revivalist, the apparent reality of his personal faith in Christ and his undeniable ability to convey a sense of that reality to many who sat in his audiences.

68. Coffin Address, Moody Mass Meeting; *Congregationalist*, 4 (March, 1875): 142 (sentence order slightly rearranged in quotation).

7

The Theology of a Popular Preacher

For those who sat beneath the railed dais where Moody preached at the revivals, this man attracted attention primarily because of his novel techniques. Nevertheless, the elements of theology which the evangelist espoused in his sermons also had their effect. At first glance, the printed versions of his sermons cause one to ponder the reasons for his success, for they were, as one of his hearers claimed, "extremely diffuse . . . unconnected, rambling and given to repetition."[1] The absence of any logical structure in his thought reflected the fact that Moody was a popular evangelist and not a trained theologian with a carefully ordered system of religious beliefs. His predecessor, Charles Finney, had received sufficient formal education and training in logic as a lawyer to be able to develop a systematic theology. Eventually Finney offered a course on the topic at Oberlin College and even published the gist of his lectures.[2] Moody's lack of disciplined intellectual training and his activist frame of mind kept him from ever preparing a comparable statement about his beliefs.

A search in Moody's sermons for his definition of the meaning of faith reveals immediately this lack of system. He defined faith in a variety of ways, usually in simple metaphors or word pictures. Once he compared the belief of the Christian with the trust of the little boy who "when his coat and pants are worn out

1. *London Daily News*, March 10, 1875.
2. Charles Finney, *Lectures in Systematic Theology* (New York, 1878). There were earlier editions than the one cited here.

believes his mother will provide him with others." Elsewhere he asserted that faith could be described as the attitude that says "Amen to everything God says," and "takes God without any ifs." At least once the revivalist spoke of faith as "an act of mind," while at other moments he conceived of it as a condition that was chiefly emotional.[3] Above all else, faith for Moody represented the presence of a feeling of personal relationship between the individual believer and God. This was a conclusion drawn not from wide reading and long hours of rigorous speculation, but from concrete experience. The roughhewn language of the quotations cited above suggest that fact.

The revivalist preached love as God's chief quality. This characterization reflected again Moody's concern that faith be viewed primarily as a personal relationship. It was in personal interaction that God's love could best be discovered. In his practical, non-analytical way, the evangelist failed to spell out fully the theological meaning of his assertion that God is love. However, the *results* of divine love, experienced concretely in his own life, he was often able to articulate. Frequently he turned to his family and drew analogies between their activities and God's love in action.[4] This seemed the most natural way for him to speak about the matter.

Some of his contemporaries worried because Moody so seldom stressed God's wrath and his concern to judge the unrighteous of the world.[5] A reduced emphasis on the somber, harsh characteristics of God fitted in well with the revivalist's overall effort to

3. *Philadelphia Evening Telegraph*, January 22, 1875; L. T. Remlap, ed., *The Gospel Awakening: Comprising the Sermons and Addresses, Prayer-Meeting Talks and Bible Readings at the Great Revival Meetings Conducted by Moody and Sankey* (Chicago, Fairbanks, Palmer & Co., 1883), pp. 220, 545; *Chicago Pulpit*, 1 (May 18, 1872): 202. See also *Glad Tidings*, (New York, 1876), pp. 171–72, 174; *To All People* (New York, n. d.), pp. 192–93; *Great Joy* (New York: E. B. Treat, 1877), p. 357. All of the books cited here are collections of Moody's sermons, reprinted usually from the stenographic reports made by newspapermen at his revivals. There is considerable repetition in these collections; therefore, citations from a limited number of these books are assumed to be representative of the sermons published in the 1870's and early 1880's.

4. *Advance*, 1 (January 9, 1868): 6; (April 23, 1868): 6; 2 (April 8, 1869): 6.

5. See, for example, *Congregationalist*, 4 (March, 1875): 143.

present a toned down, rather sedate message and personal image. He did not disturb his audiences to the degree that camp-meeting evangelists had with their fiery utterances. Failure to preach about the wrath of God was also consistent for a man of essentially optimistic temperament like Moody. Yet to argue in this manner is to miss the full significance of Moody's understanding of God. "Preaching the mere goodness of God might have been weak and dangerous," a preacher-friend of the evangelist once commented. The safeguard in the revivalist's preaching, however, "lay in its intensity." Gripped by a special, private vision of faith, Moody had somehow been able to translate that experience into quite powerful expressions of God's love that went beyond affirmations of simple goodness or benevolence. Moody preached instead "the compassionate, suffering . . . sacrificing, agonizing love of God," an insight that seemed "entirely compatible" with the "deepest and most solemn view of sin." [6]

The individual's response to Christ was another equally important method of defining relationships with God. As the revivalist stated it once during his early days in Chicago, "we may be very devout and worship God, but it is counted as nothing unless we honor his Son. Christ must be all in all." Or as he was inclined to say much later, "Faith in [is?] a person, and that person is Jesus Christ. It isn't a creed about Him but it *is* Him." [7] A distinction needs to be made here between faith and belief. Belief constitutes assent to established facts — to the authority of a logical construction of the mind that fills with meaning past events or, perhaps, religious activities. A Christian, for example, can believe in, but not have faith in, the creeds of a particular church or denomination. Faith is much more than this. Faith means participation in the object of one's ultimate concern, totally and completely. Moody clearly understood this fundamental difference between belief and faith. When he spoke in the Hippodrome in New York in 1876 he thought back a short time and noted his own shift from belief to faith. "During the last few years I was not occupied

6. Lyman Abbott, "On Preaching Christianity as a Gospel," *Andover Review*, 15 (April, 1891): 431.

7. *Advance*, 2 (April 15, 1869): 6; *Moody's Latest Sermons* (Providence, R.I.: The News Company, 1894), p. 77 [italics added].

with the person of Christ; it was more about the doctrine and about the form. But lately Christ is more to me personally. And it would be a great help to you to cultivate His acquaintance personally, and come to Him as the personal Saviour, and be able to take Him and look up to Him and say, 'He is my Saviour.' " [8]

For Christians, therefore, the suffering of Christ on the cross, his death, and his emergence from the grave, must be caught up vicariously into the immediate experience of every generation of the faithful. Historically conditioned though Christ's life, death, and resurrection were, these events must be felt existentially, gripping the totality of one's existence, and not affecting merely the intellect, the will, or the emotions. When Moody proclaimed that faith "isn't a creed about Him but it *is* Him," or when he saw Christ serving as his "personal Saviour," he was expressing exactly this understanding of the issue. Jesus Christ was for him the power that shaped and moved life, at the same time that he was Moody's "ultimate concern." Here the evangelist's instincts and perceptions seem profound indeed.

Not too surprisingly, the figure of Christ was also an important matter for evangelicals generally. In 1856 one of the leading Methodist periodicals in the midwest sought to explicate the principles on which revivals should be predicated. The series of articles began with an essay entitled "Preach Jesus." Ministers were urged to "Preach Jesus first, not subordinately. A system of theology, without Jesus in the center, would be as a system of solar astronomy that left out the sun." At the national convention of the YMCA in 1869, a lengthy and heated debate over what constituted the essence of evangelical theological principles ultimately centered on christological problems. Even when judging Sunday school literature the convention felt that the figure of Christ was of central importance, for an adequate understanding of the meaning of Christ was essential to the proper education of children. Thus "whatever tends to explain or illustrate the character and

8. *Glad Tidings: Comprising Sermons and Prayer-Meeting Talks Delivered at the N. Y. Hippodrome, by D. L. Moody* (New York: E. B. Treat, 1876), p. 110. See also *Great Joy*, p. 241. Paul Tillich, in *The Dynamics of Faith* (New York: Harper and Bros., 1957), offers an illuminating brief discussion of this general topic.

mission of Jesus, whatever can be made tributary to the function and growth of Christian character in children," was "appropriate" to the programs conducted in the evangelical Sunday schools.[9]

The centrality of the problem of salvation for the evangelicals makes it easy to understand why Christ, and not God, stood in the forefront of their schematization of the faith. Jesus as the Christ stood as the divine instrument by which individuals were brought to God and transformed into the people of faith. From this point it was easy to go on to view his work as directly related to the whole spiritual life of the individual. "The dealings of God" with men, asserted a Presbyterian in Moody's day, "compels [sic] them to turn . . . to the man Christ Jesus, for sympathy, to the Saviour, Christ Jesus, for atonement and pardon; to the Intercessor, Christ Jesus, for an answer to prayer; and to the glorified Christ for a heavenly inheritance." Moody's thoughts closely paralleled these expressions.[10]

If Christ were the bearer of salvation, as Moody reiterated again and again, the need remained to show how he accomplished salvation for the believer.[11] Whenever the evangelist tried to explain Christ's work in saving men, he turned to Jesus's death and resurrection. "I must die for my sins," he once declared, "or

9. *Northwestern Christian Advocate*, 4 (January 30, 1856): 18; 17 (June 23, 1869): 197; *New York Evangelist*, 40 (July 22, 1869): 4; *Advance*, 3 (September 9, 1869): 4. See also *New York Observer*, 43 (June 22, 1865): 193; *Independent*, 4 (December 2, 1852): 194; *Interior*, 5 (November 5, 1874): 2.

10. *New York Observer*, 43 (June 22, 1865): 193. R. W. Dale, an English supporter of Moody's and an able theologian, was struck by the evangelist's emphasis on Christ as mediator of salvation. "That Christ wants to save men, and can do it, is the substance of nearly all of his discourses." (*Congregationalist*, 4 [March, 1875]: 143.)

11. While not unimportant to his thinking, Moody said little about the Incarnation. Only once or twice did he speak distinctly of Jesus as "God-man," and his thinking advanced little beyond that phrase. Probably this was because the Incarnation was for the average evangelical an assumed tenet of the faith that was never seriously questioned. There are frequent passages in Moody's sermons attesting by implication to his support of the doctrine. For direct references to "God-man," see *The Great Redemption*, p. 280; *New Sermons, Addresses, and Prayers* (New York: Henry S. Goodspeed, 1877), pp. 387–88. Implied references to the Incarnation are in *Great Joy*, p. 190; *Glad Tidings*, p. 483.

find some substitute to die in my stead. I cannot get this man or that man to die for me, because they have sinned themselves, and would have to die for their own sins. But Christ was without sin, and therefore He could be my substitute. . . . He voluntarily gave Himself up. He died as your substitute and mine, and that is my hope of heaven." It was, then, Christ's vicarious death which made him the central object of Moody's faith. Thus the evangelist could assert that "because he died for me, I love Him. Because He died for me I will serve Him. I will work for Him, I will give Him my very life." [12]

Here Moody was attempting to express his understanding of the atonement, to suggest the meaning this doctrine should have for the faithful. The evangelist's sermons suggest that his views on the atonement were in the tradition of what theologians have called the "moral influence" theory. This doctrine has had a long life in the history of Christian thought, traceable back through the debates over Arminianism and Socinianism at the beginning of the seventeenth century to the work of the great medieval thinker, Peter Abelard. As a conservative American theologian of the early twentieth century, himself a critic of this school of thought, once wrote, the moral influence theory of the atonement in its most popular forms "has always been that in which the stress is laid on the manifestation made in the total mission and work of Christ of the ineffable love of God for sinners, which, being perceived, breaks down our opposition to God, melts our hearts, and brings us as prodigals home to the Father's arms." [13]

In contrast to this point of view, Calvinistic supporters of the Anselmic — Anselm was another medieval theologian — or penal theory of the atonement saw Christ's death as a transaction between God and his Son relieving sinners from the wrath of God, releasing them from the demands of God's law, and testifying

12. D. L. Moody, et. al., *Calvary's Cross: A Symposium on the Atonement* (Chicago: Bible Institute Colportage Association, 1900), pp. 26, 31. See also *Glad Tidings*, pp. 80, 82.

13. Benjamin W. Warfield, "The Atonement," in Samuel M. Jackson, ed., *The New Schaff-Herzog Encyclopedia of Religious Knowledge*, 15 vols. (Grand Rapids, Mich.: Baker House, 1951–55), 1:353.

to God's justice at work even as he forgave the sins of man.[14] The penal theory presupposes that the atoning work of Christ has its primary effect upon God, and its secondary effects upon man. The moral influence theory reverses the emphasis. More important yet for Moody's thought, Anselmic theory views God as principally stern, wrathful, judging, and righteous, whereas the Abelardian viewpoint softens the image of God into loving kindness and tenderness — a deity who melts the heart because of what he has done by his sacrifice of his Son on the cross.

In Protestant thought these two interpretations of the atonement reflect a classic conflict between Calvinistic and Arminian world views. In a revealing autobiographical statement made in 1875, Moody showed clearly where he stood in relation to the two theories:

> I remember for the first few years after I was converted I had a good deal more love for Christ than for God the Father, whom I looked upon as the stern Judge, while I regarded Christ as the Mediator who had come between me and that stern Judge, and appeased His wrath; but when I got a little better acquainted with my Bible these views all fled. After I became a father and woke up to the realization of what it cost God to have His son die, I began to see that God was to be loved just as much as His Son was. . . . Oh, think of the love God must have had for this world, that He gave His only begotten Son to die for it, and that is what I want you to understand." [15]

14. For attempts to characterize the two schools of thought discussed here, in addition to the Warfield article, see W. Adams Brown, "Expiation and Atonement (Christian)," in James Hastings, ed., *Encyclopedia of Religion and Ethics*, 13 vols. (New York: Charles Scribner's, 1914–27), 5:645–50; Hastings Rashdall, *The Idea of Atonement in Christian Theology* (New York: Macmillan Co., 1919), pp. 369–73, 397–420, 435–39; Oliver C. Quick, *Doctrines of the Creed: Their Basis in Scripture and Their Meaning Today* (New York: Charles Scribner's, 1938), chap. 21.

15. *Glad Tidings*, pp. 244–45. For those lacking easy access to Moody's sermons, a representative sample of his preaching, stressing the theme of God's love, is reprinted in H. Shelton Smith, Robert T. Handy, and L. A. Loetscher, eds., *American Christianity: An Historical Interpretation With Representative Documents*, 2 vols. (New York: Charles Scribner's Sons, 1963), 2:320–24.

It is easy to see how the moral influence theory of the atonement, stressing the effects of Christ's act on the believer, and the need for a response of faith and devotion to the divine act of sacrificial love, would be highly compatible with the popular evangelical perspective of the 1870's, which viewed the conversion experience and forthright expressions of religious sentiment as the normative aspects of faith. Speaking of the Saviour or of God in this context evoked deeply felt emotional dispositions that worked against viewing the deity as the cold, righteous object of belief. Thus, when christological issues arose, some popular evangelical writers could maintain with Moody: "We want the religion of intellect, of will, of conscience, but, underlying all, the religion of personal devotion. . . . What should be our love of Christ? *Supreme*, of course. We must love him more than we love ourselves or any other object." In a similar vein, the Calvinist view of a legal transaction that Christ carried out with God to save men was denied. "The Christian life is not an engagement by contract between a master and his servant. It is the union of two hearts — that of the Savior with that of the saved — by the enduring ties of the most intimate love." [16]

It should not be construed from this evidence that a manifestation of God's love was *always* the convicting agent that led to personal faith. Emphasis by evangelicals on the conversion experience could heighten or bring to the fore those attributes of God, *negative as well as positive*, which seemed efficacious in the work of redemption. Probably this double focus or emphasis grew out of the strong sense many evangelicals possessed of God's sovereignty over their lives. A contemporary of Moody's, writing for a Congregational periodical in the 1850's, suggested that by beginning with the "truth of God's sovereignty," one could come to an understanding of how to develop "conviction." Because of his sovereignty, God "leads each soul in the way that pleases him, some he quickens through fear, some through conscience,

16. *Advance,* 9 (March 23, 1876): 547; *Northwestern Christian Advocate,* 15 (January 23, 1867): 25. For similar expressions, see *Independent,* 4 (December 2, 1852): 194; *New York Observer,* 43 (June 22, 1865): 193; *Interior,* 5 (January 22, 1874): 1.

some through benevolence, some through affection, and some through all of them combined." [17]

Thus the preaching of God's wrath, as well as of his love, was entirely possible within the general context of evangelical attitudes. And indeed for many in the evangelical community the sense of a judging Lord as a regenerative agent, revealed to men in the death of Christ, was as strongly felt as was his sympathy and tenderness. Supporters of this point of view differed, of course, from those who accepted the moral influence theory of the atonement. Yet neither were these people advocates of the ancient penal theories, since Christ's saving acts still related primarily to men and not to the appeasing of God. It was in essence a middle way between two extremes, and was a position preached in the revivals on the frontier and even by Charles Finney in the 1830's. Moreover, many of the most widely recognized theologians of evangelical persuasion, both in this country and in Britain — especially Congregationalists and New School Presbyterians — espoused this so-called "governmental" theory of the atonement.[18]

In so far as he was an exponent of the moral influence theory of the atonement, Moody cannot be considered in the mainstream of evangelical apologetics and theology in either England or the

17. *Independent*, 4 (February 5, 1852): 22. The importance of God's sovereignty to the evangelicals and especially to their immediate forebears, the Puritans of the colonial period, is a major theme in the work of H. Richard Niebuhr, *The Kingdom of God in America* (New York: Harper and Bros., 1959). See chap. 2 and *passim*.

18. The "governmental" or "rectoral" theory of the atonement originated with the great European jurist of the seventeenth century, Hugo Grotius. In the United States the theory gained acceptance in the eighteenth century, especially as it was formulated by Joseph Bellamy, Jonathan Edwards, Jr., and other representatives of the New England theology. It continued to flourish in the nineteenth century in the writings of Nathaniel Taylor, Albert Barnes, and other Congregationalist and New Light thinkers. Especially through the work of John Miley, the theory deeply affected Methodist attitudes in this country. In England, Moody's friend R. W. Dale and another Congregationalist, Albert Cave, both wrote studies of the atonement that embraced the governmental point of view. For further comments see Warfield, "The Atonement"; Brown, "Expiation and Atonement," *Encyclopedia of Religion*; John Miley, *Systematic Theology*, 2 vols. (New York: Hunt and Eaton, 1894), vol. 2, chap. 7; Frank H. Foster, *A Genetic History of the New England Theology* (Chicago: University of Chicago Press, 1907), pp. 113–17, 177–82, 200–206, 210, 213–15.

United States. Indeed, at the time of the evangelist's greatest success as a popular preacher, people who embraced the moral influence theory of the atonement — Horace Bushnell is a qualified, but well-known example in the United States — were laying the foundations for the "liberal" theology that swept through the Protestant churches at the end of the nineteenth and the beginning of the twentieth century. This does not mean that Moody is now to be transformed into a thoroughgoing advocate of "liberal" theology. Rather, on the one issue of the atonement he must be viewed as varying both from the standard expressions of evangelical theory and from the Anselmic, penal theories still characteristic of certain groups of scholastic Calvinists in this country.[19]

Why, then, did Moody choose to place himself alongside those who stressed primarily the efficacy of God's love as a saving power over men? The evangelist's autobiographical statement quoted at length earlier provides some clues to an answer. If we are to take his words at face value, Moody derived his verification of God's loving nature in part from study of the *Bible*, and, perhaps more important, from the concrete facts of his daily existence in family and home.[20] Undoubtedly by the 1870's, when he uttered

19. Charles Hodge, whose dogmatics greatly influenced the thinking of conservative evangelicals and whose ideas served as antecedents to the more recent Fundamentalist movement, is a good representative of this latter group. For Hodge's views on the atonement, see his *Systematic Theology*, 3 vols. (New York: Charles Scribner's, 1875), vol. 2, chaps. 6–9. Note especially *ibid.*, p. 589: "The [church] fathers constantly speak of Christ as a priest, as a sacrifice, and as a ransom."

20. The manner in which Moody educated himself on theological questions is a rather important matter which deserves some comment. Evidence to illuminate the problem is limited, but the outlines of his procedures are clear enough. It is questionable whether he read consistently and systematically in the secondary sources on theological and religious issues. But he pored over the *Bible* with great intensity, and not infrequently gathered with religious leaders better educated than he to "pick their brains" in impromptu bull sessions. This latter tactic was especially suited to his temperament; probably what little he learned about formal theological matters was grasped in sessions of this sort. For one of the few descriptions of one of these meetings of the evangelist and his friends, see Marjory Bonar, ed., *Andrew A. Bonar: Diary and Letters* (London: Hodder and Stoughton, 1894), pp. 309–10. Other comments on his study habits are in Paul D. Moody, *My Father: An Intimate Portrait of Dwight Moody* (Boston: Little, Brown and Co., 1938), pp. 38–39.

these words, his deeply-felt second conversion experience added further confirmation to his already existing perceptions about God's inner essence and Christ's role as Saviour of men. Here was a revealing example of how the Word of God and immediate experience acted and reacted on each other to produce the special understanding that Moody possessed of the central elements of the Christian faith. The Word of God and the world of everyday experience were, indeed, the controlling elements in every phase of the evangelist's existence. Inextricably intertwined, they constituted reality for him and suggested the manner in which life was to be lived.

In the revivalist's framework of ideas, the power and work of the Holy Spirit were of almost equal significance to that of Christ. Not surprisingly, the two figures were closely related. It was the Spirit that made Christ a reality for men of different epochs. "It is through the Holy Ghost that we get life," the evangelist asserted. "We would in reality not know Christ but for the Holy Ghost." And to testify of Christ was also to "tell us of God." Thus it was that Moody could say that one of the principal works of the Holy Ghost was "to impart love." The Holy Spirit functioned before, during, and after the conversion experience. Prior to that radical turnabout, the Spirit sought to sensitize the individual to his misdeeds and wrongdoings, and to prepare him for open reception of the message of salvation. Then, as the agent of Christ and of God in the present age, the Spirit served to regenerate men. Conversion meant to be born of the Spirit. Moody made this point very clear. "There is no life or power for a man to serve God until he is first born of the Spirit, until he has been quickened by the Holy Ghost, until he has been raised as Christ's dead body was raised." [21]

Also important, however, was the work of the Spirit following conversion. For Moody the third person of the Trinity manifested himself in the world chiefly as the love of God shining in and through individual Christian lives. As he once put it: "You can sum up all the fruits of the Spirit on one word – Love."

21. *Glad Tidings*, pp. 275–76. See also W. H. Daniels, ed., *Moody: His Words, Work, and Workers* (New York: Nelson & Phillips, 1877), pp. 365–88.

There were also more exact ways of denoting the presence of the Holy Spirit. The Christian possessed "joy," which was "only love exulting," "peace," which was "love in repose," "long-suffering," which was "love enduring," and "goodness," which was "love in action." Here the evangelist was cataloging those "graces of the Spirit," which bespoke some of the most exalted conditions associated with Christian faith and life. It was these feelings and sentiments which provided the recently converted with "assurance" of their new life in Christ.

Perhaps most deeply felt was the new perception of liberty that came with the inrush of the Holy Spirit. This condition provided a special sort of freedom. This was not mere political liberty, or freedom from possible governmental or societal coercion upon the individual. Rather, Christian liberty expressed an openness to all the experiences of life, a freedom in any and all personal relations, that could be achieved only when men fell in love with the absolute goodness of their Creator and loved that goodness for its sake alone. A rebirth of the whole man was required to achieve such liberty. This had been the condition of many evangelicals earlier, and Moody also seemed to possess it. As the evangelist once expressed it, "God wants all his sons to have liberty. He does not want us bound, as so many of us are bound, by a sort of fear. The Holy Ghost casts out fear. It is the Spirit of Love and Liberty." It was this "perfect liberty" of the Holy Spirit that the evangelist thought should be present in all gatherings of the churches and denominations, and which sustained him in all of his daily activities. Speaking from the depths of his own experience, he asserted for all those who possessed true assurance "there is no uncertainty about it. *We know*." [22]

Inevitably Moody had to return to his central task, which was the obligation to evangelize the world. Here, too, the Holy Spirit had a service to perform. The revivalist spoke often of the "gift of the Holy Spirit for service," a special dispensation given to those

22. *Christian* (June 26, 1884): 18; *Glad Tidings*, pp. 278, 279–80; Daniels, *Moody: Words, Work, Workers*, pp. 392–93. Niebuhr's *Kingdom of God in America*, pp. 95–99, has been quite suggestive on this aspect of Moody's thought, as it relates to the larger spectrum of evangelical attitudes.

Christians who, in evangelical terminology, had "power." Proof of "power" varied from situation to situation. It was frequently used to point to a minister who was especially effective in his preaching, or to churches which were under the spell of a special season of revivals. But above all else, for the evangelicals the phrase was used to point to those men of faith who seemed best able to bring new converts into the church. This was the ultimate proof that one possessed "power." Moody reported to his close friend, D. W. Whittle, a conscious inrush of just such a vital force at the time of his second conversion experience, and it was this "power" which sustained much of his work thereafter. In turn, the evangelist constantly exhorted those to whom he preached to search and pray for similar "enduements of the Spirit." To spread "power" throughout the evangelical denominations was an oft-repeated, primary goal of his.[23]

True to his profession and to the perspective of evangelical Protestantism, Moody seemed almost preoccupied with the process of conversion. Since his primary function as a revivalist was to draw people into, or back into, the religious community by means of conversions, it is not at all surprising that he dwelt so often on the need for decision and the blessings that were available when one took such action. Of overriding significance was the means by which one came to believe. Moody always maintained that conversions were instantaneous. Still, the individual usually did not make his decision without some preparation.

There appeared to be three steps to salvation. First, one had to be "convicted" of sin; that is, one must become conscious of wrongdoing. Moody underscored the importance of this step when he said that "the best title that you can have to salvation is to

23. An important discussion of Moody's understanding of the work of "power" under the Holy Spirit by one of his earliest biographers, William H. Daniels, appears in the *New York Christian Advocate*, 51 (December 12, 1876): 393. For Moody's own use of the term, see *Glad Tidings*, pp. 275, 286–87; *Boston Evening Transcript*, January 14, 1897; Daniels, *Moody: Words, Works, Workers*, pp. 369, 373, 381, 390, 396–97. Whittle's comments are in Whittle Diary, September 4, 1875, October 2, 1875, May 22, 1876. Expressions similar to those of Moody by other evangelicals are in *Northwestern Christian Advocate*, 24 (January 5, 1876): 6; (February 2, 1876): 1; *New York Christian Advocate*, 47 (September 5, 1872): 284.

find out that you are lost." "Conviction" was followed by "repentance." Moody once described repentance as "turning right about," or, in the lingo of the foot soldier, "right about face." Such action brought the individual face to face with God. Then it was only a short step into the circle of faith, by believing in Christ and accepting him as a personal savior. This was the act of "regeneration." The evangelist saw Christ's role in the act of conversion to be present in the words " 'Follow me' — two words; and if there is a man today out of Christ, if he will take these two words they are enough." [24]

These words do not, however, convey fully Moody's perceptions. Merely listing and describing the steps leading to conversion makes the process too mechanical. In the evangelist's mind there was much more to it than that. For example, he tried to make clear to his audiences that repentance was not a superficial, temporary act or thought. "Repentance is not feeling," he warned a mass of people in Cleveland who were highly susceptible at the moment to precisely such a state of mind. People think, he went on, "that they have to feel very bad, very sorrowful — got to weep a good deal and then they will be in a condition to come to God." For him this was an inaccurate portrayal. Rather, repentance grew out of the fact that "man is born with his back towards God." Thus "when he repents he turns right around and faces God. Repentance is a change of mind. Repentance is an afterthought. . . . You see repentance is deeper than feeling. It is action. It is turning right about. And God commands all men everywhere to turn." [25]

Because he spoke of repentance as a "change of mind," this suggests that he knew that the Greek word for that phrase, *metanoia*, was the term used in the New Testament to designate repentance. In addition, when Moody asserted that "repentance is an *afterthought* [emphasis added]," he repeated the literal English equivalent of one of the classical Greek uses of the term *metanoia*. When the early church writers used this Greek

24. *Glad Tidings*, p. 129; *The Great Redemption*, pp. 86, 89; *To All People*, p. 248.
25. *Cleveland Plain Dealer*, October 14, 1879.

phrase they sensed that in repentance the individual lamented his misdeeds of the past only briefly. The primary emphasis of Paul and other apostolic Christians was on an immense inward movement of the whole person to grasp the power of God that ruled life. *Metanoia*, then, signified a fundamental change or reorientation of the will — of the inner man — toward God.[26] It professed a newly discovered state of enthusiasm, of ethical awareness, and of forward-looking anticipation that contrasts sharply with the usual thought of repentance as chiefly sorrow for sins committed and a turning away from the past. A fusion of the freely acting human being and the grace of the Lord working in the individual effected repentance and made one ready for conversion and the new birth in Christ. It seems clear from the words of Moody just quoted that he understood repentance in exactly these terms, and that his insights at this point were linked closely with his general understanding of the meaning of faith and the work that Christ performs in the believer's innermost being.

In his preaching Moody often shortened the procedure leading to salvation by emphasizing only the last step. Thus it was that he could argue that "salvation is instantaneous," that it was just as sudden as a man walking through a doorway. "One minute he is on this side, the next he is on that side." He expressed the idea vividly once to a mixed audience of Negroes and whites, comparing the process of conversion to the freedom a former slave achieved by crossing the boundary between the United States and Canada with his southern master in hot pursuit. "One minute a slave, the next a free man," Moody concluded triumphantly. "That is instantaneous, isn't it?"[27]

26. Paul depicts this wholehearted turning to God as crucifixion and coming to life again in Christ (Galatians 2:20); as living in Christ (Colossians 2:6–7); as taking off the soiled garment of the old nature and putting on the new (Colossians 3:9–17). The idea of new birth prominent in the Johannine epistle also embodies this same understanding (John 3:3–6). For a recent and forceful expression of how Jesus and the writers of the Gospels understood the idea of repentance, see Gunther Bornkamm, *Jesus of Nazareth*, (New York: Harper & Row, 1960), pp. 82–86.

27. *Glad Tidings*, p. 226; *Cleveland Leader*, November 1, 1879. See also the *St. Louis Globe-Democrat*, March 25, 1880. For one of Moody's rare statements contradicting the idea of instantaneous salvation, see *To All People*, p. 417.

In an interview in 1880 in St. Louis, the revivalist asserted that on such "essentials" as "Arminianism, Calvinism . . . and other matters," he "eschewed these, or reference to them, as not being essential to salvation." Such an observation was thoroughly in accord with his concern to play down differences between his hearers from the various denominations, but it did not reflect his real feelings. Moody did seem to take a stand that tended to support Arminian theories of redemption. His attitudes reflected in part the general shift in thinking that had occurred in Protestant circles in the nineteenth century regarding the universal possibility of salvation, and the means to be used to achieve that state of grace. The revivalist espoused Arminianism even more openly than did Finney a generation earlier. In the 1860's, when speaking of the old Calvinist doctrine of election, Moody dismissed it quickly by saying, "you need not . . . stumble over that doctrine into hell." [28] There was no doubt in his mind that salvation was open to all. After repudiating the doctrine of election, Moody went on to imply that man, not God, was ultimately the one to determine the precise moment when the act of salvation was to occur. Indeed, his whole revival system was predicated on exactly that assumption. By the 1870's he was making this claim quite explicit in many of his sermons.[29] At the same time, however, he tried to hold on to the traditional understanding of the meaning of grace — God's love bestowed without merit on man, a sinner — and sometimes he spoke of salvation as a gift of that grace.[30]

Such a combination of thoughts seemed to produce nothing but confusion. Moody asserted, for example, that "if you desire to be saved you can be saved, but you must be saved through Christ. You cannot work out your own salvation unless you are first saved." Utterances of this sort left some of his hearers puzzled. One woman approached him in New York and said: "I have been trying to be a Christian and yet you have been telling me

28. *Advance*, 1 (August 6, 1868): 6; see also *Glad Tidings*, p. 339.

29. *Glad Tidings*, pp. 105, 106, 233; *To All People*, pp. 209, 211, 385; *New York World*, March 30, 1876; *Philadelphia Evening Telegraph*, December 15, 1875.

30. *To All People*, pp. 205–06, 385; *The Great Redemption*, pp. 193–94.

to-night not to try. . . . I can't understand it." [31] One way of explaining these apparent contradictions is to suggest that the old Calvinist notion that God alone saves still hung in the air — the phrases at least — and occasionally the evangelist repeated these phrases at the very moment he was urging sinners to take matters into their own hands.

Yet it may also be true that Moody preached in such a manner, and saw no ultimate contradiction in what he was preaching, because this was a truly Biblical approach to the question of salvation. After all, Saint Paul uttered words several times whose import is strikingly similar to the phrases used by the evangelist. "Work out your own salvation with fear and trembling," said the apostle, "for God is at work in you, both to will and to work for his good pleasure." Or, "God was in Christ, reconciling the world to himself . . . We beseech you on behalf of Christ, be reconciled to God." [32] If Moody was confused, so was Paul. The Biblical message, in other words, is not reductionist, does not make the act of salvation an either-or proposition as both strict Arminians and Calvinists would have it. Instead, the Pauline approach is to view God's action and the action of men locked together, in tension with each other. Thus is salvation achieved. It is in this dynamic sense, perhaps, that Moody sometimes conceived the matter.

Still, one cannot ignore the evidence that shows that much of Moody's preaching, and especially the mechanics he devised in his revivals, placed tremendous stress on man's agency in achieving salvation. In the milieu in which the evangelist preached, in which simplicity of expression and action was at a premium, it was exceedingly difficult to espouse clearly and consistently the paradoxical insights concerning salvation which the New Testament seems to suggest. All the pressures generated by the revival atmosphere supported Arminian expressions in the sermons of the evangelist. Sometimes the preacher and his hearers slipped into

31. *To All People*, p. 387; *Glad Tidings*, pp. 157, 158. See also Daniels, ed., *Moody: Words, Works, Workers*, pp. 443, 445. A sermon on "Regeneration," which Moody preached many times, contains these thoughts as a central theme. See, for example, *Glad Tidings*, pp. 90–92, 94, 95.
32. Philippians 2:12–13; 2nd Corinthians 5:19–20. See also Galatians 3:26–27, 4:4–7, 8–12.

an extreme manifestation of this point of view; that is, if the individual sinner believed he was saved, forthwith the act occurred. In Philadelphia Moody learned of a woman who came to one midday service determined to be saved before she left the building. Three meetings and twelve hours later, she came to Moody and acknowledged that she would soon find assurance. Later the evangelist extolled this woman as one who came to the meetings "expecting to be saved," and was. "When we search for God with all our hearts," he went on, "we are sure to find him." [33]

There seems to be a degree of irony hidden in these assertions of the revivalist. If it is true that at certain points in his preaching Moody revealed that he had taken firm hold of the biblical understanding of salvation, it is likewise the case that these profound perceptions were simultaneously obscured and even undermined by the machinery and sentiments of mass revivalism that Moody was helping to create. This is an ancient and frequently repeated theme in the history of the Christian churches: the mixing of dross with the gold — the unwitting tarnishing of the faith by precisely those most committed to its advancement.

Closely connected with conversion were its fruits. Particularly important in this respect was the change salvation wrought in man's essential nature. Moody accepted the traditional Christian belief that before conversion, man's will, his thoughts, and his acts, were fundamentally flawed because of his sinfulness. The revivalist promised a substantive change with salvation. In an effort to underscore the importance of the saving act he often dramatized graphically the distinction between "before" and "after." The saved and the unsaved seemed to be inhabitants of separate worlds. "The devil puts his mark upon his own," he once said, "and the Lord Jesus puts his stamp on his own. You take the two and draw the contrast." In another instance he viewed the natural world as a "vast hospital" in which "everybody is sinning," though the "great Physician, who is able to cure all diseases of soul and body," was at hand.[34]

Moody's apparent radical separation of believer from unbe-

33. *Glad Tidings*, pp. 224–25.
34. *The Great Redemption*, p. 114; Daniels, ed., *Moody: Words, Work, Workers*, p. 413. The evangelist never attempted to define the

liever led him along the road to perfectionism, although he probably would have denied an explicit belief in that doctrine. Recognition of the ability of the converted to sin, or not, following regeneration was crucial to any acceptance of perfectionist attitudes. On this point Moody's public statements are ambiguous. In Chicago at the Illinois Street Church he preached that "when God puts a new nature in man there is a struggle, a war and continued battle. . . . The old man is at war with the new, is continually struggling with it." And in New York City in 1876 he said he believed "that every child of God has two natures . . . and there is a battle always going on between the worlds of light and darkness." [35] Yet statements of this sort, which lead away from perfectionism, can be counterbalanced by other comments of the evangelist which move in a different direction. In 1879, for example, he said that when regeneration occurred, and "Christ formed in me the hope of glory . . . I become a partaker of the divine nature. Then I have got a nature that I can serve God with, that is as pure as God Himself. That nature can not sin. This is holy." For some of his hearers in the 1870's, the intent of his preaching on this issue was unmistakable. "He dwells on what Christ has done in words which imply that absolutely nothing is left for man to do." [36] Such statements could turn Moody rather easily into a perfectionist.

If the revivalist harbored perfectionist sentiments, they were not consistently espoused on the public platform. Nevertheless, the presence of these scarcely suppressed ideas may partly explain why in the 1880's and 1890's Moody called increasingly for evan-

nature of sin carefully. Nevertheless, the many examples of drinking, gambling, prostitution, and callous disregard of family responsibilities that he used as illustrations whenever he spoke on the topic left no doubt as to his understanding of the problem. Here, too, he accepted conventional and quite practical criteria.

35. *Chicago Pulpit*, 1 (May 18, 1875): 197; *Glad Tidings*, pp. 363–64. John Farwell, in *Early Recollections of Dwight L. Moody* (Chicago, 1907), pp. 110–11, recalls a moment during the campaign in England when Moody explicitly denied to his friends that he embraced perfectionism.

36. *St. Louis Globe-Democrat*, December 31, 1879; undated newspaper clipping, Moody Collection, Mount Hermon Library, Mount Hermon, Massachusetts. See also *Glad Tidings*, p. 250; *The Great Redemption*, pp. 84, 312, 219.

gelical Christians to separate themselves from the corrupt, secular world. This was a pessimistic, otherworldly attitude which at first glance does not square with his essentially optimistic, practical outlook on life. Yet if the evangelist made sharp distinctions between the saved and the unsaved, and at times viewed the aftereffects of salvation as a life lived without sin, in such a context it would not be too difficult to develop an attitude demanding total separation of the faithful from the sinful outside world. A latent perfectionism, then, had its effects on Moody, not only on his preaching in the 1870's, but also on the changing perspectives of his later years.

There were also deficiencies in Moody's thoughts about the nature of the church and its work in the world. In a strict sense he did not possess a doctrine of the church. If he had, he might have outlined more precisely than he did what the role of the Christian was to be following conversion. He might also have been clearer concerning the relation of his work as an evangelist to the ongoing life of the local churches, a point to which he seldom addressed himself. He did not, however, dismiss the church entirely. Rather, he simply paid little attention to it in a formal way, for his concern was to achieve conversions and to work with individual believers.[37] Nor was he totally unconcerned with converts once they had made decisions for Christ. He espoused a doctrine of "work" which both substituted for a doctrine of the church and provided rough guidelines for the future activities of the newly converted. For Moody work was the "outward sign of faith." The test of the true believer was his ability to demonstrate his salvation in good work. To believe otherwise was, according to to the revivalist, to stake one's faith "on some creed, some church . . . and not on Christ." [38]

These attitudes caught the spirit of a point of view that was widespread among evangelicals. Because of the strong emphasis

37. One of the few public statements Moody made on the meaning of the church is in *Great Joy*, p. 500. His ideas seem to be the beginning of a valid argument, but are too brief to be of real assistance in determining what he believed about the church. Other brief comments of his on the subject appear in *Harpers Weekly*, 20 (May, 1876): 37; *St. Louis Globe-Democrat*, March 25, 1880.

38. *Great Joy*, p. 500.

1. Dwight L. Moody as a young man of 23

2. Dwight L. Moody at age 45

3. Mrs. Dwight L. Moody at about age 30

4. Mrs. Betsey Holton Moody and her nine children, 1862. Seated, left to right: Isaiah, Mrs. Moody, and George. Standing, left to right: Edwin, Cornelia, Samuel, Dwight, Elizabeth ("Lizzie"), Luther, and Warren

5. Moody and Sankey at the Brooklyn Rink, 1875 (From *Frank Leslie's Illustrated Newspaper*, November 13, 1875, pp. 156–57)

6. Dwight L. Moody and his grandson, Dwight L. Moody (son of Will Moody), who died in 1898 at about 1 year of age (probably taken in 1897)

7. Dwight L. Moody at Mt. Hermon, watching sports with some of the students

8. At home in Northfield — the evangelist in informal attire

9. Dwight L. Moody at Northfield with a group of Mt. Hermon students. One of his grandchildren rests in his arms. (About 1895)

on individual effort and striving, it was natural that the average Protestant seldom thought too seriously about the church in its corporate form and his relation to it. Moreover, Moody's concept of "work" and his substitution of it for a doctrine of the church was not unique among the evangelicals of his day.[39] His idea of "work" also reflected the old Puritan belief in the sanctity of labor and hard work, and perhaps even recalled the frugality and moments of hardship that spotted his memories of childhood. At the same time it demonstrated anew his practical, activist spirit. All of these influences, stemming from his personal experiences and from the larger cultural milieu, were bound up in Moody's assertion that "we don't read Resolutions of the Apostles, but the Acts. We must *work* and not talk." [40]

Occasionally the evangelist seemed to use the idea of work in a generalized manner to suggest the specific secular vocation to which God calls all Christians. It was, he said "the necessity of every Christian" to do "the work which God had set him, no matter how insignificant it might seem. If . . . the truth were known, every man and woman had His work laid out for him." But in reality Moody looked at these words in a particular way. "Work," like the "power" of the Holy Spirit, was an idea possessing special meaning. To begin with, a person could not work until he was converted. The revivalist tried to make this clear to his audience. "Those who have heard me know I never stir

39. Observations about the evangelicals' use of the term "work" are to be found supra, pp. 83–84. The lack of statements in the popular religious press dealing explicitly with the doctrine of the church is perhaps the best evidence supporting the observations made above. Probably it would be safe to suggest that among the major evangelical denominations in Moody's day, the Presbyterians retained more fully than others a sensitivity toward the problem of the church, followed by the Congregationalists, with the Methodists and the Baptists being least concerned. In support of this observation, see *Northwestern Christian Advocate*, 4 (March 12, 1856): 42; *Congregational Herald*, 5 (April 16, 1857): 2; *New York Observer*, 43 (March 9, 1865): 73; *Zion's Herald*, 28 (August 13, 1868): 391. The evangelicals put great stress upon the family as a pillar of the ongoing life of local churches and denominational activities. These familial concerns may have partially replaced, or at best diverted, the attention of the evangelicals from a full consideration of the nature and function of their corporate religious community.

40. *Proceedings, Fourteenth Annual National Convention, Y.M.C.A.* (June, 1869), p. 44.

a man up to work before he's saved, for a man can't work his way into heaven." Effective work was only possible as a fruit of conversion. It was a natural outpouring of the new spirit that surged through the recently confirmed believer. The intimate connections between salvation and "work" were obvious to Moody. "Why after a man's saved he can't help working for God." The evangelist even felt that willingness to work for the Lord's purposes in the present world was one of the truest indicators of conversion. "So when a man says he has faith, without work his faith is useless, for it is dead. . . . If he has not the spirit of work he has not the spirit of God, and without the Spirit of God he can never enter heaven." [41]

Of course, the best and most effective work was that directed toward further evangelization. This meant seeking new converts, holding cottage prayer meetings, maintaining the YMCA and the tract and benevolent societies. Those persons most clearly and lastingly converted in Moody's revivals went out immediately and began to convert others; that is, they exhibited the "power" of the Holy Spirit. The highest expression, then, of the ability to "work" was to show "power" in one's daily life. To "work" as Moody understood it was to "carry the revival spirit in your bosoms . . . throughout all the year." [42] Here the missionary spirit of the evangelical community expressed itself with great force and intensity.

The ultimate purpose of the evangelical churches was to Christianize the nation — indeed the world. For Moody this task was so great that it demanded an end to internal divisions within the church universal. "I hope," he exclaimed, "to see the day when all bickering, division, and party feeling will cease, and Roman Catholics will see eye to eye with Protestants in this work. Let us advance in a solid column — Roman Catholics, Protestants, Episcopalians, Presbyterians, Methodists — against the ranks of Satan's emissaries." There was also a terrible urgency about his missionary program. We must try to save souls, he said, "and do it now. We won't have the opportunity by and by." For all evangelicals this same sense of the lateness of the hour suffused their thoughts about the need to evangelize the nation.

41. *New York Times*, February 11, 1876, April 20, 1876.
42. *Ibid.*, November 20, 1875; *Great Joy*, pp. 494, 497, 499.

An anonymous Presbyterian writing in 1874 shared Moody's feelings. "We contemplate it [America] with a feeling of awe, and even of apprehension. It must be reached by the Gospel. It must be evangelized by self-denying effort. The idea of its being left to itself is simply appalling. . . . We have a thousand mission fields at home, the story of which fairly told, might stir our hearts within us like the blast of a trumpet." [43] To work, then, was a task of the highest responsibility for every church member, for what more glorious role was there to assume than one which helped to bring a mighty nation like America to its knees in repentance and submission to God?

Yet for Moody work went beyond mere duty — something one did because there was a general responsibility to move the church forward in its efforts at evangelization. It was, ultimately, the manifestation of God's love at work in the individual, a love which transcended and rendered irrelevant any considerations of duty. As the evangelist once put it, love "should be the spring of man's service to God. Men should work for God for love, not for duty." God's service was to be performed because men "love Him, and want to do something for Him, not because they have a duty to perform." For many evangelicals these were high standards to live up to, but the words express quite well Moody's own attitude toward *his* "work," his full giving of himself physically and mentally to the tasks of the church. "Men don't feel work which they love to be any burden," he asserted.[44] The sure confirmation of that assertion appeared in his own career and in his personal attitudes toward his daily tasks.

Another aspect of Moody's thought deserves special consideration. This was his belief in Christ's second coming, and his acceptance of premillennialism. Since the late colonial period most American Protestants who advocated the doctrine of Christ's second coming were postmillennialists. That is, they believed the millennium would come first, usually as the fruit of the present

43. *New York Times*, April 20, 1876; *New York Evangelist*, 45 (May 21, 1874): 4. For expressions of similar feelings, see *Independent*, 4 (June 10, 1852): 94; *Northwestern Christian Advocate*, 3 (January, 1855): 2; *Zion's Herald* 28 (August 19, 1857): 130; *Congregationalist*, 18 (January 26, 1866): 14.

44. *New York Times*, November 8, 1875.

Christian agencies at work in the world, and that the last judgment and the second appearance of the Lord on earth would then follow. Such an attitude suited well the optimistic, buoyant spirit of the country in the early decades of the republic. Everyday events seemed to confirm the upward surge of mankind toward this long-awaited kingdom of the spirit. Significantly, Charles Finney, in many ways a representative citizen of the age of Jackson, was a postmillennialist.[45]

Either during or shortly after the Civil War, premillennialism experienced a resurgence in this country. Pessimism characterized this doctrine. Those who embraced it emphasized the corruption of the present age and waited the judgment of God because of the vices and evils they saw in the world. Premillennialists believed the millennium would occur *after* the present world had been destroyed by the avenging hosts that accompanied Christ upon his return to earth. Moreover, they saw only radical discontinuities, not similarities or differences produced by slow evolution, between the present state of the world and the reign that would follow the coming of the King in glory.

Moody did not publicly espouse this doctrine until the 1870's. It is impossible to pinpoint exactly when he first came under the sway of premillennialism, but probably the Plymouth Brethren were among the first to affect him. They had been one of the most influential groups in the transatlantic community in the nineteenth century to propagate millennial beliefs. Actually the Brethren advocated a very special brand of the premillennialist faith, called dispensationalism, which was to become one of the most important intellectual roots of the Fundamentalist movement at the end of the century.[46] Particularly in the 1880's and 1890's American dispensationalists became some of Moody's closest friends. It

45. William G. McLoughlin, *Modern Revivalism: Charles Grandison Finney to Billy Graham* (New York: Ronald Press, 1959), pp. 105–06. An important exception to this rule about pre–Civil War millennial movements was the Millerite movement. William Miller and his followers are probably the best known of the anti-bellum millennialist groups, and they were premillennialists. For a detailed, sympathetic account of their activities, see Leroy E. Froom, *The Prophetic Faith of Our Fathers*, 4 vols. (Washington, D. C.: Review and Herald, 1951–54), 4:429–876.

46. For an illuminating discussion of dispensationalism in this country, and its connections with the Fundamentalist movement, see Ernest R.

is questionable whether the evangelist ever became a thorough-going dispensationalist; for the 1870's perhaps it is sufficient to say that dispensationalists, both English and American, had helped considerably to confirm Moody in his decision to adopt the position of premillennialism.

As noted earlier, members of the Brethren traveled widely in this country after the Civil War. John N. Darby, one of their most long-lived and vigorous leaders, was especially active. He had already visited this country on four separate occasions by the end of the 1860's, and returned again in 1872, just before Moody left to go to England. Certainly in the latter year, and possibly in 1868, he was in Chicago for extended visits with evangelical leaders.[47] Darby propagated his beliefs primarily through informal study sessions with recognized leaders within the churches, not through public preaching to large audiences.[48] This was precisely the kind of method for study of biblical and theological questions that appealed to Moody. It is entirely possible that Moody came under Darby's direct influence in 1868, and certainly no later than 1872. Moreover, many evangelical Protestants read the writings of Darby, and other Brethren — they were prolific publicists — like William Trotter, William Kelly, and C. H. MacIntosh. Fleming H. Revell, the brother of Moody's wife, published many of the books and tracts that the Brethren chose to distribute in this country.[49]

By the mid-seventies adherents of premillennialism, led by the

Sandeen, "Towards a Historical Interpretation of the Origins of Fundamentalism," *Church History*, 36 (March 1967): 66–83.

47. *Letter of J. N. D.* [John N. Darby], 3 vols. (Oak Park, Ill.: Bible Truth Publishers, n.d.)1:518, 2:189–93. See especially Darby's comments in 2:193, where he refers critically to "the active man at Chicago, lately in England."

48. *Ibid.*, 1:470, 486, 495; 2:189, 193.

49. James E. Baer, "Historic Premillennialism," *Union Seminary Review*, 40 (May, 1944): 218–19; C. Norman Kraus, *Dispensationalism in America* (Richmond, Va.: John Knox Press, 1958), p. 43, chap. 2. Moody once stated that he was "in the church fifteen or sixteen years" before he "ever heard a sermon" on the second coming of Christ. Assuming 1856 as a starting point, in 1871 or 1872 he first came in contact with premillennialist thought. The coincidence of dates with the known visit of Darby to Chicago is interesting. (*New Sermons, Addresses and Prayers*, p. 529.)

dispensationalists, were beginning to hold "Bible and prophetic conferences" to promote the exchange of ideas on the general subject of pessimistic millennialism. The first such conference was held in Boston in 1868, under the leadership of George C. Needham, a young evangelist from Ireland who eventually became one of the pastors of the Chicago Avenue Church which Moody had founded in the Windy City. Under Needham's direction other regional conferences eventually convened in Philadelphia and Chicago. In the winter of 1878, just as Moody was reaching the peak of his success as a revivalist, the first national "Bible and prophetic conference" gathered in New York City. Although the evangelist was too busy with revival campaigns to attend, many of his closest friends did. The list of delegates included C. M. Morton, who was then pastor of the Chicago Avenue Church, T. W. Harvey and B. F. Jacobs, two close associates of the revivalist in the YMCA in Chicago, D. W. Whittle, one of his closest personal friends, and John Wanamaker. Whittle made a major address at the closing session of the conference.[50]

The spread of premillennialist sentiments reflected in part the gradual disillusionment of many people with the new America being spawned by industrialism in the post–Civil War period. The doctrine was a judgment on society; at the same time it offered hope of eventual deliverance from the harsh realities of the present age. At the conference in New York in 1878, this disillusionment remained a muted theme;[51] but eight years later, when the second national prophetic conference was held in Chicago, nearly every speaker commented on the worldliness of America, exhorted men to separate themselves from the world, and rejoiced that their belief in the imminence of Christ's second coming and the subsequent destruction of existing society gave promise of speedy release from the trials of earthly existence.[52]

50. Elmer W. Powell, "Plymouth Brethrenism," *Crozier Quarterly*, 14 (January, 1939): 38; *New York Tribune*, October 31, 1878, November 2, 1878.

51. Nathaniel West, ed., *Premillenial Essays* (Chicago, 1879), *passim*. All the remarks and papers offered at the gathering in 1878 in New York are printed in this book.

52. See, for example, the addresses of E. F. Stroeter and A. T. Pierson in the *Chicago Inter-Ocean*, November 17, 1886. Moody did not attend the second conference because of prior obligations in Wheeling, West

The Theology of a Popular Preacher

During the seventies Moody's support of premillennialism followed a fairly predictable pattern. In each of his major campaigns he preached at least once, usually at the end of the revival, on Christ's second coming.[53] In certain ways it is hard to understand how the evangelist, with his essentially optimistic temperament and his deep love of men and things of this world, could be attracted to such a pessimistic, world-denying doctrine. However, a careful reading of his sermons on the second coming suggests that at least initially premillennialism served Moody as another weapon of evangelism. It was a way of urging sinners to turn from their too exclusive concerns with the world to contemplate more important matters of the spirit. "The moment a man takes hold of the truth that Jesus Christ is coming back again to receive His friends to Himself," he asserted, "this world loses its hold upon Him; gas-stocks and water-stocks, and stocks in banks and railroads, are of very much less consequence to him then. His heart is free, and he looks for the blessed appearing of his Lord." Moreover, sure knowledge of Christ's return to this world had its effect on the evangelist as well as on the evangelized. It imparted yet more urgency to an already tense race with time to bring the nation under the banners of God. Moody expressed his feelings clearly on this point: "I have felt like working three times as hard ever since I came to understand that my Lord was coming back again. I look on this world as a wrecked vessel. God has given me a life-boat, and said to me, 'Moody, save all you can.'"[54]

Here again the revivalist seemed to be embracing ideas whose essential meaning contradicted many of his personal attitudes and

Virginia, but he wrote a letter of commendation to the conference which was read at the opening session. (*Ibid.*, November 18, 1886.)

53. D. W. Whittle Diary, May 3, 1876, Moody Bible Institute, Chicago: *The Great Redemption*, pp. 201–12, 338–39, 392; *To All People*, pp. 449–514; *New Sermons, Addresses, and Prayers*, pp. 529–36.

54. *New Sermons, Addresses, and Prayers*, pp. 529–30, 535. The reasons which led Moody to embrace premillennialism apparently worked throughout the evangelical churches. In 1875 writers for the *New York Evangelist* noted the rapid spread of this doctrine among "the most earnest Christian workers — evangelists and missionaries," primarily because these people "make the speedy coming of Christ a prominent method to lead men to repentance." (*New York Evangelist*, 46 [September 2, 1875]: 6; [August 19, 1875]: 6.)

feelings; ignoring the posssible inconsistencies, he used these ideas for his own purposes. The pessimism inherent in premillennialism and his own progressive, optimistic outlook appeared fundamentally at variance. But the evangelist did not let that fact worry him. To his mind premillennialism seemed to strike a proper note of urgency about the need for winning souls to Christ, and to him this was crucial. Even in this area of concern he evidently ignored what some evangelicals thought were the limiting effects of premillennialist doctrines upon any belief in universal salvation.[55]

As the years passed, however, premillennialism increasingly grasped the mind of the evangelist and shaped it, rather than the reverse. As the problems of industrialization and a secularized world grew rather than diminished, the undertone of pessimism and doubt in Moody's thought came to the fore more often. By the nineties he was lashing out at specific evils and promising that Christ's arrival would bring an end to the wrongs that so clearly afflicted the world. In 1894, in Lowell, Massachusetts, the evangelist announced solemnly that "God is going to reign here and then there will be a great change in things. There will be no Tammanys in New York then and no chicanery. There will be no men seeking office." [56] The appearance of new social and economic tensions in the body of American society, and a religious doctrine that seemingly offered an escape from these tensions, had had their effect upon Moody. Perhaps in a small way the shift in emphasis in his espousal of premillennialism reflected changes in attitude going on among a much larger group of Protestants who came to embrace these same millennial sentiments.

The pronouncements of the premillennialists in the late seventies also reflected the early rumblings within church circles in this country over questions of the authority and inspiration of the *Bible*. Although this issue was not a central concern at the New York prophetic convention, the delegates based all their theological arguments and eschatological interpretations on a verbally-

55. For evidence of opposition to Moody's preaching of the second coming and premillennialism in Chicago and Boston, see *Northwestern Christian Advocate*, 26 (January 10, 1877): 1; (January 17, 1877): 4.

56. *Lowell* [Mass.] *Daily Citizen*, December 22, 1894.

inspired *Bible* and publicly proclaimed their support of that authority.[57] Since the time of the Reformation, in any debate over authority all Protestant groups had assumed that the *Bible* was of primary significance. Indeed, the Reformation itself was in large part a debate over where ultimate authority for the believer resided. In their rejection of the primacy of church tradition, the earliest reformers turned logically and inevitably to the *Bible* as the rock to which faith and daily action were to be anchored. *Sola Scriptura* was a phrase known and understood as to meaning and significance by knowledgeable Protestants in all the generations that followed Luther and Calvin.[58]

Evangelical Protestants, whether believers in premillennialism or not, were certainly within this tradition. In both England and the United States the evangelical communities viewed the *Bible* with a special reverence and intensity that transcended even the usual Protestant biblicism. The chief student of this phenomenon in England has sensed this attitude and stated it succinctly:

> Bound up inextricably with every phase of the religious experience of evangelicals, an experience that touched their lives at every significant point, was the Bible — a Bible that was not merely a source book for the early history of their religion, but a Bible that was the authoritative and infallible Word of God. Faith in the Bible was to the early evangelicals as fundamental as faith in God, and they made little distinction between the two.[59]

57. The first two resolutions in a series adopted by the delegates at the close of the New York conference clearly reflected this feeling. (*New York Tribune*, November 2, 1878.) This set of resolutions was accepted as the guiding principles for the second conference held in Chicago in 1886. (*Chicago Inter-Ocean*, November 22, 1886.)

58. Helpful comments on this broad, but important, historical topic are in S. L. Greenslade, ed., *The Cambridge History of the Bible: The West from the Reformation to the Present Day* (Cambridge, England: Cambridge University Press, 1963), chaps. 1, 5, 7, 8. William E. Moore has written a helpful survey of the question, with special reference to developments in the United States, in "American Identity and the Decline of Biblical Religion," (unpublished paper read at the meeting of the Society for Religion in Higher Education, August, 1966).

59. Willis B. Glover, *Evangelical Nonconformists and Higher Criticism in the Nineteenth Century* (London: Independent Press, 1954), p. 16.

In the United States the feeling was perhaps as intense. For American evangelicals the primacy of the written Word took on special power and significance when disestablishment and the coming of denominationalism ended any influence that ecclesiastical authority and church tradition possessed over people's lives. Most of the denominations regarded the *Bible* as the historical guide to be used in re-creating in their own church bodies replicas of the Apostolic Church. One of the largest denominations by 1860, the Disciples of Christ, had been founded on precisely that principle. Nor were Moody's contemporaries in any doubt as to the importance of the book. Presbyterians could assert that "the Bible alone" was the "religion" of the denomination; indeed, the "venerated formulas of the Westminster Assembly are so venerated just because they so squarely stand on the Bible as their basis, and ask to be received only as they conform to the Bible." Congregationalists quoted with approval these words: "The Book will live when we are dead. It is immortal. We ought to link ourselves so closely with its everlasting texts and chapters . . . that when we are gone our memory will continue green by being forever associated with God's undying truth." And Methodists claimed rhapsodically that the *Bible* was "the source of thought, the spring of feeling, whence gush forth perpetually thought and heart . . . vitalizing human nature, and beautifying all good institutions that have been, or are, or can possibly be." [60]

One of the keys to Moody's power as a preacher was that he seemed to express so frequently the full intensity of the spirit evangelicals felt when contemplating the *Bible*. Shortly after his death one of his close friends summarized his general attitude toward the written Word. "The plenary authority of the Bible was the fulcrum of his work. . . . On his platform it was not subject to dispute or debate, though it always was strongly defended as well as affirmed. . . . He knew that there were difficulties to be

60. Sidney Mead, "Denominationalism: The Shape of Protestantism in America," *Church History*, 23 (December, 1954): 296–99; *New York Evangelist*, 46 (October 14, 1875): 4; *Advance*, 9 (February 24, 1876): 463; *Zion's Herald and Wesleyan Journal*, 28 (June 17, 1857): 94. See also *ibid.*, (December 2, 1857): 190; 29 (January 20, 1858): 9; *Independent*, 4 (January 15, 1852): 10.

accounted for in Scripture as we have it. . . . [But] he believed that the Bible not only claims a Divine authority for all of its teachings, but vindicates its own claims." In a practical sense, too, the *Bible* was of overriding importance to him. It was the only book that he read and reread constantly. His personal copies of the Scriptures were dog-eared and heavily thumbed, and they contained innumerable marginal notes in the owner's sprawling handwriting.[61]

Consequently it was understandable that a churchgoer who sat in one of his services commended Moody's preaching to others because it was "so intensely *Biblical*." What, exactly, did this mean? The observer went on to write that the revivalist's message was "saturated with Scripture, in its spirit and aim. . . . The Bible is continually in his hands, and his incessant use of it cannot but affect the style of sermonizing hereabouts." [62] The first phrase in the quotation remains a bit vague, but it takes on additional meaning when one reads Moody's sermons for oneself and sees the frequent and vivid use of Bible stories and Biblical texts as illustrative material. This technique, moreover, represented a manner of thinking which shaped in a fundamental way Moody's whole framework of ideas. The revivalist was being true to Biblical language generally in his sermon illustrations, for the Biblical mode is to speak in concrete, personal terms. Thus it was natural for him to go on and speak of God, of Christ, and of the Holy Spirit, in the same manner. God was love, but love actualized in highly personal expressions and word images. Christ the man was the bearer of God's love and salvation.

Moody's long and persistent encounter with the *Bible* could not help but affect the way he thought about theological questions and about his whole experience. Moreover, it appears that he read the *Bible* without preconceived notions about what it *should* say — with a freshness that let the book speak *to him*. In 1886,

61. Henry W. Rankin to A. P. Fitt, April 19, 1900, Henry M. Rankin Papers, Mount Hermon School Library, Mount Hermon, Massachusetts. Sentence order is slightly rearranged for clarity. One of Moody's much-used personal *Bibles* is in the collection of his materials at Moody Bible Institute, Chicago.

62. *Advance*, 9 (March 30, 1876): 574. See also *ibid.*, 19 (January 21, 1886): 37; (January 28, 1886): 60.

speaking to a group of college students in Northfield, he tried to tell his young friends how they should go about studying the *Bible*. His words were very revealing, especially of his own techniques chiseled out of the hard rock of years of experience and practice. "When you read the Bible, the word of God talks to you," he said. "Become an independent reader and feed yourselves and grow in strength. Too many Christians everywhere get their religious food by ecclesiastical spoon-feeding. They take only that which is fed them from the pulpits one day in the week. Take, read, feed on the whole word of God. Don't throw this and that passage in the book aside. If you can't explain, can't understand it, don't try; don't worry because of it. There are depths in the Bible no one, however acute his theology, can sound." [63]

The evangelist never broke away entirely from the intellectual framework in which most evangelicals of the late nineteenth century felt at home.[64] But at times he did seem to reach out and grasp in quite a profound way portions of the Biblical message. He saw and understood in part because of the way in which he read — in a manner which many people, including ministers and theologians far more sophisticated than he, were not willing or able to follow. In any case this openness to the Biblical message on its own terms helps to explain both the rather frequent profundity of his comments and his ability to establish a deeply felt rapport with many of his listeners, people who were often as diligent and devout in their study of the *Bible* as he.

Finally, before leaving this point, we must consider again some of the problems Moody's understanding of the Biblical message covertly posed for his work as a revivalist. There is a glimpse offered of the possible effect when one returns to what the evangelist said to an audience in Cleveland about repentance. Perceiving the full truth of the Biblical message about repentance,

63. *Springfield* [Mass.] *Republican,* July 26, 1886.
64. The context in which Moody uttered the statements just quoted above about *Bible* study illustrates the point beautifully. In the same talk Moody opposed the work of higher criticism and its pernicious effect on the churches. To the evangelist the work of the new generation of biblical scholars seemed like nit-picking. He expressed his feelings neatly and vividly: "I pity those men who are all the time picking away in the difficulties, running their plow into roots, and letting it stick there." (*Ibid.*)

Moody marched to the pulpit at his revival and cautioned thousands of people to eschew emotionalism, weeping, and superficial sentiments about sad events in their past. Yet ironically, the machinery of the revival which he was creating and manipulating oftentimes tended to produce conditions in which repentance was to be viewed *precisely in the manner Moody was criticizing.* This could not help but create tensions for the evangelist, although he remained largely unconscious of the fact. Yet, as we shall see later, these hidden contradictions may well have had an effect upon him when he turned partially away from revival work in the 1880's and thereafter.

When the first tentative expressions leading to modifications of biblical authority appeared in theological circles, a tremor of uneasiness ran through the evangelical ranks. Because they felt so passionately about the subject, any hint of an alteration in assumptions about the written Word seemed to raise immediately the threat of obliteration of faith itself. Although the full fruits of the work of the continental higher critics was not widely known in the United States until the 1880's, and the great controversies that rent denominations asunder occurred still later, heretical views were sufficiently abroad in the late 1870's to affect the most sensitive evangelical groups. Thus it was that the people attending the "Bible and prophetic conference" in New York in 1878 placed at the head of a list of five principles of the faith their belief in "the supreme and absolute authority of the written Word of God on all questions of doctrine and duty." In like manner, Moody took his stand. Late in 1879 in St. Louis he stated peremptorily that "when a minister or messenger of Christ begins to change the message because he thinks it is not exactly what it ought to be, and he is wiser than God, God just dismisses that man or woman. . . . We haven't any authority to take out just what we like, what we think appropriate, and let dark reason be our guide." [65] These words indicate a considerable misunderstanding of the intentions and work of the higher critics, but at the same time the evangelist's phrases make it

65. *New York Tribune*, November 2, 1878; *St. Louis Globe-Democrat*, December 3, 1879. One of the earliest avowals of support for the higher criticism in a popular American religious periodical appeared in a guarded manner in the *Northwestern Christian Advocate*, 17 (January 20, 1869): 22.

clear that on this question he was fully in sympathy with orthodox evangelicals.

Any careful, sober assessment of both Moody's revival techniques and the thoughts presented in his revival sermons is a study in contrasts. Technique seemed to be Moody's great strength as revivalist and preacher, theology a noticeable weakness. His success in the revivals of the 1870's and later came chiefly by creating a mood or special frame of mind that seemed to speak of God, Christ's love, and the need to be saved. This mood was the result of the use of right techniques primarily, and not the outcome of intellectual pyrotechnics. Frequently Moody's methods largely determined the special emphases to be found in his theological statements. The doctrine of "work," his peculiar use of the word "power," even his acceptance of premillennialism and his special understanding of God's love and Christ's work of atonement, were all concepts conditioned by the needs of evangelization, of missionary efforts, and of bringing about the conversion experience. If there was any common element in Moody's technique and in his sermons, it was the evangelist's consuming interest in grasping converts for the Lord. The need to save souls seemed normative in all phases of Moody's thought and work. And the conversion experience, while not without theological content and significance, was principally a function of technique.

When technique occupies the place it did in Moody's work, and when one is dealing with great masses of people, as he certainly did, the almost inevitable result is that the low-level, rather indiscriminant standards of the popular culture are so catered to that they tend to be incorporated bodily into preaching and practice. Popular revivalism in the United States was vulnerable from the beginning to this charge, and Moody certainly embraced secular practices as completely as any popular religious leader. To the man with carefully defined and earnestly defended theological principles, Moody's revivals would appear as nearperversions of the faith because of their tendency to embrace too willingly the corruptions of the present world. The doughty Englishman John Darby, a man of strong convictions, apparently viewed Moody in such a context. Indeed, his picture of the entire American religious scene was of the gloomiest sort. For American churchgoers "activity, organization, mending the world, mixing with it, is all that is known, hence also the word has little authority." [66] For Darby, technique had triumphed over truth rigorously examined, and scorn was the only appropriate response. From theologians and many secular historians since his time, Moody has deserved the same sort of criticism.

Yet one cannot leave the evangelist here, at the mercy of his critics, and feel that full justice has been accorded him. His technique was not the sole basis of his appeal. Embedded in his sermons are bits of information that point to a man of faith who knew intimately and in a profound manner what it was to be grasped by the love of God as revealed in Jesus Christ. Perhaps it was long and unremitting study of the *Bible*, perhaps it was a conversion experience that shook his personality to its very roots in 1871, perhaps it was daily living among family and friends, more probably it was the intermixing of the three, that enabled Moody to possess the personal conviction and the authority that he did. But there is unmistakable evidence that he had grasped a sense of the richness, the fullness, the complexity, the sheer joy and exultation of life, that has characterized deeply-committed Christians since the days of the primitive church. Perhaps in the last analysis it was this impression projected to his audiences that made the greatest impact and helped mightily to draw people to his side.

66. *Letters of J. N. D.*, 2:193. There are numerous comments of this sort scattered through Darby's correspondence of the late sixties and early seventies.

8

Gauging the Fever of Spiritual Enthusiasm

"Few are converted under the sermon," Moody once said, "they are only impressed; that is sowing the seed and the personal conversation is the reaping." [1] These words suggest that even in the handling of the crucial issue of bringing his hearers to a decision for Christ, the evangelist proceeded more cautiously than had many of his predecessors on the frontier and in the small cities of the West. Finney had his "anxious bench" whereby potential converts were brought to the front, placed directly under both the baleful eye of the revivalist and unseen group pressures, and then exhorted further to conform to God's ways. Never did Moody make a final plea for converts in one of his large general meetings. He undoubtedly realized that the intimacy associated with small gatherings in churches or other limited physical surroundings had disappeared completely in his vast undertakings. Finney's tactics simply were not appropriate.

But it is also true that Moody personally would not have been fully sympathetic with the kind of high-pressure tactics associated with the "anxious bench." This was largely because of his sensitivity to individual feelings. In the one known attempt he made to justify his procedures in print, he placed great emphasis on the need throughout the churches for an openness and freedom between preachers and parishioners. This same spirit he hoped

1. *Springfield* [Mass.] *Republican*, February 21, 1878.

to place at the center of the work in the inquiry rooms. It violated the integrity of the penitent individuals seeking help to force them to parade their inward feelings and to make a crucial decision about the Christian faith under the noses of a curious mass of five thousand onlookers. Therefore, people were invited to the after-meetings at Moody's revivals in a "friendly, confidential way," and this sentiment animated the proceedings that followed.[2]

Interestingly, in the early stage of his careeer as a revivalist, Charles Finney had met regularly with potential converts in after-meetings that served the same purpose as did Moody's gatherings for inquirers. The parallels are quite striking.[3] Probably the younger man did not copy the tactics of the older evangelist directly, but something similar to an inquiry room was not unknown among the evangelicals of Moody's day. The noonday prayer meetings conducted by Moody for the Chicago YMCA in the 1860's bear a certain resemblance to his later work, with their emphasis on testimony, prayer for individual sinners, and personal exhortation. Procedures of this sort were common in the YMCA in England as well as in the United States. In any case, Moody began using the inquiry room from the moment he became a revivalist. In Newcastle, England, where he began his career, the gathering was called an "after meeting," but the primary intent of the revivalist to establish *"personal contact* with those who are unconverted," was perfectly clear. In Scotland many initial errors were corrected, and by the time the Americans reached London early in 1875 the methods to be used in the inquiry room from then on were functioning smoothly.[4]

Because, as one participant in the revivals phrased it, the inquiry meetings "were the true thermometer of the movement," Moody paid the closest attention to what went on there. He actively participated, attending to even the smallest details. There was a conscious effort to locate the gatherings outside the main

2. *Christian*, 5 (June 18, 1874): 3; *San Francisco Chronicle*, January 30, 1889.

3. Charles G. Finney, *Memoirs of Charles G. Finney* (Chicago, 1875), pp. 74, 160–61.

4. *Christian*, 4 (January 23, 1873): 27; (November 6, 1873): 6; *Church of Scotland Home and Foreign Missionary Record* (April 1, 1874): 18.

auditorium where the huge public services were held. Ideally the rooms for inquirers adjoined the public concourse, as in Philadelphia, New York, and Chicago; but if such facilities were not available, the people walked to the nearest evangelical church, never more than a block or so away.[5] The meeting usually began with a nod from the evangelist to a nearby cluster of singers who started the group singing. Soft and gentle tones were usually deemed most appropriate. "Just as I am, Without One Plea," was a hymn often used at this moment. After the last stragglers wandered in and the doors closed, Moody usually proceeded with a short talk or prayer. Workers then were free to scatter about the room to engage the "anxious" in quiet conversation. "While the gospel is still ringing" in the penitent's ears, enthused an admirer of Moody's work, "while his heart is softened," and "his conscience tender," then is the time to learn "what are those doubts, and fears, and difficulties which are keeping the poor sinner from Christ." [6]

In knots of four or five, those seeking help conversed earnestly with Moody and his helpers. Usually the workers mentioned a few Gospel texts as a means of assistance, or simply prayed with the lost and discussed their spiritual problems as best they knew how. If the gathering were small, the revivalist made an effort to talk at least briefly with every inquirer. He moved constantly about, overseeing the progress of the meeting and making it possible to shift his forces instantly to wherever he thought they were needed. Heated theological disputes with nonbelievers or with those who came to bait the workers were never allowed. One person correctly summed up Moody's approach: "The only people wanted are those who wish to become Christians." A newspaper reporter who slipped into the meetings seemed impressed with the enthusiasm of the workers and with how "quietly and sys-

5. *Philadelphia Inquirer,* November 20, 1875; *New York Times,* January 9, 1876; *Northwestern Christian Advocate,* 24 (September 20, 1876): 6; *Boston Evening Journal,* January 26, 1877. In Brooklyn, where facilities were inadequate, portions of the balcony in the hall where Moody preached were curtained off and changed quickly into inquiry rooms at the end of each service. (*Brooklyn Eagle,* October 25, 1875.)

6. *Chicago Tribune,* December 20, 1876; *Homiletic Review,* 36 (September, 1898): 205; *Christian,* 5 (November 12, 1874): 9.

tematically the work was performed." At least by the time he reached America, it appeared as though Moody's techniques usually functioned rather effectively and projected an image that fitted reasonably well with his own professed aims for the inquiry room.[7]

There were distractions, however, and the revivalist never overcame them fully. In Catholic Dublin a newspaper half-seriously called these gatherings a "Protestant confessional." Moody would have chuckled at such a phrase for its seeming aptness, but it missed the mark a bit. Words of this sort implied that there was considerable privacy in the inquiry meetings; in fact, they always remained semi-public gatherings. Among the hundreds who moved daily into the after-meetings, there were the insincere curious as well as those honestly moved to seek "assurance." The crush of numbers sometimes made it impossible to maintain the decorum and quiet that Moody felt was essential to his work. Once the evangelist was overheard complaining to bunches of spectators knotted up around the door that "they made it seem more like a town-meeting than anything else." Often, then, it was impossible to make the sudden transition from the giant public meetings with their mass conviviality and surface excitement to the imtimacy of face-to-face talks between sinners and saved.[8]

Perhaps the biggest obstacle was the chronic shortage of qualified workers. Moody was clear enough in his own mind as to what qualities he was looking for in his assistants. He once said that they should be people who had had "a religious experience themselves," and who would "work with their Bible in their hands, showing the seekers about Christ, instead of telling of themselves." Knowledge of the *Bible* was particularly important, for "if men are brought into the kingdom on top of a text of scripture, they have a sure foundation." Using informal screening procedures devised in Scotland, the inquiry-room workers usually ended up

7. *London Times*, March 26, 1875; J. Mackinnon, *Recollections of Dwight L. Moody* (privately printed, 1905), pp. 121–22; *Chicago Tribune*, December 20, 1876.

8. *Christian*, 5 (November 5, 1874): 710; *Springfield* [Mass.] *Republican*, February 22, 1878; *Philadelphia Evening Telegraph*, December 8, 1875.

being local ministers and a select group of laymen recommended by these selfsame clergy. It pained Moody that the supply of workers qualified to carry out "this most delicate and difficult service," always seemed inadequate.[9] Indeed, one of his principal reasons for establishing the Bible Institute in Chicago in the mid-eighties was to meet the obvious and pressing need for "Bible-educated" laymen who could assist him and other evangelists in the inquiry-room work connected with their revivals.

Once again we discover a gap existing between the ideal and the real in Moody's revivals. Surely the revivalist was sincere, and correct, to try to take those last moments leading to basic personal decisions about the Christian faith out of public view and to place them in more secluded surroundings. But this phase of his work, especially the assumptions on which the after-meetings were constructed, simply did not mesh fully with all the efforts to generate mass interest and excitement that had gone before. The tidal wave of public curiosity and enthusiasm could not be dissipated quickly; instead it washed in and through the inquiry meetings, destroying the privacy sought and deemed essential to the work there. Moody was caught in contradictions produced by separate phases of his work and he was never able to resolve the conflicts entirely successfully.

To the unknowing, however, the sight of hundreds of people streaming into the inquiry rooms at the close of daily services augured well for the success of Moody's revivals. But the mere presence of large numbers in the after-meetings was no sure sign that a bountiful harvest of souls was being reaped. Many who came forward were repeaters who relished the excitement of the occasion and the public attention they received. More important, a large number of the penitent were not new converts, but backsliders who had long associations with the church. One of Moody's most experienced assistants once privately recorded his observations of an inquiry meeting. He estimated that a third of those engaged in conversation were not connected with any church and that two thirds were "church members who had

9. *Philadelphia Evening Telegraph*, February 21, 1878; *Christian*, 5 (October 1, 1874): 634; *Church of Scotland Home and Foreign Missionary Record* (April 1, 1874): 18.

back slidden or who never had assurance." In England a religious periodical strongly supporting Moody's work admitted that a large majority of the inquirers had been "previously under religious convictions" and that nearly all were "members of Bible classes, congregations, or even churches." In Chicago in 1876, at an inquiry meeting of 150 people, when workers asked all Christians present to stand, most of the audience rose to their feet. Some eventually admitted they were backsliders, but when the inquiry room leader asked how many present were "sinners who anxiously desired to be saved," only three persons stood up.[10]

Moody would not be entirely unhappy with these developments. He adopted the view long advocated by revivalists, that their function was twofold — to gather in new members and to enrich the existing life of the denominations. Thus he once stated that "unconverted church members" were "the first class who should visit these meetings." Somehow they had dropped out of sight after joining the church and had become "mere stumbling blocks" rather than militant Christians embued with the converting power of the Holy Spirit.[11] Revivalists and ministers should devote as much energy to these people as to those approaching the church for the first time. This attitude created, needless to say, a real point of tension between evangelists like Moody and the local clergy, the latter feeling that professional revivalists were working in yet another way to usurp their responsibilities in the local parish.

There was also some question as to the immediate effectiveness of the work in the inquiry rooms. Understandably, not all those who entered went away convinced. In Chicago, for example, a young man came for advice and went away "greatly encouraged," though "he could not really tell whether he was converted or not." In London, workers fired questions indiscriminately at those present. At the close of meetings they even asked children, who had little real understanding of the query, if "Christ was

10. D. W. Whittle Diary, January 22, 1884, Moody Bible Institute, Chicago; *Christian*, 6 (January 7, 1875): 9; *Chicago Tribune*, December 20, 1876.

11. *Springfield* [Mass.] *Republican*, February 21, 1878.

precious to them." Moody himself sometimes complained of the lack of tact that some of the workers exhibited.[12]

In spite of these inadequacies, however, the work in the inquiry rooms had an effect upon people. Conversions *did* occur, and examples could always be cited later of words spoken in these meetings which eventually bore spiritual fruit. Of course, the extent of these delayed-reaction cases and their ultimate significance can never be measured precisely. Nevertheless, for many of Moody's contemporaries, conversions at the revival meetings were specific and numerous enough to provide substance to the claims that the revivals were highly successful. The evangelist himself consistently refused to keep a public tally of those converted. In doing so he differed noticeably from later members of his profession. As a more businesslike approach to revivalism developed, professional revivalists determined the number of converts or "trail hitters" — Billy Sunday's phrase — quite carefully and then used the figures to advantage in publicizing the success of a revival. Moody often asserted that he did not consider numbers important because the reality or lasting quality of claimed conversions could never be judged accurately. Thus he usually dismissed questions about the number of converts garnered in a revival by saying, "that record is on high." [13]

Still, the nature of Moody's enterprise forced him to think often in terms he sought consciously to avoid. Mass revivalism could not exist unless there was a noticeable numerical response to the pleadings of revival leaders. People in the local community who gave the revivalist essential backing demanded success, which they judged in large part by the size of audiences that gathered and the number of conversions that were produced.[14] Half uncon-

12. *Chicago Tribune*, December 20, 1876; *London Times*, July 16, 1875; *Christian Register*, 45 (February 17, 1877): 1.
13. *Christian Register*, 45 (February 17, 1877): 2; *Christian*, 6 (February 11, 1875): 103; *New York Evangelist*, 46 (March 4, 1875): 6; *New York Times*, November 14, 1875; *St. Louis Globe-Democrat*, March 25, 1880; William G. McLoughlin, *Modern Revivalism: Charles Grandison Finney to Billy Graham* (New York: Ronald Press, 1959), pp. 334–35, 336, 414–15.
14. For representative expressions of this sort see Whittle Diary, March 10, 1884; J. V. Farwell to E. W. Blatchford, September 6, 1876,

sciously, Moody accepted such reasoning. Long experience in handling crowds provided him with rough numerical yardsticks which he used privately to gauge his forward progress.[15] Newspapermen and many of the evangelist's supporters were much less reticent than he to brag about the number of conversions. Public discussion usually centered around the estimates published of the numbers attending the special converts' meeting which Moody held at the end of each of his major campaigns. In Philadelphia 3,000 came to this gathering, in New York 5,000, in Chicago 6,000.[16] These figures were probably roughly accurate as an index to the number who had formally professed regeneration and assurance during the course of a given campaign.[17]

"Professed convert" remained a very imprecise distinguishing mark. There were ways to test for religious enthusiasm, and when this was done the insincerity of some quickly revealed itself. In Chicago, workers distributed cards at the final gathering of converts to secure the names, addresses, and church preference of those attending. When local ministers later checked some of the residences listed, they proved to be fictitious, or, reflecting the sense of humor of bogus converts, were the sites of breweries and saloons. Many of those who signed a card, upon reflection appar-

quoted in John V. Farwell, *Early Recollections of Dwight L. Moody* (Chicago, 1907), p. 163.

15. See for example his concern for statistics regarding the results of revivals in St. Louis and Colorado in D. L. Moody to H. N. F. Marshall, April 10, 1880, Moody Papers, Mrs. E. M. Powell, East Northfield, Massachusetts; W. J. Fisher to D. L. Moody, December 12, 1898, Moody Papers, Moody Bible Institute, Chicago.

16. W. H. Daniels, *Moody: His Words, Works, and Workers* (New York, 1877), pp. 53, 55, 60; *New York Christian Advocate*, 51 (April 27, 1876): 133; *New York Tribune*, November 20, 1875. In Brooklyn it was estimated that 2700 to 3000 people "sought advice and help" in the meetings. It may well be that no final converts' meeting was held when the revivalist felt results were not quite up to his expectations. (*Independent* [New York], [November 25, 1875]: 14.)

17. Some of the neophyte Christians lived in distant towns. For this and other reasons some missed the final gathering of new converts. On the other hand, a few ministers and all the inquiry-room workers were invited to this meeting. (*Christian*, 11 [May 21, 1874]: 328; *Springfield* [Mass.] *Republican*, March 10, 1878.) Perhaps it is fair to say, then, that losses balanced gains and that the new disciples were to be numbered at approximately stated attendance figures.

ently repented of the act, or simply lacked the desire to push the matter further. Not being contacted by church people, they dropped from sight.[18] The evidence is too meager to do much more than note examples of this sort, but at least it means that the official conversion totals cannot be accepted at face value.

The natural concern of local church groups was to reap the field "made white for the harvest" by Moody's activities. In this instance the revivalist's oft-expressed hesitancy about guiding new sheep into the fold was a stumbling block. As one writer for a religious journal put it, the evangelist's job was "to break up the ground and sow the seed, leaving it to the regular preachers to water, protect and gather in such as are influenced." The previously noticed inadequacies of his doctrine of the church partly explain this attitude. But Moody also recognized that he ran the risk of charges of favoritism to particular churches or denominations if he worked too vigorously to link new converts with local evangelical groups. The need to preserve the nondenominational emphasis of his revivals overruled other considerations at this point.[19]

Yet even with these self-imposed handicaps he did try to assist local churches in the task of attracting new members. Collections of vital statistics about the converts, to be passed on to local ministers, were an important service. Moody experimented with this idea, but did not follow it consistently. The systematic use of pledge cards came later, initiated by B. Fay Mills at the turn of the century. Moody was always eager to help the churches "maintain the revival spirit." Indirectly this too eventually meant expanding membership rolls. Usually following a special invitation, associates of the evangelist remained in an area at the close of a campaign to preach and to hold special services. In addition Moody invariably supported plans to continue any of the special meetings begun during his revivals.[20]

18. *Northwestern Christian Advocate*, 25 (February 21, 1877): 4.
19. *Church Times* [Eng.] (February 12, 1875): 82; *St. Louis Globe-Democrat*, March 25, 1880.
20. McLoughlin, *Modern Revivalism*, p. 334; *Brooklyn Eagle*, November 22, 1875; *Northwestern Christian Advocate*, 24 (December 13, 1876): 1; *Zion's Herald*, 54 (May 10, 1877): 148; *Hartford Courant*, February 8, 1878; *Record of Christian Work*, 6 (November, 1887): 5.

Claims and counterclaims concerning gains in church membership resulting from the revivals are as difficult to judge fairly as is the evidence about the newly converted. The first flush of enthusiasm often led local religious leaders to view Moody's work as fully successful.[21] But if we take a hard look at the number of new members added to church registers following the revivals, the picture is less clear. Probably the most reliable statistics available at the time were those on church membership published annually by the major denominations. At least two intensive studies of data of this sort have been published which include quantitative estimates of Moody's impact on particular cities. The two analyses agree in their broad conclusions. Accessions of new members rose dramatically for a year or so following one of Moody's campaigns, but then an extended downswing occurred which eventually offset the gains made shortly after the revival ended.[22]

A third examination of this material, using a more comprehensive sample, agrees only partly with the previous findings. In two of the three denominations studied there were close correlations with earlier compilations. In a third instance, however, Moody's revivals seem to have produced more positive effects on church membership in several cities than had previously been indicated.[23] The evidence can be summarized roughly as follows: in terms of church membership the revivals had a negative cumulative effect on the Congregational and Presbyterian denominations, and a mixed, or perhaps slightly positive, effect on the Methodists. As a result of the influx of new members, Moody undoubtedly

21. Examples of this sort of rhetoric are in the *Chicago Tribune*, January 9, 1877, January 16, 1877.
22. Samuel W. Dike included statistics on Moody's revival in Boston in 1877 in "A Study of New England Revivals," *American Journal of Sociology*, 15 (November, 1909): 361–78. Lefferts A. Loetscher studied Moody's impact on Presbyterianism in Philadelphia in "Presbyterianism and Revivalism in Philadelphia since 1875," *Pennsylvania Magazine of History and Biography*, 68 (January, 1944): 56–84. William McLoughlin has relied heavily on the conclusions of these writers in his discussion of Moody's effect on church membership in *Modern Revivalism*, p. 266.
23. James Findlay, "Dwight L. Moody: Evangelist of the Gilded Age," (Ph.D. dissertation, Northwestern University, 1961), pp. 190–95, and appendix.

promoted new life and vigor in *some* churches in the cities he visited. But the claim can also be made that probably a larger number of churches were hurt by a decline in membership that occurred after the excitement of the revival wore off.

In 1896 newspapermen went to a number of ministers in New York City who had participated in the great revival there twenty years earlier and asked these men to comment on what seemed to be the long-range effects on the churches of that special moment of religious excitement. Although the observations were generally critical of the results of the revival, even these quickly assembled reflections tended to support the conclusions drawn from the broad statistical materials mentioned above. Moody's critics admitted that several specific churches profited considerably by a large-scale influx of new members. But many other churches were less fortunate over the long run and were hurt when enthusiasm waned. Evidently there is enough substance in the primary data to support the claims of both Moody's supporters and his detractors, although the critics seem to possess a stronger case. For the historian, who must perforce accept the long view, one of the New York ministers interviewed in 1896 perhaps provided an appropriate summary comment, though with mixed metaphors: "I have, in my twenty-six years' pastorate here, added to my church 3,000 members. I have done it by hard, steady work, not by fireworks and hurrah methods. New York is so big that shelling the woods doesn't do much good. It is the steady work, directed intelligently, that counts." [24] At the most, mass revivals provided only temporary uplift. The burden of maintaining a vital church membership rested ultimately, as it always had, in the hands of local churches and ministers.

Perhaps it is more significant to consider precisely who it was that came to Moody's revival meetings. As in England, the evangelist seemed to attract chiefly people from the middle class. The crowds that flocked to the Hippodrome in New York looked to one newsman "like an audience able to pay its way, to ride in horsecars, or even on rapid-transit lines." It seemed impossible to enter one of the meetings without noticing that Christianity ap-

24. *New York Times*, October 13, 1896.

parently had become the religion of the comfortable and the well-to-do. One critic of Moody characterized a typical supporter of his, a bit excessively perhaps, as "a stockholder in a wealthy and flourishing corporation." In 1880 while in St. Louis, Moody himself admitted that in that city it was "principally the middling class" that had come under this influence.[25] Many of Moody's hearers also seemed to be regular churchgoers. Numerous bits of evidence confirm that fact. In Brooklyn one evening the revivalist applied a familiar technique, asking those who considered themselves already saved to stand. Four fifths of the audience rose to their feet. Frequent complaints about the "selfishness of excitement-seeking professed Christians" who crowded into the revival meetings, thereby squeezing out nonbelievers, also attested to the social origins of many in his audience.[26]

Moody worried a great deal about criticisms of this sort, for he had often stated that he had come to serve and preach to all classes of men. In Philadelphia he resumed the practice begun in England of issuing tickets of admission to the large revival services, hoping to give irregular churchgoers a better chance to see and hear him. This did not help the situation much. Tickets were always easy to obtain, and it soon became clear that front-bench regulars continued to exclude the unsaved. Indeed, distribution of tickets probably acted as a barrier as much as it did an aid in attracting the secularized masses to the meetings. Many who might have gone to the services possessed neither the time nor energy to go in search of tickets. More important, those with admission tickets oftentimes were seated conspicuously in front, placed under the scrutiny of thousands of curious eyes. A person unfamiliar with or hesitant about attending religious services would think twice before entering into such a situation. One

25. *Nation*, 21 (November 8, 1875): 321; 22 (March 9, 1876): 157; *St. Louis Globe-Democrat*, March 25, 1880. See also *Brooklyn Eagle*, October 29, 1875, November 11, 1875, November 16, 1875; *Philadelphia Evening Bulletin*, January 11, 1876; *Northwestern Christian Advocate*, 24 (October 18, 1876): 1. For a somewhat different assessment of the social composition of the audience at Moody's first meeting in New York City, see the *New York World*, February 8, 1876.

26. *Christian Register*, 44 (November 20, 1875): 2. See also *Independent*, 27 (November 25, 1875): 14–15; *Philadelphia Evening Bulletin*, November 20, 1875; *Nation*, 21 (November 18, 1875): 321.

of Moody's supporters sensed the difficulty when he said that "the trap is set somewhat too publicly, and with something too much of congratulation. It is not 'the leaven *hid* in the meal.' " [27]

Thus the revivalist never devised procedures that enabled him to minister substantively and effectively to lower-class groups. His audiences continued to be chiefly regular churchmen and businessmen, young and old, all of them people of the middle class who comprised the backbone of most evangelical congregations in the cities he visited. These people were, of course, attracted to him because he preached a familiar revival message. But Moody also appeared as a sympathetic figure because his attitudes toward the world at large tallied so closely with those of his hearers.

Nearly twenty years ago Henry F. May documented with considerable thoroughness the conservative temper of the evangelical denominations on social and economic issues at the time of Moody's first revival campaigns in this country. "In 1876," asserted May, "Protestantism presented a massive, almost unbroken front in its defense of the social status quo." [28] The revivalist's outlook on social affairs fitted into this perspective very well. His ideas were shaped first by personal experiences, starting with childhood and extending into his mature years. A boyhood spent in the petty-bourgeois, individualistic environment of small-town New England, the word and example of an upright, determined mother, and countless other events in his early years meant that Moody grew up embracing the principles of the Puritan ethic of his forebears. His strong religious commitments acquired later did nothing to unsettle these basic convictions.

One of his cardinal beliefs was that laziness and idleness were a blight upon personality, not unlike sin in their origin and effect. In the 1860's Moody stated with assurance, "I never knew a lazy man to become a Christian. . . . It is the devil whose workers are idlers." A decade later his attitude was unchanged. "If you can get only twenty-five cents a day go to work for that. . . . Work

27. *Independent*, 27 (November 25, 1875): 15; *Baltimore Gazette*, November 19, 1878; *Northwestern Christian Advocate*, 24 (October 18, 1876): 1; *Chicago Tribune*, October 8, 1876; *Nashville American*, January 23, 1886.

28. Henry F. May, *Protestant Churches and Industrial America* (New York: Harper and Bros., 1949), p. 91.

is honorable. Any honest work is better than idleness." [29] Moody also had a ready explanation for poverty that made it appear as though it was the inevitable outcome of laziness and wasteful habits. Gifts to the poor, then, had to be handled with care. Be cautious in aiding these people, Moody once warned, for too often "the money would go into their pockets to get whiskey with." Unless the poverty-stricken were willing to help themselves, Christians had little obligation to contribute to their support. Certainly it seemed the case that if people "get a good living without work, they will never work." And an easily discovered Biblical sanction — "God has decreed that man shall earn his bread by the sweat of his brow, and not live on other people" — turned this notion into truth for the evangelist.[30]

In Moody's eyes, hard work and personal honesty walked hand in hand with piety. One of his sermon illustrations made this point clear. A defaulter whose conscience bothered him eventually came to his senses and repaid all his debts, though ultimately it cost him all that he possessed. "Then friends gathered around him and helped him. He is now a successful businessman. God forgave him and his employers forgave him." Not too surprisingly, Moody went on elsewhere to assert that "you will succeed if you follow Him. Whenever you find a man who follows Christ that man you will find a successful one." [31] The centrality of the conversion experience to his thinking obviously affected how he looked at social and economic issues. Unbelief seemed to be a major cause of economic difficulties and social dislocation. The revivalist insisted once that he had never known a man or woman who was "a consistent member of the Christian church" who had "come to want."

29. *Advance*, 1 (July 30, 1868): 6; 2 (October 10, 1869) 6; *Northwestern Christian Advocate*, 25 (January 17, 1877): 5. See also *Glad Tidings*, pp. 237–38, 239, 384; James B. Dunn, ed., *Moody's Talks on Temperance with Anecdotes and Incidents* (New York: National Temperance Society and Publication House, 1877), p. 84.

30. *50 Evenings at the Great Revival Meetings Conducted by Moody and Sankey* (Philadelphia, 1876), pp. 391, 392.

31. *The Great Redemption*, pp. 98, 160; *Great Joy*, pp. 348, 343. See also *New York Times*, December 11, 1896; *Glad Tidings*, p. 384; *To All People*, p. 43. Moody at times suggested that he used the same criterion to judge his success as a worker for Christ. (See Daniels, *Moody: Words, Work, Workers*, p. 431.)

Men were in need because "they are living in rebellion to God; they have turned their backs on God." It was also true that "there would not be a drunkard walking the streets," or "a harlot walking the streets, if it were not for unbelief." [32]

Moody's pronouncements, which seem harsh and insensitive to readers of a later era, were faithful reflections of the way a large majority of evangelicals of his time thought. Possessing a theological and ethical framework that placed great stress on individual striving and effort, Moody and his supporters found highly appealing the sentiments of the middle classes on social and economic questions, sentiments which possessed a parallel accent on individualism. Other tendencies in Moody's thought led in the same direction. His emphasis on "work" connected with evangelistic concerns was compatible with secular notions about self-help. Perhaps even more relevant was the evangelist's frequent cry that Christians should "separate themselves from the world." This otherworldliness grew largely out of his pre-millennialist beliefs and his latent perfectionism. Negatively it became a way of dealing with contemporary issues. Moody actually defined "separation" in legalistic terms, advising Christians to avoid all contact with those who drank, danced, played cards, or frequented theaters. This was a familiar point of view, propagated energetically by evangelical Protestants since the pre–Civil War period.[33] Needless to say, it was not a very realistic way of dealing with the problems being created by a complex, interdependent industrial society.

But some premillennialists pushed the demand to divorce oneself from the world to extremes, so that it became a total critique of society. Separation was urged upon people because absolute and thoroughgoing corruption characterized the present world. Christians, therefore, should have nothing to do with the sinful

---

32. *New Sermons, Addresses, and Prayers*, p. 248; *Power From on High; or, The Secret of Success in Christian Life and Work* (London, 1882), p. 77.

33. *To All People*, pp. 43–44, 46; *Glad Tidings*, pp. 317–18; *New York Times*, November 20, 1875; January 11, 1897. Clifford S. Griffin, *Their Brothers' Keepers: Moral Stewardship in the United States, 1800–1865* (New Brunswick, N. J.: Rutgers University Press, 1960), pp. 99–151, has some interesting comments on evangelical attitudes of this sort and their uses in the pre–Civil War period.

machinations of politics or business affairs. Moody usually did not carry his argument for separation from the world this far. Yet this idea, implicit in premillennialism, reinforced by Moody's very strong belief that evangelists had no other duty but to preach the Gospel and save souls, made it easy for him to avoid making critical judgments about current social, economic, and political practices in the nation. Thus whenever the evangelist mentioned publicly the crucial issues facing society, these items usually served as an added emphasis to drive home some basic point of his sermon. In the eighties he easily dismissed politics by saying: "Now, my friends, we will not bring up this question of parties. I have nothing to do with that, I only use it as an illustration." In 1897, engaged in giving advice to ministers, he was even more explicit about his feelings. Lumping domestic and foreign affairs together, he urged his co-workers not to have "anything to say about capital and labor. You don't know anything about it." Moreover, he went on, "What right have you to criticize President Cleveland [about Cuba]. You had better preach the gospel and let him deal with questions of state about which you know nothing." [34]

Unable, or unwilling, to examine and discuss critically from an independent point of view the major historical developments of his time, Moody easily and naturally came to share the attitudes of the American middle class, of which he was such an excellent representative. Although in public he professed a lack of concern for politics, in private he was a staunch Republican. When Bryan and the Populists offered a serious threat to the political status quo in 1896, he strongly supported McKinley. At least once during that campaign he broke his rule about speaking openly on political issues to say to an audience in New York that he "didn't believe a thing" Bryan said. In private correspondence he was less guarded in his comments. Three weeks before the election he had become so fearful of the outcome that he told a friend he had advised a leader of a group from England visiting him that "if the country goes for silver he had better take his Boys Home."

Even more inadequate were his suggestions for helping the de-

34. *New Sermons, Addresses, and Prayers*, p. 223; *Great Joy*, p. 18; *Boston Evening Transcript*, January 7, 1897.

pressed classes in the crisis years of the mid-nineties. Small individual acts of kindness were the best way to surmount unemployment and economic hardship. In this spirit he exhorted one of his middle-class audiences in 1896 to "go and act the Good Samaritan and . . . send your carriages out and give poor people a drive in the park once in awhile and they'll call you an angel, I'll warrant." [35]

Moody's social ethic rested entirely on individualistic assumptions. Only if businessmen and other men of power *as individuals* violated community standards of right and wrong were they to be criticized. The evangelist never questioned in any ultimate sense the values of the ruthlessly acquisitive society that characterized America in his adult years, nor the men who governed that society. Paul Moody recalled the time when his father, serving as a lobbyist of sorts supporting the closing of theaters on Sunday, secured an appointment to speak to Richard Croker, the notorious leader of Tammany Hall. Moody's son observed, "I have often wondered since whether it was really Father's interest in the defeat of this bill . . . as much as it was to find a pretext for meeting the great Tammany chieftain which prompted him [in his action]." [36] In this instance Moody largely ignored personal ethical conduct, judging Croker more on the basis of technical competence in his work and on the fact that out of the struggle of life the politician seemingly had emerged a victor. Croker was, like himself, a "success," to be admired because he had reached the top. Middle-class values, not religious convictions, shaped the evangelist's response. The same attitude, of course, explains a great deal about Moody's relations with successful businessmen, who were his closest supporters everywhere.

When forced to confront the race issue, Moody experienced a sharp conflict between his religious convictions and the pressure

35. *New York Times,* October 6, 1896, November 9, 1896; D. L. Moody to A. F. Gaylord, October 10, 1896, Moody Papers, Moody Bible Institute. See also D. L. Moody to Reuben F. Torry, February 1, 1896, and handwritten comments of Moody added to Torrey to Moody, January 25, 1894, in Moody Papers, Moody Bible Institute.

36. Paul D. Moody, *My Father: An Intimate Portrait of Dwight Moody* (Boston: Little, Brown and Co., 1938), pp. 47, 46, 117.

to conform to local customs and practices. After his return from England in 1875 he made a number of trips into the South to conduct revival meetings. Negroes and whites vied for his attention and racial tensions inevitably developed. One of the earliest difficulties occurred in April, 1876, when the evangelist and his family went to Augusta, Georgia, for some rest after his arduous campaign in New York City. During this vacation he agreed to hold a series of open-air meetings for the people of Augusta. The meetings began on an unsegregated basis, but when Negroes filled many of the front seats at the first services, railings were put up to divide blacks from whites. Moody opposed this move initially and reportedly made pointed comments in public about whites who "might possibly be astonished some day to see these blacks marching into the kingdom of heaven while they themselves were shut out."

Quickly local white politicians seized on the affair and tried to use it for personal political ends. Caught in a rising tide of feeling and emotion, Moody recoiled as indignant white Georgians assured him the "contempt and abhorrence of our entire people" if he had come South "endeavoring to change the relation of the black and white races." [37] The criticism heaped upon him by this southern community taught him a lesson he never forgot. Whenever he campaigned in the South thereafter he preached either to segregated audiences, or, more often, held services in separate buildings for the two races.[38] The evangelist had deter-

37. *Liberal Christian*, 30 (May 20, 1876): 9; letter to the *Atlanta Constitution* (no date), quoted in the *New York Times*, May 10, 1876.

38. Moody's friend, D. W. Whittle, who accompanied him to Georgia and who had been in the state at the end of the war as a captain in Sherman's army, first suggested the plan that the revivalist followed to mollify the white population of Augusta. Whittle later defended himself, asserting that "not to have done it would have . . . kept the white people away." There was, he felt, "no way we could carry on the meetings" without such an arrangement. (Whittle Diary, April 28, 1876.) For evidence of Moody's policies of segregation in other southern cities, see the *Richmond Dispatch*, January 6, 1885, January 7, 1885; *Memphis Avalanche*, February 5, 1886, February 9, 1886; *New Orleans Times-Democrat*, February 14, 1886, February 15, 1886; *Mobile Register*, March 12, 1886, March 13, 1886; *Charleston News and Courier*, March 17, 1886, March 26, 1886; *Nashville American*, February 10, 1896; clipping, Moody Collection, Mount Hermon Library.

mined his position on social issues in southern states by conforming to prevailing community standards, just as he did concerning economic questions in the North.

At times Negroes had the courage to protest in public about Moody's treatment of them. During a month-long revival held in Louisville, Kentucky, in 1888, the evangelist followed his usual procedures, holding union meetings in which blacks and whites sat in separate parts of the auditorium. In an effort to mollify the Negro churches, however, Moody offered to return to Louisville six months later to conduct a revival exclusively for blacks. Negro church leaders made no move to accept the offer. The embarrassing silence was soon explained by one of the ministers: "Any union meeting where the people are classified according to race or color will be a failure as far as the colored people are concerned. . . . I recognize no color line in the church of God, and it must come to that in the end." At about the same time the evangelist faced similarly outspoken ministers in Jacksonville, Florida. A year earlier, following the completion of a long tour of southern cities, in which segregation practices were followed, Moody was attacked by Negro leaders of the African Methodist Episcopal church in New York. One spokesman asserted heatedly that the revivalist's conduct "toward the negroes during his Southern tour has been shameless, and I would not have him preach in a barroom, let alone a church." [39]

Moody was not entirely unaffected by these criticisms and by the moral accommodations he made by following the procedures he did in the South. In August, 1876, his initial response was to defend the right of blacks to attend his services in an unsegregated capacity, and it was only after strong urging from close advisors that he agreed somewhat reluctantly to the change in policy.[40] His offer a decade later to the Negro community in Louisville of a special revival in their exclusive interest revealed the

39. *Louisville Courier-Journal*, February 13, 1888; *New York Times*, June 11, 1887. See also *Record of Christian Work*, 7 (March, 1888): 1; undated clipping, "Speaking Up for Their Race," Moody Collection, Mount Hermon Library. Ira Sankey hinted at racial difficulties in Chattanooga, Tennessee, in *My Life and the Story of the Gospel Hymns* (New York, 1906), p. 80.

40. Whittle Diary, April 28, 1876.

guilt feelings he harbored because of the moral compromises he was making over the race question. Nevertheless, his staying power in support of the Negroes was really quite limited when the full weight of advice from friends and the possible loss of his white audiences pressed down upon him.[41] Even though privately Moody might have been interested in bringing about a degree of racial justice, he could not risk the unpopularity of such a stand in public. To remain a popular religious hero he had to conform to national secular standards on this social issue, and he did so, accompanied only by an occasional hesitation or guilty afterthought.

Moody also gave unswerving support to the crusade against intemperance, a movement for social control directed by representatives of the middle class. This fight had long been considered a special concern of evangelical Protestants. Originating in the pre–Civil War era as a temperance crusade, and becoming later a struggle to blot out all use of intoxicating liquors by the public, this was one way Christians attempted to reshape society to conform more closely with their concepts of personal behavior. In the post–Civil War era it seemed natural for the denominations to support the mounting attack on the liquor problem. Drunkenness was highly visible, a concrete evil against which the churches could level criticism without appearing too radical. For many church people, support of this crusade also became a gratifying, though much oversimplified, response to the complicated, confusing social questions related to the new mode of urban living. According to the average temperance worker, elimination of "demon rum" promised an end to such widespread social ills as poverty, crime, insanity, divorce, and the general disintegration of the American family.[42]

41. The extent to which the evangelist was willing to go to remain in the good graces of white southerners revealed itself in his attempts to deny in 1885 in Richmond, Virginia, circulated reports that he had made disparaging remarks about Robert E. Lee and Stonewall Jackson. Seeking "a union of hearts and hands in this work" of revival, Moody pleaded that "if he had at any time said in any of his sermons anything which has given offense to people of the South," he asked "the forgiveness of his brethren." (*Richmond Dispatch*, January 6, 1885.)
42. Griffin, *Their Brothers' Keepers*, chap. 2, suggests some of the attitudes that animated the efforts of evangelicals in temperance work in

The evangelist supported the movement chiefly by incorporating meetings devoted exclusively to temperance into his revival campaigns. In his major crusades of the seventies he held such meetings once each week, usually modeled after the familiar prayer meetings that all church people had frequented at one time or another. Often these services included lengthy testimony from reformed drunkards, each one attesting to the work of revivals and the Christian faith in helping to shatter the power of John Barleycorn over his life. Some of these witnesses spoke in several cities, following the evangelist as he moved about the country.[43]

Moody was not as single-minded, however, about the matter as were the most ardent advocates of total abstinence. The primary aim of a confirmed crusader like Frances Willard, who assisted Moody in his revival in Boston in 1877, or Frances Murphy, another national temperance leader who dabbled occasionally in revival activities, was to get people to sign the pledge of abstention. Religious faith was designed primarily to stiffen the will, thereby preserving the pledge. In contrast, Moody never mentioned the pledge. Instead he reversed the order of precedence, always making the conversion experience primary, abstinence a manifestation of that experience. To preach temperance and no more was to go only halfway in solving personal problems. Salvation of men's souls was the only true cure for drunkards. One participant in a revival campaign in Massachusetts saw this distinction clearly: "To drinking men, as to everybody else," he said, Moody's one message was " 'Believe on the Lord Jesus Christ and thou

the pre–Civil War era. Winfred Garrison, in *The March of Faith: The Story of Religion in America Since 1865* (New York: Harper and Bros., 1933), p. 158, has some hints that help to explain the movement's widespread popularity after the Civil War. An illuminating recent study, stressing the changing social attitudes and aspirations of middle-class supporters of temperance is Joseph Gusfield's *Symbolic Crusade: Status Politics and the American Temperance Movement* (Urbana: University of Illinois Press, 1963).

43. *Zion's Herald*, 52 (March 15, 1877): 84; *Philadelphia Evening Telegram*, December 3, 1875, December 10, 1875, December 24, 1875; *Springfield* [Mass.] *Republican*, February 16, 1878, February 19, 1878, February 23, 1878; *Hartford Courant*, January 24, 1878, January 26, 1878; *Baltimore Gazette*, March 31, 1879.

shalt be saved.' " [44] Perhaps this was a minor difference; in any case Moody remained fully identified with the anti-liquor forces throughout his adult years.

Speaking before an audience in his hometown late in 1876, the revivalist observed that the nation hears "every few years the cry of 'Reform!' 'Reform!' " What sort of response should Christians make to such an appeal? Moody's answer was both unequivocal and predictable. "Man, away from God, is not to be trusted, and there is no reform until God has been found." [45] These words represented a basic assumption that determined many of the evangelist's responses to the economic and social issues of his time. When coupled with his natural tendency to embrace the individualistic, conservative values held by businessmen friends and by the great majority of those in his audiences, it becomes easy to understand why he was liked and respected so much by the people who came to hear him preach. He was one of them, not a critic but a strong supporter of their way of life. And probably if his views had been much different he would not have been the popular hero that he certainly was after 1875.

From the vantage point of the second half of the twentieth century, Moody appears as a conservative, a man who was frequently naive and sometimes uncomprehending of changing realities when dealing with the difficult social and economic problems that crowded the national stage in his later years. But if these words, and the examples of his attitudes and practices just cited, leave one solely with the impression of a person who was callous and insensitive to the deprived and broken people in society, then the image is unfair. Historically evangelical Protestants were activists, involved deeply with the world as they sought to transform it to the greater glory of God. Evangelicals like Moody did not necessarily ignore social ills; rather, they dealt with these problems

44. *Springfield* [Mass.] *Republican*, February 16, 1878. This attitude of Moody's probably explains why he reprimanded Miss Willard in Boston when he found her working in every spare moment to advance the cause of temperance, to the neglect, he thought, of her assigned tasks in the non-temperance phases of his revival. (See Frances Willard, *Glimpses of Fifty Years* [Chicago, 1889], p. 358).

45. *Greenfield* [Mass.] *Gazette and Courier*, October 11, 1876. See also the *New York World*, March 9, 1876.

chiefly in individual, not institutional or organic, terms. More-over, it must not be forgotten that the evangelist personally laid great stress on love as the essence of the Christian faith, and that he persistently illustrated that love with anecdotes drawn from the personal side of life. Christian love for him was not some-thing in the abstract but something quite concrete, bound up in all the manifold dimensions of face-to-face contacts.

In such a context it would not be surprising if a man like Moody frequently exhibited deeply-felt social concerns. There springs to mind the revivalist's earliest efforts in an evangelical denomination as a neophyte missionary administering to grimy urchins and their shabby families living on Chicago's near north side. The evangelist's taste for work with young people and in-volvement with urban missions in England in the 1870's, his later deep interest in secondary education in New England, his estab-lishment of a school to train people for work among the poor in Chicago, and his support of the Student Volunteer Movement, which attracted hundreds of college-age youth into overseas mis-sionary endeavors, are additional hints that he was a person with considerable human sympathy and a certain large-mindedness who embraced, and then struggled valiantly to deal successfully with, the problems of the world. Remembrance of these personal attributes and activities tends to blur somewhat any image of Moody as a flinty, rugged individualist caring little for those fel-low human beings forced to face, with few defenses, the onrush of industrialization and urbanization.

On the other hand, careful analysis of the evangelist's words and deeds must underscore finally the glaring inadequacies of an individualistic social ethic in an age of consolidation and growing interdependence. It is sad but true that most of Moody's efforts to deal with social problems were doomed to at least partial frus-tration and defeat because of fundamental weaknesses in the assumptions on which he predicated his actions, and because of an unwillingness to alter these assumptions in any significant way when novel social conditions appeared. This was, in a sense, the nature of traditional evangelical Protestantism's response gen-erally to the outside world late in the nineteenth century. The response was sincere and earnest, but inadequate, and often it did not comprehend even minimally the significance of the revolutionary changes which all citizens faced as industrialization inexorably worked its will on the country.

Few of his supporters at the time worried over Moody's interest in social questions, or the lack of such concerns. But in the 1870's and ever since many people have puzzled over the reasons for the great outpouring of public enthusiasm for the revivalist and his work that welled up following his return to this country in 1875. For example, in December, 1876, the *Chicago Tribune* undertook to explain the causes of the successful revival then going on in the Windy City. This analysis emphasized Moody's technique — his "plainness of speech," his "conversational style," and his "earnest manner." In a reply to this editorial, printed in the letters-to-the-editor column of the paper a few days later, a reader made an important observation. When the revivalist had lived in Chicago only a few years earlier he had possessed all the traits the *Tribune* deemed essential to his present success, yet he had failed then to bring the city to its knees. Indeed, asserted the critic, if his memory served him rightly, Moody had "often exhorted to nearly empty houses." [46] Clearly the newspaper's examination of the question was insufficient. Considered historically, the factors discussed by the Chicago editorial writer cannot be ignored. But it does seem that much more must be added if we are to understand fully the dynamics of the situation that resulted in Moody's emergence as a popular religious leader.

A key fact to begin with was the existence of an aroused, receptive public, stirred to consciousness about Moody and eager to see and hear him because of his successes in Great Britain. This man was unique among all the American evangelists of the nineteenth century in that he did not have to prove himself by a long period of preparation in this country. His years in Chicago working in closely related fields provided him with essential personal contacts and a backlog of necessary experience. But by being in England when he reaped the first rewards of his efforts in mass evangelism, he was able thereafter to burst seemingly fullblown upon the American scene as a revival leader of national significance. His apparent meteoric rise confirmed for many

46. *Chicago Tribune*, December 11, 1876.

church people the appropriateness of his calling — that he had been "chosen by God" — and this attitude surely eased his way. For the merely curious, the public notoriety created by his and Ira Sankey's conquests overseas was an initial attraction to the meetings.

A touch of chauvinism, too, inevitably got mixed into popular expressions of sympathy and delight concerning the adventures of the two American evangelists in England. When the highborn as well as the run-of-the-mill Londoner turned out to hear preaching interlaced with New England colloquialisms and the singing of catchy American gospel tunes, it was time to applaud and point with pride at the triumph of democratic manners abroad. The spectacle of New World simplicity gaining new respect and popular support in the bosom of a sophisticated, aristocratic Old World culture was a pleasing sight to any American possessing an ounce of national pride. The *New York Herald* shrewdly pointed out the general tendency of Americans "to adore any successful countryman who returns from Europe." The newspaper went on to predict, quite correctly, that for this reason Moody and Sankey's popularity in Great Britain would work to their advantage in the United States.[47]

A factor influencing the success of the revivals mentioned before, yet a point that deserves reemphasis, was the identification of Moody with the businessmen of the day. A prominent religious leader in Brooklyn wrote just before Moody launched his campaign there that the secret of the revivalist's success in England lay in the fact that he "conducted his meetings on business principles." The assumption was that for the same reasons success could be expected in the United States.[48] Moody did conduct

47. *New York Herald,* August 11, 1875. Theodore L. Cuyler, a popular preacher in New York, explicitly articulated this attitude. Commenting on Moody's triumphs in England in 1874, Cuyler observed that "last week . . . the Duke and Duchess of Sutherland invited" the evangelist "to their splendid Castle. . . . There are hundreds of our American millionaires who would give a thousand pounds for the honor bestowed on a humble minded evangelist whose life-work is to preach 'Jesus only.'" (*Christian Cynosure* [October 15, 1874]: 12.)

48. *Christian Cynosure* (October 9, 1875): 5. See also the *London Globe and Traveler,* March 10, 1875; *New York Evangelist,* 46 (October 28, 1875): 8; *Harper's Weekly,* 20 (March 25, 1876): 247; *Universalist,* 59 (February 24, 1877): 2.

his services with promptness and dispatch. He and Sankey appeared precisely on the hour, began with a minimum of fuss, and moved the service along at a brisk rate. Vigorous preaching added to the sense of forward movement. This attitude was in line with the evangelist's oft-repeated belief that church services should never be allowed to lag, for to do so was the quickest way to kill interest in the audience. This was a businesslike efficiency, with which the personal mien and dress of the evangelists blended well, and which seemed so clearly to speak of the splendid qualities of the industrial leaders who had come to personify the age.

The revival meetings also had just a touch of refinement. The portly Sankey with his smooth delivery, his relatively handsome features, his fashionable burnside face whiskers and careful dress, created part of this image. The mildness of Moody's preaching also contributed its effect. Although not lacking in earnestness and intensity, his sermons seemed a far cry from the vigorous denunciations and thunderous exhortations of the frontier evangelists. These were no backwoods revivals. The new spirit fitted the atmosphere of the large city. The revivalist had even selected appropriate physical structures in which to hold his meetings. Although not necessarily esthetically pleasing to the connoisseur of religious architecture, the use of business buildings, railroad depots, skating rinks, and large exhibition halls in the heart of downtown areas was quite appropriate in a world that was business oriented and rapidly becoming urbanized. Moody searched continuously for ways to make religion a vital force at the center of society. Perhaps one of his most daring efforts, symbolic of this attempt, was his willingness to abandon traditional church buildings in order to take his work to the very heart of the industrial towns and cities mushrooming throughout the country.

There were yet other ways that the revivals reflected big city life. Many people with no abiding religious interests came simply to look and see, to participate in the public spectacle. Nearly all newspaper accounts remarked that these people made up a sizable percentage of the crowds, particularly in the earlier stages of a campaign. A wag in New York had reasons for attending which probably expressed the tongue-in-cheek attitude of this group fairly well. "I visited the Hippodrome when Barnum ran it, and I thought it would be just about as amusing under Moody's management, so I came." [49] Whether because of these people or for other reasons, a carnival spirit sometimes permeated the crowds. In London, those who lined up early for admission to the meeting hall brought picnic lunches to munch while waiting. Around the fringes of the meeting place sprang up knick-knack booths, cut-rate eating shops, and souvenir stands, all of which are now a recognizable part of the paraphernalia of large public gatherings. In Liverpool, England, colporteurs erected book stalls at the entrances of the tabernacle and disposed of hymnbooks, *Bibles,* and religious pamphlets. Because of Moody's objections, places for booksellers were not included in the buildings where he conducted meetings in the United States. But vendors swarmed on the streets nearby, hawking pictures and cheap biographies of Moody and Sankey, and copies, for a few pennies apiece, of the hymnbooks used at the services. [50]

The crowds that gathered inside the giant building used for a meeting place possessed a power of their own that seemed to work in favor of the evangelists. People reported later their awestruck feelings in looking around at the vast audience or in hearing for the first time the sound of 5,000 to 8,000 voices engaged in congregational singing. Here is a description penned by one minister:

> The greatest power of the music . . . has lain in the sweeping, surging, irresistible, overwhelming, singing of the congregations. . . . And you, too, though you have only gone

49. Quoted in the *New York Evangelist,* 47 (April 20, 1876): 4.
50. *Christian,* 6 (February 11, 1875): 104; *London Globe and Traveler,* March 10, 1875; *Philadelphia Evening Bulletin,* November 29, 1875; *New York World,* February 8, 1876; *Boston Post,* January 30, 1877. Partly because he knew the results would be exploited commercially, Moody was extremely camera shy throughout his life. (Paul Moody, *My Father,* pp. 80–81.) Although the revivalist opposed publicly the crasser forms of profit-making which linked up with his revivals, certain of his actions made it easy for these practices to flourish even without official sanction. The Moody and Sankey hymnbook was used exclusively in all the meetings, and the evangelists controlled the royalties from the sale of these penny hymnals. Although none of these monies were used personally by the two men, it was understandable that they were not overly concerned if the books were distributed near the revival meeting place.

in as an indifferent and critical spectator, before you know it you too are drawn into the enchanted current, and are being borne with strange intoxication on the bosom of the wild but wondrous song. . . . Only he knows that who has himself stood in the midst of the great multitude, awed and borne away by the strange power of its mighty choruses.[51]

Questions might be raised as to the truly *religious* sentiments being stirred by such manifestations of mass feeling and movement, but nothing can illustrate more accurately the kind of world in which revivalism now operated. Bigness and increasing systematization and efficiency of operation became a part of the religious practice, as well as the business enterprise, of the day. This congruence of attitudes could not help but influence people and attract them to Moody's meetings.

For native Americans, Moody's revivals served as part of their acculturation to urban life. Thousands of people sucked up from farms and small towns into the maelstrom of the city discovered in the words, songs, and techniques Moody and Sankey used something relevant and meaningful to them personally. Thus the revivals served as a constructive force in the urban centers of the 1870's helping to bridge the cultural chasm that lay for many of the revivalist's hearers between early rural or small-town experiences and the later years of metropolitan living. It may also be the case, however, that the revivals were surface manifestations of deep-seated anxieties and uncertainties developing in the religious community of Moody's day.

"[Although] this age is, on the whole, no worse than other ages, things are changed," averred an evangelical journal in 1870. "As in warfare, the forms of attack are different. . . . books that once were valuable, have lost their power. Forms of work that once availed, are useful no more." The same journal's reply to

51. J. T. Sunderland, *Orthodoxy and Revivalism* (New York, 1876), pp. 111–14, as quoted in Marie Hochmuth, ed., *A History and Criticism of American Public Address*, 3:245. See also J. M. Mackinnon, *Recollections of D. L. Moody and His Work in Britain, 1874–1892* (Privately printed, 1905), p. 55; *London Times*, March 16, 1875; *New York Evangelist*, 46 (June 17, 1875): 1.

a world in flux was to urge loyal church people to "anchor themselves upon the Bible . . . trusting most to the sword of the Spirit, which is the word of God." [52] This was the instinctive response of any right-thinking evangelical to fundamental challenges levelled against long-held commitments and beliefs. Indirectly the words also suggested something about the source of the external challenge. It seemed clear that evangelical Protestantism was approaching a crisis in the realm of ideas, centering chiefly in the threats posed by a rapidly spreading scientific world view. Especially in the guise of Darwinian evolution, the higher criticism, and the comparative study of religions did the techniques and principles of science appear most unsettling to the American religious community. All three of these movements tended to undermine the authority that orthodoxy exerted over the popular mind. Evolution and biblical criticism questioned the infallibility of the *Bible*, while the comparative study of religions raised doubts regarding the primacy of Christianity as a system of ethical and religious belief. [53]

Although historians have been correct in claiming that none of the attacks on traditional views touched wide segments of the churchgoing populace until 1880 or later, the new ideas were sufficiently abroad before that date to produce measurable, and unnerving, effects. As early as 1869 Washington Gladden, then a young minister of thirty-four, was writing in one of the major denominational periodicals that "theology is and must always be progressive. The parable of the mustard seed applies not only to the numerical increase of the church, but also to the growth of its doctrine. There never was a time," he went on to say, "when Orthodox men did not depart from the standards of Orthodoxy; there never was any attempt to maintain an inflexible standard." Less than three years later a Methodist worried out loud that Henry Ward Beecher and Horace Bushnell, with "their some-

52. *Advance,* 4 (May 12, 1870): 2. See also *Western Christian Advocate,* 41 (September 16, 1874): 292; 42 (March 17, 1875): 81; *Northwestern Christian Advocate,* 23 (March 3, 1875): 1.
53. Bert J. Lowenberg, "Darwinism Comes to America, 1859–1900," *Mississippi Valley Historical Review,* 28 (December, 1941): 339–68; Ira Brown, "The Higher Criticism Comes to America," *Journal of Presbyterian History,* 38 (December, 1960): 193–212.

what indefinite and erratic" doctrinal notions, made "it fashionable for young ministers to copy" them. Reports that people were growing "impatient of doctrinal discriminations," that among evangelical Christians the "gospel truth has lost its savor," that "religious sentimentalism, vague and undefined . . . has usurped the place of a sound religious faith," — such words and phrases frequently appeared in the denominational periodicals.[54]

Care must be used in attaching too much significance to jeremiads of this sort, since religious leaders in America have always inveighed against threats to their influence. This was true in New England in colonial days, and ministers spoke similar words to every generation thereafter. Yet the evidence is sufficient to indicate that disquieting thoughts were not far from the surface in the years that Moody was preparing himself for revival work. Moreover, it was not simply that young theologians and Biblical scholars upset people when they devised arguments that departed from the "old gospel." A few evangelicals sensed that somehow a whole generation was growing up for whom the traditional word symbols that always evoked deep feelings no longer possessed the authority they once had. A Methodist, commenting on Moody's preaching in vivid, nearly literal language about "the Blood" of Christ's atonement, noted that "some of our familiar Christian phrases of a figurative nature, which thus are the very alphabet of religion, convey no clear idea to those who have not been brought up under evangelical influences." It was, the writer concluded, "quite possible that one might so repeat the words 'blood of Christ' . . . as to bewilder, rather than enlighten or persuade. Many . . . in this Christian land, if told to 'wash away his sins in the blood of Christ,' would wonder what

54. *Advance*, 3 (November 18, 1869): 1; *New York Christian Advocate*, 47 (April 4, 1872): 108; (January 4, 1872): 2. See the editorial by C. H. McCormick in *Interior*, 5 (February 5, 1874): 4, pointing to the "disrelish for strong doctrinal convictions, too apparent in ministers and people," and the need for the "whole evangelical press [to] stand firmly for the common cause, and against the assaillants of the *infallible* Word of God." For other expressions of the same sort, see *Advance*, 8 (March 11, 1875): 494; (June 3, 1875): 682; *Interior*, 6 (September 9, 1875): 4; (September 16, 1875): 4; *New York Christian Advocate*, 51 (March 2, 1876): 68; *Congregationalist*, 21 (April 9, 1879): 114–15, 116; (May 21, 1879): 160.

in the world he was to do." [55] This was certainly a state of affairs that could cause concern among dedicated supporters of the evangelical denominations.

At the moment when Moody appeared on the national scene, doctrinal disputes probably were not the most disturbing development that faced the churches. Indeed to the Methodist worrying about the continuing potency of a symbol like "the Blood," this decline in the authority of religious symbols pointed ultimately to the growing secularism of the world, not just to the assaults of science on the prevailing religious world view. "Worldliness," a vague though menacing word, appeared increasingly in the comments of church people whenever they spoke about those forces that seemed to threaten their way of life. Worldliness had produced "above-all, the ebb-tide of spirituality in the church"; the task of the church was that "she must first conquer the worldliness of the age, and this she can do only by her spiritual power." [56]

The epithet standing by itself remains vague and brings to mind similar exhortations by the godly in earlier times. Moody's friends and supporters, however, were usually specific enough about the nature of their fears. Some disliked the nearly exclusive identification of the most influential denominations with middle-class America. This meant increasingly the loss of warmth of fellowship — the "sociality of early days." This earlier friendliness "did not wait for parlors, or appointed occasions, but beamed out on all places, and at all times." In contrast, complained a Presbyterian, "our congregations are generally of a wealthier class, and as men grow rich they grow cold." The conclusion was that "a 'fashionable' church is about as frozen a place as one may find any place this side of the North Pole." [57] The worldliness and lack of interest in religious matters was in part, then, the fault of the churches themselves, particularly when Protestants became so much a part of the middle class that they forgot about other rapidly expanding segments of the society.

55. *Northwestern Christian Advocate*, 24 (February 2, 1876): 5.
56. *Interior*, 6 (August 26, 1875): 4; *New York Christian Advocate, 51* (August 17, 1876): 260.
57. *New York Evangelist*, 40 (January 14, 1869): 1. The same article refers to similar criticism being directed by a Methodist leader against his denomination.

Gauging the Fever of Spiritual Enthusiasm

As early as 1855 an astute observer put his finger on one of the most baffling and most disquieting tendencies that affected the churches. There was a certain kind of "popular infidelity" which was "not outspoken, which hides itself in silence." This was the subtle though steady undermining of popular support for religion that occurred as materialistic concerns increasingly grasped the hearts and souls of even the most lowly individuals. The products of an industrial technology that poured over the land like an expanding river at flood stage were first objects to be desired and owned, and then ultimately sources for edification and guidance of popular opinion. "The very marvel of the daguerreotype, the steamship, the telegraph, the railroad and the locomotive," wrote this commentator from the 1850's, "has, doubtless, weakened the popular faith in the old-fashioned order of human restoration and amelioration." For many people these fantastic material achievements were to be considered, "without question, as the effective agents of a social millennium near at hand." The evangelical writer's response to all this seemed unequivocal. "Sad and fatal mistake!" Yet uncertainty remained, for he concluded, "but still the popular belief obtains, that men are actually to be made better by steam and electricity, rather than by the Spirit of God." [58] Twenty years later these social tendencies were yet more strongly in evidence, and were penetrating to the heart of daily life in America. Few churchmen of the 1870's divined the forces at work in society as clearly as did their compatriot in 1855, but probably more of them felt uneasy and uncertain as the new mode of existence pressed insistently in upon them, demanding alterations in established patterns of thought and styles of life.

Several times in the early seventies the popular religious journals felt called upon to point out to their readers the increasing number of "great offenses against the peace of society," that were occurring, especially in urban areas. Crime and vice in the cities, both real and imagined, had always been a target of the evangelicals, but what seemed particularly bothersome at this point was the seemingly large number of young men and youths — "juvenile

58. *Northwestern Christian Advocate*, 4 (December 26, 1855): 206.

delinquents" in more modern parlance — who participated in these nefarious activities. A writer for a widely-read Congregational newsweekly attempted to describe these "young scoundrels" and their way of life. They usually were "boys who live nowhere, stealing when they cannot beg a precarious sustenance, and sleeping when night overtakes them in the nearest box or barrel or in some back cranny or underground burrow — street *gamins*, over whom nobody watches, and for whom nobody cares." A Methodist journal, defending the law requiring all children to attend public schools in New York City, asserted that this great metropolis of the nation "virtually rests upon a volcano composed of the neglected, vicious, ignorant children who haunt its streets by day and night." [59]

The spectacle of homeless, wandering waifs touched a particularly sensitive nerve. There was a connection here with a point that the evangelicals had always put great stress upon — the importance of the family. This primary social group was the place where Christian education in its fundamental and most effective forms was to be pursued. Within the bosom of the family children learned the civilizing obligations of moral duty and responsibility, and presumably observed Christian love at work in the minds and hearts of parents and fellow siblings as they all slept, ate, and worked together day after day, year after year. The family was a house of worship as well. Here children learned their *Bible* verses and received their initiation into the ritual of prayer and hymn singing, guided by converted and religiously dedicated parents. Family worship, usually led by the father, was a daily occurrence that served a whole series of educative and spiritual functions. Indeed, the family seemed to become in many ways the church for the individualist-minded evangelicals. Religious periodicals, particularly those read by rank-and-file members of the denominations, were crammed with an astonishing array of articles, stories, anecdotes, and memorabilia of various sorts, extolling or commenting upon the family. The cen-

59. *Congregationalist*, 25 (January 2, 1873): 4; *New York Christian Advocate*, 50 (February 11, 1875): 44. See also *ibid.*, (March 25, 1875): 92.

tral importance of this social institution in the life of the evangelical groups should never be underestimated or overlooked.[60]

Remembering this, it becomes easy to understand the shock and dismay expressed by religious leaders when they contemplated the growing number of rootless youth roaming the streets of urban centers throughout the country. These young people seemed to contradict everything the evangelicals had assumed was right and proper about what should be done with the early years of a person's life. Although historians have usually looked at the words of spokesmen for religion in this period as simply expressions of an extreme conservatism, their words often meant more than that. In some instances their pronouncements also revealed fears for the proper continuance of one of the most cherished and fundamental institutions of society. The strong dislike for these street urchins was as much a distaste for their *home environment*, or lack of it by evangelical standards, as anything else. The Methodist quoted earlier made his sentiments clear when he spoke of the homes of lower-class children who he thought were such a threat to society. These youngsters, he said, were "born in the abodes of the most squalid poverty, or dens of infamy, and brought up in lanes and alleys. . . . Springing like weeds from among the very stones . . . they live like rats, from

60. One can dip into the weeklies the evangelicals published at almost any point and observe their concern for the family. Citations included here are highly selective and are no more than a partial indication of the source materials that are available for study and exploitation. For comments about the role fathers and mothers were expected to assume, see *Interior*, 5 (July 16, 1874): 4; (March 19, 1874): 2; *Northwestern Christian Advocate*, 15 (July 24, 1867): 234; *New York Evangelist*, 46 (May 20, 1875): 5. The significance of family worship and some of its educative functions are suggested in articles in the *New York Observer*, 30 (September 30, 1852): 314; (October 21, 1852): 340; *Northwestern Christian Advocate*, 3 (January 3, 1855): 1; (March 21, 1855): 45; *Interior*, 6 (February 18, 1875): 4. Stories for children, all with educative and moralizing purposes in mind, are legion. There are, for example, one or more such items in every issue of *Interior* from January 22, 1874, to March 19, 1874. Some interesting discussions of the position and purpose of the family within evangelical activities generally are in the *Northwestern Christian Advocate*, 15 (July 17, 1867): 226; *New York Christian Advocate*, 50 (May 27, 1875): 164; 51 (January 13, 1876): 12; *Advance*, 21 (January 7, 1886): 1.

their casual stealings and plunder. Their home is the wide world, and they are in continual conflict with all about them." Cast adrift without the moral and civilizing influence of a "normal" home life, one evangelical at least deemed these young people "a dangerous class" growing up "to confront our children in the future with the most fearful problems of our social organization." [61]

The special interest evangelical Protestants took in the family reflects to a considerable degree the larger perspective of respectable Victorian society. By the 1870's the interpenetration of Christianity with American culture had occurred at so many points that at times churchmen came perilously close to equating the two; at least they felt Protestantism to be an absolutely essential prop underneath the secular society. A Methodist said as much in 1872. "The great bulwark of our liberties," wrote this man, "and the pledge of our continued national welfare is, under God, in our Protestant Christianity. It is this that has made us what we are, and the nation's greatness cannot long survive that by which it has hitherto lived and grown." Presbyterians echoed these sentiments. For them the commonly accepted standards of public morality in the United States were really nothing more than Christian precepts. Beginning with the idea that "the standard of public morals is established by the recognized religion," it was easy to go a step further and assert that "the present nation, the majority of whom as we think, are believers in Christianity, have a right to recognize Christian morality as binding on the people." This meant that although church and state were "formally separated," they had to be "harmonious in general policy," if the people of America were going "to live as a nation." [62]

A few evangelicals were not willing to stake out claims for their

61. *New York Christian Advocate*, 50 (February 11, 1875): 44.
62. *Ibid.*, 47 (July 4, 1872): 212; *Interior*, 5 (February 12, 1874): 1. Similar statements linking evangelical Protestantism with the national culture were common in the popular literature of the denominations. See, for example, *Northwestern Christian Advocate*, 3 (January 17, 1855): 10; (May 30, 1855): 85; 24 (March 22, 1876): 1; 17 (August 25, 1869): 268; *Zion's Herald* (May 7, 1868): 223; *Interior*, 5 (January 8, 1874): 5.

faith that were quite as sweeping as this. One writer in the *New York Christian Advocate* began somewhat differently. "Ours is a Christian government," he asserted, "only because the almost universally prevalent predilections of our people are Christian. Let any other form of religion prevail in like degree, and, without any formal change of our Constitutions and laws, our government would be in like manner Mohammedan, Buddhist, or Jewish. In *spirit* our laws are pervaded by the Christian element; in *form* they are without definite religious expression." [63] Although historical perspective shows this to be close to the truth, not many evangelicals in the 1870's were prepared to accept, or to face fully, all the implications of the insight this observer possessed.

For the religious scene *was* changing. Evangelical Protestants were already finding their cultural hegemony challenged by Irish, German, and Italian Catholics, and later there would be threats posed by a great rush of Jews, chiefly from eastern Europe, to this country at the end of the nineteenth and the beginning of the twentieth centuries. Almost unthinkable to Protestants in Moody's day was a third challenge — that of a completely secularized world, in which public expressions of religious sentiments, whatever the form, would tend to be eliminated. While this latter alternative was somewhat removed from the scene in the 1870's, there were manifest even then tendencies that led in this direction. The central point, however, was that almost without exception evangelical Protestants in the immediate post–Civil War era refused to consider any other ultimate basis for their nation but a religious one, and that basis was, of course, predicated on Protestant beliefs and doctrines.

Thus when challenges to this assumption occurred, Protestants nearly always reacted heatedly and defensively. One issue, for example, which always seemed to raise evangelical tempers to the boiling point was the question of Sabbath desecration. For many church people a decline in the spiritual uses of the Sabbath was as ominous a warning to the religious community as any intellectual questioning of the *Bible*. Reserving Sunday solely for rest and the exercise of the common religious activities of the com-

63. *New York Christian Advocate*, 47 (January 25, 1872): 28.

munity had become a seemingly immutable principle that was the sheet anchor of an orderly, respectable, and law-abiding society. In 1869 Philip Schaff, himself a first-generation American, illuminated feelings about the seventh day of the week in this country by comparing our practices with those in Europe. "The European Sabbath is a simple holiday; the American a holy day. The European idea is to devote it to pleasure, the Anglo-American, to piety and rest. In Europe it is the day on which revelry and vice have full sway[,] in America, it is designed that virtue and religion should be promoted by it." [64]

Native Americans justified their convictions about the Sabbath in several ways. First, and most obviously, the *Bible* offered a full justification for Sabbatarianism. A convention of evangelicals that gathered in Wisconsin late in 1866 to ponder the problem of the decline of the Sabbath published a set of resolutions headed by the following statement: "We recognize the Christian Sabbath as appointed of God . . . we recognize the fourth commandment as implying the previous existence of the Sabbath, and we believe that it was created when man was created." Some referred back to the early days of the nation and discovered national origins and Sabbath observance indissolubly tied together. The foundations of the country "were laid deep in the Sabbath," asserted a Congregationalist. "It was the Sabbath in its purity and power, that made us what we are as a free people." Others took hope in the belief that the Sabbath was a moral institution, and thus it became the cement of any progressive society. Its very nature, as defined by the evangelicals, was its own justification. Thus "human nature demands it. Public morals demand it. Civilization demands it, and its observances." [65]

Such absolute identification of religious conviction with care-

64. *Northwestern Christian Advocate*, 17 (May 12, 1869): 146.
65. *Ibid.*, 16 (January 16, 1867): 19; 4 (August 20, 1856):134; *Independent*, 4 (July 18, 1852): 110. See also *Zion's Herald* (March 19, 1868): 135; *Northwestern Christian Advocate*, 17 (January 13, 1869): 14; (February 3, 1869): 38; *New York Christian Advocate*, 47 (May 16, 1872): 156; 51 (June 1, 1876): 172. Philip Schaff's analysis previously cited also contains a number of interesting comments about the evangelical rationale for Sabbatarianism.

fully prescribed cultural standards encountered difficulties when the substance of the national culture changed. Indeed, the vehemence with which churchmen argued their case showed that conditions already had changed considerably. As early as the 1850's evangelicals were flailing away at twin specters — immigrants and material progress — that threatened traditional Sabbath practices.[66] As industrialization advanced and immigration continued in the post-war years, the pressures increased. There was no end to the dilemma of the churches, and their attacks on violators of the Sabbath continued unabated.[67] Largely unconsciously, in 1868 a writer for a Presbyterian journal revealed the contradictions existing at that moment in the evangelical mind. As a proud American he embraced enthusiastically the material progress he saw epitomized in the advance of the railroad across the continent. "Railroads are great civilizers, extending commerce, wealth, and literature in every direction, populating the wilderness, and binding the extremities of our vast country with stronger ties than standing armies could do." Yet in the next breath railroads were reviled because they "override the laws of God, deprive thousands of their employees of their only day of rest and the pleasure of Christian worship," and "train the communities through which they pass in habits of Sabbath desecration." [68]

By 1870, then, the denominations were beset with anxieties and internal contradictions as their traditional patterns of thought and behavior seemed more and more out of line with secular historical

66. *New York Observer*, 29 (January 2, 1851): 4; *Congregationalist*, 4 (March 19, 1852): 46; *Independent*, 4 (July 15, 1852): 114; *Congregational Herald*, 1 (August 5, 1853): 2; (September 2, 1853): 2; (September 23, 1853): 2; *Northwestern Christian Advocate*, 3 (February 14, 1855): 25; *Zion's Herald and Wesleyan Journal* (May 20, 1857): 77.

67. *Advance*, 1 (October 10, 1867): 2; *Northwestern Christian Advocate*, 15 (August 28, 1867): 276; (September 4, 1867): 284, *Interior*, 5 (November 26, 1874): 4; (December 31, 1874): 1; *New York Evangelist*, 46 (July 22, 1875): 6; (September 16, 1875): 4. "O! If this [railroad] traffic could be stopped on the Lord's day, . . . it would do more towards bringing men to the churches, and bringing them to the Saviour, than even all that Moody and Sankey are doing." (*Ibid.*, 47 [January 13, 1876]: 6.) See also *New York Christian Advocate*, 51 (June 1, 1876): 172; (July 27, 1876): 236; *Congregationalist*, 31 (October 29, 1879): 346, 348.

68. *New York Evangelist*, 39 (December 10, 1868): 1.

trends. It was too soon, perhaps, to expect the great mass of church people to break away from inherited attitudes enough to grapple effectively with the radically new conditions which science, technology, and massive immigration were thrusting upon them. The natural tendency initially was to reiterate ancient understandings as a sure source of comfort, authority, and guidance. In a number of ways Moody was an ideal man to effect this renewal of mind and spirit for the average member of the evangelical fellowship. Although his theological pronouncements possessed certain unique elements, on such all-important matters as instantaneous conversion, the authority of the *Bible* in determining the sources and dimensions of faith, and the urgency of the church's missionary responsibility to the outside world, Moody was fully orthodox. Combining religious views tied to the past with a polished technique that utilized fully mass-oriented promotional and organizational tactics, the evangelist appeared to offer an effective bridge for many people between the old and the new in American society.

Moreover, the revivalist often seemed the incarnation of a middle class businessman, both in body and mind. This image provided assurance for people who often viewed businessmen as their peers, gentlemen to be listened to and followed. When his hearers feared for the stability of the family in the guise of unrestrained children running amok in city streets, thoughts of Moody's own loving circle at home, the idea the evangelist may have projected of a strong, Victorian-father type,[69] and his support of most of the traditional evangelical attitudes on the general subject of the family could easily combine to soothe jangled nerves. Perhaps most important, his efforts for many carried the stamp of a special spiritual authority. Perhaps this came from a particular baptism with the power of the Holy Spirit, perhaps people sensed his peculiar grasp of the biblical message which sometimes leaped beyond the purely mechanical sentiments and contrivances of the

69. Bernard Weisberger, *They Gathered at the River: The Story of the Great Revivalists and Their Impact upon Religion in America* (Boston: Little, Brown and Co., 1958), pp. 217–18, offers brief, but stimulating, comments on this topic.

revival to profounder depths of meaning and feeling. Nevertheless, these charismatic tendencies, and the spiritual authority they represented, might be especially appealing to church people who were unnerved because the unifying principles of life that rested on God seemed to be disappearing in the dense undergrowth of a new way of existence springing up on all sides.

Moody's revivals represent one of the earliest institutionalized, nationwide responses of the churches in the post–Civil War era to the giant transformations brought on by the industrial revolution. Because the revivals came at a relatively early date in the general efforts of the nation to adjust to new social and economic realities, almost by definition the substance of the response would be conservative in nature, couched in traditional terms. This was true of Moody's work.[70] He did not alter in any fundamental way the main course of theological developments, although he had much more to say on theological matters than commentators in the past have been willing to recognize. Neither did the evangelist produce a radical transformation of the polity or ecclesiastical structure of any of the evangelical denominations. His most lasting contribution as a revivalist was to lay down the methodological and operational foundations of mass revivalism. He, like the leading figures in the business world of his time, was chiefly an innovator in organization and management. And his con-

---

70. There may be historical significance in the close proximity in dates of the spiritual excitement touched off by Moody in this country and the first national prophetic conference held by the premillennialists in New York late in 1878. Like Moody's revivals, premillennialism in its post–Civil War form has recently been shown to be a movement rooted in the cities. (Ernest R. Sandeen, "Towards a Historical Interpretation of the Origins of Fundamentalism," *Church History*, 36 (March, 1967): 75–76, 77.) Despite the conservative and traditional aspects of both of these movements, they represent honest and legitimate efforts on the part of the churches *in the urban environment* to respond to industrialization. Both secular and church historians have tended to ignore these early, perhaps less attractive, developments, concentrating instead on the reform movements within the denominations of later years. Perhaps now is the time to broaden the scope of our studies and thus render a fuller and more precise understanding of the church's work in the late nineteenth century.

tributions in this area enabled revivalism to survive in an urban, mass society.[71]

71. Differences in motivation which attracted people to Moody's meetings in the United States and in Great Britain deserve a brief comment. The popularity of the two American evangelists in England was partly tied to a rising spirit of democracy, a factor which was absent in the United States. Although tensions arising from industrialization affected people in the British Isles, the industrial revolution probably was a more pervasive "first cause" of Moody's successes in the United States. These differences illuminate the uniqueness of national development and the variations in response in different countries to the broad social and economic movements that have swept over the western world in the last two hundred years. There were other aspects of Moody's campaigns on both sides of the Atlantic which, on the surface at least, seemed to evoke similar responses. We need to know more about the common aspects and the elements of disparity — institutionally and ideologically — of the Anglo-American religious community of the nineteenth century. Suggestive materials in this regard are in Jerald C. Brauer, ed., *Reinterpretation in American Church History* (Chicago: University of Chicago Press, 1968), pp. 153–67, 207–12.

9

New Approaches to Evangelism: Schools in the East and in the Midwest

Beginning late in 1878 Moody changed some of his basic tactics as a revivalist. Instead of concentrating his efforts in a centrally located tabernacle or public auditorium, he divided the cities he visited into sections, and held meetings in each for several weeks. A leisurely campaign lasting several months replaced the eight to ten weeks of rather frantic activity of the earlier revivals. He had precedents for the changes he made. In 1875 he had followed somewhat similar procedures in London, and he had considered seriously the idea of such a program in the early stages of the planning for the Chicago revival in 1876.[1]

The actual shift came in Baltimore, where the evangelist went with his family in October, 1878, to rest and study. But "rest" as ordinary people know it was not a part of Moody's experience for very long. Less than a week after his arrival he had begun to meet with local ministers and laymen who sought help in their work. The series of small meetings that developed eventually were in part shaped by Moody's continuing desire to adhere as much as possible to his original purpose in coming to Baltimore. He felt he had strength to devote only a limited amount of time to revival work. He agreed, therefore, to conduct one service a

1. J. V. Farwell to D. L. Moody, February 8, 1876, quoted in John V. Farwell, *Early Recollections of Dwight L. Moody* (Chicago: Winona Publishing Co., 1907), p. 149.

day in one of the evangelical churches of the city. In the seven months that followed, his new approach to revivalism unfolded. Usually he stayed a month or so in an area; by May, 1879, he had canvassed the city thoroughly.[2]

Moody's alteration in technique was partly a response to an immediate situation. Pragmatic adjustment to current circumstances was typical of the revivalist, but this does not explain entirely the reasons behind his change in working habits. In a practical sense he was utilizing the existing denominational facilities more fully than before and thus was able to omit the high costs of a central meeting place. By working more directly through church groups he both minimized the exhausting and time-consuming labor of setting up the separate structure of a revival and cut down further on expenses. But the format introduced in Baltimore was not merely a short-lived attempt to tinker with the machinery of mass revivalism. Evidently the evangelist felt the new methods were of permanent value, for he continued to use them after leaving that city. He did preach from a central meeting place in a short revival held in Cleveland late in 1879, and he nearly always used a large public building to house the brief revivals he conducted in small cities and towns throughout the country after 1881. But because he had more time in St. Louis in the winter and spring of 1879–80, he again used his new methods. A year later he followed the same procedures in San Francisco.

Evidence of this sort suggests that Moody was revising considerably his assumptions about revivalism. His interest in new techniques may have developed out of a growing concern over the failure of many professed converts to become effective church members. He spoke revealing words in Cleveland in 1879 to

2. Emma C. Moody to "Mother," November 11, 1878, Mrs. Frank R. Smith Collection, Library of Congress; *Baltimore Sun*, October 9, 1878, October 14, 1878, October 15, 1878, November 2, 1878, May 17, 1879; *Baltimore Gazette*, October 30, 1878. It was hard to break away from familiar patterns of operation. When tensions arose in November, 1878, Baltimore ministers considered seriously a proposal to build a tabernacle in an appropriate location and to continue the meetings there. Eventually, however, they discarded the plan. (*Baltimore Sun*, November 14, 1878, November 26, 1878.)

justify his new approach. "The plan of holding meetings in the Tabernacle centralizes the interest and possibly draws out larger crowds," he vouchsafed to a reporter, "but the churches are the places to do effective work." Thus he concluded that by "holding our meetings in the different churches," these selfsame groups "would receive additions" which they might "otherwise lose." [3]

These words recall to mind once again that nearly all revivalists have envisioned their work as two-fold — to convert sinners outside the church and to revitalize backsliders within. In this instance Moody was shifting emphasis from the external to the internal problem facing the evangelicals. He wanted to spend less energy trying to convert the masses, devoting more time instead to the quickening of regular churchgoers. Through these reawakened church members, who would work vigorously in the world as bearers of the gospel and savers of souls, Moody might well have a greater cumulative impact than previously. Although at the moment this rationale for his new techniques appeared only occasionally in print, it was a point of view that increasingly affected his activities in the last two decades of his life.

These developments may well be related to the point made earlier about the hidden yet powerful tensions developing in Moody as his understanding of the Biblical faith deepened and in some instances came to contradict the visible results of his work as a revivalist. Perhaps it was true that his vision of the Christian faith and what it should mean to individuals and the world no longer squared with what he thought he could achieve through revivalism. If so, such shifts in altitude help to explain both Moody's change in revival procedures in 1878 and his simultaneous development of interests in public projects entirely apart from revivalism. Not that revivalism was a failure to him — for he continued to work strenuously as a revivalist until the last few days before his death. Rather, his faith was dynamic, and this forced him constantly to seek other ways, in addition to revivalism, to bring the Word to the world, and the unsaved to Christ. Although there is no evidence of the kind normally available to

3. *Cleveland Leader*, November 9, 1879. See also *St. Louis Globe-Democrat*, March 25, 1880.

historians to support such claims as these, internal logic and the nature of Moody's public activities after 1880 make this a plausible interpretation of his actions.

Beginning in 1879 the evangelist began yet another career, outside the ambit of revivalism. This was a job devoted chiefly to Christian education. Specifically it involved the establishment of the Northfield School for Girls in 1879, Mount Hermon School for boys in 1881, and the Bible Institute in Chicago in 1886, which after Moody's death was renamed Moody Bible Institute. This new work included other projects of importance, usually relating in one way or another to his three schools. He established summer Bible conferences at Northfield both for adults and college age youth, he supported the Student Volunteer Movement, which got its start officially at Northfield in the summer of 1886, and he became a publisher of religious periodicals and pamphlets. These new tasks permanently altered the course he took in public affairs.

The new activities, rooted as they were in the evangelist's innermost thoughts and beliefs, undoubtedly were related as well to changes in public attitudes toward revivalism. Unless he were to retrace his steps, by 1880 Moody had practically exhausted the territory in which he could conduct revivals on the scale of the campaigns of the previous five years. In the decade that followed he preached again in Chicago, New York, Boston, and Brooklyn, as well as in many other towns both large and small throughout the country. But in none of the large cities did he stir general public interest and enthusiasm to the degree he had in his campaigns of the seventies. Perhaps this was a hint that his power as a revivalist was waning. The evangelist himself admitted privately that the results of his trip to England from 1881 to 1884 were probably not as great as were those of the highly successful tour of 1873–75.[4] His growing interest in new methods of evange-

4. Paul D. Moody, *My Father: An Intimate Portrait of Dwight Moody* (Boston: Little, Brown and Co., 1938), p. 180. See also D. W. Whittle Diary, February 23, 1884, Moody Bible Institute, Chicago. A close reading of the printed accounts of two interviews with Moody in Cleveland and St. Louis in 1879 and 1880 contain veiled references to lessening public interest in those two cities. (*Cleveland Leader*, November 9,

lization inevitably produced divided loyalties that distracted him from his previous single-minded concern. The result was less emphasis on, if not less interest in, his career as a professional revivalist. All of these developments point to the conclusion that by the early eighties Moody's greatest days as a revivalist were over.

There were several possible explanations for the fading of revival fervor after 1880. All popular movements like these revivals run the same risks that any fad does which grasps the public mind for a period of time. The season of spiritual refreshment generated its own momentum, and once it reached a peak an inevitable downswing in public support began. The techniques Moody used to ballyhoo his work undoubtedly accentuated this tendency by building enthusiasm dramatically and thus making the downswing more drastic when it finally came. Moreover, the problems connected with industrialization, from which Moody's simple message seemingly offered some release, grew in complexity and number. Revivalism was unable to provide fully satisfying and lasting answers to these problems and thus many of Moody's followers, and the revivalist himself turned to other expedients. By 1890 some had joined the incipient social gospel movement, and some banded together around the ballot box to promote local crusades for reform. Others, still within the church, expressed themselves more conservatively, like certain Methodists who broke away from the main denominations to form splinter holiness groups, and like the adherents of premillennialism and dispensationalism who attended the annual Niagara Conferences in the 1890's.[5] These latter groups asserted that they were reacting

1879; *St. Louis Globe-Democrat,* March 25, 1880.) See also the *Cleveland Plain Dealer,* November 13, 1879; D. L. Moody to H. N. F. Marshall, November 13, 1879, April 10, 1880, deposited in a collection of documents relating to the early years of the Northfield Schools, Alumni Office, Northfield School for Girls. The last item cited above indicates the public response improved by the end of the St. Louis campaign.

5. Timothy L. Smith, *Called Unto Holiness: The Story of the Nazarenes: The Formative Years* (Kansas City, Mo.: Nazarene Publishing House, 1962); Emory S. Bucke, ed., *The History of American Methodism,* 3 vols. (Nashville: Abingdon Press, 1964), 2:608–27; Ernest R. Sandeen, "Towards a Historical Interpretation of the Origins of Fundamentalism," 36 (March, 1967): 71–72.

to the corruption evident in America as the nation moved toward secularization.[6]

For a variety of reasons, some of them measurable, others not, it appears that the attitude of the nation toward revivalism was shifting as the eighties began. Moody, with his great sensitivity towards popular moods and feelings, may have sensed this shift intuitively and realized that his message, and the tactics that accompanied that message, would have to change. After all, each of the crucial junctures of his career rested on just such a sudden veering into new paths. The move from Boston to Chicago, the shift from business to full-time religious work, the determination to leave the midwest for England and big-time revivalism, were all a part of a pattern of decision-making based on hunches that seems quite appropriate when applied again in 1878 and 1879. It may also be that he was the kind of man who liked to drop something once he had it going, moving to new fields of endeavor as others continued to build upon the foundations he had constructed.

Between the autumn of 1879 and the early months of 1881, Moody embarked formally on his new course of action. During that time he founded the Northfield Seminary, a preparatory school for girls, and then Mount Hermon School for boys. Together they quickly became known as the "Northfield Schools." It was probably no more than accidental that the girls' school appeared first. A philanthropist-businessman in Boston, Henry Durant, probably helped to crystallize Moody's thoughts into

6. After the 1870's, mass revivalism did not lie in ashes for long. Moody's continuing activities in this capacity cannot be ignored. In addition, evangelists of lesser stature, men like Reuben J. Torrey, Sam Jones, Wilbur J. Chapman, William Biederwolf, Charles Alexander, B. Fay Mills, and "Gypsy" Smith, helped to nurse the revival tradition along, making important contributions in perfecting the techniques first devised by Moody. Scarcely a decade after Moody's death, in the same cities where the New Englander preached, Billy Sunday drew great crowds into his wooden tabernacles to hear the familiar gospel messages, and a new round of nationwide religious enthusiasm had begun. For details of all these developments, see William G. McLoughlin, *Modern Revivalism: Charles Grandison Finney to Billy Graham* (New York: Ronald Press, 1959), chaps. 6, 7; Bernard Weisberger, *They Gathered at the River: The Story of the Great Revivalists and Their Impact upon Religion in America* (Boston: Little, Brown and Co., 1958), pp. 220–43.

action. The two men had first met in the sixties, and the evangelist stayed at Durant's home during the Boston revival of 1877. A leading proponent of higher education for women, Durant had founded Wellesley College in 1875. Moody visited Wellesley several times and saw there a college grounded on the *Bible* and a strong program of self-help. His own schools were soon to reflect a similar spirit.[7]

The evangelist undertook the task of establishing the girls' academy with typical suddenness and directness. Another close businessman friend from Boston, H. N. F. Marshall, visited Moody at Northfield for the first time early in 1878. During this visit the revivalist broached his idea of a school to his visitor, and with customary persuasiveness soon had the Bostonian enthusiastically enlisted in his cause. With Marshall's backing Moody purchased a tract of land near his home immediately, then expanded these holdings in the months that followed. In August, 1879, workmen began construction of the first building on the new campus, a combination recitation hall–dormitory designed to accommodate one hundred students.[8] Since it was expected that the school would open before the building was completed, Moody made alterations in his own home during the summer of 1879, and here the ladies' seminary opened officially on November 3 of the same year. Twenty-five girls lived and attended classes in the evangelist's household until the new building was available a month later.[9]

7. Thomas Coyle, ed., *The Story of Mt. Hermon* (Mount Hermon, Mass.: Mount Hermon Alumni Association, 1906), pp. 10–11. Moody became a trustee of Wellesley College and Durant returned the favor by serving on the first board of trustees of the girls' school. (William R. Moody, *D. L. Moody* [New York: Macmillan Co., 1930], pp. 305–06.)

8. *Handbook of the Northfield Seminary and the Mt. Hermon School* (Northfield, 1889); D. L. Moody to H. N. F. Marshall, May 6, 1879, October 10, 1879, October 15, 1879, October 31, 1879, typewritten copies of original letters, Documents, Northfield Schools; *Greenfield* [Mass.] *Gazette and Courier*, June 2, 1879; *Franklin County* [Mass.] *Registry of Deeds*, 344:112, 123, 124, 125.

9. *Handbook of Northfield Seminary*, pp. 16–18; *Greenfield* [Mass.] *Gazette and Courier*, August 18, 1879, August 25, 1879, November 24, 1879. The school did not receive its official incorporation papers until February 12, 1881. A handwritten copy of the charter is in the W. R. Moody Papers, East Northfield, Massachusetts.

Moody had always included the idea of an academy for boys in his plans. In November, 1879, when a choice plot of ground just across the Connecticut River from Northfield was put up for sale, Marshall, acting as an agent for the evangelist who was preaching at the moment in the Midwest, made the necessary arrangements and purchased the land. Not until a year later, however, when Moody received a gift of $25,000 from Hiram Camp, a well-to-do clock manufacturer from New Haven, did the plans for the boys' school materialize fully. This money enabled the evangelist and his friends to purchase additional land and to renovate farm buildings included in these purchases into classrooms and living quarters. The Mount Hermon School for boys opened its doors on May 4, 1881.[10]

The idea that came to fruition in 1879 had long been germinating in Moody's mind. As part of his work at North Market Hall in Chicago during the Civil War, he had given some thought to a plan for starting a school in which the boys of his mission might be trained in elementary English and the *Bible*. But this was no more than a pipe dream. Twenty years later, however, Moody was a famous man, able to attract men willing to assist him and large sums of money to finance his schemes. These were factors that transformed the earlier dream into reality.[11] Moreover, there were plenty of backcountry youngsters in and around Northfield who might respond to an offer of education at nominal costs, and since the town had no high school, there would be little competition.

10. *Handbook of Northfield Seminary*, pp. 135–41; *Franklin County Registry of Deeds*, 343:104–07; 345:227; *Greenfield* [Mass.] *Gazette and Courier*, September 1, 1879, November 17, 1879, October 4, 1880. Incorporation papers were filed on September 14, 1881. A copy of these papers is in Documents, Northfield Schools.

11. The contributions of Camp and Marshall underscore the importance of the support of businessmen in enabling Moody to bring his plans to fruition. Other Boston and New York business leaders also played prominent roles in the founding of the two schools. Moody himself once thanked Marshall for his efforts. In a letter written in late 1879 he told his friend that he had never "even *thanked* you for all your time in this matter but I want to do so with all *my* heart. I am quite shure the girls' school never would have been up if you had not taken hold of it." (D. L. Moody to H. N. F. Marshall, October 31, 1879, Documents, Northfield Schools.)

Thus one of the purposes for the founding of the two sec. ondary schools was to afford opportunities for young men and women "whose means could not permit them to attend some of the excellent schools now in progress." [12] Perhaps recalling his own poverty as a youth, Moody sought to give a boost to young people held back by lack of money. Costs at the schools were kept to a minimum, aided in part by a work program for the students. This program was particularly emphasized at Mount Hermon where the boys ran a farm connected with the school and also provided most of the school's janitorial service.[13] In such a way was Moody able to implement his belief that special virtues were learned by those who were willing to work hard. Officials at Mount Hermon made this purpose quite explicit in their school catalogue. The primary aim of the work program was "to provide for physical culture . . . form habits of industry, and inculcate right views of manual labor." [14]

The practical success achieved in implementing these aims can be ascertained in part by a report from a visitor to the schools in 1886. About half the Hermon boys remained in Northfield in the summer months to provide the many services demanded by the hundreds of conference-goers who flocked to Moody's town at that time. There seemed to be a special spirit in the way they went about things, however. "There are no sluggards in Mr. Moody's school," wrote the observer. "Give one of these boys a letter for the train, the station is a mile away, and it gets there if it is a possible thing." Moreover, the spirit of enterprise seemed to affect the whole lot of youths. "They have organized a boot-black brigade, set up a barbering establishment, run two or three news-stands for the sale of the *Republican* every morning, wait on the tables in the white, large dining hall and in countless ways minister to the comfort or necessities of the visitors and make an honest nickel for themselves. They are," the writer concluded,

12. "Prospectus, Northfield Young Ladies Seminary, 1879," included in *Northfield Seminary Calendars, 1879–1889.* See also *Mt. Hermon Catalogue,* 1886 (Boston, 1886).

13. *Handbook of Northfield Seminary,* p. 191; circular entitled "Northfield Young Ladies Seminary," bound in *Northfield Seminary Calendars, 1879–1889; Mt. Hermon Catalogue, 1886,* pp. 7–8.

14. *Mt. Hermon Catalogue, 1886,* p. 8.

"a very promising set." Obviously Moody's young friends were learning, in the apt phrase of one of the evangelist's friends, not to "eat the bread of idleness." Nursed at Northfield on ideals of thrift, diligence, and Godliness, possessed of an education that would help them to rise above their obscure origins, the students would soon qualify as the best of the self-made men and women of their day.[15]

The religious purposes of the two schools were of great significance to the founder. The first announcement of the Seminary made Moody's intentions clear by asserting that "the Bible is intended to form the basis not only of the belief, but of the life, of the institution." The Biblical and theological courses soon became the core of the curriculum of the two academies. Gradually there also developed a distinctive spirit which affected the entire community of the two schools. This was perhaps a deeper reflection of this religious concern. In 1894 a committee of Harvard professors visited Mount Hermon and were particularly struck by these conditions. One examiner commented on the "unpolished earnestness" of the faculty that "commands respect and keeps it." Another noted that school officials believed that the religious instruction should bind the students together "into a harmonious working force and certainly that result is, in some way or other attained."[16] Evidently Moody's hope that personal piety and religious commitment might find strong expression in his new institutions of learning was being realized even in the more informal expressions of daily life of faculty and students.

The evangelist also entertained more specific ideas about the role his schools ought to play in the larger religious community. He hoped that they would become schools for the training of evangelists like himself who would spread the gospel effectively throughout the country. This idea was of fundamental significance to him. Mount Hermon was to be the chief training center

15. *Springfield* [Mass.] *Republican*, July 10, 1886; *Evangelistic Record*, 1 (April, 1882): 14.
16. The first quotation in the paragraph comes from the circular, "Northfield Young Ladies Seminary, 1879." The statements of the Harvard professors are quoted in Richard W. Day, *A New England Schoolmaster: The Life of Henry Franklin Cutler* (Bristol, Conn.: Hildreth Press, 1950), pp. 108, 109.

in the East.[17] The idea also became the principal motivation behind the founding of the Bible Institute in Chicago later in the decade. In 1886, as Moody began his campaign to open the Institute, he talked publicly about the common function of all of his schools. He described the students at Mount Hermon and the Bible Institute as "sort of middlemen to stand in the breach; men who will give their time to visiting the homes of the people, hold cottage meetings and meetings in halls and stores . . . men who will strike night after night, and follow up the work among the people."[18]

These words of the evangelist confirm again his changing attitude toward evangelization. The Northfield schools, and later the Bible Institute, were to be another means by which he could inject new life into the church. Perhaps in this way the ultimate effect on the world at large would be greater than by his direct, personal assaults through revivals upon religious indifference. It does not seem a mere coincidence that he was conducting his revivals in Baltimore and St. Louis, campaigns which emphasized reviving the churches before arousing the unsaved, at the very moment that he and his friends were swinging wide the doors of the academies in Northfield.

There was also a more practical need for workers of the sort suggested here, growing out of Moody's experience as a revivalist.

17. See the description of a separate curriculum for "students preparing for special Christian work," in the *Mt. Hermon Catalogue, 1886*, p. 11. A statement made in 1882 by Miss Harriet Tuttle, then head-mistress of the Seminary, expresses her understanding of the purposes of the girls' school. Miss Tuttle said nothing about mission work which the young ladies were to undertake, like the boys at Mount Hermon. (*Evangelistic Record*, 1 [March, 1882]: 13.) Compare Miss Tuttle's words with those of a supporter of Mount Hermon about that school's general purposes, *ibid.* (April, 1884): 4.

18. *Record of Christian Work*, 5 (March, 1886): 1. Moody was entertaining thoughts of this sort long before he opened his schools. His experience in England once more influenced him a great deal. As early as 1874, while in the British Isles, Moody published a letter which showed that his ideas on the need for practical training of lay people to make them effective urban evangelists were already fully developed. This earlier appeal for such training programs directly affected the thoughts of T. J. Barnardo and William Booth, two of the best-known urban evangelists among the English evangelicals in the late nineteenth century. (*Christian* [June 11, 1874]: 6; [June 18, 1874]: 6.)

One of the major problems the evangelist faced in the inquiry rooms was an adequate number of qualified assistants. He felt acutely the lack of lay people with ample knowledge of the Scriptures who could converse effectively with inquirers. By the eighties his ideas had broadened somewhat and he recognized the necessity to prepare people for evangelistic work outside, as well as within, revival campaigns. But the need remained the same. In 1888 a close friend, writing a formal letter to raise funds for the evangelist's many projects, spoke Moody's mind for him. Out of the two schools in his hometown the revivalist hoped to draw "helpers" in evangelism, "well equipped for their work." Although not all the graduates of the schools were destined to enter into religious vocations directly, the writer concluded that "the central original and underlying purpose is always kept in sight of in these schools, offering the favorably [*sic*] general education for those whom God shall call, as helpers in the special field of evangelistic work." [19]

Given the environment in which he chose to work, it was not too surprising that Moody first tried to implement his new ambitions by means of two private academies. Northfield was located in a region of western Massachusetts which, even in the nineteenth century, was known for its fine educational institutions. One of the evangelist's college-age friends, John R. Mott, dramatized this fact in 1889. Describing a trip to the summit of Mount Tom, a landmark in the Connecticut River Valley, Mott was struck by the vista of educational institutions which stretched out before him in the valley. "From Nonotuck [Mount Tom] you see the grove that just hides from the eye Mr. Moody's Mt. Hermon School for Boys and his Ladies Seminary. A few

19. T. W. Harvey to "friend," November 16, 1888, Nettie Fowler McCormick Papers, Wisconsin State Historical Society, Madison, Wisconsin. The fact that Harvey wrote the letter as Moody's representative suggests that the letter writer did not misstate the evangelist's basic ideas. Further evidence supporting the assumptions expressed in Harvey's letter is in an unsigned form letter (presumably another of Moody's "begging" letters sent to many acquaintances), in the papers of Henry M. Rankin, Mount Hermon School Library, Mount Hermon, Massachusetts; and in the comments of R. C. Morgan during a visit to Northfield in 1881, printed in *Christian* (September 1, 1881): 10.

miles South you see the Mass. Agricultural College. A mile from it stands Amherst College. . . . To the left lies Smith College from which pass annually scores of consecrated young women. Williston Seminary is only a few miles off. . . . Looking Southward one first sees Mt. Holyoke Seminary — or college. . . . The eye readily takes in Hartford where old Trinity College . . . stands. Away to the South & to the right — just out of sight — lies Wesleyan University." [20] The Northfield Schools began as they did in part because of their proximity to many schools of a similar sort. Moody was not so ambitious as to think of starting a college, but private secondary schools like his own were also typical of the area and were patterned in many ways after the system of collegiate education that flourished throughout the Connecticut Valley.[21]

Once established as secondary schools, the competitive environment forced Moody's institutions to follow certain paths to survive. Of primary importance would be an educational program of high quality. The early years at Mount Hermon confirmed this need fully, when a combination of untoward developments precipitated a great deal of confusion. Moody left Northfield in September, 1881, to begin another extended revival campaign in Great Britain. For the next three years, excepting the summer of 1883, he was outside the country. This absence worked a greater hardship on Mount Hermon than on the Seminary, for the boys' school had just opened when he left, whereas the girls' school was already a going concern. Significantly, too, Mount Hermon had no headmaster for the first two years of its existence. Initially a personal friend of Moody's, Julius J. Estey, a businessman in nearby Brattleboro, Vermont, tried to oversee operations, sandwiching visits to the institution into his daily schedule. The first headmaster, secured in 1883, fell ill shortly after assuming his duties and retired after one year. Not until 1884, when Henry E. Sawyer, a graduate of Dartmouth College, became superin-

20. John R. Mott to "Mother," October 10, 1889, John R. Mott Papers, Yale Divinity School.
21. Little work has been done recently on the history of the academy movement in this country. A brief survey of the nineteenth century, with helpful footnotes, is in Theodore Sizer, ed., *The Age of the Academies* (New York: Columbia University Press, 1964), pp. 1–48.

tendent, did the school receive much direct and sustained guidance at the top.[22]

Chaos was almost inevitable. Mount Hermon was without a graded system of study until 1885. Admission requirements were practically non-existent, and as a result few of the early students were prepared for work at the secondary level. In the first two years, half of the student body were less than twelve years old. Many were orphans, and students from countries overseas, attracted by Moody's fame, added to the difficulties. By 1886 administrative officials began to reverse the tide of affairs, however, by setting minimum age standards for entering students, organizing the faculty into departments, and systematizing the curriculum on a basis quite similar to that of the Seminary across the river. On June 28, 1887, the first graduating class at Mount Hermon marched across the platform, further evidence that the school was achieving stability.[23] Yet as it became more effective educationally it also became more like the other academies in the area. Whether desired or not, the future course of the school was being determined in fundamental ways by these events.

Leadership at the two academies also shaped the contours of historical development. From the beginning the Seminary had close associations with Wellesley College. Henry Durant served on the first board of trustees of the school, although his death in 1881 prevented him from making further personal contribution to

22. *Handbook of Northfield Seminary*, pp. 145, 151, 154–55, 156.
23. Coyle, *Story of Mt. Hermon*, pp. 24, 25, 143, 145–46, 177; "Report of the Superintendent to the Board of Trustees, Mt. Hermon School, 1884," handwritten MS, and "Rules," typewritten copy of regulations concerning student conduct, approved by board of trustees of Mount Hermon, March, 1882, Documents, Northfield Schools; *Mt. Hermon School Catalogues*, 1886–1890. The educational program at both academies developed around the so-called "scientific" and "classical" courses. The scientific course, emphasizing English literature, composition, history, and mathematics and some natural science, was intended for those with no further educational plans. The classical course served to prepare qualified students for college. This program stressed Latin and Greek, eliminating such courses as bookkeeping, civil government, and many of the natural science offerings. (*Mt. Hermon Catalogue*, 1886, pp. 11–12; *Catalogue of the Officers and Students of Northfield Seminary, 1882–1883* [Boston, 1882], pp. 12–15.)

the work at Northfield.[24] The first teacher and principal had been a student at Wellesley and was recommended personally by Durant to Moody. During the first decade, almost half the teachers at the girls' school were either graduates of or onetime students at the parent college. By the mid-eighties the boys' school was also attracting college-trained people to its staff. About half the teachers had some college experience, including former students at Amherst, Bowdoin, Mt. Holyoke, Oberlin, Wellesley, and Williams.[25] Given the tasks they were to perform and the reasonably good educational backgrounds they possessed, it was to be expected that teachers and administrators conceived of the two schools' progress chiefly in terms of improved educational standards.

Moody's personal influence on his schools left clearly identifiable marks. Since he lived in Northfield it would be expected that he would play a special role in the life of the institutions there. All the evidence indicates that he strongly impressed his personality on the minds of most of the students, faculty, and administrators. His personal example contributed a great deal to the distinctive atmosphere that permeated the academies. Having grounded his own life on study and daily application of the *Bible,* he established a similar emphasis in the everyday activities at his schools. The evangelical Sabbath was observed in all its rigor. In order to avoid keeping anyone from observing the Lord's day properly, cooks prepared Sunday meals on Saturday, and at Mount Hermon no classes were held on Monday to allow the boys to study the secular subjects they were asked to avoid the preceding day.[26]

In a variety of ways Moody sought to inculcate in the students his personal belief in piety, hard work, and scholarship. At commencements he personally awarded formal prizes for improve-

24. There is no record of monetary gifts to the schools in these early years. Durant continued on the board until his death. He also spoke at the cornerstone-laying of the first building on the Seminary campus in 1879. (Copy of original charter, Northfield Seminary, in W. R. Moody Papers; *Greenfield* [Mass.] *Gazette and Courier,* August 25, 1879.)

25. W. R. Moody, *Moody* (1930), pp. 305–06; *Handbook of Northfield Seminary,* pp. 195–96, 201–02.

26. Day, *New England Schoolmaster,* pp. 98–99, 103; Coyle, *Story of Mt. Hermon,* pp. 59–65.

ment in handwriting, deportment, and excellence in *Bible* study. More informally, he once invited a group of students with outstanding records to join his family on a two weeks' trip to the White Mountains. Graduates could later recite endless stories of small monetary rewards that the evangelist impulsively handed out when he discovered a student in need or one whose work particularly pleased him. He preached frequently in chapel at both schools. The first Sunday night of every term was reserved especially for him, as was the baccaleureate sermon at the close of the school year each spring. Frequently before starting on a major evangelistic mission he would call a prayer meeting so that students could pray with him for his success. For a number of years he had a "Hermon Male Quartette" assist him in his evangelistic tours. In this way he gave the students a sense of sharing directly in his work.[27]

Besides the direct effect he had on students and faculty at Mount Hermon and the Seminary, Moody raised most of the money needed to finance daily operations at his schools. This was a familiar task, reminding one of similar work he did for the Chicago YMCA in the 1860's and for many local associations when he "passed the hat" for them at the end of his revival campaigns in the seventies. Throughout the eighties and nineties Moody also raised thousands of dollars annually to finance the student work of the International Committee of the YMCA.[28] Thus it was logical that he tried to assist his educational institutions by performing tasks he knew he could handle. His success in financing the two schools in Northfield and eventually the Bible Institute in Chicago was indeed a major achievement. From 1879 until his death twenty years later his total solicitations for

27. The files of the student newspaper, *The Hermonite*, published jointly by the schools, are particularly revealing about these aspects of Moody's relations with the students. See especially the issues for October 5, 1888, June 7, 1889, September 27, 1890, February 17, 1894, October 6, 1894, May 18, 1895. See also Coyle, *Story of Mt. Hermon*, pp. 30, 48, 49–50, 51–53, 56; *Advance*, 20 (February 19, 1885): 118.

28. "Letters in the Interest of College Work Sent by Mr. Moody, 1885–1896," mimeographed copies, YMCA Historical Library, New York City; Richard C. Morse to George H. Stuart, William E. Dodge, and John V. Farwell, April 10, 1883, R. C. Morse to W. E. Dodge, April 10, 1883, YMCA Historical Library.

the three schools amounted to about $1,800,000.[29] It was chiefly through the evangelist's personal attempts at fund-raising that the schools remained solvent during this time.

In spite of his essential contributions to the ventures in education in Northfield, Moody's day-to-day role was a rather nominal one. Occasionally the founder recommended someone for the teaching staff, and he frequently influenced the selection of outside speakers who appeared at the schools. The latter were often his personal friends. He also unhesitatingly recruited students whenever possible.[30] But he never actively intervened in the daily

29. This figure is only roughly approximate, since all statistics used are imprecise. A large portion of the money came from a "hymnbook fund" representing the royalties from the sale of the Moody and Sankey hymn book. The trust fund was administered by three nationally-known businessmen. After 1880 the Northfield Schools received nearly all of the proceeds, which were applied to current expenses and the construction costs of new buildings. In addition Moody raised a great deal of money by personal solicitation, which he also poured into the operational budgets of the schools, and later of the Bible Institute. ("Statement of the Treasurer, Mt. Hermon School [1888–1889]," Documents, Northfield Schools; *New York Tribune,* June 6, 1894; Thomas K. Cree, unpublished typewritten MS [no date, no title], YMCA Historical Library, p. 10; John R. Mott, *The Larger Evangelism* [New York, Nashville: Abingdon-Cokesbury Press, 1944], p. 51.) For examples of Moody's "begging letters" to prospective donors, see D. L. Moody to "Mr. Dwight," September 22, 1888; September 22, 1892; May 23, 26, 1894, all in Moody Papers, Moody Bible Institute; D. L. Moody to "Mr. Aylsworth," December 22, 1892, Emma C. Moody to Mrs. Billings (no date), typewritten copies of originals, Moody Papers, Powell. Strong support for the Northfield schools also came from England. Gifts from Moody's friends there made possible several of the buildings on the two campuses, and additional donations in the form of money and a herd of cattle for the Mount Hermon farm came from overseas. (Elsie Scott, "Educational Pioneering in New England," [unpublished typewritten MS], Northfield Seminary Library, pp. 57, 61; D. L. Moody to H. N. F. Marshall, October 10, 1879, May 28, 1884, Documents, Northfield Schools, Northfield, Massachusetts; *Advance,* 20 [February 12, 1885]: 98, [February 19, 1885]: 117.)

30. *Handbook of Northfield Seminary,* pp. 200–204; Coyle, *Story of Mt. Hermon,* p. 149; *Greenfield* [Mass.] *Gazette and Courier,* May 17, 1880. Already by 1882 the seminary drew its student body from New York, Delaware, Connecticut, New Hampshire, and Vermont, as well as from many parts of Massachusetts. The first listing of students at Mount Hermon in the catalogue was in 1892. In that year boys came from 29 states and 14 foreign countries. (*Catalogue of the Officers and Students of Northfield Seminary, 1882–1883* [Boston, 1882], pp. 2–3;

running of the academies. The saving grace of his common sense told him to let college-trained educators do the actual administration. And this meant that the evangelist's distinctive personal stamp could not be impressed as deeply on these institutions as it had been on the edifice of mass revivalism created in the 1870's.

Although his spirit manifested itself in a hundred different highly personal ways on the campuses of the two academies, over the years the founder's vision of the Northfield Schools as training centers for practical evangelism seemed increasingly farther from realization. At least until his death in 1899 this vision served as the general purpose of the schools. But a carefully worked-out program of studies designed to implement the evangelist's idea never achieved the primacy he intended in Northfield. In 1889, in a draft of the *Handbook* describing the schools and their brief history, Henry W. Rankin, a young faculty member at Mount Hermon, had asserted that "the supreme aim" of the boys' school was "to provide an academy training, either English or Classical." Henry B. Sawyer, the headmaster, administered a rebuke to the young man by repeating his understanding of Moody's purposes for the schools. The evangelist "had no desire to start another academy or high school like the many excellent ones already existing," said Sawyer. Rather, it was "Mr. Moody's desire to send out from Mount Hermon, . . . men of deep piety and with more knowledge of the Bible than most Christian laymen have, to tell or sing the story of the cross in neglected old towns, on the far and new frontiers, and in the degradation of city slums." [31]

Clearly Sawyer had grasped Moody's intentions and was defending them vigorously. On the other hand, Rankin's words, which never found their way into the final version of the *Handbook,* perhaps struck closer to the historical truth of what was happening in Northfield. The tension caused by the divergence between hopes and reality was thus made explicit. With these

Catalogue of Mt. Hermon School, 1891–92 [Mt. Hermon, Mass., 1892], pp. 15–22.)

31. Henry B. Sawyer to Henry W. Rankin, June 9, 1889, Rankin Papers, Mount Hermon School Library. Sawyer quotes Rankin's words concerning the purposes of the school before attempting to refute them.

developments in mind, it is easier to understand why Moody chose to launch another school in 1886, this time in Chicago. Not that the academies in Northfield had failed him, but rather that friends in Illinois seemed to be offering him the opportunity to organize an institution that came to grips more directly and immediately with the problems of city evangelization, an issue that weighed heavily on his mind. Thus it was that the evangelist went back to the Midwest and tried again, much more specifically and concretely than in the East, to implement his concept of a school for evangelists. Chiefly because the environment and the leadership in Chicago were different, Moody's plan was carried out more successfully this time.

A number of the evangelist's Chicago friends had long harbored the hope that Moody would return to their city to spread the gospel in some more lasting way than by a brief revival campaign. A group of such supporters existed within the business community, chiefly men who had been associated with Moody in the Chicago YMCA in the 1860's. The circle included people like Turlington W. Harvey, a millionaire lumber dealer, E. G. Keith, a banker and real estate investor, Nathaniel S. Bouton, owner of a large foundry and iron works, Moody's close friend John V. Farwell, and the family of Cyrus H. McCormick, the famous farm implement inventor and manufacturer. These men possessed more than ordinary financial resources and were ready to stand behind any proposal Moody might make to advance his cause in Chicago.[32]

Another person with hopes and ambitions linked to the evangelist was Miss Emma Dryer. She was a woman of considerable ability — for her day an unusual individual. She had graduated from college and had been on the faculty of Illinois Normal University in the 1860's. Deeply religious, with a desire to "do good" in the world, she came to Chicago about 1870 to set up a home for wayward girls in the slums of the city. She soon met Moody and thereafter frequently attended meetings at the young evan-

32. Emmet Dedmon, *Great Enterprises: 100 Years of the YMCA of Metropolitan Chicago* (Chicago: Rand McNally, 1957), pp. 41–42; Bernard R. DeRemer, *Moody Bible Institute: A Pictorial History* (Chicago: Moody Press, 1960), pp. 18–20.

gelist's tabernacle on the near north side. In the spring of 1873, with encouragement from her friend, Emma Dryer established a school of "Bible Work," devoted to a program of personal evangelism among the poor, including house to house visitations, women's prayer meetings, and tract distribution. "Sewing schools" for young women were also held weekly; the number of girls thus trained "to habits of neatness and industry" were "very large." The Bible Work began in Moody's church, but moved eventually to quarters in the YMCA building further downtown.[33]

Although the evangelist left Chicago permanently only a month or two after Miss Dryer established her little school, the two people maintained contact with each other. They met in New York City in 1876 in the midst of Moody's great revival at the Hippodrome and laid tentative plans for the establishment of a permanent home for Miss Dryer's work near Moody's old church, now rebuilt and renamed the Chicago Avenue Church. The evangelist also encouraged Miss Dryer to visit England, in order to observe the manifold activities of the evangelicals there in the field of urban evangelism. She carried out his suggestion in 1879–80, living for a number of weeks at the Deaconess House at Mildmay, accompanying the women of that institution on their round of duties in London. With Moody's help she also contacted his friends associated with the Central YMCA in London and thus was able to study firsthand many facets of the work of the evangelical groups in the great English metropolis.[34]

The crushing burden of work associated with his revival campaigns in the late seventies, and then his deep involvement in the new developments at Northfield in the early eighties, kept Moody from bringing to fruition the long-held promises he had made to Miss Dryer to widen her work in Chicago. But she never

33. W. H. Daniels, *D. L. Moody and His Work* (Hartford, Conn.: American Publishing Co., 1875), pp. 187–88; Emma Dryer, "Reminiscences of the Founding of Moody Bible Institute," (unpublished typewritten MS., January, 1916), in the possession of Mr. Gene Getz, Moody Bible Institute, pp. 1, 2, 5–6, 10, 12; circular entitled "Bible Work," Nettie Fowler McCormick Papers; *Interior*, 5 (November 19, 1874): 2; *Evangelistic Record*, 1 (December, 1881): 11; (March, 1882): 5.
34. Dryer, "Reminiscences," pp. 11, 17, 20.

gave up hope that the evangelist would return some day and help his friends with their efforts among the city poor. Throughout the first half of the eighties a number of Chicagoans maintained their importunities. They held meetings with Moody in 1884, just after his return from a second revival tour of Great Britain, to consider opportunities for evangelism in Chicago. And a religious journal published in the Windy City by a close relative of the revivalist, Fleming H. Revell, occasionally dropped pointed comments about the need for Moody's return.[35]

Suddenly, early in 1886, the evangelist came to Chicago to launch a new effort in evangelism. On January 22, 1886, at a midday meeting in the Loop especially designed to attract the city's businessmen, Moody set forth his plans. He hoped to establish a "training school for Christian workers," chiefly for city missions. With characteristic boldness he asked the people in his audience to raise $250,000 to assure the success of his venture. Not until Chicagoans had raised that sum would he commit himself further. But this did seem to be the call to action that his friends had long been awaiting to deal with the "unsaved masses" of their city.[36]

In those years, whenever evangelical Protestants with middle-class standing invoked the phrase "the masses," it seemed to convey a scarcely suppressed sense of unease about disorderly, uneducated ruffians who clogged the streets of cities. Or at best the

35. *Ibid.*, pp. 17, 21–24; *Chicago Inter-Ocean*, January 23, 1886; *Record of Christian Work*, 4 (October, 1885): 1; 5 (January, 1886): 1. The businessmen previously mentioned were all connected in one way or another with Miss Dryer's Bible Work at the downtown YMCA. See list of members of board of trustees included in circular intitled "Partial Summary" (report on the activities of Miss Dryer's organization, first quarter, 1886), in Nettie Fowler McCormick Papers.

36. *Record of Christian Work*, 5 (January, 1886): 1, provides a detailed account of Moody's speech. There is some evidence to suggest that Moody entered the meeting in Farwell Hall lacking preconceived notions that at this moment his plans were about to jell. Another account suggests that enthusiastic responses from his audience to his talk on the need for city evangelization caused him to seize his opportunity and propose the fund-raising plan that he did. The spontaneity of the meeting, and Moody's ability to capitalize upon such feelings, would accord fully with the way he had often worked in the past. (*Advance*, 21 [January 28, 1886]: 57.) Other reports of the gathering are in the *Chicago Tribune*, January 23, 1886; *Chicago Inter-Ocean*, January 23, 1886.

phrase cast into the limbo of stereotype the working-class elements of the population that were beneath them in the social order. For a few evangelicals, perhaps, the phrase meant merely all those people outside the church, who could be found "in splendid mansions along the fine avenues" of any city, as well as among the poor set apart in special sections of the great urban centers.[37] Moody's understanding of the term sometimes seemed to approximate this latter definition.[38] But he was never exact and consistent in his application of terminology, and thus frequently he assumed the more prevalent attitude that the urban "masses" were lower-class people — chiefly immigrants, the poor, and industrial laborers. In any case the unchurched in the cities, whatever their social backgrounds, were of great concern to Protestants in the post–Civil War era.[39] Consequently Moody's special appeal to establish a training school for missionaries to the urban masses was bound to fall generally on receptive ears.

The evangelist's concern with missionary work in the cities is known to be of long standing. His visits to the great industrial centers of England in the early seventies seemed to have had a special effect upon him in this respect. By the time he reached the great steel center of Sheffield in northern England, the appalling social conditions he had witnessed forced him to cite statistics about Sheffield — 150,000 people who "never go near a place of worship, but for whom there is actually no church accommodation provided, even if they are willing to take advantage of it." This was an "appalling state of things," the more so because it implied "thousands of dead and slumbering Christians," who were "rubbing shoulders with" these people every day, yet "never as much as lifting up a little finger to warn them of death,

37. *Interior*, 23 (September 1, 1892): 11.

38. *Christian*, (April 10, 1884): 6; *Chicago Inter-Ocean*, January 23, 1886.

39. For examples of discussion of the problem of city evangelization and the "masses" in evangelical periodicals, see *Zion's Herald*, 45 (January 9, 1868): 19–20; (June 11, 1868): 283; *Northwestern Christian Advocate*, 17 (August 11, 1869): 252; *New York Evangelist*, 40 (July 8, 1869): 1; (September 9, 1869): 6; (November 4, 1869): 6; 45 (September 3, 1874): 2; 47 (May 18, 1876): 2; 46 (March 18, 1875): 6; *New York Christian Advocate*, 17 (May 2, 1872): 140; *Interior*, 5 (April 2, 1874): 1; 6 (September 2, 1875): 4; (November 18, 1875): 4.

and eternity, and the judgment to come. . . . What is to be done about the masses?" Moody asked rhetorically. "Let us all contribute to the answering of it, and contribute in deeds as well as in words," was his immediate reply.[40]

These last words were bravely spoken but they lacked specific content. We have traced a few of Moody's efforts to fill his words with content — his encouragement of Emma Dryer's work in Chicago, his own efforts with the academies in Northfield — and there is evidence that he struggled elsewhere to devise some way other than the sweeping impulse of the mass revival to reach the thousands in the cities languishing outside the churches.[41] Now in 1886 came the opportunity to build a school with the mission field at its doorstep. This seemed to be a real step forward in the battle to overcome the forces of evil in the great urban centers of the nation. And it simplified a problem which plagued Moody in Northfield, that of initiating the students into city missionary activities while they were still involved in their studies. The students in Chicago could be thrust immediately into evangelistic work, and thus they could learn by doing. The possibility of linking urban evangelism directly with the program of his school undoubtedly appealed to Moody, and provides a partial explanation of why he returned to the Midwest to help create the new institution.[42]

40. *Christian* (January 21, 1875): 6. Moody's statements made in England in 1875 were subsequently circulated in this country, reprinted in their entirety in the *New York Evangelist*, 46 (February 18, 1875): 6.
41. *London Daily News*, March 25, 1875, March 31, 1875; *Methodist* [London], 2 (April 23, 1875): 4; Emma Moody to Edwin Moody, April 19, 1882, Moody Papers, Moody Bible Institute, Chicago.
42. Moody occasionally connected urban evangelism with the Northfield schools. See the *New York Tribune*, August 4, 1892; undated, unsigned letter (probably dictated by Moody), Rankin Papers. On the other hand, see the statement by the evangelist comparing the purposes of Mount Hermon and the Bible Institute in Chicago in *Record of Christian Work*, 5 (March, 1886): 1–2. In this instance he emphasized urban evangelism when referring to the work in Chicago, but omitted this emphasis from his words about Mount Hermon. For additional comments by Moody and his friends about the Bible Institute's concern for urban evangelism, see *Chicago Inter-Ocean*, January 23, 1886; D. L. Moody to "gentlemen," June 17, 1887, Moody Papers, Moody Bible Institute; T. W. Harvey to "friend," November 16, 1888, Nettie Fowler McCormick Papers; *Record of Christian Work*, 8 (March, 1889): 2.

The general economic and social conditions in the mid-eighties in Chicago also made this an appropriate moment for the evangelist's reappearance. For a long time tension had been growing between working-class groups and the managerial segments of the city's population. The depression of the seventies had caused intense distress among the laboring people, as it had throughout the nation. Chicago's large immigrant population also included a small number of men who openly espoused anarchist and Marxist views. These factors provided the seedbed for a flourishing radical movement among the city's lower classes in the eighties.

Following a brief economic upturn between 1881 and 1884, Chicago like the rest of the country headed into a new tailspin. Wages fell, unemployment figures grew, and strikes again became common in 1884 and 1885, centering at the Pullman Palace Car Company and at Cyrus McCormick's harvester works. A renewed interest in the eight-hour day, first advocated vigorously in the 1860's, also stirred labor circles in the city. Early in 1886 friction developed again between management and the workers at the McCormick plant. The conflict smoldered until early in May when discontent flashed up into the open and culminated ultimately in violence and the horror of the Haymarket riot. The fears of Moody and his friends of social upheaval seemingly had become a reality, and they viewed the future apprehensively, seeing in this whole chain of events a mounting threat to law and order and their own favored position in society.[43]

The task of urban evangelism now assumed an added sense of urgency. In March, 1886, the evangelist made his position clear.

43. Bessie Pierce, *A History of Chicago*, 3 vols. (New York: Alfred A. Knopf, 1937–57), vol. 3, chaps. 7, 8; Henry David, *The History of the Haymarket Affair: A Study in the American Social-Revolutionary and Labor Movements*, 2nd ed. (New York: Russell & Russell, 1958). Almost three years earlier, in the fall of 1883, while speaking at a Christian convention in Chicago, Moody outlined plans for a "training school" to prepare "a band of men and women," who would "stand in the gap" between the working classes and the church. His appeal fell on deaf ears at the time, however. It is hard not to resist the conclusion that further labor upheavals in the intervening period was a major factor in producing the very different response from Chicago businessmen in 1886 when Moody espoused his ideas once again. (*Evangelistic Record*, 2 [October, 1883]: 7–8.)

"Either these people are to be evangelized or the leaven of communism and infidelity will assume such enormous proportions that it will break out in a reign of terror such as this country has never known. It don't take a prophet or a son of a prophet to see these things. You can hear the muttering of the coming convulsion even now, if you open your ears and eyes." Moody's friends agreed with him entirely. In a letter written to publicize the evangelist's return, one of his closest advisors in Chicago sought to explain why church people should give the new institute strong support. His conclusion was that "the depressing consciousness of the extent and danger of the communistic element in our midst" had caused "many earnest Christian people" to feel that "the only way to convert this dangerous element into peaceful helpful citizens was through the transforming power of Christ." [44]

These words revealed a great deal about the motivation which lay behind the founding of the Bible Institute. The fusion of evangelism and stark conservatism is not suprising, given our knowledge of the social and economic views of Moody and of the respectable people in the churches who were his close friends and supporters. Moody's attitude corresponded perfectly with the general pattern of thought and feeling of those whom he served. It did mean, however, that the evangelist was far from free to attempt radically new methods in dealing with the deep divisions created in society by industrialization. To his friends, his work in Chicago seemed a fresh start, a promising departure from past evangelical practices of talking, yet doing relatively little about the unchurched masses in the cities. From the perspective of a later day, however, his venture in the Midwest seems much less of a challenge to existing conditions than people at the time considered it to be.

Nevertheless, the evangelist had perceived a real social need, and in spite of the limitations of his perspective, he was struggling to devise a way to come to grips effectively with that issue.

44. *Record of Christian Work*, 5 (April, 1886): 3; T. W. Harvey to "friend," November 16, 1888, Nettie Fowler McCormick Papers. See also form letter signed by Moody, March 15, 1889, and typewritten copy of form letter, D. L. Moody to "gentlemen," June 17, 1887, Moody Papers, Moody Bible Institute; *Record of Christian Work*, 5 (June, 1886): 2; *Chicago Inter-Ocean*, November 21, 1886.

He was fairly clear as to the broad purposes of his new school. He hoped the institution would produce workers without seminary degrees, yet with some formal theological training, who would go into city mission work. Appropriately enough, Moody dubbed these followers of his "gapmen." They were to be "men who know the Word" and who were to "go into the shops and meet these bareheaded infidels and skeptics," to appeal to them "in the name of Jesus Christ" so that their hearts would "soften under His precious Gospel." [45] This was to be the old missionary enterprise of the evangelical churches at work among the newly created urban masses.

Those inclined to be hostile to these proposals could quickly advance the argument that Moody was creating an institution which falsely led young men to believe they now had a chance to get a seminary education more easily and cheaply than had been true previously.[46] The evangelist did his best to counteract such claims. He argued that the need for workers in the cities was so overwhelming that laymen, as well as trained ministers, could be used immediately. His school, he once asserted, was strictly to "fit laymen for Christian work," and was not intended in any way to compete with the seminaries and their task of education.[47] Nevertheless, Moody's new work could easily be viewed as another effort of professional evangelists to undermine the regular structure of church organization. The historic antagonism that existed between lay evangelists like Moody and the ordained ministry might come to the surface once again. Moody recognized there were dangers in his new undertaking, but the urgency of the problem evidently overrode all other considerations.[48]

45. *Record of Christian Work*, 5 (February, 1886): 6.
46. For criticisms of this sort see *Interior*, 19 (October 10, 1889): 1; (October 17, 1889): 4; (October 24, 1889): 1.
47. *Ibid.*, 6 (April, 1887): 1; 9 (May, 1890): 6. There is an example of Moody's explicit criticism of seminary training vis-a-vis urban problems, *ibid.*, 8 (September, 1889): 3.
48. In 1916 Emma Dryer remembered that early in the 1870's, when she and Moody first discussed possible projects like the Bible Institute, even then the evangelist recognized the implicit threat such an undertaking would pose to the seminaries. Partly for that reason he first supported Miss Dryer's Bible Work, which dealt exclusively with women, and avoided any plan that included the education of young men. (Dryer,

Certainly there were ample historical precedents for Moody's "gapmen." Indeed that term is another way of describing the lay preacher who had long played a crucial role in evangelical groups both in England and America. The teachers in Wesleyan Sunday schools in eighteenth century England, the Methodist and Baptist circuit riders and farmer-preachers who crisscrossed the American frontier, the dozens of lay evangelists who plied their trade in the nineteenth century in both countries, all could be called "gapmen." Although Moody sought to make a bit more formal the preparation of these unordained workers for the Lord, the connection is clear between his "gapmen" and the historic Protestant tradition of carrying the gospel to the world through specially qualified and interested laymen.

The "gapmen" of earlier days had always been practical-minded. In Moody's eye his new school, much more than the two he had recently established on the East Coast, would have this practical emphasis. The evangelist himself described the program of the new school as "practical work" in "learning how to reach the masses." Students were certainly expected to study the Scriptures carefully, but Moody saw no need to burden them with some of the frills included then in seminary training. "Never mind the Greek and Hebrew," he declared. "Give them plain English and good Scripture. It is the sword of the Lord and cuts deep." Moreover, he felt the plan of study for each student should vary according to individual interests and special abilities. In his inimitable way the evangelist asserted that he did not propose "to make a regular groove . . . and break every bone in a man's body to make him fit it. Men have been spoiled that way," he went on, and he wanted to develop them, not spoil them.[49] Thus there was to be a looseness, a flexibility, and a practical orientation to the new school's program which had never quite been true of the work in the academies in Northfield.

"Reminiscences," p. 10.) The change in attitude a decade later is perhaps one indication of an alteration in power relationships. Moody could act in 1886 because he knew his public prestige was great enough to cause official church voices to hesitate before criticizing him openly. Such was not the case in the seventies.

49. *Record of Christian Work*, 5 (February, 1886): 5; 8 (September, 1889): 3; *Chicago Inter-Ocean*, January 23, 1886.

The self-help theme, stressed so vigorously at the schools in Massachusetts, reappeared in Chicago. Here, too, Moody wanted to encourage young people who, despite the handicap of meager beginnings, sought to make something of themselves. But this time self-help was to be linked more specifically to the cause of Christ. He wanted, he said, to make it possible for "a man without any education," who had "a passion for souls" and no "means to get 'em," to get the education he needed to work effectively for God. Combining a modicum of *Bible* study with evangelistic fervor, Moody was convinced his workers would soon find themselves transformed into successful missionaries. The evangelist summarized his point of view in a typically pungent phrase: "We want men who can do something uncommon. Any man can eat soup with a spoon, but the man who can eat it with a one-tined fork is a marvel." [50]

In the year following his first appeal to Chicagoans, Moody did little in a tangible way to bring his proposals to fruition. The $250,000 he deemed necessary was pledged during this time, yet in January, 1887, the school was still nothing more than Emma Dryer's Bible Work somewhat expanded. Something more grandiose had to be achieved. What seemed a promising first step came on February 12, 1887, when Moody and his friends chartered the Chicago Evangelization Society. Through this society the work of building the training school was to be carried out. Cyrus McCormick, Jr., T. W. Harvey, N. S. Bouton, E. G. Keith, and John Farwell were charter members. Miss Dryer and the mother of Cyrus Jr., Nettie Fowler McCormick, were also active in the group. Moody became the first president.[51] This was the first major

50. *Chicago Tribune*, September 27, 1889.
51. *Ibid.*, January 2, 1887; *Record of Christian Work*, 6 (April, 1887): 1; MS copy of charter, Moody Papers, Moody Bible Institute; Minutes, Board of Trustees' meetings, Chicago Evangelization Society, handwritten extracts in Moody Papers, Moody Bible Institute, February 17, 1887; hereinafter cited as Trustees' Minutes, C. E. S. In spite of his assertion that he would do nothing in Chicago until the businessmen of the city raised the money he demanded, Moody participated actively in the fund-raising program. He and his friends sought contributions from such prominent Chicagoans as Levi Z. Leiter, Potter Palmer, the Armour brothers, and Marshall Field. Nearly all were asked for $50,000 apiece. (D. L. Moody to N. F. McCormick, February 10, 1886,

step in creating the school which became Moody Bible Institute in the twentieth century.

From 1887 to 1890, however, the new society's efforts languished. Not until the fall of 1889 was the first building of the Bible Institute completed and the school officially opened. Lack of physical facilities in turn hindered the development of a consistent, long-range program by the Evangelization Society.[52] The greatest barrier to progress, however, lay in disagreements among the leaders. These controversies damaged all efforts to create an effective organization and program. Indeed, in the late summer of 1887 tension was so great that the entire project threatened to collapse in confusion.

Emma Dryer and the work she directed were at the heart of the difficulties. Precise and exact to a fault, she consistently demanded high standards of performance of herself and her associates.[53] Along with these characteristics went an outspoken, mercurial temperament. This combination of personality traits often led her to be openly critical of those who did not meet her exacting standards, and sometimes she wounded the feelings of fellow workers in driving toward desired ends. It was understandable that she was not always easy to work with.

The members of the Evangelization Society had assumed that

February 19, 1886, Emma Dryer to N. F. McCormick, March 19, 1886, October 20, 1886, T. W. Harvey to C. H. McCormick, Jr., May 5, 1887, Nettie Fowler McCormick Papers.)

52. Activities consisted primarily of occasional month-long conferences or "Bible Institutes" held in the Chicago Avenue Church or in Farwell Hall in downtown Chicago. In the summer the Evangelization Society also organized daily tent meetings in different parts of the city. (*Chicago Tribune*, September 27, 1889, January 17, 1890; *Record of Christian Work*, 6 [June, 1887]: 1, 2; 7 [January, 1888]: 1; 8 [January, 1889]: 2; D. L. Moody to D. W. Whittle, May 24, 1889, W. R. Moody Papers, Northfield, Mass.)

53. Some idea of the meticulousness of her work can be gained from Emma Dryer to N. F. McCormick, February 1, 1887, Emma Dryer to C. H. McCormick, Jr., June 15, 1887; circular entitled "Partial Summary of Work, 1st quarter, 1886," Nettie Fowler McCormick Papers. The manuscript diary of Miss M. J. Moore, also in the Nettie Fowler McCormick Papers, provides a detailed record of the daily visitations made by the Bible Work Society in 1886. This journal demonstrates the care with which Miss Dryer marshalled her forces and trained them in their duties.

their organization would eventually absorb Miss Dryer's work as they moved toward the creation of a larger school for city missionaries. Shortly after incorporation, the trustees of the society took the first steps in this direction.[54] From the outset, however, Miss Dryer questioned the plans and intentions of some of her associates. With her precision and passion for organization, she quite naturally hoped to see the new group operate efficiently. But she saw little evidence of such qualities in the work of Moody and his closest advisors.[55] Her worries were also probably a reflection of an unspoken fear that her Bible Work would not be accorded what she conceived to be its proper place in the activities of the society.[56] Finally, Miss Dryer's intense feelings caused her to develop personal animosities toward particular members of the group. She especially disliked Turlington W. Harvey, who was Moody's most intimate advisor on society matters. Like the evangelist, Harvey was slow to accept the drudgery of working out organizational details and more eager to support workers already in the field. Because he could not work with Miss Dryer effectively, he simply avoided her as much as possible. Apparently Harvey possessed no malicious motives, but Miss Dryer, highly sensitive and introspective by nature, dwelt on each suspected slight. Eventually she came to view Moody in much the same light, as the two men worked so closely together.[57]

Moody helped to complicate matters by his long absences from

54. A committee was appointed to work out the details of the merger and the trustees voted Miss Dryer an annual salary of $1000 under the new arrangement. (Trustees' Minutes, C. E. S., February 17, 1887, March 5, 1887.)

55. Miss Dryer became openly critical of Moody scarcely a month after the society was organized. Writing to Mrs. McCormick, she said that the evangelist "astonishes me, by the evidence he exhibits, that he *forgets* what he says and does. . . . Some of the things he did and said when he first came here he seems to know nothing about and his reasons for certain doings are amusing." (Emma Dryer to N. F. McCormick, March 22, 1887, Nettie Fowler McCormick Papers.)

56. Hints of such a concern are to be found in Trustees' Minutes, C. E. S., March 5, 1887.

57. Emma Dryer to N. F. McCormick, February 1, 1887, February 17, 1887, February 27, 1887, March 22, 1887, October 19, 1887, October 26, 1887, Emma Dryer to C. H. McCormick, Jr., June 15, 1887, Nettie Fowler McCormick Papers.

Chicago. He continued his annual tours about the country conducting revivals throughout the eighties, and whenever he was
not on the road he spent most of his time in Northfield. Thus it
was almost impossible for him to be well-informed about events
taking place in Chicago. Equally troublesome was the fact that
the evangelist inevitably held the final veto over all major policy
decisions. Everyone knew that without his approval and support
the Evangelization Society could not survive. Thus most important issues had to be brought to him for final settlement. In some
instances he acted without understanding fully all the factors involved. It is easy to see how his actions, too, could aggravate
tensions almost to the point of an explosion.

The climax of the differences of opinion came in late July,
1887. Mrs. McCormick, who had tried to serve as a mediator between conflicting factions, had reservations regarding certain
powers delegated to the board of trustees which she felt might
hinder efficient operations. She also thought there was a lack
of "any clear provision for the ladies work" in the society's constitution. Accordingly, she sent a letter to Moody at Northfield with
suggestions for alterations in the constitution.[58] Moody mistook
mere suggestions for a *demand* that changes be made. Irritated
and upset, the evangelist quickly wrote Mrs. McCormick, tender-
ing his resignation from the society, because, as he put it, "for
six months I have had to oppose some of the dearest friends I
have ever had, and I am tired and sick of it." [59]

His supporters in Chicago were aghast. Mrs. McCormick hastily
wrote him another note offering her own resignation in place of
his and pointing out what was obvious to everyone but Moody —
that his leaving the society "would dissolve it at once." A steady
hand in the East also worked to restore order. Moody's wife, who
acted as the evangelist's secretary frequently, soon learned of the
controversy. Immediately she wrote Mrs. McCormick a long per-

58. N. F. McCormick to D. L. Moody, July 15, 1887, *ibid*. See also
N. F. McCormick to N. S. Bouton, July 12, 1887, *ibid*. Copies of the
original constitution of the society and several drafts of a revised document seeking to incorporate Mrs. McCormick's suggestions are also
ibid.

59. D. L. Moody to N. F. McCormick, July 18, 1887, *ibid*.

sonal note, assuring the latter of her husband's good intentions and his desire always to serve the group's best interests. Probably she had a hand in causing Moody to wire Mrs. McCormick a reversal of his original intentions.[60] The latter individual, too, remained in the society and on the surface matters seemed to return almost to normal.

In several ways this was an illuminating incident. First, it revealed how Moody acted under stress. It demonstrated again his headstrong, sometimes impetuous nature, not yet fully curbed even in middle age. Perhaps even more important, this moment showed him responding to criticism in a familiar way. His abrupt offer to resign recalls an earlier impatience with those who disagreed with him, and particularly it suggests again a sensitiveness to criticism that was very near the surface. At the same time his quick reversal of himself indicates an openness of mind that also was one of his essential characteristics. All of these traits manifested themselves at other times in his life, but perhaps nowhere in quite as clear and unmistakable a fashion as at this moment. It is also one of the few times that the historical record provides us more than a fleeting glimpse of Moody's wife at work. Everything that has been said about her devotion to her husband, yet her counterpoise to his occasional impetuosity, seems confirmed by what she did when the Evangelization Society found itself in this crisis.

The events that transpired in the summer of 1887 created divisions of feeling and opinion that could not be bridged fully in the months that followed. Outwardly the dispute seemed a thing of the past, but in reality the acrimony continued to hold back any forward movement of the group. Mrs. McCormick was one person who was affected seriously. She had made major financial contributions to the undertaking, and had tried with considerable success to keep the antagonisms among her friends at a minimum until the final blowup occurred in 1887. Greatly offended by Moody's precipitous action when she questioned his plans, she hes-

60. N. F. McCormick to D. L. Moody, undated letter, July 21, 1885 (1887), Emma C. Moody to N. F. McCormick, July 26, 1887, telegram, D. L. Moody to N. F. McCormick, July 27, 1887, *ibid.*

itated to continue her active role in the Evangelization Society. Thus an important figure in the inner circle gradually withdrew.[61] Emma Dryer's response to Moody's temporary resignation did not help either. As impetuous as he and harboring many more frustrations, she sat down immediately, before consulting her more moderate friends, and penned him a long letter which defended in acid tones Mrs. McCormick's actions in the crisis.[62] Acting in this manner, Miss Dryer destroyed any effectiveness she might yet have possessed in the society.

Affairs continued to bump along with little direction. Only occasionally did the society hold meetings; even when a quorum gathered disputes broke out.[63] The wounds could not be healed. Eventually Miss Dryer and her supporters were forced to leave. As one member realized at the time he resigned, "no great Christian work can be accomplished, until the Society is reorganized and entire harmony of purpose prevail [sic]." Under pressure, Miss Dryer herself finally left in May, 1889. Perhaps it was significant that at the meeting of the board of trustees where her connections were severed officially, the board took the initial steps toward building the first permanent quarters for the society. In October, 1889, the Chicago Bible Institute officially opened its doors to students.[64] Although the Evangelization Society and the Institute

61. N. F. McCormick to Mary Blatchford, August 29, 1887, *ibid.* Mrs. McCormick had pledged $50,000 to the organization and offered a piece of property on which the school was to be built. Eventually half of her gift, which was to be used to support the women's work, was returned to her. (Minutes of the Board of Managers, Chicago Evangelization Society, extracts in Moody Papers, Moody Bible Institute, March 26, 1887; Trustees' Minutes, C. E. S., April 20, 1887, May 11, 1887; N. S. Bouton to N. F. McCormick, May 14, 1887, Nettie Fowler McCormick Papers.)

62. Emma Dryer to D. L. Moody, July 25, 1887, Nettie Fowler McCormick Papers.

63. Emma Dryer to N. F. McCormick, October 19, 1887, October 26, 1887, November 14, 1887, *ibid.*

64. N. S. Bouton to N. F. McCormick, August 16, 1888, *ibid;* Trustees' Minutes, C. E. S., May 16, 1889. For events leading up to this action, see the Trustees' Minutes, C. E. S., October 1, 1888, November 26, 1888, December 11, 1888; "Report of Meeting Held October 1, 1888," folder in Nettie Fowler McCormick Papers; Emma Dryer to N. F. McCormick, November 15, 1888, John V. Farwell to N. F. McCormick, December 18, 1891, *ibid.*

had their ups and downs thereafter, never again was their existence so severely threatened.

This sharp clash of personalities marked a sad beginning for Moody's educational experiment in Chicago. The bitter arguments of 1887 and later stood in sharp contrast to the high hopes with which the evangelist and his friends had embarked on their venture. Besides illuminating once again certain aspects of Moody's personality, and explaining the delays in establishing the school in Chicago on firm foundations, the controversies also pointed to other important changes occurring in Moody's life at this moment. Assessing the evidence from Emma Dryer's point of view, one of the chief difficulties had been the seeming confusion, the backing and filling, that characterized the evangelist's actions almost from the beginning. Several reasons have already been advanced to explain these developments — Moody's disinterest in organizational details, the personality differences that impaired cooperation, the long absences of the evangelist from Chicago. Yet it may be that the confusion primarily reflected the fact that Moody's projects were creating challenges that he was unable to encompass and deal with adequately.

By the end of the 1880's the evangelist was involved deeply in several enterprises, each of which separately would have demanded the full time of an ordinary mortal to administer properly. These projects were scattered across the country. The absence of the instant transportation and communications of the jet age made it doubly hard to remain in proper contact with supporters toiling in different locales. In addition, Moody was determined to spend a good part of each year continuing his work as a revivalist. He followed a routine similar to that which he had developed in the 1870's, which meant leaving home in October or November and, with a few exceptions, remaining on the "circuit" until the following March or April.[65] This burden of duties was at times simply too much for him. He was perfectly

65. Each year he tried to cover a different part of the country — the South in 1886, the West Coast in 1888, New York and New England in 1890 and 1891. Typed lists of the towns where he preached and the corresponding dates are in a loose-leaf notebook entitled "Sermons," Moody Papers, Mrs. E. M. Powell, East Northfield, Massachusetts.

capable of organizing the program of the Chicago YMCA in the 1860's, and even the great mass revival campaigns of the 1870's, but he had neither the time nor the ability to administer in detail the various programs he initiated in the 1880's. This point will become even clearer when we consider in the next chapter additional activities in Northfield that occupied his thoughts during the eighties.[66]

Moody's problems were not unique, however. The great empire builders in business belonged chiefly to the 1870's, and as has been noted several times, Moody was their religious counterpart. In the late eighties and nineties these men were giving way to the planners and technicians who were making a science and a corporate bureaucracy out of American business. Moody, the robust man of imagination, belonged to an earlier, less complex, age. The confusion that characterized the early history of the Bible Institute in Chicago, and Moody's divorcement from the actual running of the two academies in Northfield as trained educational "experts" took over these enterprises, indicate an experience that merely typified the social changes occurring generally at that time.

Despite his inadequacies, however, Moody's accomplishments in the 1880's outside of revivalism were real and lasting. The founding of his three schools was the most significant of these achievements. For a man with no more than a grade-school education to establish three educational institutions, and then for the last two decades of his life to give sustained financial, moral, and administrative support to these same schools, says a great deal about his

---

66. That the difficulties in Chicago were not indicative of general administrative incapacities on Moody's part is suggested in notes written by one of his supporters to Mrs. McCormick following the resolution of the crisis over the Bible Institute. The letter writer visited Northfield late in the summer of 1887 to study Moody's "success as an *organizer* — remembering the statements I had heard that he was not successful in that capacity." The outcome of this visit was a complete vote of confidence for the evangelist as one who, in Northfield at least, was "able to plan widely — to secure means in abundance, and to choose and inspire workers who carry out his undertakings in the same generous Christian spirit in which they are conceived." (Mary E. Blatchford to N. F. McCormick, August 7, 1887, September 13, 1887, Nettie Fowler McCormick Papers.)

vision and breadth of view. His ultimate purpose in all three instances was to pursue the traditional task of evangelism that churches and professional revivalists had had as a primary goal throughout much of the nineteenth century. But he had departed noticeably from the usual approaches of revivalists both before and after him in his work in the 1880's. This willingness to strike out in new directions in itself sets him apart from even the best-known of his successors in the revival tradition. That these schools flourished and grew once he had set them in motion enhances his achievement. Although not the personal triumph that characterized his revival work of the seventies, these efforts of the following decade should now be fully recognized for the considerable accomplishments they were.

10

The Evangelist at Home

In November, 1879, a young minister, H. B. Hartzler, was assisting Moody in Cleveland by leading one of the prayer meetings held in conjunction with the revival in that city. Following established practice, the evangelist sat in a front pew, ready to participate in the service. Hartzler later wrote that in the midst of the meeting Moody emerged from prayerful reverie, cast a glance at the platform "as tho struck with a bolt," then rushed to his friend in front at the close of the service to pour out plans suddenly formulated for a conference for lay churchmen which he hoped to hold at Northfield the following summer.[1]

We know this to be a time when Moody was rethinking generally his vocational concerns. Thus it is not surprising that at the exact moment when he began to alter his approach to revivalism, and when he began his first efforts with the schools in Northfield, the evangelist also struck out in another direction. In this instance his idea was to set up a series of summer conferences to educate and inspire the laity of the churches so that they might take their religious responsibilities more seriously. These conferences were to be focused on *Bible* study and discussion of methods of work in both home and overseas missionary endeavors, and were to be a time for "the promotion of individual consecration to Christ."[2]

1. H. B. Hartzler to W. R. Moody, February 22, 1900, Moody Papers, Mrs. E. M. Powell, East Northfield, Massachusetts.
2. Circular entitled "The Northfield Conference," describing the adult conference for 1886, in scrapbook entitled "Conferences," Moody Museum, Northfield School for Girls, Northfield, Massachusetts.

These stated purposes were all familiar concerns of the evangelist. Moreover, the plan for the summer conferences was in line with Moody's growing conviction that spiritual renewal must occur within the church before the nation at large could be approached with the gospel.

The full scope of the new hopes and intentions that worked themselves out into concrete programs in the eighties and nineties now becomes apparent. First, the evangelist did not intend to forget revivals entirely, but instead sought to put them in a new context. Whenever feasible he lodged these operations within the institutional framework of the churches, expending more time in the communities he visited, as well as working more systematically, more quietly, and with less public attention. Undoubtedly this was attractive to local church people, and in the long run may have been conducive to more lasting results. Second, Moody established training schools for young people to augment the forces of the denominations seeking to evangelize the world. He tried to put his peculiar stamp upon these schools. They were not to be seminaries, but halfway houses of theological education, training laymen like himself through some *Bible* study and much practical effort to handle their duties as "gapmen" with greater sureness, and thus with greater success. And their work was to be directed toward the cities, where the "unsaved masses" resided in great numbers — in Moody's eyes the chief threat to the continuing viability of the evangelical faith. Finally, he arranged for summer conferences at Northfield, to be viewed as exercises in adult education and moments of spiritual renewal for the rank-and-file members of the evangelical churches. This was a comprehensive plan of action that attempted to serve the Protestant community at several levels and in different parts of the nation and the world.

It is wrong to assume, however, that Moody thought consciously in the context proposed here. There is no specific documentation that reveals him thinking in these broad terms. More likely he thought, and acted, in several isolated instances and never glimpsed fully the grand design that seemed in time to emerge. Yet the specific institutions and programs mentioned are all historical facts; so also is the fact of their simultaneous emergence in 1879 and 1880. What *is* certain is that Moody's reworking of his vocational intentions during these years produced a series of new enterprises that show him planning and thinking in terms quite beyond the narrow confines of mass evangelism. Undoubtedly he was hampered in his response to industrialization by the traditional ideology of evangelical Protestantism, which he embraced so constantly and willingly. But it does not appear that this man was content merely to follow popular religious opinion, viewing the dislocations of his day with fear or despair and doing little in a constructive way to deal with these difficulties. Despite his traditionalism, Moody perceived the problems of his age and earnestly tried to grapple with them.

Possessing a commanding presence in the evangelical community made it relatively easy for the evangelist to call people to his side and transform the ideas conceived in Cleveland into reality nine months later in Northfield. The first summer conference lasted only ten days, beginning September 1, 1880. About a hundred people attended, most of them being housed in the recently completed women's seminary recitation hall. Formal meetings were held three times daily, with the women gathering in the seminary building, the men in a huge tent pitched on the grounds of the campus nearby where delegates squatted or sat cross-legged on the straw-matted ground to listen to speakers and to pray. Moody and some of his evangelist friends were the principal preachers. The emphasis in every session was on reconsecration to a sounder Christian life — on the "surrender of the will," as Moody put it, to "sacrifice all for the Master." [3]

An acquaintance of the evangelist wrote later that this first conference was unique in its emphasis on the "earnest cry to God for the recovery of that pentecostal power," the power of the Holy Spirit.[4] Moody's efforts may have been less unusual than some people thought. The few words available which describe what was preached and taught at this first summer gathering in

3. *Greenfield* [Mass.] *Gazette and Courier,* September 6, 1880, September 13, 1880. See also D. L. Moody to "Currier," July 2, 1880, Moody Papers, Powell; *Christian* (August 25, 1881): 7.

4. S. F. Hancock to Henry Rankin, September 18, 1896, Moody Papers, Powell.

Northfield suggest that the evangelist and his friends were participants in a post-war revival of holiness teachings in this country. Holiness sentiments had always been championed by the Methodists, both in this country and in England, because of their strong leanings toward the doctrine of sanctification. But the holiness movement in pre–Civil War America was an interdenominational phenomenon, and this was no less true of the movement in the seventies and eighties. In England, for example, the Keswick Conventions, which began in the 1870's and which bore a considerable resemblance to the conferences at Northfield, were interdenominational gatherings from the outset. Moody knew about these conventions in England, since some of his supporters in the revivals of 1873–75 had actively participated.[5]

It is questionable whether the evangelist personally viewed his conferences as a distinct part of the movement that sought "the higher Christian life." Moody himself never made the connection explicit, and the uncertainty that exists concerning his support of the doctrine of sanctification further clouds the issue.[6] It cannot be denied, however, that speakers invited to Northfield, and often the people who came as delegates to the conference, were friendly to holiness opinions and sentiments. Suffice it to

5. Timothy Smith has pioneered in the historical analysis of holiness movements in this country, both in the pre– and post–Civil War periods. See his *Revivalism and Social Reform: American Protestantism on the Eve of the Civil War* (New York: Harper Torchbook, 1965), chaps. 7–9, and *Called Unto Holiness: The Story of the Nazarenes: The Formative Years* (Kansas City: Nazarene Publishing House, 1962), especially chaps. 1, 2. See also John L. Peters, *Christian Perfection in American Methodism* (New York: Abingdon Press, 1956). For Moody's interest in holiness gatherings in England in the seventies, see Stephen Barabas, *So Great Salvation: The History and Message of the Keswick Convention* (London: Morgan and Scott, 1952), pp. 23–24.

6. Some of Moody's most explicit statements denying support of perfectionism and "entire sanctification" were uttered at one of the summer conferences at Northfield in the 1880's. (T. J. Shanks, ed., *College Students at Northfield, or, A College of Colleges, No. 2* [New York: Fleming H. Revell Co., 1888], pp. 186–88.) On the other hand, if the holiness movement is viewed as concerned principally with achieving "enduement with power" (of the Holy Spirit), Moody may be considered more fully within its orbit. For comments by the evangelist on this subject, see *ibid.*, chap. 11. See also his sermon, "Overcoming Faith," printed in *Evangelistic Record*, 2 (July, 1883): 3, which casts doubt on his maintaining holiness or perfectionist sentiments.

say that expressions of holiness were a recognizable part of the general atmosphere of spiritual enthusiasm and personal reconsecration that Moody sought to kindle among those who visited Northfield during the summer conferences.

The general format of the summertime gatherings in Massachusetts was not entirely new to Moody's experience. These meetings were partial reminders of the many Christian conventions the evangelist had attended as a young man in Illinois and other midwes.ern states. The pastoral scene at Northfield was perhaps equal to the natural beauties associated with the Keswick movement in Great Britain. As previously noted, this English precedent may have been in Moody's mind as he laid his plans in 1880. Probably an even more direct influence from England was the remembrance the evangelist had of Mildmay and the great annual conferences held there for all evangelical groups throughout the islands. Moody had participated in these mass meetings directly, and he admitted their influence upon him to some of his friends in America.[7] The parallels between Mildmay and Northfield are also striking.

The second conference was held at Northfield in August, 1881. This time the meetings lasted for a month, with people coming and going at intervals, the constituency fluctuating almost daily. Friends from England visited for part of the conference, presumably to assist Moody in his preparations for another prolonged visit to Britain that was soon to follow. Indeed, since the evangelist and Sankey left with their families early in September for overseas, it must have been difficult to concentrate fully on the immediate task of bringing the summer program to a successful conclusion. Moody was in England for three years, and during that time the summer conferences were not held in Northfield. But in 1885, after his return, the activities resumed.[8] Soon

7. Emma Dryer, "Reminiscences of the Founding of Moody Bible Institute" (unpublished typewritten MS, January, 1916), in the possession of Mr. Gene Getz, Moody Bible Institute, p. 7; W. Y. Fullerton, *F. B. Meyer: A Biography* (London: Marshall, Morgan and Scott, 1929), p. 41.

8. *Christian* (August 25, 1881): 7; A. P. Fitt, "Outline History of the Northfield Summer Conferences" (typewritten MS, no date, in possession of Frank Piersall, Northfield School for Girls). Andrew Bonar, a

after, the evangelist expanded these summer conferences to include a month-long gathering for college students. This new undertaking marked again his growing interest in the younger generation of the country, which was also manifested in his work for the YMCA.

Moody's abiding concern for the national YMCA was the outgrowth of a mutually supportive relationship. The reader can recall how local associations and their members performed yeoman's service in most of Moody's revivals in the seventies and later, and how the evangelist always tried to reciprocate in some helpful way whenever possible. In addition to fund-raising carried on from coast to coast, he had helped to organize new associations in some of the towns where he preached. And in recognition of his many contributions to the national movement, Moody was elected national president of the YMCA in 1879 at the annual convention in Baltimore.[9] Probably because of his growing interest in his schools in Northfield, in the early eighties the evangelist began to focus his attention on the work of the International Committee of the YMCA which was responsible for the college youth program of the national organization. Prior to 1883 this committee received annual gifts of a thousand dollars or more from Moody's hymnbook fund to help underwrite its work. After the hymnbook royalties were devoted exclusively to the Northfield Schools, the evangelist personally solicited $5000 each year from 1885 to 1896 to support student YMCA work on college campuses throughout the country.[10]

Scottish churchman and supporter of Moody in his earlier campaign, was the chief speaker at the second conference (*Greenfield* [Mass.] *Gazette and Courier,* August 8, 1881).

9. *Hartford Courant,* February 8, 1878; C. Howard Hopkins, *History of the Y.M.C.A. in North America* (New York: Association Press, 1951), p. 754; *Proceedings of the Annual National Convention, Y.M.C.A.,* June, 1879, pp. 70–76, 95–101, 106–09; *Watchman,* 5 (June 1, 1879): 121, 127, 131.

10. In exchange for aid from the hymnbook fund, YMCA officials solicited money for the Northfield Schools and YMCA secretaries assisted Moody in his revival work in the eighties. (Form letter included in "Letters in the Interest of College Work Sent by Mr. Moody"; Richard C. Morse to George H. Stuart, William E. Dodge, and John V. Farwell, April 10, 1883; Morse to Dodge, April 10, 1883, YMCA Historical Library; Luther E. Wishard, "The Beginning of the Student

Until 1880 the collegiate members of the YMCA were expected to attend the annual convention of the parent body instead of holding a separate meeting of their own. In reality, students seldom went to these large national meetings, for the agenda usually ignored college activities and the conferences convened at the end of the school year when young people had their minds on other problems. By the late seventies, however, the YMCA had become sufficiently specialized that some departments began to hold their own national meetings. The professional leaders of the youth division, especially C. K. Ober and Luther Wishard, supported by Richard C. Morse, the general secretary of the International Committee, aggressively sought to implement a similar convention for college students. Wishard in particular was eager to experiment, and by 1883 he was holding student conferences on the state and regional levels independent of the national organization. By the summer of 1885 the separate conference for the intercollegiate YMCA had become a well-established procedure.[11]

Long before this date Wishard had shrewdly begun a campaign to draw Moody into close association with the student movement. Although the revivalist had had little direct contact with young people in his evangelistic work after he left Chicago, Wishard sensed that Moody's personal vitality and vivid preaching would produce great enthusiasm in the collegiate ranks. Undoubtedly he also realized that there would be other advantages, perhaps financially, and certainly in terms of prestige, if a man of Moody's reputation could be induced to support the student work directly. As early as 1877, during a revival in Providence, Rhode Island, he had approached the evangelist about speaking before college students. Again in Baltimore in 1879 he made overtures. These early efforts all met with curt rebuffs. Moody was especially sensitive about speaking to college students because of his own lack of education. Apparently he honestly felt he had little to offer them in terms of either personal or intellectual stimulus. But events in the early eighties — the educational work in Northfield, and especially a series of successful contacts with students at Oxford

Era in Christian History" [unpublished typewritten MS, YMCA Historical Library], pp. 139–40.)

11. Hopkins, *History of the Y.M.C.A. in North America*, pp. 294–95.

and Cambridge during his tour of England — caused Moody to modify his views a bit. Wishard maintained his entreaties, first during the summer of 1885 at Northfield, then again the following year. In April, 1886, he went to Atlanta to assist Moody in a revival. Here Wishard first broached the specific proposal of a student conference, to be held at Northfield the following summer. Using all of his powers of persuasion, he overcame Moody's still-lingering doubts about his ability to appeal to college students, and the two men laid tentative plans for a student gathering the following July.[12]

Preparations now had to be rushed, for there were less than three months before the conference was scheduled to open. Wishard, with C. K. Ober's help, had circulars printed and mailed to all the college associations in the country. The two men also visited many of the colleges clustered in New England, New York, and New Jersey, where campus YMCA's flourished most strongly, and where they knew they would have to get most of their delegates. This personal appeal was especially effective, and ultimately over 200 students came to Northfield, a majority of them from the East Coast.[13]

Although staff members of the YMCA, particularly Luther Wishard, played key roles in making this student gathering function properly, Moody's contributions were of singular significance. Wishard himself had told the revivalist in Atlanta that it was "his name and his alone that would draw the students." [14] Despite his lack of experience, the evangelist's boyish enthusiasm, his great seriousness about religious convictions, as well as the magnetism of his name, made him into a natural student leader. Correspond-

12. Luther Wishard, "D. L. Moody and the Origin of the Student Volunteer Movement," *Christian Workers Magazine* (no date), pp. 90–92, clipping in files of YMCA Historical Library; Wishard, "Beginning of the Student Era," pp. 138–39, 146–48.

13. Hopkins, *History of the Y.M.C.A. in North America*, p. 296; Wishard, "Moody and the Origin of the Student Volunteer Movement," p. 92; Wishard, "Beginning of the Student Era," p. 149; "Souvenir, College Y.M.C.A. Summer School for Bible Study," undated pamphlet in files of YMCA Historical Library, New York City, p. 7; circular in scrapbook entitled "Conferences," D. L. Moody Museum, Northfield School for Girls, Northfield, Massachusetts.

14. Wishard, "Beginning of the Student Era," p. 148.

ingly, Moody soon discovered in this impressionable and warm-hearted group as potent a revival spirit as had animated any audience in his large urban revivals. Soon after the conference began, the students eagerly voted to hold prayer meetings, led by the revivalist, each morning at six A.M. The "question and answer" approach to the daily lectures, a favorite technique of his, also met with a hearty response. Moody personally led many of these lecture sessions, although other speakers, specially invited by the evangelist, helped out.[15]

Above all else, however, was the impact of Moody's personality upon the boys. The afternoons were devoted chiefly to recreational activities. Despite his huge bulk, the evangelist threw himself into the games and sports of the students. Foot races were his specialty, with the proviso, laughingly added, that all his young challengers had to carry ballast equal to his own considerable poundage. In a later conference he took a special interest in Amos Alonzo Stagg, then a delegate from Yale and later a famous football coach, whose athletic prowess was already much in evidence. Spiritual enthusiasm lasted even into the closing moments of his first student conference, and Moody as usual was at the center of things. As the camp broke up on the first day of August, the delegates marched in a body to the Mount Hermon railroad depot a mile from the campus. Moody drove through the straggling procession in his buggy for a final farewell. In this moment of cheering and singing, instinctively he seized upon the occasion and turned it into a "meeting" at the roadside. The camp choir director happened along, and was pressed into service for more gospel singing and even a short address to the boys. In moments like these the evangelist probably made his most indelible impressions and captured the hearts and energies of the young men who had come to Northfield.[16] Wishard, Ober, and the other YMCA leaders could not have asked for more than that

15. *Springfield* [Mass.] *Republican*, July 7, 1886, July 8, 1886, July 9, 1886; "Souvenir, College Y.M.C.A. Summer School," p. 8; *Greenfield* [Mass.] *Gazette and Courier*, July 12, 1886, July 19, 1886, August 12, 1886.

16. P. D. Moody, *My Father*, pp. 90–91, 92; *Springfield* [Mass.] *Republican*, July 8, 1886, August 3, 1886.

the evangelist just be himself with these youngsters. This he had done, and thereby he assured the success of the first student conference.

Yet Moody's larger purposes were never forgotten. He could see this collegiate gathering serving as a starting point for the ultimate evangelization of American institutions of higher education, turning even the "great state and national universities" into "Christian institutions," which in turn would send out "thousands of trained Christian workers into the pulpits of our land, the foreign mission fields and into business and the professions." [17] In part this was grand rhetoric that had to accompany the frequent "begging letters" he sent to friends and acquaintances. But the intentions behind these words did not differ much from the purposes that animated his other activities.

In other somewhat unexpected ways, however, the student conference assumed a direction that varied from Moody's primary interest. Much of the fervor that the evangelist helped to generate at this first Northfield gathering focused finally in a desire to draw more workers into foreign missions. The circulars sent out in advance of the conference made no mention of any such special emphasis, and there is no evidence that Moody was thinking along these lines as the plans for the summer program evolved. [18] There is considerable evidence to suggest, however, that Wishard and his cohorts in the YMCA hoped that something would develop during the conference that would directly benefit mission work. Wishard personally had harbored for some time a strong interest in the missionary tasks of the church, and he dreamed of drawing the student movement of the YMCA directly into the mainstream of efforts at overseas evangelization. He asserted once that aleady by 1886 this dream had taken the concrete form of a plan to spend personally several years in "missionary lands," the better to

17. D. L. Moody to C. H. Ingram, December 22, 1892, C. H. Ingram Papers, Wisconsin State Historical Society. See also "Souvenir, College Y.M.C.A. Summer School," p. 8.

18. In support of this statement note especially the detailed account of Moody's comments made at the first formal gathering of the conference delegates, printed in the *Springfield* [Mass.] *Republican*, July 8, 1886.

prepare himself in promoting "foreign missionary devotion in the colleges" of the United States.[19]

He and C. K. Ober had boldly prepared a tentative outline of a program for the summer conference which included specific consideration of missions. Apparently Moody did not desire to be tied down to such a detailed agenda, and thus these plans were quickly abandoned. But Wishard was a hard man to deny, and by more roundabout means he worked toward his goal. At least one of the speakers, A. T. Pierson, had shown an interest in missions earlier and could be counted upon to press these questions at the conference.[20] The YMCA secretary also took pains to seek out and invite college men who already showed strong interests in missionary activities.[21] A number of such students, some already committed to work in missions after graduation, came to Northfield. Finally, a half dozen representatives of foreign countries had thoughtfully been invited. Once the interest in missions

19. Wishard, "The Beginning of the Student Era," p. 116. For additional details of his pre-1886 hopes and experience with missionary work, see Clarence Shedd, *History of the World's Alliance of Young Men's Christian Associations* (London: S. P. C. K., 1955), p. 278; Clarence P. Shedd, *Two Centuries of Student Christian Movements: Their Origin and Intercollegiate Life* (New York: Association Press, 1934), pp. 254–55.

20. As early as 1882 Pierson was writing articles in an evangelical journal published by Moody's brother-in-law in Chicago urging the American churches to take their missionary responsibilities overseas more seriously. One piece of his was entitled "The World May Be Evangelized Within Twenty Years" and urged that "by the year 1900, the Gospel shall be preached to every living soul. Of course, to evangelize is not always to convert; it is simply making known the Gospel." The ideas, if not the words, are strikingly similar to those used by the Student Volunteers a few years later. (*Evangelistic Record*, 1 [March, 1882]: 2.) See also *ibid.*, 2 (April, 1882): 5–8. For Pierson's activities on behalf of missionary work at the Northfield meeting in 1886, see the *Springfield* [Mass.] *Republican*, July 19, 1886.

21. Wishard especially sought out Robert Wilder, then a student at Princeton, active there in the student YMCA and well-known for his interest in missions, perhaps in part because his father was a missionary in India. Wilder came to Mount Hermon and played a key role in arousing the student interest in overseas evangelism. (Shedd, *Two Centuries of Student Christian Movement*, pp. 258–59; Robert Wilder, *The Great Commission: The Missionary Response of the Student Volunteer Movements in North America and Europe; Some Personal Reminiscences* [London: Oliphants, 1936], chaps. 1, 2.)

manifested itself at the conference, all of these young men helped to spread the enthusiasm.

A few days after the meetings began, a small band of delegates who were interested in the mission field began to hold special sessions of their own. The group proselytized vigorously; a dramatic mass meeting for the entire conference occurred midway through the four-weeks' session in which "hearts were thrilled" by testimony from the foreign students and from the sons of missionaries attending.[22] Thus a missionary "gusher," as Ober later described it, erupted. Before the conference closed about one hundred students — later known as the "Mount Hermon Hundred" — pledged themselves to work in the foreign mission field after completing college.[23] Deputations that were formed at the summer conference toured college campuses during the succeeding academic year urging fellow students to join the movement and commit their lives to Christian service overseas. By the time of the next conference at Mount Hermon, held in June, 1887, over 2,000 students had been swept into the movement. This was the beginning of the Student Volunteer Movement, seeking "the evangelization of the world in this generation." [24]

22. "Souvenir, College Y.M.C.A. Summer School," p. 9. John R. Mott, soon to become one of the central figures in the Student Volunteer Movement, attended the conference not having given much thought previously to missions. In the 1890's he recalled vividly how he, and others, eventually fell into line. Robert Wilder and his supporters, he said, "had the spirit of propagation. Probably Wilder himself did not secure more than eight or ten. They got one another. . . . Men talked missions everywhere — running, tramping, eating. One parlor meeting, unannounced, was continued in prayer, the lights out, till midnight. Gradually this missionary group became the spiritual . . . center of the conference." (Quoted in Shedd, *Two Centuries of Student Christian Movements*, p. 260.)

23. The exact number of students who pledged themselves to missionary work cannot be determined with absolute certainty from the available records. In "Souvenir, College Y.M.C.A. Summer School," pp. 16–22, there is a listing of all the delegates at the first student conference, including vocational preferences. Only forty delegates planned missionary careers. However, many others stated an intention to enter the ministry and were probably among the one hundred said to have banded together at the conference. See also John R. Mott, *Addresses and Papers: The Student Volunteer Movement for Foreign Missions*, 6 vols. (New York: Association Press, 1946), 1: vi, 6.

24. *Springfield* [Mass.] *Republican*, August 3, 1886, clipping in the

Although Moody did not foresee that the student conference would take the turn it did, it was not too difficult for him to endorse this new surge of interest in missions, which soon affected American Protestantism and the world far beyond the confines of collegiate ranks. The Student Volunteers, who were the spearhead of the movement, reflected his own prejudices and interests in many ways. The Student Volunteer Movement was, first of all, closely connected with the YMCA; like that latter organization it possessed a broad nondenominational bias and was led by vigorous laymen whose greatest talents were centered on organizing and administering people and programs. The Student Volunteers were also an expression of the transatlantic evangelical community. A constant flow of students between Britain and the United States for missionary and collegiate conferences occurred throughout these last years of the nineteenth century. In 1888, for example, the Northfield Conference hosted sixteen young men from England and Scotland, fourteen the following year. A student leader who had supported Moody's efforts to reach the undergraduates at Cambridge in the early eighties, J. E. K. Studd, came to this country in 1885 to tour the land speaking to college students about mission work. Studd helped to prepare the way for the first conference at Northfield with its special concern for missions.[25] These Anglo-American ties were also a part of Moody's experience and he undoubtedly looked upon such developments with approval.

The Student Volunteer Movement, especially in its programs at Northfield each summer, was also shaped by theological movements with which the evangelist sympathized. As noted earlier, the speakers were nearly all personal friends of Moody, and the majority of them shared his views. At the first conference in 1886 all of the principal speakers — D. W. Whittle, J. H. Brooks, W. G.

files of the YMCA Historical Library; Hopkins, *History of the Y.M.C.A. in North America*, pp. 296–99; *Greenfield* [Mass.] *Gazette and Courier*, July 26, 1886; "Souvenir, College Y.M.C.A. Summer School," pp. 8–9; Mott, *Addresses and Papers*, 1:4–7.

25. Shanks, *College Students at Northfield*, pp. 287, 290, 294; Fred L. Norton, *A College of Colleges Led By D. L. Moody* (New York: Fleming H. Revell Co., 1889), p. 286; Shedd, *Two Centuries of Student Christian Movements*, pp. 238–40.

Moorehead, A. T. Pierson, and A. J. Gordon — were strong supporters of premillennialism and, indeed, of dispensationalism.[26] Brooks evoked strong criticism from the students because he vigorously advocated a rigidly literalistic view of the *Bible*; in later conferences Moody took pains to include as speakers William Rainey Harper and Henry Drummond, men who represented a more liberal position on questions of Biblical criticism.[27] But the premillennialist view of the speakers rubbed off on those who sat at their feet. Robert Wilder and Robert E. Speer, two young college graduates who became leading spokesmen for the Student Volunteer Movement, embraced premillennialism. Indeed, it might well be argued that the Student Volunteer Movement itself was an attempt to carry out the urgent demands that emerged from premillennialist beliefs. The movement possessed a sense of expectation, of the nearness of Christ's second coming, which made immediate efforts at evangelization of the heathen necessary. This feeling of urgency was present in premillennialism and caught up in the motto of the Student Volunteers — "the evangelization of the world in this generation." [28]

Finally, the Student Volunteer Movement and Moody's participation in it must be placed in a broader historical perspective. In the late seventies and especially in the early eighties there was a noticeable upsurge of missionary interest among Protestants throughout Western Christendom. Students in particular were in the vanguard of this movement. The academic year 1883–84

26. "Souvenir, College Y.M.C.A. Summer School," pp. 12–15.

27. *Springfield* [Mass.] *Republican*, July 13, 1886, July 14, 1886, July 20, 1886, July 22, 1886; T. J. Shanks, ed., *A College of Colleges: Led by D. L. Moody* (Chicago: Fleming H. Revell Co., 1887), chaps. 3, 5; Shanks, *College Students at Northfield*, chap. 6; Norton, *College of Colleges*, chap. 10.

28. Brooks preached a sermon to the students at the first conference on the second coming of Christ. A. T. Pierson spent much time on prophetic themes in his talks, themes directly related both to premillennial and dispensationalist thinking. And A. J. Gordon, another speaker at the conference, clearly revealed dispensationalist and premillennialist sentiments in his preaching. (*Springfield Republican*, July 15, 1886, July 17, 1886, July 19, 1886, July 20, 1886, July 21, 1886, July 23, 1886. See also William Beahm, "Factors in the Development of the Student Volunteer Movement for Foreign Missions," (unpublished Ph.D. dissertation, University of Chicago, 1941), pp. 57, 186, 188.

saw five student missionary organizations created — in Britain, Norway, Sweden, Denmark, and North America. Four undergraduates at Princeton, including Robert Wilder, took the lead in the United States, although even their work had precedents since the Inter-Seminary Missionary Alliance had been organized in 1880 among divinity school students scattered along the eastern seaboard.[29] Foreign missions, whether originating in Europe or in America, possessed obvious links to the massive outthrust of Western civilization into the less developed areas of the globe in these last few years of the nineteenth century.[30] The enthusiasm with which American college students embraced the watchword of the Student Volunteer Movement and responded to the call of duty in foreign lands shows how closely America was tied to this general impulse in the West. In this country the most powerful popular expressions of expansionism outside our existing territorial boundaries did not come until the 1890's. The beginnings of the SVM, therefore, were a significant portent of this impending change in attitude. And it is not at all surprising that Moody, a man who had served so frequently as a barometer of popular religious feelings, was associated intimately with this movement from the outset.

At one point, however, Moody's normal interests conflicted with those of the young volunteers for foreign missions. This concerned the choice of the field in which to labor. Although Moody was not opposed to evangelism throughout the world, he clearly felt that home missions, particularly in the cities, were of primary importance. It may be that the slight reticence that one senses in Moody's commitment to this new cause stemmed from this latent clash between his career and beliefs about evangelism, and the direction his young friends were taking by going overseas. Certainly it is true that both Moody's work in the seventies and eighties, and the emergence of the Student Volunteer Movement, signified

29. Wilder, *Great Commission*, pp. 13–14; Shedd, *Two Centuries of Student Christian Movements*, chap. 13; Beahm, "Factors in the Development of the Student Voluntary Movement," p. 44.

30. For a recent study which shows the linkage between power politics and the expansion of Christian missions in Africa in the late nineteenth century, see C. P. Groves, *The Planting of Christianity in Africa, 1878–1914* (London: Lutterworth Press, 1955), 3, part 1.

as clearly as anything could that the old pre–Civil War emphasis of the evangelical churches on missionary work in the West and on the frontier was at an end. America had changed, and the church had to adjust accordingly. But with the advantage of hindsight, it may well be that Moody's plan to work in the great urban centers of America and Britain was a more acute judgment of where Christians could be most effective, than was the decision of those who became foreign missionaries. Foreign missions were an exciting opportunity, and the spirit of American optimism and expansiveness in the world enticed young people to enlist in the ranks of those going to Asia and Africa. Now we know how woefully unprepared to work in non-Western lands, how naive about other cultures and ways of life these young missionaries were. They may have done their cause greater harm in the long run than if they had stayed at home to work in an environment in which their burning desire to convert people to Christ traditionally possessed some meaning and significance.[31] In this sense Moody's personal program of evangelism, with all of its inadequacies, seems more realistic than did the notions of the Mount Hermon Hundred and those who followed in their footsteps.

Above and beyond these somewhat impersonal considerations was the evangelist's lasting personal impact on the students who came to the Northfield conferences. The collegians who visited the evangelist's home each summer were to provide the leadership not only of the YMCA, but to a large degree of American Protestantism up to World War I. Moody deeply influenced men like John R. Mott, Robert Speer, Robert Wilder, and Sherwood Eddy, all of them great lay leaders in the pre-war era. Mott, prob-

31. For analyses by historians which offer substantive conclusions concerning the success of American missionaries in converting non-Western populations to Christianity in the nineteenth century, and indications of the impact the missionaries made in these non-European cultures, see Paul A. Varg, *Missionaries, Chinese, and Diplomats: The American Protestant Missionary Movement in China, 1890–1952* (Princeton: Princeton University Press, 1958); Paul A. Cohen, *China and Christianity: The Missionary Movement and the Growth of Chinese Antiforeignism* (Cambridge: Harvard University Press, 1963); Kenneth S. Latourette, *A History of the Expansion of Christianity: The Great Century in North Africa and Asia AD 1800–AD 1914* (New York: Harper and Bros., 1944), 6.

ably the best known of these men, became directly involved in planning the Northfield meetings, and for a time after 1893 shouldered most of the responsibility. At the same time this energetic young man was building a career in national and international church circles that would make him a leading American spokesman in the world ecumenical movement in the first quarter of the twentieth century.[32] Mott and the others inherited the best of Moody's outlook. The warmhearted spirit and enthusiasm of evangelical Christianity shaped their deepest personal predilections; at the same time they possessed an ecumenical viewpoint that would have pleased their mentor in Northfield, and by which they tried to overcome the frictions, theological and otherwise, that affected American Protestantism in the pre–World War I period.[33]

Even though Moody seemed to be engaged in a welter of activities in the early and middle eighties, during this time he somehow also thought it feasible to spend about two and a half years in England. In September, 1881, he and Sankey and their families set out once again for overseas, this time to be welcomed to the British Isles by a host of friends, and to be besieged by churches

32. Basil Mathews, *John R. Mott: World Citizen* (New York: Harper and Bros., 1934), p. 105; John R. Mott to D. L. Moody, May 23, 1899, Mott Papers, Yale Divinity School Library; D. L. Moody to Ambert Moody, May 22, 1892, letter in a collection of materials gathered by Mrs. Esther Loos and now on deposit in the Library of Congress. Moody's close relations with Mott culminated in an offer in 1893 to the young man of the directorship of the Bible Institute in Chicago. Mott refused, but evidently for a time worked closely with the officials in Chicago and even located some of the offices for the Student Volunteer Movement in the Institute buildings. See John R. Mott to "parents," February 2, 1893, May 30, 1893, January 10, 1894, April 23, 1894, John R. Mott to "Father," May 27, 1895, Mott Papers.

33. Sherwood Eddy has given some indications of Moody's influence on him in *Eighty Adventurous Years: An Autobiography* (New York: Harper and Bros, 1955) pp. 26–27. John R. Mott recognized Moody's significance for the pre-World War I generation in *The Present-Day Summons to the World Mission of Christianity* (Nashville: Abingdon Press, 1931), pp. 240–41. See also chap. 3 of his *The Larger Evangelism* (Nashville: Abingdon-Cokesbury Press, 1944), which is a tribute to Moody as "the greatest evangelist of the last century," and his eulogy delivered at a mass meeting in New York City shortly after the death of his friend, printed in J. Wilbur Chapman, *The Life and Work of Dwight L. Moody*, (New York: W. E. Scull, 1900), pp. 463–66.

in both England and Scotland for a place on their itinerary.[34] The plan was to hold revivals first in Newcastle, then to move north to Edinburgh and Glasgow. Much of the year 1882 was spent in northern climes, almost six months in Glasgow alone. Except for a brief interlude in Ireland at the end of 1882, from September of that year to April, 1883, the two Americans wandered through the provincial towns and industrial centers of England. Moody returned to America in April and remained there until October, to oversee directly the development of his schools in Northfield and to rest from his arduous labors of the preceding months. Then he sailed back to England, spent a few weeks with Sankey in certain small Irish cities, and finally in November, 1883, crossed back to English shores to launch another extended campaign of religious activities in London. Not until late June of the following year did he consider his duty done in the great metropolis, closing the doors of his worship houses and preparing for the final trip home. He arrived back in this country late in July, 1884.[35]

In some respects this tour of Britain seemed an exercise in nostalgia. The itinerary itself, at least until Moody left in mid-1883 for his visit to Northfield, paralleled the route the two Americans had followed in their triumphal passage in the 1870's. Familiar procedures were used in the smaller towns of petitioning Moody for a visit, and of assuring him the united support of religious groups in backing the preaching and singing he and Sankey would initiate.[36] Yet there were significant changes which

34. *Christian* (September 29, 1881): 12; (October 6, 1881): 12.

35. Moody and Sankey's itinerary can be followed by paging through the files of *The Christian* during this three-year period. This journal, still closely supporting the two Americans in their work, printed in almost every issue reports of the movements of the revivalists. An especially detailed itinerary covering the period from June, 1882, to April, 1883, is to be found in the issue of July 6, 1882, p. 47. See *Evangelistic Record*, 2 June, 1883): 6, for comments explaining why Moody returned to America in the middle of 1883. This magazine contained detailed monthly reports of the progress of Moody and Sankey beginning with the December, 1881, issue. See also Emma C. Moody to "Mother," February 28, 1883, March 28, 1884, Mrs. Frank R. Smith Collection, Library of Congress.

36. *Christian* (October 13, 1881): 8; (November 29, 1883): 5.

occurred in the American's tactics. Whenever the evangelist moved into the large cities, and particularly when he was in London, he used procedures which showed again that he had altered his theories about revivalism in a fundamental way. In an interview with a writer for a leading London journal just before he departed for home in the summer of 1884, Moody made it clear how his thinking had changed. He praised the churches of England because of their ability to utilize so effectively the "great principle of divide and conquer." This meant that "the Church has discovered that in order to get at men it must attack them in sections. It is of no use trying to get at men in the mass. You must split them up and deal with them in detail." [37]

In London Moody made a noticeable effort to implement his new approach to evangelism. He began by doubling the length of his visit to the great capital in comparison with that of 1875, from four to eight months. In the seventies he had preached in four parts of the city. Now he broke up the metropolis into twelve smaller units and moved his troupe slowly from one section to another. Borrowing an idea from earlier, the evangelist's supporters assembled two portable, corrugated iron tabernacles, which could be put up and torn down easily, each of which contained seating for over 5,000 people, and which even had extensions on one side that were to serve as inquiry rooms. As he and Sankey preached and sang in one of the structures, the other squat, low-hanging building was being erected in another section in anticipation of their next move. Finally, a carefully devised ticket system was installed, tickets being issued for particular services through the ministers of the local district to the people of the parishes, "especially non-churchgoers," and not "mere visitors from other parts of London." The object, it appeared, was "to get nearer to the people," or better expressed perhaps in terms Moody might have used, "not to create a sensation, but to get at individual souls," not to seek "vast assemblies," but "audiences of manageable size that can really hear" the evangelist, and "that he can get thoroughly into his grasp." Moreover, it does seem true that he spent a great deal of time in working-class districts as well as

37. *Pall Mall Gazette*, 40 (July 12, 1884): 2.

in middle and upper-class sections of London, and that he was reasonably well-received in these working-class areas.[38]

As was true of all of the evangelist's other revivals, there have been mixed judgments about the success of his tactics this time. The traditional yardstick continued to be applied, that of calculations based chiefly on estimates of attendance made by newspapermen and other informed observers. Certainly the public excitement was not as great as in the seventies — this was admitted even by Moody's most ardent supporters — but that does not necessarily mean that the cumulative impact of his presence in England was less significant than previously.[39] Perhaps it is time to dismiss as futile the attempts to ascertain Moody and Sankey's "success" as revivalists. Instead it seems best to remember the campaigns in England in the 1880's as perfectly consistent with what Moody had been thinking about and doing almost simultaneously in the United States. The consistency of purpose that undergirded all of his public activities in this period is once again dramatically illustrated. In that observation probably rests much of the historical significance of the revivals he organized and promoted on this second lengthy trip overseas.

One other important consequence of the visit to England was Moody's first and sometimes stormy contacts with English undergraduates at Oxford and Cambridge. Almost as soon as he arrived

38. The quotations are from an article first published in *Congregationalist* (February, 1884) reprinted in *Christian* (February 7, 1884): 8; (November 15, 1883): 10. See also *Christian World* (November 8, 1883): 772; (November 15, 1883): 800; (November 22, 1883): 816; (November 29, 1883: 835; (December 6, 1883): 855; (December 13, 1883): 882. Moody and his supporters also tried to improve their efforts to link inquirers and converts with the local churches. The names of all inquirers and the churches they attended were asked for, and then all were to be "thoroughly visited under the direction of the central committee, and every effort made to house them." (*Christian* [February 21, 1884]: 10.)

39. Even a cursory review of newspapers and journals of opinion at the time reveals the lack of public interest in Moody and Sankey between 1881 and 1883. Only a few religious periodicals devoted any space at all to comments about their work. The secular newspapers, which had followed their progress closely in the seventies, offered isolated and extremely limited coverage. See, for example, *The London Times*, October 12, 1883, November 5, 1883. For comments by Moody's supporters about this fact, see *Christian* (February 7, 1884): 8.

in Britain, interested students at the latter school wrote to him asking that he visit them. As time passed and the entreaties piled up Moody gave in and accepted an invitation to visit Cambridge for eight days early in November, 1882. This visit was followed immediately by a trip westward to Oxford and meetings with students there. Moody and his singing partner approached this new task with a certain amount of reluctance. The evangelist openly acknowledged later his uneasiness in facing, as a common, uneducated American, a crowd of young men from the citadels of English higher education and social respectability. Unfortunately, perhaps unknowingly, he made his first talk to Cambridge students on Guy Fawkes' Day, traditionally a time for revelry and pranks throughout the country. The students were eager to honor the tradition at the expense of the two strangers from abroad. At the first service Sankey's music produced, instead of the usual deathly stillness and rapt attention, shouts of "Hear, hear!" and a steady tattoo on the floor with umbrellas and canes. Moody's New England accent provoked a volley of mimicked cries and guffaws from the students. Eventually, by maintaining his composure and by exhibiting a good-natured willingness to continue his efforts to the end, several days later Moody seemed to have made friends among a number of the students who came to hear him.[40]

In Oxford the evangelist faced the same treatment at the beginning. At the first meeting he was forced to stop his reading of the book of Ezekiel to await the end of the stamping and shouting of the undergraduates. This time he adopted more direct methods of rebuke. The next night he opened his service with comments about how "ungentlemanly" his hearers had acted, and that apologies were in order. Ever quick to press an advantage shrewdly gained, Moody went on to say that the students could demonstrate their apologies most clearly by attending the gathering the following night and listening quietly to his remarks. A description of that later meeting conveys again to the reader something of the personal magnetism and authority that Moody pos-

40. J. C. Pollock, *Moody: A Biographical Portrait of the Pacesetter in Modern Mass Evangelism* (New York: Macmillan Co., 1963), chap. 25; *Evangelistic Record*, 2 (December, 1882): 10.

sessed, even in as inauspicious surroundings as those in Cambridge and Oxford. It was

> no spun-out manuscript sermon from decorous surpliced preacher in a distant pulpit, but here a man, a very honest and earnest man, face to face with them [the students], searching them with his glance, pointing at them personally, unveiling their hearts to them in a way that is strange, because it is new. At the end, Mr. Moody says: "I'm much obliged to you men for giving me a hearing; there's thirty or forty of you here who promised me you'd come to-night and listen fair, and you've done it." [41]

He had their attention, and perhaps their respect, if not always a commitment to Christ. Later analyses agree that he made the greater impact at Cambridge, in part because the evangelical groups were more strongly represented in the student body there than at Oxford; thus interested undergraduates were better organized and initially more ready to receive the kind of message Moody tried to bring to them.[42] In any case, these visits to the English establishment in higher education did not so unnerve him that he was never again to consider working with college students. As we have seen, the visits evidently had the reverse effect, helping to open the way for his extended service to the collegiate YMCA and the Student Volunteer Movement in the United States.

Questioned before he left England about what Americans might contribute to the understanding and general uplift of the population in Britain, Moody replied with thoughts that at first seem

41. *Christian* (November 23, 1882): 11.
42. Pollock, *Moody*, pp. 235–36, 238; Peter B. Morgan, "A Study of the Work of Four American Evangelists in Britain from 1873–1905 and of the Effect Upon Organized Christianity of Their Work There," (unpublished typewritten B. Litt. thesis, Oxford University, 1958), pp. 258–61, 508. Pollock has written an account of a group of Cambridge graduates who formed a famous missionary band and stirred a renewed interest in missions in England, partly as a result of their involvement in the Moody meetings at the University in 1882. (John C. Pollock, *The Cambridge Seven: A Call to Christian Service* [Chicago: Inter-Varsity Press, 1955].)

a bit strange. The greatest need in London, he argued, "is homes. . . . there, that is your great lack." Strange, perhaps, but not from an American point of view, as the evangelist quickly made clear. He went on to assert that "at present your poor people shift aimlessly from place to place. A man may be in a room to-day, and out of it to-morrow. There is no sense of permanence of ownership such as we have in America, where nearly every man owns his own house and has his own bit of land. . . . What you want to do is to give them a stake in the country. Let them feel that they have a fixed home out of which they cannot be turned by anyone." [43] The statement reveals as much about popular American attitudes as it does about legitimate comparisons between England and the United States. Moody's words echoed beliefs that were widely held in his homeland concerning the importance of private property, of the opportunity to own such property, and the civilizing influence — the stabilizing of social relations — which resulted from such ownership. It was appropriate that a popular hero like Moody should espouse ideas containing the scarcely concealed materialistic and democratic biases so common to American thought generally.[44]

He justified his thoughts on other grounds as well. "The home was founded before the church," he believed, "and you in England stand more in need of homes than you do of churches." [45] Here his evangelical biases peeped through. Earlier it was noted that the sanctity of home and family was a touchstone of belief whenever evangelical Protestants confronted social questions or considered how society was to be ordered. Moody was no exception to this rule. He said what he did to his English friends in part because of this special perspective, and his words would strike

43. *Pall Mall Gazette*, 40 (July 12, 1884): 2.
44. Following hard on the heels of the observations just cited, were words in which Moody made his democratic assumptions more explicit, and in which he engaged a bit in twisting the lion's tail. "In America," he maintained, "the sense of ownership is a great stimulus to the development of manhood; and I think our institutions also contribute to sharpen the intelligence of the working man. He has a vote, and so he reads the papers to see which side he should vote upon, and the result is that, on the whole, I think our working classes are more intelligent than yours." (*Ibid.*)
45. *Ibid.*

fire in many Englishmen precisely because they shared with him a common attitude. When Moody thought of the home as the cement of society, or as an institution of considerable moral and religious significance, he was not speaking cant — he was deadly serious. He tried to act upon these beliefs in everyday life. Certainly he and his wife worked to establish their family's daily existence in some such context as this.

All of the children and Mrs. Moody had accompanied the evangelist on the second long tour overseas. This was nearly always the practice when Moody was gone from Northfield for an extended period. For much of the time spent in England, Emma Moody and the three children took lodgings in London, a city where they had many friends. Emma and Will were now both teen-agers and spent part of their time in boarding schools or in private tutoring with Fannie Holton, a young relative from Northfield who came to England to serve as a sort of governess for the children. Occasionally the mother left the children with Miss Holton and joined her husband as he preached outside London, but this was not often. Thus even here the family was at times separated, and the absence of the sturdy, warmhearted father from the small circle was felt very much.[46]

"Home" for Moody was partly bound up in the close relations between him and his family, but it also was a word closely associated with Northfield. He had been in Britain only a few months when his wife wrote to relatives that her husband was "very homesick for Northfield often . . . especially on bright spring days" when he was reminded of home. No other kind of work except his

46. Emma C. Moody to "Mother," November 2, 1881, February 20, 1882, Smith Collection; Emma C. Moody to "Mother," January 24, 1883, June 5, 1884, Moody Papers, Powell. During the first part of 1882, which Moody spent in Scotland, the family came north and settled in Glasgow in order to be near the head of the household. There are a few comments on the Moodys' life together during those six months in J. Mackinnon, *Recollections of Dwight L. Moody* (Privately printed, 1905), pp. 125, 135–36, 180. See also Emma M. Powell, *Heavenly Destiny: The Life Story of Mrs. D. L. Moody, by Her Granddaughter, Emma Moody Powell* (Chicago, Ill.: Moody Press, 1943), pp. 142–43, and Emma C. Moody to "Mother," December 2, 1881, Emma C. Moody to Henry Rankin, May 17, 1882, Moody Papers, Powell; Emma C. Moody to H. N. F. Marshall, December 22, 1881, Documents, Northfield Schools.

present campaigns in England, Mrs. Moody concluded, "could induce him to remain away from Northfield one summer." [47]

The family home in Massachusetts was a beautiful spot, situated on one of the main roads into Northfield, commanding a sweeping view of the Connecticut River. The meadows sloped down to the river's edge in front, and the tree-shrouded foothills of the Green Mountains edged almost up to the doors on the other sides. The property adjoined that of his mother, Betsey Holton Moody, and by the mid-1880's it was further encircled by the land purchased for the school for girls. The evangelist had bought the home plot of ten acres, including the house and the outbuildings thereon, early in the fall of 1875, shortly after he returned from the first great campaign in England.[48] This purchase signified his intention to make Northfield his permanent residence for the rest of his life.

The "Old Home," as it came to be called by some members of the family, was a spacious New England farmhouse, with large windows on three sides downstairs that afforded glimpses of the magnificent scenery all about. Like many of the homes in rural areas of the region, the outbuildings were strung out behind the main wing of the house — harness room, carriage sheds, carpenter's shop, covered sheep pens and hen house, and the barn with its three-story hay loft. All of these were linked together to permit easy passage from human to animal living quarters in the winter months when bitter cold and deeply drifted snow slowed all outdoor activities. The back portion of the house had a section running along under the eaves which was converted into tiny rooms, "about as big as pennies," to house the first group of girls who came to the Seminary in 1879 before the first building on the

47. Emma C. Moody to Henry Rankin, May 17, 1882, Moody Papers, Powell.

48. Moody bought the land on October 11, 1875, from a member of the Alexander family, long-time residents of Northfield, for $3,500. Subsequent smaller purchases of land were made between 1877 and 1887. Nearly all of this property abutted on the real estate acquired in 1875; all of the land purchases were deeded to Moody's wife. (Franklin County [Mass.] *Registry of Deeds*, 310:355; 333:46; 369:240; 396:33; D. W. Whittle Diary, June 30, 1876, Moody Bible Institute, Chicago; *Greenfield* [Mass.] *Gazette and Courier*, October 4, 1875.)

campus was completed. Forever afterward the family called this area Penny Alley; eventually it became a place for storing unused paraphernalia and many of the exotic gifts sent to the evangelist from all over the world — an attic of sorts containing unaccountable mysteries for grandchildren to explore on rainy days.[49]

This setting obviously was one the evangelist dearly loved. His letters attest to his feelings. At the beginning of the visit to England he wrote to his mother urging her to "slip out of the County paper all the Northfield news," to keep the family fully informed about activities at home. In London in June, 1884, Moody wrote to a brother in Northfield that he was "just longing to get home. As spring comes on I get homesick." He requested his relatives in Massachusetts that they "tell me all about the farms." The letters he asked for he dubbed "farm letters." Almost every communication from him to his farmer-brothers, George and Edwin in Northfield, was filled with inquiries about every phase of their work, and thus they became "farm letters" themselves. At a much later date Paul summarized his father's feelings with the assertion that each year, "as winter wore away," Moody wrote often to his family in Northfield and these notes were "pathetic in their expression of a genuine homesickness, and he was counting the days and weeks until he could get back." [50]

Northfield offered the evangelist a sense of security and personal identification that in many ways was unique among his contemporaries. Because of his comparative well-being after 1875,[51]

49. For descriptions of the evangelist's house see the accounts of Paul D. Moody in *My Father: An Intimate Portrait of Dwight Moody* (Boston: Little, Brown and Co., 1938), pp. 36–37, and of his granddaughter, Emma Powell, in *Heavenly Destiny*, pp. 108–10.

50. D. L. Moody to Edwin Moody, June 13, 1884, Moody Papers, Moody Bible Institute; D. L. Moody to George Moody, April 10, 1880, March 8, 1881, September 23, 1881, December 3, 1881, January 22, 1882, July 25, 1882, September 19, 1882, D. L. Moody to "Mother," October 22, 1881, Moody Papers, Powell; D. L. Moody to Ambert Moody, December 9, 1892, Esther Loos' Collection, Library of Congress; Paul Moody, *My Father*, p. 38.

51. In the 1880's the evangelist's personal income continued to be based chiefly on the donations handed to him privately at the end of each revival campaign. This helps to explain why he continued to work as a revivalist until his death, for it was the one job for which he was paid. Apparently he also received occasional gifts from friends, unre-

Moody was able to actualize what many Americans of his day often thought about and longed to do — to return to the certainties of a small-town milieu which they remembered from childhood. The evangelist's birthplace, then, and the manifold activities in his later years associated with the family home there, tended to confirm in him many of the deepest prejudices and feelings he had clung to throughout his life, such as the need for unity among social groups and a faith in simple personal virtues. A deeply embedded conservatism was a force which drew him back to Northfield in 1875, and then was reinforced by many of his ensuing experiences there. Perhaps these associations caused him to cling too much to the past, but they helped to make him what he was. His life and thought cannot be understood fully apart from this influence.

At home Moody was able to relax completely and lapse into informality. He let his beard get scraggly, he often moved about in somewhat shabby clothes, and he spent much of his time puttering in the vegetable garden, or among a large flock of chickens in which he took great pride. In addition he oversaw the manifold duties of a household with many guests in the summer, or simply participated in the round of conferences held at the schools each year between June and September. The evangelist never did any large-scale farming. His acreage was not really big enough to plant any crops of substance, and his evangelistic work drew him away from Northfield too often to make it worthwhile becoming a full-time tiller of the soil. His financial resources were sufficient to maintain his family comfortably, and thus he became a "gentleman farmer," able to indulge his special whims and agricultural interests without having to farm profitably. Indeed, much of the work of caring for the animals he owned and the few crops

lated to his revival work. All of these gifts were unsolicited in any formal sense. His granddaughter has reported that the Moodys also owned stock in Morgan and Scott, a publishing house in England, and in the publishing firm of the evangelist's brother-in-law, Fleming H. Revell. These investments provided a small but steady flow of income. (F. G. Ensign to unknown, May 6, 1887, Robert Scott to C. H. McCormick, Jr., May 10, 1887, Nettie Fowler McCormick Papers, Wisconsin State Historical Society; conversation of author with Mrs. Emma Powell, February 17, 1958.)

planted each year was done by hired help drawn from the surrounding community.[52]

An example of special interests best pursued in a pastoral setting was his love of horses and the opportunity to drive them over the winding country roads in and near Northfield. When friends learned of this interest, Moody, like famous men everywhere, received horses as gifts, although he also purchased his own steeds from time to time. Each child in the family had his own horse or colt to ride, and Paul Moody remembered one moment in his childhood when there were fourteen animals tied up in the barn, all of them driving horses.[53] The passion to drive horses seemed to many observers to be purely an extension of the evangelist's personality, for he always loved to push the beasts along at top speed. The pell-mell rush over the landscape in a horse-drawn buggy was an unnerving and unforgettable experience for visitors who happened to participate. Often Moody disregarded roads and drove through fields and down the sides of hills. As in his evangelistic work, he always sought the most direct route to a desired end. A friend once described a typical buggy ride with him: "The last day I was with him he drove me from the Conference Hall over ground so irregular and uneven that every moment I expected we should be overturned. But we came out all

52. Paul Moody, *My Father*, pp. 18–19, 25–26, 32–33, 99–101. Moody's nephew, Ambert Moody (the son of George), took over much of the responsibility of supervising the work done in and about Moody's place while still in his teens. He remained a trusted advisor to the evangelist until the latter's death, running the Northfield Hotel in the 1890's and assisting in the management of the summer conferences. Indications of the nature of the relationship that developed between Ambert and his uncle can be seen in the following letters: D. L. Moody to Ambert Moody, April 1, 1878, February 28, 1881, April 1, 1882, January 2, 1892, March 9, 1895, September 28, 1895, letter with no date, although probably written sometime in the spring of 1892, May 25, 1892, June 14, 1892, June 15, 1892, March 5, 1895, March 9, 1895, April 2, 1895, Esther Loos' Collection, Library of Congress.

53. Paul Moody, *My Father*, pp. 12–16. Moody was known to like animals generally, and this provoked a flood of exotic gifts from both England and the United States. The children recalled the presence from time to time of swans, a pair of English mastiff hounds, a peacock, pheasants, donkeys from Palestine, merino sheep (eventually passed on to Moody's brother George), and a deer in a paddock behind the house. (*Ibid.*, pp. 16–17, 20–21.)

right, at the gate we wanted, and it was certainly the shortest cut." [54]

Somehow Moody's driving at breakneck speed implied a flourish and daring, an instinct for the dramatic, that was also a part of his revival work and preaching. In addition, the way he commanded a team of horses pointed to his love of doing things on a grand scale. The same trait explains in part his diligently maintained flock of hundreds of uneconomic laying hens, and his annual cultivation of a four acre vegetable garden. When he perceived a need in his house, real or imagined, he moved to remedy that need with gargantuan orders. What he thought at one time to be a lack of china produced barrels of it for use thereafter; a shortage of suspenders caused him once to buy a *gross* of white, large-size elastics so that he would be certain never to have to face that difficulty again. His taste for art, while not very discriminating, fitted the same mold. Paul reported that once on a trip West his father saw a series of paintings he liked. Not willing to take the time to select one or two that were particularly appealing, he bought the lot of about twelve oils and sent them to Massachusetts for hanging in his own home and eventually in the homes of his children.[55]

While there is quite a little of the philistine revealed in these acts, they also suggest again his painfully straightforward way of approaching all difficulties, and even something of his rather delightful unpredictableness. Perhaps, too, these deeds reflected half-unconsciously Moody's feelings about long-departed years when material possessions had often been lacking. Certainly he did not compensate for the impoverished experiences of youth as extravagantly as did some of the first-generation millionaires of his own time. He was in no economic position to do that, and his ethical scruples would assuredly have restrained him. But an observer of a later day must not be judged too severely if he seeks to read into these acts, and others like them, personal mo-

54. Unsigned clipping (probably written by F. B. Meyer) from the *British Weekly* (December 29, 1899), Moody Museum, Northfield School for Girls. See also George Pentecost, "Dwight Moody: A Criticism and an Appreciation," *Independent*, 52 (January 4, 1900): 11–12; Paul Moody, *My Father*, pp. 14–15.
55. Paul Moody, *My Father*, pp. 29–31.

tivations linked unavoidably to the privations of the evangelist's early life.

Moody's willful nature was bound at times to affect negatively friends and supporters who moved more slowly than he. He had a brusqueness that offended some people, and he also injured feelings because of his direct, precipitous methods. Yet the hint of his underlying softness of heart is suggested by the fact that there were also times when he seemed vague and indecisive, unable to tell a person gracefully that his services were no longer wanted. The latter was particularly the case with Emma Dryer and Mrs. McCormick in Chicago, and there were hints of similar difficulties in his relations with the headmaster at Mount Hermon in 1890.[56] In all these instances he stepped on toes and hurt people. Although he never intentionally wounded the feelings of anyone, his occasional insensitivity did cause some friends to turn away, indignant at what they felt was unwarrantably rude and unbrotherly treatment.[57]

On the other hand, if the evangelist discovered that he had hurt someone, he nearly always tried to apologize profusely. These near-abject recantations were sometimes made in public and must have cost him something to make, but such was his instinctive response.[58] Although he tried hard to achieve humility,

56. In the spring of 1890 Moody decided that Henry Sawyer should be relieved as principal at Mount Hermon and he agreed that Henry F. Cutler should fill the post temporarily. The evangelist delayed, however, making any public announcement of the change. This temporizing left Cutler in uncertainty for several months. Finally he asked Moody directly to make a decision. As a result Cutler received the job permanently. (Richard W. Day, *A New England Schoolmaster: The Life of Henry Franklin Cutler* [Bristol, Conn., 1950], pp. 90–91.)

57. Wishard, "Beginning of the Student Era," p. 137; Pentecost, "Dwight Moody," p. 11; Emma Dryer to N. F. McCormick, September 14, 1887, Nettie Fowler McCormick Papers; *Homiletic Review*, 36 (September, 1898): 206; Whittle Diary, April 26, 1876.

58. A good example of one of these incidents occurred once at one of the summer conferences when an impetuous young man interrupted Moody while he was speaking. Stung by the interruption, the evangelist chided the young delegate by saying that he was "too young to be heard here. You better wait till your beard is grown." Soon after he realized his mistake and got to his feet before the meeting ended and apologized both to the young man and to all present for his rudeness. "To have been betrayed into nasty and unjust speech was deplorable," wrote an observer later, "but to have atoned for it so promptly

his outspoken habits of mind caused him always to fall short of the mark. Perhaps it is true that he drew closer to the ideal of Christian humbleness in his later years; certainly his struggles over this question drew out of hiding some of the more engaging aspects of his personality. Writing to a friend in 1884 about his career, he displayed himself in his deeply earnest way, now putting on, now tearing off, his sackcloth and ashes. "Whenever I think of businessmen who have become wealthy . . . and the worldly influences that surround them and their families I feel so thankful to God for being right out of the whole of it. What should I want of their moneys? I have had more money to give away to the cause of Christ during the past ten years from the Hymn Book fund than the wealthiest of them."

Perhaps more in true humility he wrote once to H. N. F. Marshall that "I do not like to see the idea of my name being at the head of all the letters [from the seminary]. I do not like to see it in print so much . . . the school is well advertised now and I do not think it is needed." His refusal to be photographed was a further expression of the same attitude. Only late in life, lured by relatives who placed irresistible grandchildren in his arms for posing, did he sit willingly for formal camera shots. As late as 1897 the *Ladies Home Journal* had to resort to whitening the hair of an earlier photograph when Moody refused to permit publication of later pictures.[59]

In his hours of relaxation at home, the evangelist's sense of humor was never far from the surface. He reveled in a good story, sometimes laughing until the tears ran down his cheeks when someone told a real rib-tickler. At the same time the mor-

and openly was both manly and Christian." (Undated clipping, Moody collection, Mount Hermon School Library.) See also *Advance*, 20 (February 19, 1885): 117.

59. Whittle Diary, February 3, 1884; D. L. Moody to H. N. F. Marshall, February 21, 1881, Documents, Northfield Schools; A. P. Fitt to Henry Rankin, June 1, 1897, Rankin Papers. Once on her own authority Emma Moody authorized one of the officials of the national YMCA in New York City to loan a picture of the evangelist to a publishing house for public use. "Send yours and I will take the blame," she said. "You will never get consent from Mr. Moody. No one ever will!" (Emma C. Moody to R. R. McBurney, October 9, 1885, McBurney Collection, Box #1, YMCA Historical Library.)

alistic tendencies so characteristic of the evangelicals meant that a *Bible* conundrum or application of Scripture to point up a jest was strictly taboo. When among friends or members of his family, his old penchant for practical jokes would often appear. He kept a platter of rubber fake fried eggs and pine shaving potato chips in the kitchen to be pulled out for foisting off on unsuspecting visitors at mealtime. There is a description of his sneaky efforts in 1875 to teach a group of boys how to "pin a dipper of water to the wall." Climbing a step-ladder with a large straight pin and a full dipper, he "inadvertently" dropped the pin. As the boys scrambled to aid by picking up the pin, Moody cascaded the water down upon their heads! Once when Paul sought to hive a swarm of bees, the pesky insects somehow got inside his clothes, stinging him severely. Paul remembered much later that worse than the pain of the bee stings was the sight of his father rolling on the ground with laughter — at a safe distance.[60] There is a touch of that lack of sensitiveness to the feelings of others, noted earlier, in these glimpses of Moody playing tricks, especially those he perpetrated on his family. Much of it was good clean fun, but occasionally the line of propriety was overstepped, and it must have been irritating to endure the effects of his mischievous acts and be unable to strike back.[61]

The Moody household in Northfield reflected outwardly the warmth and expansiveness of its head. The latchstring was always out to visitors. In the summer, especially at conference time, the house was full of guests. Informality always seemed to prevail. This spirit particularly sparked the scene at noon each day when "company" and the family gathered in the library before lunch. At this moment the evangelist usually opened his daily mail. He delighted in thrusting freshly opened letters into the hands of his guests accompanied by a brusque "Answer that!" Often he

60. Whittle Diary, May 2, 1876, May 12, 1876; Paul Moody, *My Father*, pp. 22–23; *Congregationalist and Christian World* (November 12, 1914): 627.

61. To be fully fair to Moody it should also be noted that he laughed at himself as well as at other people. His son, especially, has made this point clear, and to illustrate his point has cited several amusing incidents that regaled Moody and everyone in his family. (Paul Moody, *My Father*, pp. 23–25.)

met with remonstrances, but his jesting snort was, "I gave it to *you* to answer! I don't intend to hire the dog and do the barking." [62] This was a New Englander's way of saying that guests were really short-term members of the family and should therefore enjoy the daily give and take of that intimate circle.

The informality people noticed when they came to Moody's home, and the oft-repeated observation that the evangelist utterly lacked pretentiousness, suggest yet another basic attribute of his. Once again it was his son Paul who perceptively remarked that his father was "democracy personified." [63] Surging forward along with a comment like this are memories of the youthful Moody breaking out of the mold of middle-class businessman to minister long hours to poor children in the streets of Chicago, of constant though never completely successful efforts to preach and talk with "the masses" in all of his revival campaigns, of attempts to build private schools designed to educate economically disadvantaged young people. Middle-class attitudes were certainly a basic part of his value system, but Moody also embraced equalitarian sentiments that constantly mitigated and hemmed in any pretensions and patronizing thoughts he might have developed from too close an identification with businessmen and the well-to-do. In this sense he was probably typically American in his responses. Yet here was also a partial key to an understanding of his personality.

His common sense and ability to spot instantly "cranks and imposters" who occasionally tried to force their attentions upon him were in part reflections of this attitude. In an unspoken, dignified manner his concern for everyone, regardless of social position, revealed itself in his daily rounds in Northfield. Driving through the streets he tipped his hat to each person he met — men as well as women. His son thought this to be an outward sign of the respect he held for all of his neighbors. He remained friendly toward the Catholics in Northfield, by then a numerous lot, at a time when most American Protestants were bitterly anti-Papist. Many of the Catholic men were hired for work at

62. *Ibid.*, p. 42. See also Gamaliel Bradford, "Dwight L. Moody the Educator," *Advance*, 52 (May 22, 1930): 675.
63. Paul Moody, *My Father*, p. 107.

the two schools, and Moody gave money for the building of a new parish church in Northfield, for which some of his Protestant friends never forgave him.[64] Probably it was true that at bottom his democratic sentiments were simply an expression of his deep love and esteem for all those with whom he worked and lived; and this love was best understood in the context of a religious faith that in its most profound moments demanded of its supporters precisely the kind of understanding of human relations that Moody seemed to practice from day to day.

Possessing a hearty, bluff manner, the evangelist's personality seemed an open book to many. In reality, few outside his immediate family ever knew him intimately. He may have been friendly but he was not familiar — not the back-slapping, back-store–companion type. He still possessed a streak of the reserve for which New Englanders have always been famous. Even in Northfield, where he was best-known, this was true. As a young man he had been *"Dwight* Moody" to the townspeople. After 1875 he was *"Mr.* Moody" only, a democratic as well as respectful title, which fitted him well. Few who lived in the town those last twenty-five years of his life laid a hand familiarly on his shoulder. Ira Sankey was always "Sankey" to him; and not until several years after their marriage could his wife speak of him as "D. L." rather than "Mr. Moody" in correspondence with family and friends.[65] Innermost feelings and the close relations of husband and

64. Pentecost, "Dwight Moody," p. 11; Paul Moody, *My Father,* pp. 103–09. For examples of the evangelist's efforts to help people in economically disadvantaged positions, see D. L. Moody to "Mr. Lundington," September 15 (no year), Salisbury Family Papers, Yale University Library; Samuel Holton to D. L. Moody, March 20, 1878, D. L. Moody to Samuel Holton, March 30, 1878, Moody Papers, Powell. A delightful anecdote dramatizing Moody's refusal to put on airs, even when introducing a mud-spattered Mount Hermon student to an English gentleman of noble birth is in the *Institute Tie,* n.s., 4 (December, 1903): 127.

65. Paul Moody, *My Father,* pp. 66–67; Pentecost, "Dwight Moody," p. 10; Emma Moody to "brother," October 5, 1866, Emma Moody to Betsey Holton Moody, September 2, 1874, Moody Papers, Powell; Emma C. Moody to "Sister Lizzie," October 6, 1876, Emma C. Moody to "Mother," November 11, 1878, November 2, 1881, Smith Collection. Emma Powell, in *Heavenly Destiny,* reprints a number of Emma C. Moody's letters not noted here, as well as excerpts from her sporadically maintained diary. The same hesitancy to speak in familiar terms about

wife, or of parents with children, were not to be put on public display. One might easily ascribe these practices to Victorian reticence, or to New England prudence, and be partially correct. But there was also an almost innate sense of modesty in Moody which seemed to transcend these cultural determinants and which aided him in the struggle to preserve the privacy of a famous person's most cherished activities and relationships. His wife, a woman of great modesty and reserve, undoubtedly sensitized and refined Moody's feelings in this respect, and surely the ethical demands of the religious faith he took so seriously had their effect upon him, too. A man like Moody, subject to many public pressures and delighting often in the limelight, deserves a great measure of respect for the discreet attitude he rigorously maintained when his deepest personal relationships were involved.

This very discreetness plagues the historian somewhat in the quest for understanding of the exact nature of relations within the family. But there is enough information available to venture a few conclusions. Strong family ties were an important factor in drawing the evangelist back to his birthplace in 1875. An older brother George and his family, as well as the mother and a younger brother, Samuel, had continued to live in the town after Moody left in the 1850's.[66] Samuel, who lived with the mother, died in 1876. Samuel had been a favorite of Dwight's, and perhaps it was the latter's thought that he could partially carry on the responsibilities of his brother if he returned to live nearby. Since his mother's property adjoined his, she was always near at hand. The historical record leaves much to be desired in informing us of her personality and of her relations with her famous son and his family. Moody's devotion to her seemed honest and continuous. Will Moody has reported that scarcely a day passed when the evangelist was absent from home that he did not send his mother a note or at least a newspaper clipping of his whereabouts and

her husband is manifest — only in the diary is the phrase "D. L." consistently used (see pp. 38, 49, 52, 58, 77, 78, 79, 82–83, 88, 90, 92, 118, 119).

66. U.S. Bureau of the Census, "Schedule I, Free Inhabitants of Northfield, in the County of Franklin, State of Massachusetts," *Eighth Census of the United States, 1860* (microfilm copy, National Archives), 11:151; Bureau of the Census, "Inhabitants in the town of Northfield," *Ninth Census 1870*, 7:326.

what he was doing. This filial bond revealed itself most clearly, strongly tinged with Victorian sentiment, in the touching tribute Moody managed to make at her funeral in Northfield in 1895.[67] Betsey Holton Moody remained throughout her son's life the symbol of family solidarity. He never forgot her determination to keep sons and daughters all under one roof early in his life when circumstances threatened to tear them apart. That determination suggested a degree of personal integrity and a familial love that he admired and responded to even in his later years.[68]

Moody's wife had relatively little difficulty adjusting to the routine of life in Northfield when the family settled there in the mid-seventies. Her desire to remain in the background of the family's affairs meant that she was happiest in her home, pursuing the traditional duties of a comfortably situated housewife. This meant endless tasks of canning vegetables and preserves from the capacious garden and the loaded fruit trees, writing letters for her husband, visiting those who needed her in the community, and entertaining her spouse's many friends whenever they stopped in Northfield or attended one of the summer conferences. All this she did self-effacingly and with dispatch. On her children she lavished the same great care and concern that characterized her relations with her husband. Perhaps it was natural that later the children would remember most vividly her responses to their moments of illness. When Paul was afflicted with measles while in college, his mother hastened from Florida to his bedside in New Haven, and spent the long waking hours reading to him. A similar concern evidenced itself at those times when Will fell ill during his student days at Yale.[69]

67. William R. Moody, *D. L. Moody* (New York: Macmillan Co., 1930), p. 510. The eulogy of the son at his mother's funeral is reprinted in *ibid.*, pp. 511–13. See also D. L. Moody to "Mother," December 23, 1891, February 14, 1893. Moody Papers, Powell.

68. Moody's relationships with his mother and both Samuel and George undoubtedly were enhanced shortly after his return from England in 1875 when all three joined the Trinitarian Congregational Church in Northfield. (Pollock, *Moody*, p. 174; Paul Moody, *My Father*, p. 73; *Greenfield* [Mass.] *Gazette and Courier*, October 16, 1876.)

69. Paul Moody, *My Father*, p. 62; Emma C. Moody to W. R. Moody, January 21, 1889, October 6, 1889, January 8, 1890, November 25, 1890,

As was the case in most evangelical households, it was the mother's responsibility to provide her children with the rudiments of the formal content of the Christian faith. The teaching procedures she followed were time-honored. Each Sunday afternoon the children undertook the task of memorizing certain of the Psalms and selected passages from the Gospel narratives. As Emma's young charges bent to their duties she remained with them, seeking to answer questions and illuminate the meaning of passages as best she knew how. She was firm and unyielding in her demands that what seemed at the time a thankless job — to young Emma, Will, and Paul at least — was to be completed in its entirety. Brought up a Baptist, she loyally joined with Moody in the activities of the Congregational Church in Northfield. It has been made plain, however, that on certain doctrines, notably that concerning baptism, privately she never departed from the perspectives of youth.[70] This does not mean that the training of her children departed in any significant way from the broad standards of evangelicalism. Rather, it simply means that she maintained a degree of individuality in her religious thoughts, quietly and almost unnoticed, that was perfectly in character.

Above all else she was loyal to her husband. This loyalty, in reality a reflection of the love that existed between her and "D. L.," could even take on overtones of hardheartedness that ordinarily was alien to her personality. A sensitive son has noted that those persons deemed "disloyal" to Moody by Emma — people who took advantage of his generous nature, or who disagreed and no longer were able to work with him — were cast into limbo in the mind of the evangelist's wife. As Paul expressed this fierce attachment, "her affection and admiration for my father were such that disloyalty to him was the unpardonable sin in her eyes, unforgivable, unforgettable, and above all unmentionable. The gentlest and kindest and most thoughtful of women, here she was implacable." [71]

Moody Papers, Powell; Emma C. Moody to W. R. Moody, February 4, 1889, October 24, 1889, Smith Collection.

70. Paul Moody, *My Father*, pp. 62–64.

71. *Ibid.*, pp. 65–66; Emma C. Moody to W. R. Moody, February 4, 1889, Smith Collection.

Moody, of course, returned her affection fully. Again, there is a veil that has been drawn across nearly all of the historical record on this account. All the evidence we possess now of this relationship between husband and wife are fading memories of one or two relatives and a few anecdotes from the pens of their children. From the family accounts it does not appear that the Moodys lived a marriage that conformed to the usual image of a stuffy, sexually repressed Victorian union. Modesty and restraint were present, but also conscious, overt affection that their children witnessed and recognized as a deeply felt, tender, and continuous interaction of two human beings who loved each other. How else does one explain the fact that even late in life this man and his wife occasionally drove off with horse and buggy into the woods and hills of the surrounding area, to be alone with each other, "going where fancy led them, having as it were a renewed honeymoon"? [72] These last words undoubtedly are romanticized too much by the admiring eyes of a child of theirs, but the actions do indicate in a dumb sort of way something of the strength of the ties that held these two individuals so closely together. [73]

The bonds between parents and children were almost as strong. One of Moody's habits when he was absent from home was to take time to write his children on their birthdays, no matter where

72. Paul Moody, *My Father*, pp. 70–71. Emma Moody evidently took great pleasure in walks and drives, especially when her husband joined her. Whenever she discovered a scenic spot in her travels with the evangelist in their later years, she easily prevailed upon him to take her on buggy rides to enjoy the natural beauties together. See especially her comments about Colorado Springs and its environs and the scenery near Santa Barbara, California, in Emma C. Moody to W. R. Moody, March 17, 1889, March 30, 1889, April 5, 1889, Smith Collection. This strongly suggests that behind Emma Moody's exterior of reserve and conventionality, a deeply romantic, even sentimental, strain existed that was not only characteristic of the age, but ran parallel to similar sentiments in the makeup of her husband.

73. The evangelist turned down an opportunity to visit Egypt and the Middle East in 1887, principally because, as he wrote to his oldest son, "I could not leave my wife." Separation from the rest of the family also figured prominently in this decision. (D. L. Moody to "Willie," January 15, 1887, Moody Papers, Powell.) See also W. R. Moody to "Mother," February 5, 1900, excerpts printed in Powell, *Heavenly Destiny*, pp. 17–18; Emma C. Moody to W. R. Moody, March 6, 1890, Smith Collection.

he was or how busy he might be. When Will reached his seventeenth birthday, his father, then in Jacksonville, Florida, penned a note asserting that "I wish I could write all I feel this morning, but I cannot, so you will have to wait until you get to be a father before you will know how much I love you. I am your loving father, with a prayer and a wish that you may see seventy good years." [74]

In 1887 the evangelist sent his daughter Emma on a trip to Norway.[75] Although he had urged this trip on his daugher, at the moment of her departure he suffered twinges of regret that she would be so far away from him for so long. He spoke openly of his melancholy in the last letter he wrote to her from Chicago before she left the country. "I must write you once more before you leave this land . . . although I have no news to tell you. But I am real lonely at the thought of your goin. It has seemed so nice to me to think of you so safe and happy at Northfield and now it seems as if a part of myself was gone and I do not know how it will seem when I get to Northfield. . . . I never loved you more than I do tonight and if I thought you were not goin to get great good I think I should telegraph you not to go. . . . May the Angels of God hover over you by day and night is my most earnest prayer." The time for the annual student conference also arrived while his daughter was gone. Moody took time out of his busy schedule to write frequent letters and to send her each day's newspaper clippings containing details of the confer-

74. D. L. Moody to W. R. Moody, March 20, 1886, Moody Papers, Powell.

75. Emma's trip to Scandinavia was one of several lengthy excursions Moody planned and underwrote for his children. Will traveled once to Alaska and Paul had been tentatively promised a globe-circling tour after his graduation from college, a proposal that had to be discarded at the time of his father's death. All were typical gestures, reflecting Moody's desire to give his offspring advantages through travel and advanced education which he had lacked as a young person. Paul argues that actually his father was torn between this attitude and a traditional desire that his children not be deprived of the "advantages" of going without. Since the evangelist had the money and possessed a generous nature, he delighted in awarding gifts to those he liked; this probably means he "spoiled the child" most frequently. Paul Moody discusses both sides of this part of his own upbringing in *My Father*, pp. 8–11, 57–60, 77, 142.

ence sessions. One of his letters shows how easily he fitted in among the young men, and reveals as well the newsy chatter he passed on to his offspring. "The Harvard and Yale and Princeton boys had a fire down on the bank of the river or in front of the woods in front of our House and Willie and myself were invited down and they sang songs and told storeys and they did have a time. . . . I must go to the six o'clock meeting so good morning." [76]

In the fall of 1887 Will began his college work at Yale.[77] After he left home his parents buoyed him with a steady stream of letters. They seemed no different than most parents today in their concern with his experiences at school. They sympathized over his difficulties with a foreign language, emphasized the dangers of scrub football — "it seems to me like running a great risk of being crippled for life for the sake of an half hour's fun and exercise" — registered shock at his first tasting of a hot toddy on a Yale outing — "If you meant it that you would take hot whiskey if you felt cold, then, I have reason to think you would take wine for the sake of not seeming cold or odd with friends. I want to beg of you Will never do this!" — gave advice about playing cards — "Will you make me a promise never to play for any gain not even a drink of soda? Will you promise me this?" — and worried over his illnesses when he was so far from home.[78]

One thread of concern ran through all their letters, however. This was the hope that their son would some day give his life fully to work for Christ. On this point mother and father were united and determined. It was a hope they cherished for all of

76. D. L. Moody to Emma Moody, April 25, 1887, July 12, 1887, Moody Papers, Powell. See also D. L. Moody to Emma Moody, April 24, 1887, July 4, 1887, July 6, 1887, *ibid.*

77. Paul reported that the "ultra-pious" were critical of his father for allowing his two sons to go to Yale when there were other colleges, especially in the Midwest, that had stronger reputations for maintaining religious orthodoxy. It is a sign of his trust in the good sense of his sons, and his own common sense, that he brushed off such comments and paid little attention to them. (Paul Moody, *My Father*, pp. 91–92.)

78. D. L. Moody to W. R. Moody, November 26, 1887, January 20, 1888, Emma C. Moody to W. R. Moody, January 21, 1889, October 6, 1889, January 8, 1890, November 25, 1890, Moody Papers, Powell; Emma C. Moody to W. R. Moody, February 4, 1889, November 20, 1889, February 19, 1890, Smith Collection.

their children, the result in part of their own deep religious convictions, but most especially the result of the special emphases that were at the heart of the evangelical persuasion. Tangible signs that their offspring were to remain close to God and would be committed Christians after they left home permanently were constantly looked for by the parents as the youngsters reached adolescence. As early as 1878, Moody's wife confided her feelings and surely those of her husband in a letter to a close friend in England. "If God will only make our dear children his *own*," she said, "*faithful and earnest*[,] it is the best that we can ask of Him for them." [79]

Apparently by the late eighties their daughter had responded to parental advice. On Christmas day, 1889, Moody wrote his eldest child a glowing letter that seemed to burst with the joy he felt when he discovered, after a long absence from home, that she was working actively in the church and launching plans to assist the poorer inhabitants of Northfield. "For thirty years I have had the secret of a happy life," he asserted, "and it was in making others happy." Now it seemed as though his daughter was beginning to taste life in a similar manner and it pleased him immensely. "You can set an example for others," he concluded, "and it seems . . . you have just commenced to live." [80]

Will appeared to be another matter. Even before he reached college he began, not unnaturally, to think independent thoughts about religion. But the slightest deviation from the path his parents thought proper drew admonitions from them. In reply to an observation as a seventeen-year-old that the Wednesday prayer meeting was uninteresting, his father suggested he "go in and make it interesting" — a familiar comment to anyone who had attended his revivals. In the same breath the evangelist asserted that Will should attend "one prayer meeting a week" if he expected to grow spiritually. These words were all a part of a continuous

79. Emma C. Moody to Mrs. J. Mackinnon, April 1, 1878, Moody Papers, Powell.

80. D. L. Moody to Emma Moody, December 25, 1889, Moody Papers, Powell. See also Emma C. Moody to J. Mackinnon, April 1, 1878, *ibid.*, for comments of the mother about the younger Emma's spiritual progress at an earlier age.

stream of advice that was handed to Will throughout his adolescence.[81]

When the young man freely admitted late in 1886 that he felt
tempted to smoke, an almost universal urge among young blades
his age, his father hastened to give him guidance and to speak more
generally about spiritual matters. Moody's words reveal with some
precision his own religious convictions and the earnestness with
which he hoped his son could achieve attitudes similar to his own.

> I have not talked much with you for fear I would turn you
> more and more againt Him, who I love more than all the
> world and if I have ever said or done anything unbecoming
> a Christian father I want you to forgive me. . . . I have
> always thought that when a mother and father are Chris-
> tians and their children were not that there was something
> decidedly wrong with them. I still think so. I have tried
> not to make religion offensive in my home and if I thought I
> had neglected to do my duty toward my three children I think
> I would rather die than live. I have tried to make your
> home life as pleasant as I can and have done all in my power
> to make you happy. . . . I have never prayed for you as
> I do now. . . . and now dear Willie take this in the same
> spirit it is written in.[82]

One finds in this passage an intricate tangle of attitudes — self-
justification, tenderness and loving concern, attempts at humility,
and driving efforts to convert the unconverted — personality
traits that have all been noted before. Needless to say, these words
say a great deal about Moody and what moved him to act, both
in public and in private.

To many present day observers, the evangelist's worries expressed in this letter would seem far out of proportion to the
seriousness of his son's "misdeeds." But this would be to misjudge
the attitude of Moody and most deeply committed evangelical
Protestants. To them the decision to accept Christ *immediately* was

81. D. L. Moody to W. R. Moody, September 25, 1886, *ibid.* For
similar statements see D. L. Moody to W. R. Moody, September 24,
1884, January 24, 1886, *ibid.*
82. D. L. Moody to W. R. Moody, December 8, 1886, *ibid.*

the most important and necessary act of a man's life. It was logical to think that young people nurtured in Christian homes and in the church were among those best qualified and most able to make this decision. To allow such individuals to slip from the fold would be almost tragic and quite inexcusable. This issue had to be faced by the parents in every evangelical family, but for Moody the problem was undoubtedly an even more urgent one to resolve. What would people say if the children of the greatest soul-saver in America turned away from Christ? The evangelist seemed to imply that he was bothered by some such problem in his comment to Will that Christian parents whose children left the church probably harbored unseen blemishes that made them more at fault than the young people. He was restating here a view often held by the most committed evangelicals, but unconsciously there was also a warning therein to his child: by accepting Christ you can prove the strength of your father's faith as well as your own. These were subtle pressures that perhaps the evangelist was not fully conscious he was exerting. But the peculiar thrust of his thinking and the special circumstances of his position within evangelical Protestantism were powerful determinants. We can sympathize with what he did, or at least understand why he said what he said, even though we may not fully agree with all the implications of his entreaties to his son.

The anxious queries of a mother and father also suggest that a Puritan conscience still worked its will in the Moody household. The agonizing of Dwight and Emma over what seems today to be trivial bits of behavior was not out of the ordinary, but quite within a long-established tradition of deep-seated emotions that New Englanders since the earliest colonial days had experienced. For the earlier Puritans there was not only the need to recognize the perfect love of God and the exemplary life of Christ that were a guide to daily action, but also there had to be frank admission that even the "saints" again and again failed to live up to their high calling. The diaries of divines of the colonial period abound in statements that reflect the inner tensions created by striving to live according to high ethical standards and the inevitable failures that resulted simply from being human. In the late nineteenth century people like Moody and his wife, deeply religious and imbued with strong feelings about what was proper as defined by the ethics of the evangelical faith, were similarly afflicted. It is probably true that by the 1880's the evangelicals were entirely too legalistic in their definitions of sound ethical behavior. At least it appears that way to an observer eight decades later. Yet our judgments should not blind us to the intensity and legitimacy of the feelings of Moody and his wife as they struggled with their son through his adolescence. Especially this is true when the parents' thoughts are placed in the context of a religious heritage extending back to the earliest practices of the Puritans both in this country and in England.[83]

In any event, the pressures on Will continued without letup. The young man began his college work in the fall of 1887. His first years at Yale continued to be a time of trial for his parents. His mother wrote to him shortly after he left of her fear of him "being in any college without reliance on the help of Christ." She went on to inform him that "Papa I know is praying and I am that Gods spirit may lead you to give up yourself to Christ entirely." Stronger exhortations followed. "I don't believe my dear boy that anything else will really satisfy you. You know what you ought to do, then do it, not halfway but out and out. . . . It

83. A sensitive brief appraisal of the workings of the Puritan conscience is in Edmund Morgan, *The Puritan Dilemma: The Story of John Winthrop* (Boston: Little, Brown and Co., 1958), chap. 1. Some of the most revealing words of Emma Moody's that have been preserved point to the anguish that accompanied her musings over the possible "corruption" of an "innocent" son by the "world" outside Northfield. Traveling with her husband in the spring of 1889, Emma wrote Will that "we have in the West seen so much of young men, some that are noble young men & some that are wrecks. My thoughts have so often gone to you with the prayer also that you might be kept from sin. I know so much more about the temptations than if I had always lived quietly at home & as I have known of case after case of young men who have gone astray while in College you dont know how I have yearned after you & prayed that you might be kept. I have a horror of strong drink & its dreadful power but I have as great a dread of a sin that I know young men fall a victim to as often & now as I write I know you wont laugh or make light of my earnest prayer for you that you may be kept from the *first* steps either in drink or in impurity. You are not stronger than other men & the temptations are ready. Dont depend on yourself but look to the same source for help in overcoming that we go to for you. May God keep & bless my dear dear boy!" (Emma C. Moody to W. R. Moody, May 5, 1889, Smith Collection.)

is not for dying alone but for right living you will need help stronger than your own." In February of the following year his father wrote him that he thought "the best birthday gift I could have . . . is the news that you have taken your stand for the Son of God. My heart goes up to God for you constantly." Still later his mother asked, "I wonder what you do on Sundays. I wish you were in some Bible class. If Prof. Harper has one — join!" [84]

As late as January, 1889, Will was still unable to make up his mind. His father castigated himself that the boy had grown up and left home "with so little knowledge of the word of God." Will's asserted "growing dislike" of the *Bible* was to the father "the greatest sorrow I have on earth." Scarcely four months later, in April, 1889, the evangelist received the news that his son had "taken a good stand for Christ." Moody quickly wrote Will his congratulations. "I do not think you will ever know until you have a son of your own how much good it did me to hear [this]," he said. Even so the parents were not satisfied to let the issue drop completely in the letters they wrote to their son. Later the same year Moody ended one of his notes to his second-born with a bit of advice. "I do hope," he said, "you will lay hold of eternal life with a firm hold. It seems to me it is the only thing worth holding on to in this life. Everything else must pass away." Written in a spirit of encouragement, rather than as an admonition, the evangelist's words did seem to reflect a change in attitude that accompanied Will's public commitment to "stand for Christ." [85]

In reality there probably was little chance that Will would have acted other than in the way he did. His deep attachment to his family all but assured the eventual outcome. Family ties at Northfield tugged as strongly and insistently at the young man

84. D. L. Moody to W. R. Moody, February 4, 1888, Emma C. Moody to W. R. Moody, November 4, 1887, October 6, 1889, Moody Papers, Powell. See also Emma C. Moody to W. R. Moody, May 7, 1888, February 4, 1889, March 17, 1889, Smith Collection. "Prof. Harper" refers to William Rainey Harper, then a leading young biblical scholar on the Yale faculty. As noted earlier, Harper had been invited to speak at the student conferences at Northfield and apparently was a favorite among the undergraduates at Yale.

85. D. L. Moody to W. R. Moody, January 12, 1889, April 6, 1889, October 23, 1889, Moody Papers, Powell.

as they had on his father. Even after three years' absence in college, Will suffered attacks of homesickness which caused his parents to worry.[86] It is not surprising that following graduation from Yale he returned to Northfield to live, marrying and raising his family there, and eventually assuming general direction of the schools his father had founded, serving them with distinction for over three decades thereafter.[87]

In the early nineties Moody's happiness grew as the family circle widened. In 1894 both Emma and Will were married in Northfield, the former on May 10, the latter on August 12.[88] Will's wife was May Whittle, the daughter of D. W. Whittle, one of Moody's closest friends since the early days with the YMCA in Chicago. Emma married A. P. Fitt, a young Irishman who came to this country to act as Moody's secretary, and who with his young wife moved to Chicago to assist in the management of the Bible Institute. Before her marriage, May Whittle had often been a visitor in the Moody home. To find a place for herself with Will and his family was not at all difficult. And it did not take long for "Percy" Fitt to gain the acceptance of his in-laws.

In his special way Moody demonstrated his attitude even before the latter couple was married. Once when young Fitt was away, his fiance sat down to write him. She was called from her room to see a friend who had come to visit, and while she was gone her father stole into her room and composed her letter for her. "My dearly Beloved Piercey I Cannot tell you with pen how very much *I love you.* Your last letter lifted me up in the clouds. . . . I

86. D. L. Moody to W. R. Moody, October 23, 1889, *ibid;* Emma C. Moody to W. R. Moody, May 5, 1889, September 19, 1889, Smith Collection.

87. In the nineties Will was handed a growing list of responsibilities at Northfield that lightened the burden on his father's shoulders and prepared the son to take over entirely the overseeing of schools and conferences after the evangelist's death. For evidence of this development, which the elder Moody promoted, see D. L. Moody to Ambert Moody, March 5, 1895, March 9, 1895, April 2, 1895, Esther Loos' Collection. At the time of Moody's death Paul was still in college. Thus other members of the family assumed command of most of the key jobs connected earlier with the great evangelist. Consequently Paul left Northfield and built a career outside Massachusetts, culminating in his tenure, until his death in 1948, as president of Middlebury College.

88. Northfield Town Records, p. 43.

find no one in Providence that will take your place. All the young men here look inferior to you. You are a boy after my own heart." Even during a serious love affair there was always room for a practical joke or two perpetrated by the evangelist to keep matters in proper perspective. Joshing aside, however, the close bonds between the father and his children remained even after marriage. A week after Emma's wedding, the evangelist wrote to his daughter that the family "did not know how much we all loved you untill you left us Monday eve." The house, he said, seemed "lonely without you and all seam to miss you more than I can tell." Pride, mixed with deep affection for his offspring, was the theme expressed in letters written to his two eldest children at this time of their great personal happiness.[89]

Late in the evening of February 4, 1888, Moody paused from a round of duties which had called him away from Northfield to write a note to his son Will. The evangelist was in a pensive mood. "I will be 51 inside of 2 hours," he wrote. "It seems strange to me to be so old. I feel as young as I did at 30. I cannot realize that I am passing off the stage and you are coming on."[90] With these words Moody caught feelings that said a great deal about his life and career at that particular moment. As the 1880's ended, the list of the evangelist's achievements continued to expand. The previous decade had been a very busy time, and, although lacking somewhat the great public acclaim that had accompanied so much of his work in the seventies, it was on the whole a very fruitful period in his career. Always a man of immense energies and indefatigable optimism, Moody could look back over what he had planned and what he had wrought and find real satisfaction for himself. Thus it was easy to understand why he could assert that he felt no more than thirty in spirit, if such were not the case in actual years.

Yet even amidst his successes, times were changing and his own responsibilities had altered enough to leave him with slight feel-

89. The undated letter to "Piercey," in Moody's handwriting with additional comments by Emma at the bottom giving an explanation, is in Moody Papers, Powell. The other quoted material is from D. L. Moody to Emma Moody, May 18, 1894, *ibid.* See also D. L. Moody to W. R. Moody, March 25, 1894, *ibid.*

90. D. L. Moody to W. R. Moody, February 4, 1888, *ibid.*

ings of uneasiness. We have already seen how the proliferating programs which Moody tried to finance and direct had created difficulties and partial failures for him, as ability to maintain close control in one person's hands became an impossibility. Moreover, as advancing years pressed in upon him, Moody would not be able to maintain the furious pace he had always set for himself. Despite his disclaimers to his son, he was *not* as young as he was at 30, and whether he liked it or not, eventually he would have to slow down. In 1892 Moody consented, while preaching again in England, to go with friends on an extended vacation to the Holy Land at Eastertime. His son Paul claimed it was probably the "only occasion" in his life "when he traveled" solely for "leisure . . . as an end in itself."[91] This may have been a hint of the evangelist's willingness to ease his schedule a bit as he moved on into middle age.

Developments at Northfield also fit easily into this perspective. The undoubted natural beauty of the locale and the presence there of his family and those public projects of his that often seemed closest to his heart made it easy for him to think longingly about the "Old Home." It is not meant to suggest that during the last years of his life Moody abdicated in any way what he felt were his public responsibilities. After all, he was vigorously leading a revival campaign in Kansas City at the time he suffered what was the first of a series of fatal heart attacks late in 1899. But his deepest emotional attachments all centered in his birthplace, and thus it is not surprising to see him appreciating more and more often in his later years the solace, happiness, and sense of security which the activities there seemed to afford him. They were activities that were less in the public eye and more of a private nature. His home life in particular seemed a serene and in many ways unruffled series of daily experiences, rooted in the economic security which the evangelist was able to provide for his family and the undoubted love that all the members of the family felt for each other. To observers of our day, the Moody household was a sunny representation of solid, middle-class family

---

91. Paul Moody, *My Father*, p. 131. There are accounts of the trip to Palestine, *ibid.*, chap. 9; Powell, *Heavenly Destiny*, chap. 14; W. R. Moody, *Moody* (1930), pp. 396–98.

life of the late nineteenth century. It would be hard for any person participating in such an environment not to enjoy it most of the time and feel at least relatively secure.

In the nineties, however, a series of untoward events disrupted the rather even tenor of both Moody's private and public life. The rapidly changing external scene in America was partly responsible for the frustrations he sometimes experienced, and the tragedy of death among young children in the evangelist's immediate family also made these trying years. Through all his difficulties, however, Moody's faith anchored his personality, which meant he retained his essentially optimistic spirit to the end. But it is true that much of the last few years of his life were spent with worries more intractable and profound than any he had had to face before. Thus his last days can be set apart in certain basic respects from much that had gone before.

11

Last Days

In June, 1884, Cyrus H. McCormick, a long-time friend of the evangelist, died. One of the ministers who spoke at his funeral tried to piece together for the mourners what seemed to be the distinguishing characteristics of McCormick's religious life. In words reprinted in the religious periodical founded in Chicago by McCormick, the speaker said first that the great businessman had "believed, without hesitation, whatever was said in the Bible." He had a settled confidence that "the whole Bible was the word of God, and that whatever it said must be true. . . . And that," came the conclusion, "is the kind of faith that makes men strong." There was a second great attribute of McCormick's faith — "his love for and his devotion to the distinctive doctrines of the gospel." And, the eulogist went on, "we all know it to be true, and it is with a feeling of utmost thankfulness that I here proclaim it, that no religious teacher . . . could ever win this man's confidence unless he taught the great leading doctrines of Christ's gospel with no uncertain sound. Justification by faith, regeneration by the Spirit, the propitiary sacrifice of Jesus Christ[,] the God man [,] the only way of salvation [—] these and kindred truths are things he loved to hear clearly stated." [1]

These words perhaps say something significant about Cyrus McCormick's religious beliefs, but they say even more about the fears and uncertainties that were manifesting themselves through-

1. *Interior*, 15 (June 22, 1884): 4.

out the Protestant community by the end of the 1880's. In stressing his subject's absolute commitment to "whatever was said in the Bible," and his "devotion to the distinctive doctrines of the gospel," the ministerial eulogist suggested that these seeming verities were now under open and sustained attack, even by people within the churches. The debate over higher criticism and its effect upon theological standards had its beginnings in this country primarily in the 1880's. Charles Briggs, a young Presbyterian Biblical scholar and theologian, deserves much credit for focusing attention on the matter by opening as early as 1881 the pages of the *Presbyterian Review*, a journal he coedited, to articles dealing with higher criticism. By the end of the 1880's, Moody's friend, William Rainey Harper, was also performing yeoman's service in the cause. Harper, although a topflight scholar, did a great deal to popularize the principles and findings of the higher critics among the clergy and forward-looking elements in the ranks of the laity. In 1882 he founded a semi-popular journal published twice monthly, the *Hebrew Student*, and later organized a series of chatauqua-like summer seminars — suspiciously like the summer conferences at Northfield — through which he spread liberal ideas concerning Biblical and theological studies.[2]

By the middle of the 1880's some of the popular evangelical journals had begun to take notice. The *New York Christian Advocate*, parent of all the smaller *"Advocates"* scattered across the country, presented a survey of the "Results of Recent Biblical Research," in 1885, and a year later discussed in detail various aspects of the controversy then raging, especially in England, over the nature and authority of the "inspired *Bible*." In the eighties, Presbyterians were also willing to print articles in their New York-based periodical, *The Evangelist*, about Biblical criticism and to struggle openly with the problems raised by the new

2. One historian has recently stated that "if Briggs was the prophet, Harper was the organizer of the crusade." (Ira V. Brown, "The Higher Criticism Comes to America, 1880–1900," *Journal of Presbyterian History*, 38 [December, 1960]: 200.) This entire article deserves a careful reading in this connection. See also William E. Moore, "American Identity and the Decline of Biblical Religion" (unpublished paper read at the sessions of the Society for Religion in Higher Education, August, 1966).

scholarship. Many of these early expressions of interest ended, however, with strong reaffirmations of traditional views. A writer for the *Christian Advocate* phrased it well. The new Biblical research, he said "has done nothing to shake the Christian believer's permanent confidence in the inspired accuracy of the sacred text." Perhaps somewhat more uncertainly he concluded that "whatever are the futher disclosures of Biblical research, God's 'testimonies are sure,' and 'the Word which he commanded for a thousand generations' will not be found obsolete or antiquated in our day." [3]

As younger ministers carefully considered the new ways of thought, and sometimes began to move to new theological positions, they came into conflict with the traditionalists. As early as 1883 local heresy trials plagued the Presbyterian denomination. A troubled editorial writer for the *New York Evangelist* pondered the meaning of all this. "When such cases become frequent, and when the defection occurs at some specific and central point in the faith, it becomes at once an important question . . . whether what appears on the surface is a revelation of a deeper current." The writer went on: "Especially does this question become significant when those who for such reasons abandon the Church . . . are . . . men exceptional in personal worth, and of high religious temper and usefulness." The answer appeared to be a thoroughgoing revision of the denomination's creedal statements, in order "to win back those who have swung from one theological extreme over into another, and to prevent further instances of doctrinal defection, and save to the Church beloved sons, especially among her younger members." [4] Biblical criticism and theological change were joining hands in a most unsettling manner. The response reprinted here represented a decided minority view among church people in the eighties, but it was sig-

3. *New York Christian Advocate,* 60 (September 24, 1885): 615; 61 (September 9, 1886): 567–68; *New York Evangelist,* 54 (January 4, 1883): 1; (January 25, 1883): 4; (February 1, 1883): 4; (February 15, 1883): 2, 4.

4. *New York Evangelist,* 54 (October 4, 1883): 4. For interest among the Congregationalists in changing theological patterns in the eighties, see *Advance,* 21 (January 28, 1886): 54; (February 18, 1886): 102; (March 18, 1886): 161; (June 10, 1886): 364.

nificant that such a position could find expression even that early in one of the leading evangelical journals.

As the century neared its end, the signs of change within the church grew greatly in number. In 1894 a series of articles published in *The Congregationalist*, the most widely-read popular journal of that denomination, dramatized what was taking place. The editors sought to provide for their readers a comprehensive understanding of what the cutting edge of thought and practice among Congregationalists had produced as the churches struggled to cope with industrialization and the impact of science and evolutionary theory upon theology. In six successive weeks the story unfolded of "new departures in our theological seminaries," including notes on changes in worship, in methods of work with the outside world, and in doctrine. Not only did these articles inform thousands of lay people of the work of the pioneers of the Social Gospel like George Herron at Iowa — later Grinnell — College and Graham Taylor at Chicago Theological Seminary, but they also attempted to summarize the tendencies toward theological liberalism, already called the "New Theology," being developed both by Frank H. Foster, then at Pacific Seminary near San Francisco, and by the proponents of "progressive orthodoxy" located chiefly at Andover Seminary on the East Coast. The results of important Biblical studies conducted at Yale Divinity School and important alterations in curriculum at the Hartford Seminary were also discussed. In short, ministerial training in all of the leading Congregational seminaries was undergoing fundamental change. A writer for *The Congregationalist*, commenting upon the series of articles, made the point quite explicit. "The leading teachers in our seminaries frankly claim to be reformers in theology. They recognize the fact that a restatement of doctrine is demanded, and they are striving to meet the demand. The theology of Edwards, Hopkins, Emmons, Taylor and Park, with its various modifications as presented by these great teachers, is no longer dominant in any of our seminaries." [5]

Perhaps it was not surprising that the Congregationalists were

5. *Congregationalist*, 79 (May 24, 1894): 718. See also *ibid*., (April 19, 1894): 550, 557–58; (April 26, 1894): 594–95; (May 3, 1894): 628; (May 10, 1894); 659; (May 17, 1894): 692; (May 24, 1894): 724.

responding as they did to the new impulses in society and the church. Historically the left wing of the denomination had shaded off imperceptibly into Unitarianism, and there had been famous Congregationalist deviants from strict orthodox evangelical positions, like Horace Bushnell, earlier in the century. But even more representative evangelical groups showed the effects of the changing times. In the *New York Christian Advocate*, open challenges were being made in the early nineties to the traditional view that the authority of Biblical writings should never be questioned. Although editorially the *Advocate* was much more conservative than *The Congregationalist*, even in its pages the frequency and the sharpness of debate over theological and Biblical questions, when contrasted with the eighties, was striking.[6]

The *Bible* had always been central to the entire world view of committed evangelicals. The new questions and suggested revisions in interpretation were deeply unsettling to many people. Here is a statement, written in 1891, which suggests the agony of unrest and spiritual turmoil that some persons were going through.

> The reason why there is so little spiritual life in the church to-day is easily found. The Bible is not to the average professor of religion the one book and the living book that it was to the saints in olden times. We believe in the Bible, we read it, we eulogize it, we go to it for texts to use as mottos for our sermons; but we do not study it and tremble or rejoice in its presence as we would if we realized that it is spirit and life. If we had this faith in the Word we would never leave our homes in the morning without taking with us in our memories and our hearts passages of Scripture to caution, comfort, and direct us through the day. We would be meditating on this divine truth as we walked the streets . . . when we came home at night we would say, Now I must invoke the keeper of the soul before I go

6. For a sampling of articles and comments about biblical criticism in the New York *Christian Advocate* in the early nineties, see 68 (January 26, 1893): 51–52; (February 9, 1893): 81, 83; (March 16, 1893): 163–64; (March 30, 1893): 195; (April 6, 1893): 217; (April 13, 1893): 230.

to sleep. I must hunt up sweet promises in the Bible to pillow
my head upon. . . . We ought to open the Holy Book, as
we would go into a sanctuary where we were sure of meeting
our heavenly Father face to face and of hearing his voice.[7]

These were words that spoke powerfully to the hearts of many
evangelicals, but they were powerless to stem the tide of change
that swept on and on.

When the traditional faith was challenged at its core, it was
inevitable that attitudes regarding everyday practices associated
for so long with that faith would change. By 1895 old-time piety
seemed to be waning noticeably. Comments of church people, both
positive and negative, underscored the fact. An observer supporting the need for change declared that the "piety" of the nineties
"is characterized by a less vivid sense of personal sinfulness and
of the inherent evil of sin than was common formerly." Such a
"fact," he said, was "not wholly lamentable." Others, however,
were quick to lament this new attitude. "The good old way of
our fathers is not popular these days," asserted a conservative Presbyterian. Significantly, he saw the dry rot of lackadaisical religious
practice first affecting the home and the Christian family. People
"used to recognize the Christian home as a church in miniature."
The family was a congregation for Bible study and for worship."
Now there seemed to be "really no time, in many homes . . .
for religion. It is relegated to the Sabbath . . . and all the piety
has been [placed?] outside the home. If this is the way we are
drifting it is time for fathers and mothers to stop and think."
Others bewailed the apparent growing lack of respect that children held for their parents, surely a reflection of the widespread
"want of reverence." The admonishment continued. " 'As a man
thinketh in his heart, so is he.' If he thinks irreverence, he will
act irreverent[ly]." [8]

By the middle of the nineties, advanced thinking in church

7. *Interior*, 22 (January 5, 1891): 4.
8. *Congregationalist*, 80 (January 31, 1895): 154; *Interior*, 17
(April 22, 1886): 4; 22 (January 8, 1891): 2. See also *ibid.*, (January 22, 1891): 2; (March 5, 1891): 4; *Congregationalist*, 79 (February 8,
1894): 186; 80 (June 6, 1895): 871.

circles was willing to stab at practices and institutions that for generations had symbolized the heart of religion for evangelical Christians. A bold editorial in *The Congregationalist* ultimately raised what had been an almost unaskable question: "Must Conversion Be a Special and Conscious Experience?" For many honest people, asserted the editorial writer, especially those "trained from infancy in Christian households and taught that they have been dedicated to God and belong to him," the "change of heart and life" usually denoted as the conversion experience "occurs almost, if not wholly, unperceived at the time." Only later did one awaken "to the fact that he has been trying sincerely for sometime to love, trust and obey his God." This was of course a perennial problem the church had had to face — witness the Halfway Covenant in Puritan Massachusetts in 1657. What was significant about this statement of the 1890's was that church spokesmen were now willing to challenge openly the long-held belief among nineteenth century evangelicals that conversion was a clear-cut, easily identifiable moment in the believer's life. This attitude simply no longer squared with people's experiences, and so it was "to be expected" that sons and daughters of Christian parents, especially, "should have no special experience of conversion and be able to specify no particular date of conversion." [9]

By the end of the century some commentators were prepared to cut the ground out from under men like Moody. In 1899, Congregationalists in Massachusetts, through a state "committee on the work of the churches," publicly questioned the wisdom of the continuing use of the revival. "The word revival must come to have a different meaning from that commonly associated with it if it is to describe any large access of mature men into church membership." That is, there should be "less emphasis on emotional experience and more on conviction of duty to be wrought out in life." Direct attacks upon revivalism also came from outside the churches. Pertinent at this point were the words spoken by Dr. F. H. Giddings of Columbia University in his presidential address to the American Academy of Sociology in 1898. Professor Giddings represented that new breed, the social scientist,

9. *Congregationalist*, 80 (March 7, 1895): 351.

who was in the vanguard of those critical of the old order. In particular he disliked the revivalists' emphasis on emotionalism. "The revival meeting is, and always has been, the chief school of impulsive action. . . . So long as revivalism is possible the overthrow of Plattism, Crokerism, and Quayism will be impossible. Let us not deceive ourselves . . . that we can make men irrational, impulsive . . . creatures for the purposes of religion, and expect them to be cool-headed, critical, rational men for the purposes of politics." [10] Giddings's linkage of revivalism with conservatism in politics and social affairs was not unfair. Indeed, Moody could easily serve as a case study in this respect. But the evangelist had also been a defender of the status quo in the 1870's. What was important was that now a public figure like Giddings was openly attacking Moody's profession for its conservatism, whereas twenty years earlier few people would have thought of doing such a thing. This was symptomatic of the altered perspective of the nineties.

In a context of this sort, characterized by expanding hopes and fears about innovations both within and without the church, a man of Moody's temperament was bound to experience difficulties. Few of the evangelist's problems seemed related directly to the work of his schools, however. The three institutions continued to develop along lines suggested by their histories prior to 1890. The schools in the East stressed academic quality but also sought to preserve the warm piety and religious enthusiasm of their founder. Moody had been fortunate in his selection of directors for the two institutions. Those in charge in the nineties were alert administrators, and were dedicated to the evangelist's ideas and purposes as well as to strong academic standards. Miss Evelyn Hall, member of the first graduating class at Wellesley, had become principal of the Seminary in 1883 and remained in that capacity until her death in 1911. Henry F. Cutler, who was to be headmaster at Mount Hermon for almost thirty years, assumed his post in 1890. The long tenure of both of these

10. *Ibid.*, 84 (November 9, 1899): 679; *Literary Digest*, September 10, 1896, clipping in Moody Collection, Mount Hermon School Library, Mount Hermon, Massachusetts.

people assured continuity of leadership during the two schools' formative years.[11]

The problems with which the officials of the academies struggled show how fully the Seminary and Mount Hermon had acclimated to the educational climate of New England. By the nineties the quantity of work demanded at both schools of students preparing for college had increased noticeably. Proliferation of courses, a widespread tendency in American education at this time because of the emergence of new fields of inquiry, also occurred.[12] By the middle of the nineties both academies were offering electives as a part of their curriculum. Indeed, at Mount Hermon a separate elective course was begun in 1894, and served as the central expression of Cutler's efforts to effect major changes in the academic program. With the headmaster's encouragement, a committee of Harvard professors visited Mount Hermon in 1893. This served as a catalyst for a general review of operations at the school. The visitation was also a part of the efforts of President Eliot at Harvard to raise standards in the preparatory schools of New England that fed so many students into his university. The chief recommendation of the university committee was that Mount Hermon institute an elective system. Cutler did not scrap the old curriculum, but merely added the elective course. Nevertheless, this new program became the one most students followed thereafter and Cutler's actions brought Mount Hermon fully into line with some of the most advanced thinking about education in America at that time.[13]

11. Mary E. Silverthorne and Paul D. Moody, *The Life Story of Evelyn Hall* (New York: Hodder & Stoughton, 1914); Richard W. Day, *A New England Schoolmaster: The Life of Henry Franklin Cutler* (Bristol, Conn.: Hildreth Press, 1950).

12. In the nineties at the Seminary courses in zoology, chemistry, psychology, bookkeeping and a more extended treatment of American literature were added to the program for those not preparing for college. Compare course offerings in *Calendar of the Northfield Seminary, 1882–83*, pp. 12–15, and *Calendar of the Northfield Seminary, 1898–99*, pp. 32–35.

13. For a description of the elective course at Mount Hermon, see *Catalogue, 1894–95*, p. 35. See also *Calendar of Northfield Seminary, 1890–91*, pp. 27–29. A detailed discussion of the development of the elective system and of the academic life at Mount Hermon generally in the nineties is in Day, *New England Schoolmaster*, chap. 5.

The Bible Institute in Chicago quickly assumed its role as a training ground for evangelists. A professional evangelist, Reuben A. Torrey, had become the superintendent even before the official opening of the school in 1889, and the first director of music, H. H. McGranahan, was also well-known on the revival circuits. An air of informality and practicality characterized the Institute. The school granted diplomas to students who remained for two years, thus completing the Biblical or musical course, and who gave the faculty evidence of "genuine Christian character and fitness for Christian work." But all classes were arranged so that people able to stay only for a short time could also participate. Students thus came and went as they saw fit. Initially there was no charge for instruction, the only costs being room and a four dollar weekly board bill.[14] These few comments suggest the differences between the schools in Northfield and in Chicago. As further evidence of these differences, a sizable number of Hermon graduates went on to seminary, but only a few went to Chicago for their preparation for Christian work.[15] Their academic training had already carried them beyond much that would be required of them if they went west. Therefore it was natural that men from Mount Hermon tended to go on to college and then to secure a B. D. degree before entering the ministry.[16]

14. *Course of Study of the Bible Institute of the Chicago Evangelization Society, 1891–92* (n.p., n.d.); *Catalogue for Men's Department, Bible Institute for Home and Foreign Missions, Chicago Evangelization Society* (n.p., n.d.); *Catalogue of Moody Bible Institute of Chicago, 1904* (Chicago: Moody Press, 1904); *Annual Report of the Moody Bible Institute, 1902* (n.p., n.d.). All of these pamphlets are in the Moody Collection, Moody Bible Institute.

15. For support of this statement see listing of graduates in *Catalogues, Mt. Hermon School, 1892–1897*.

16. In October, 1890, Moody started a third school in Northfield which bore striking resemblances in its methods of operation to the Bible Institute in Chicago. This was the Northfield Training School for Girls, occupying the Northfield Hotel (owned and run by the evangelist and his friends) during the winter months when there were few visitors in the town. The school's stated purpose was "to meet the needs of ladies who desire . . . to reach needy homes in a practical way, and who wish to equip themselves for more efficient work as Bible teachers." This sounded very much like a small copy of Emma Dryer's Bible Work, and later the Bible Institute. One of the teachers from Mount Hermon taught a course in the *Bible*; otherwise there was a practical emphasis on dress-

One important project that Moody started in 1894 illustrates again the down-to-earth approach of the Chicago school. Because of depressed economic conditions that year, students at the Institute were hard pressed financially and sought means of earning money. Someone suggested that a "Colportage Association" be created to distribute religious books and tracts throughout the country. The prospect of combining the talents of a salesman with the work of evangelism had an irresistible appeal for Moody. Thus it was that he and his friends founded the Bible Institute Colportage Association. The new organization was an instant success. Its stated purpose was to help "stem the flood of vicious literature that is now in circulation, by supplying clean, healthy, and helpful literature at a low cost." The Asssociation's "clean, healthy" publications were all surefire best sellers — Moody's sermons — and there was a mass market to be exploited — the millions who had attended Moody's revivals or who sympathized with his work.

The evangelist also devised a colorful method of merchandising his product. Horse-drawn "Gospel Wagons," manned by students from the Bible Institute and arranged as miniature sleeping cars with kitchen attachments, fanned out from Chicago into the hinterland of Iowa, Illinois, and Wisconsin during the summer months. Wherever they stopped the students sold books in the morning, then conducted religious services from the wagon steps for children in the afternoons and for adults in the evening. Apparently this was the religious equivalent of the itinerant

making, cooking, drawing, music, and "talks on Hygiene and the care of the sick." Part finishing school for young Northfield damsels, part evangelistic training center, it tried to do what was not possible at the Seminary. It provided a program of self-help and practical evangelistic training for young ladies that corresponded with what had previously been offered for boys at Mount Hermon, and later at the Chicago Institute. It also confirms conclusions presented earlier that the Seminary never fitted into Moody's conception of his schools as training "gapmen" to work in the mission field quite as precisely as did Mount Hermon and the school in Chicago. (*Record of Christian Work*, 7 [April, 1888]: 7; [September, 1890]: 3; D. L. Moody to "Miss Holbert," September 12, 1890, Moody Papers, Moody Bible Institute, Chicago; *Northfield Training School Catalogue*, [n.p., n.d.]; clipping from *Advance* [April 7, 1892]; clipping and catalogue in box, "Northfield Training School," Mount Hermon Library; *Institute Tie*, n.s., 1 [September, 1900]: 17.)

patent–medicine man with his wagon load of medicinal notions and geegaws. The "Gospel Wagons" were a perfect expression of Moody's willingness to fuse the skills of the huckster and the seeker of souls. It was appropriate, too, that the Bible Institute should be the place where this new method of evangelism was devised.[17]

In some ways Moody's personal control over the Bible Institute was always much greater than in the instance of the academies in Northfield, for he was an acknowledged expert in most of the activities for which the Institute offered courses and training. Even when he was absent from Chicago the evangelist strongly influenced the daily activities there by means of a voluminous correspondence. He helped to decide whom to hire and fire, he worried along with school officials about declines in enrollment, changes in curriculum, and the inevitable budgetary problems. A friend of his who knew the situation in Chicago well, observed shortly after Moody's death that because the evangelist had the "fullest confidence of the Trustees he had gathered around him, he was left by them to have absolute freedom in the control of the institution." [18] Yet this was an oversimplification of the truth. Simply because he was not in Chicago much of the time, subordinates on the spot unavoidably shaped the Bible Institute as much as he. Thus in Chicago, even as in Northfield, he could not make his personal impression quite as lasting as was the case with earlier enterprises of the seventies and sixties.

It is true, however, that as long as the evangelist lived, the three schools retained a degree of common purpose and identity. During the nineties the student newspaper at Mount Hermon carried regular notices of activities at the Bible Institute. Reuben Torrey, the head of the Chicago school, served on the

17. *Annual Catalogue, Bible Institute, Chicago, 1895* (n.p., n.d.), p. 26; *Calendar, Bible Institute of the Chicago Evangelization Society, 1898*; these two items are in the Moody Collection, Moody Bible Institute; *Congregationalist*, 81 (November 5, 1896): 671. The Bible Institute Colportage Association was the forerunner of the present-day Moody Press.
18. *Institute Tie*, n.s., 1 (September, 1900): 1. See also D. L. Moody to T. W. Harvey (no date), D. L. Moody to Miss Strong, October 13, 1896, D. L. Moody to Reuben Torrey, January 16, 1889, March 11, 1899, D. L. Moody to A. F. Gaylord, December 13, (no year), June, 1895 (?), November 4, 1898, October 7, 1899, Moody Papers, Moody Bible Institute.

boards of trustees of both Mount Hermon and the Seminary from 1894 until well after Moody's death, and he was often invited to speak at those schools, both during the academic year and at the summer conferences. In Chicago, a Northfield alumni club held occasional meetings at the Institute, and a few students from the academies went to the Midwest for additional religious training.[19]

In the early years of the twentieth century, however, the three institutions were increasingly affected by the great conflict that broke out in the denominations between modernists and fundamentalists. The Bible Institute came to serve as a standard bearer for the conservative groups in American Protestantism. Renamed Moody Bible Institute shortly after the founder's death, the Chicago school became one of the centers for the propagation of fundamentalism and was a training ground for many of the professional revivalists that flourished in the twentieth century. Reuben Torrey himself turned to full-time work as a revivalist shortly after Moody's passing, feeling a call to carry on the latter's work in this area.[20] The school officials at Northfield, contrary to a widely-held view today, were slow to move in the direction of liberalizing the religious tone on their campuses. Partly this was because of the relatively conservative theological views of leaders like Will Moody and Henry Cutler and, more important, because much of the financial support of the schools came from friends of Moody and alumni who were outspoken friends of fundamentalism. The people in Northfield were much more reluctant, however, than their counterparts in Chicago to become involved in the raging controversies that divided the churches. It was not really until the 1920's, when a new generation began to take over administration of the two institutions in Massachusetts, that truly liberal tendencies in the teaching of theology and the *Bible* were introduced there.[21]

If the turmoil that struck the American churches in the 1890's

19. *Hermonite*, 3 (January 4, 1890): 54; 4(May 2, 1891): 115; 7 (November 18, 1893): 87; (April 21, 1894): 273; *Catalogue, Mt. Hermon School, 1895–96*, pp. 11, 54; *Calendar of Northfield Seminary, 1894–95*, p. 71; *Calendar of Northfield Seminary, 1903–04*, p. 9.

20. William G. McLoughlin, *Modern Revivalism: Charles Grandison Finney to Billy Graham* (New York: Ronald Press, 1959), pp. 366–67.

21. *Ibid.*, p. 274, repeats the tale of the theological liberalization of

had only a nominal effect at that time on the fortunes of Moody's major educational endeavors, the same could not be said of other efforts of his. In particular his revival campaigns, still at the heart of his public activities, were subjected to growing critical scrutiny. Within the church, *The Congregationalist* again seemed to take the lead, making pointed comments about the evangelist's ineffectiveness in a revival he conducted in New York City early in 1897. Secular newspapers that had supported his revivals in the seventies now attacked him for his Biblical literalism and the inadequacy of his methods in dealing with urban problems.[22] The greatest revival the evangelist conducted during the decade occurred in 1893 in conjunction with the Chicago World's Fair. Supporters at the time pointed to the thousands who participated in this campaign as proof of Moody's continued potency as a preacher and soul-winner. However, their claims are difficult to uphold. This revival depended upon more contrivances than any of his great campaigns of the seventies. Moreover, Moody did not generate the crowds by himself, but relied to a great extent on the magnet of the world's fair to attract an audience. His work did not reflect a genuine religious upsurge in Chicago, but was more nearly a part of the general public excitement created by the fair.[23]

As traditional evangelical practices and beliefs, and even Moody's revival work, came under increasing attack, the evan-

the Northfield Schools soon after Moody's death. There is a good discussion of the religious developments at the schools during these years in Day, *New England Schoolmaster*, pp. 126–28. H. F. Cutler to William Norton, March 2, 1926, Moody Papers, Moody Bible Institute, shows that Will Moody questioned Harry Emerson Fosdick personally on what the latter conceived to be the essentials of the Christian faith before allowing Fosdick to speak at Northfield late in 1925. The fact that Fosdick *did* speak, however, suggests that Will was more open-minded than some conservatives of that same period.

22. *Congregationalist*, 82 (April 21, 1897): 598–99; *Boston Evening Transcript*, January 9, 1897; *New York Times*, September 29, 1898, October 11, 1898, October 12, 1898, May 4, 1897, February 7, 1898; *New York Tribune*, November 12, 1896; *New York Sun*, May 3, 1897, clipping in Moody Collection, Mount Hermon School Library.

23. See circulars and clippings in scrapbook entitled "World's Fair, 1893," Moody Museum, Northfield School for Girls, Northfield, Massachusetts; *Chicago Tribune*, May 8, 1893, June 12, 1893, November 1, 1893.

gelist reacted strongly to all of these criticisms. In 1894 in Providence, Rhode Island, he hurled thunderbolts against those who claimed the "old gospel" had lost its power. "I don't believe one word of it," he said. "There is a lot of stuff that men call the gospel that has no more gospel in it than there is wheat in sawdust; . . . I want to say, if you put the old gospel straight and square it has as much effect as it ever had." His attacks upon the growing secularization of the Sabbath, while not new to his thinking, became more vehement and occurred more frequently than in his earlier years. In Boston he proclaimed that "people tell me they cannot believe in the Bible! They don't read it. . . . They read the Sunday newspapers." Or he would ask his audience, "Is not this great country giving up the Sabbath? Aren't all these big cities making Sunday a day for a picnic? . . . When a nation has forgotten God and has gone after other gods, have they not gone to ruin? . . . If we had a revival of righteousness we would have no more hard times. We are turning away from the Lord." [24] Moody's words also constituted an implied criticism of the church itself, related to earlier sentiments of his which, when used to justify the founding of his Institute in Chicago, served as scarcely veiled criticism of current seminary training for work among the masses in the cities. He had felt for some time that the church was in decline, and that recognizable standards of practice were disappearing. Again and again in the nineties he called for a new "baptism of the Church of Christ" with "the spirit of Christ," which for him meant new revivals and recapturing the enthusiasm of an earlier day.[25]

But in many places the church refused to listen to his pleadings. Rumors of plans for a summer revival in New York City in 1897 provoked strong criticism from local ministers. A year earlier, when Moody conducted a series of meetings at Cooper's Union,

24. *Moody's Latest Sermons* (Providence: The News Company, 1894), pp. 120–21; *Boston Traveler*, January 6, 1897, January 20, 1897; *Boston Evening Transcript*, January 13, 1897, January 14, 1897; D. L. Moody to "Miss Strong," December 21, 1895, Moody Papers, Moody Bible Institute.

25. *New York Tribune*, August 4, 1896. See also *ibid.*, February 27, 1890; *Boston Globe*, January 9, 1897; *Cincinnati Enquirer*, March 11, 1897; *New York Public Ledger*, February 16, 1896; D. L. Moody to "Miss Strong," December 21, 1895, Moody Papers, Moody Bible Institute.

the *New York Times*, a paper that had taken great interest in his revival of 1876 in New York, now criticized his work editorially, bluntly asserting that "we are unable to believe that these meetings, if conducted on the lines made familiar by Mr. Moody, will be of any permanent advantage to the cause of religion or will promote the happiness . . . of any large number of men and women of this city." For the *Times* at least, the conclusion seemed obvious. "The day of the evangelist has passed, at least in modern cities and [under] modern sociological conditions." The paper further emphasized its point by interviewing clergymen in the city, some of whom had participated in the revivals in the seventies, nearly all of whom now questioned Moody's methods.[26]

One of the clearest indications of the shift in attitudes toward Moody came from the YMCA. By the 1890's the older tradition in that organization which had emphasized personal evangelism was weakening. The national Association now placed greater stress on developing social services and recreational facilities for the local communities. The younger officials of the YMCA also entertained theological views which men like Moody disliked. Conflict was almost inevitable. In 1890, a dispute broke out between Moody and leaders in the student movement over the evangelist's efforts to interest college students in Kansas and Oklahoma in the mission field. A major bone of contention were theological differences. The YMCA secretaries with liberal theological opinions were irritated with Moody's frequently-expressed utterances about the literally inspired *Bible* and premillennialism. These disagreements symbolized the rift that was developing.[27]

It seemed the supreme irony that the trouble between the evangelist and the YMCA came to a head in Chicago. During the eighties, under the dynamic leadership of young L. Wilbur Messer, the Chicago YMCA launched a program which emphasized its secular services and facilities in the city, and largely dis-

26. *New York Times*, May 4, 1897, October 11, 1896, October 13, 1896. For a more sympathetic attitude toward Moody, see *New York Tribune*, November 12, 1896.

27. C. Howard Hopkins, *History of the Y.M.C.A. in North America* (New York: Association Press, 1951), pp. 353–54.

pensed with the old-time evangelism which had marked the work of the Association since Moody's heyday in the 1860's. During the nineties, however, Reuben Torrey, the superintendent of the Bible Institute, had held weekly Sunday School classes under the auspices of the local association in the auditorium of the Central YMCA in the Loop. Apparently this was an effort to allow Moody's point of view to continue to be represented in the program. Suddenly, in the fall of 1898, Torrey's services were cancelled. A newspaper account of the affair claimed that the policy board of the Chicago Association felt that "the Rev. Mr. Torrey and his old-fashioned gospel was [sic] not quite what the YMCA people wished." In public, Torrey attributed his dismissal to personal differences between Moody and Messer. Whatever position people took, the action was generally regarded as a slap at Moody and his followers.[28]

A statement prepared for publication by the board of managers of the YMCA confirmed the surmise that conflicts over doctrine had figured prominently in the decision to cancel Torrey's lectures. Nevertheless, conflicting stories explaining Torrey's ouster continued to circulate.[29] In an effort to clear the air, the officials of the YMCA finally agreed to meet and discuss the matter with Moody and his supporters. The meeting was held in Chicago in April, 1899. Besides the evangelist, those attending were Torrey, A. P. Fitt — Moody's son-in-law and an officer of the Bible Institute, and Richard C. Morse from New York, a member of the International Committee of the YMCA.

Throughout the conference, Torrey and Fitt asserted that Messer had acted because of a personal pique toward Moody, and the evangelist generally supported them in their accusations. Messer vigorously denied the charge and offered documentary proof that the changes were made primarily because the YMCA

28. *Chicago Daily News*, November 4, 1898.
29. The statement of the board is printed in *Minutes of the Board of Managers, Chicago Y.M.C.A.*, November 25, 1898. Messer had the full support of the directors of the association in the action he had taken. See also *Minutes of the Board of Managers*, November 8, 1898. Torrey's attitudes are revealed in letters between him and Richard C. Morse in folder entitled "Torrey-McBurney Correspondence," files of the YMCA Historical Library, New York City.

no longer desired to endorse Torrey's theological views.[30] The meeting eventually broke up without any agreements between the two camps; indeed, the heated debate had appeared only to exacerbate the hard feelings that existed on both sides.

Records that have been preserved, both of this conference and of other discussions among the participants, show clearly that Moody was meeting opposition not only in Chicago but throughout the national organization.[31] The evangelist's attitude was an unchanging one toward the new theological and organizational questions being considered by the YMCA. He himself stated his position perfectly in the heat of the conference in Chicago. "I am an old man," he said, "too old to change and positive in my convictions." [32] The spectacle of Moody engaging in furious debate with former friends, largely refusing to listen to the arguments of his opponents, and in essence being led astray by the claims of his associates, served as a sad ending to his work and relations with the Chicago YMCA. The organization which had provided him with a springboard to fame had now all but repudiated him. What had come to pass cast into bold relief all the questions that had been raised by critics of Moody's techniques concerning the adequacy of his responses to the challenges of the nineties.

In yet another area Moody found his views challenged in his last years. He could not avoid getting involved in the controversies growing out of the attempts of liberal churchmen to reconcile theology and biblical studies with the findings and methodology of science. By 1890 the conservative counterattack was gathering momentum in nearly all the denominations against the advocates of higher criticism and evolutionary theism. We have already seen how, as early as the 1870's, this opposition began to take shape in the first national prophetic conferences, where supporters of premillennialism and the literally inspired *Bible* sought a common cause. The Northfield Conferences, both student and adult gatherings, in the 1880's and afterwards brought

30. Memorandum signed by J. F. Oates, April 8, 1899, L. W. Messer to D. L. Moody, June 24, 1899, in folder entitled "Messer Papers; Letters, etc., of Interest," Historical Records, File C, Archives, Chicago YMCA.
31. J. F. Oates's memorandum, W. J. Parker to L. W. Messer, July 14, 1899, I. E. Brown to L. W. Messer, April 7, 1899, Messer Papers.
32. J. F. Oates's memorandum.

Moody into yet more frequent and close contact with the most adamant opponents to the new tendencies in the denominations.

A particularly aggressive group of churchmen were those advocating a set of ideas known as dispensationalism. This strain of thought had also developed in the context of the transatlantic evangelical community. Many of the basic ideas of the dispensationalists originated in the preachings of the Plymouth Brethren, and especially in the ideas of their aged leader, John Darby. We know of the influence of the Brethren in this country and on Moody in particular, extending back to the 1860's. Dispensationalism was so-called because its adherents believed that the *Bible* revealed time as divided into distinct ages or dispensations. Although the number of these dispensations differed depending on the writer, they were crucial in constructing the theological systems of the adherents of the movement. Dispensationalists revealed their conservative temper in their dogmatic adherence to premillennialism and a verbally inspired *Bible*.[33] Not too surprisingly, many of them had participated in the prophetic conferences, and one needs only to cite the names of A. J. Gordon, A. T. Pierson, James Brookes, W. G. Moorehead — all of them dispensationalists and all regular speakers at the Northfield Conferences — to realize the influence these people exerted on Moody and his work in his last years.[34] Moreover, C. I. Scofield, author of the Scofield Reference

33. For analyses of dispensationalism see Ernest R. Sandeen, "Towards a Historical Interpretation of the Origins of Fundamentalism," *Church History*, 36 (March 1967): 67–82; C. Norman Kraus, *Dispensationalism in America* (Richmond, Va.: John Knox Press, 1958); Clarence B. Bass, *Backgrounds to Dispensationalism: Its Historical Genesis and Ecclesiastical Implications* (Grand Rapids, Mich.: Eerdmans, 1960).

34. The vehemence and sense of urgency with which some of these men argued their case can be seen in the statements of Dr. James Brookes made at the first student conference at Northfield in 1886. On July 12 he said to his young listeners, "You will go back to professors and instructors whose shoe latchet I am unworthy to unloose; but I beg of you, earnestly, prayerfully, to study the word for yourselves, and then, if these men give you one learned teaching or another against its inspiration, tell them you have studied for yourselves and you cannot agree with them." The next day Brookes continued, "If I could see you young men permeated with this thought of the verbal inspiration of the scriptures, I should have more hope of the future. . . . [The words of the *Bible*] are the words of Jesus. If you can't believe them as such, young men, give up your faith! Give up your faith, I say, and pass on to judgment and hell! I'm tired to death at hearing these poor worms of the

Bible, a major vehicle for the expression of dispensationalism after 1900, was the pastor of the Northfield Congregational Church in the nineties, which Moody attended regularly.[35]

One careful student of the dispensationalists has pointed out that strict Calvinists seemed to become the strongest supporters of the movement. In this country at least, few Methodists were sympathetic.[36] After the Civil War, however, there did develop in the latter denomination a movement which contributed to the growing conservative bloc in the evangelical churches. This was the holiness movement. The Methodists with their long-held sympathies for sanctification and perfectionism would be naturally inclined toward holiness sentiments. As was noted earlier, holiness movements were rife in the evangelical churches in the pre–Civil War period and experienced a resurgence in the post–Civil War period. Ultimately, new denominations like the Church of the Nazarene, coming into being about 1900, became the center of much of this post-war activity. An emphasis on otherwordliness, the desire to separate individual believers through personal sanctification from the corruption that seemed widespread both in the church and the world at large, made holiness teachings appealing to frustrated and disillusioned churchgoers struggling to maintain a footing in the shifting bogs of change in the late nineteenth century. We know that advocates of holiness were at the first Northfield conferences in 1880 and 1881, and they returned in even greater strength in the nineties. One of the best indications of this fact was the regular appearance at Northfield of representatives of the Keswick Movement in England, another manifestation of international evangelical co-operation. The Keswick Movement was, in its own right, an influential holiness gathering.[37]

dust sit in judgment on their Lord and Master Jesus Christ!" (*Springfield* [Mass.] *Republican*, July 13, 1886, July 14, 1886.)

35. For references to Scofield in Northfield and other dispensationalists at the summer conferences in the nineties, see *Northfield Echoes*, 1 (1894): 4–6; 2 (1895): 3; 6 (1899): 78–83; Sandeen "Towards a Historical Interpretation," pp. 76–77. The effect of the dispensationalists at the conferences in the nineties is suggested in *Congregationalist*, 84 (August 17, 1897): 212.

36. Sandeen, "Towards a Historical Interpretation," p. 71. This statement has been confirmed generally by this author's research.

37. F. B. Meyer, Andrew Murray, and H. W. Webb-Peploe, leaders

Since prominent dispensationalists were numbered among Moody's closest friends, they undoubtedly affected his thinking on theological issues considerably. It is not correct to assume, however, that he was an outright advocate of dispensationalism. A careful search of his published sermons reveals him using only once or twice the term "dispensation," and he never developed, as did the dispensationalists, a structured series of ages through which the world had to pass in order to reach the millennium. He was not enough of a theologian to worry about such fine details.[38] Perhaps it is proper to say that if his dispensationalist friends did not capture the evangelist's mind entirely, they did help to establish more firmly his generally conservative outlook on theological questions. He approached the holiness movement in the same spirit. When in England in the early nineties, he visited one of the Keswick meetings, but he did not appear to be an especially ardent advocate of the movement.[39] Strong mystical tendencies present from the seventies in his personal

at Keswick, came to Northfield several times in the nineties to participate in the conferences. (*Northfield Echoes*, 1 [June, 1894]: 4, 6; 2 [1895]: 419–44, 619–21; 3 [1896]: 357, 528–29; 4 [1897]: 21–30; 5 [1898]: 5–25; 6 [1899]: 42–50, 448–70; *New York Tribune*, August 14, 1896; circulars in "Northfield Conferences" box, in the files of Mount Hermon Library; Henry W. Rankin to Andrew W. Murray [duplicate of original], April 24, 1895, Rankin Papers, Mt. Hermon School Library, Mount Hermon, Massachusetts. See also D. L. Moody to Ambert Moody, May 25, 1892, June 14, 1892, June 15, 1892, March 5, 1895, Esther Loos Collection, Library of Congress. Care must be used, however, in relating the Keswick Conventions to holiness groups in this country. Although Americans like Phoebe Palmer, Robert Piersall Smith, and his wife were instrumental in establishing the Keswick movement, over the years Keswick developed a style and emphasis exclusively its own. Strong Calvinistic tendencies in the theology of the movement, for example, might distinguish it somewhat from groups like the Nazarenes in America. See Stephen Barabas, *So Great Salvation: The History and Message of the Keswick Convention* (London: Morgan and Scott, 1952), chaps. 2, 3.

38. William H. Daniels, *Moody: His Words, Works, and Workers* (New York: Nelson & Phillips, 1877), pp. 448–78; D. L. Moody, *The Second Coming of Christ* (Chicago: Bible Institute Colportage Association, 1896), p. 27; D. L. Moody et. al., *Calvary's Cross: A Symposium on the Atonement* (Chicago: Bible Institute Colportage Association, 1900), p. 17; C. Norman Kraus to author, March 25, 1960.

39. See especially the comments recorded in John C. Pollock, *The Keswick Story: The Authorized History of The Keswick Convention* (Chicago: Moody Press, 1964), p. 66.

theology, the product of his unforgettable second conversion experience in 1871 and of his great emphasis on the importance of the Holy Spirit to the everyday life of the believer, created natural affinities between him and the holiness groups. But he also refused to embrace openly the doctrines of entire sanctification and perfectionism which were fundamental to most holiness thinking in the United States. If the advocates of holiness influenced him, once again it was primarily in broad terms, in his belief in the literally constructed *Bible* and in his concern over the corruption of the present world, especially the activities within the churches.[40]

Through the years Moody remained firm in his advocacy of premillennialism and the verbally inspired *Bible*. In the nineties the justification for his beliefs was the same as it had been twenty years earlier: "I cannot understand what these people mean who come to me and say that they cannot believe in the Old Testament, but can believe the New. Now, both Testaments come from the Lord, and both are entitled to the same credence. . . . If you can't rely on this book, what can you rely on . . . ?" For those preaching the "New Theology" he could only say that "they choose a text and then they go up in a balloon whizzing away above the heads of the people. You call it metaphysics, but I don't know what it is." [41]

40. At Keswick there was much greater hesitation to embrace perfectionist doctrines than was the case among holiness people in the United States. This may help to explain why Moody was interested in the movement. People who went to Keswick were also strong believers in the present corruption of the church and the need for reform therein. With this attitude, too, Moody — and many holiness advocates in this country — would heartily agree. See Barabas, *So Great Salvation*, pp. 30–31, 98–100. For the evangelist's comments about the corruption of the church, see the *Boston Globe*, January 8, 1897; *New York Tribune*, February 27, 1890; note 25 on p. 402.

41. *Boston Traveler*, January 5, 1897; *Boston Evening Transcript*, January 7, 1897. See also *Boston Globe*, January 7, 1897; *Moody's Latest Sermons* (Providence, R. I.: The News Company, 1894), pp. 149, 91–92, 93, 94–96. Compare these views with earlier and similar statements of Moody in the *St. Louis Globe-Democrat*, December 3, 1879; *New York Times*, October 14, 1884. See also Henry Rankin to A. P. Fitt, April 19, 1900, Rankin Papers, for relevant comments on Moody's theological opinions.

More often, however, he dismissed the agitation by advocates of the higher criticism as irrelevant to the principal task of preaching the gospel and seeking converts. Using the pungent metaphorical language of a rural New Englander, Moody described once his reactions to a divinity school student who said he had been studying a year to discover the author of the Pentateuch. "If a man has got the colic, what difference does it make to him where the mustard was grown that relieved him." Or, as he once said to a friend in the liberal camp when the latter voiced worries about interpretations concerning the authorship of the Book of Isaiah: "See here, it doesn't make much difference who wrote the book anyhow. God could have used half a dozen Isaiahs." [42]

These comments of the evangelist depict his anti-intellectualism, his inablility to respond to a fundamental intellectual challenge that now confronted the church. Yet the evidence that has just been presented also possesses another dimension. Moody's persistent tendency to hold back from an absolute commitment emotionally and intellectually to his conservative dispensationalist and holiness friends reaffirms that his viewpoint was more catholic than theirs. It was largely personal characteristics which kept him out of the rut of religious bigotry and gave him the broad outlook that many of his friends lacked. This spirit of open-mindedness is reflected in the words of participants in the dispute between Moody and the Chicago YMCA. One witness at the meeting in Chicago, unsympathetic to the evangelist, said he "was struck by the magnificent spirit displayed by Mr. Moody. . . . Although he spoke at times vehemently, as is his wont, and . . . stated that he thought Mr. Messer had done him a great injustice and ought to apologize . . . at the close he . . . did not even suggest that an apology was due him." Another person also

---

42. *Boston Evening Transcript*, January 5, 1897; *Boston Globe*, January 8, 1897; words of Henry Sloane Coffin paraphrasing Moody in address by Coffin included in folder entitled "Moody Mass Meeting, Carnegie Hall," John R. Mott Papers, Yale Divinity School. At the summer conference in 1891 Moody raised a laugh from his audience, when in responding to a technical question of biblical interpretation, he asserted "I would say as the Scotchman did when he found a difficult passage, 'Brethren, we will look it full in the face and pass on.' " (*Springfield* [Mass.] *Union*, July 6, 1891, clipping in the files of Mount Hermon Library.)

noted that "Mr. Moody . . . desired to be fair and brotherly." [43] Even when forced to reject Moody's ideas, men could continue to admire his large-heartedness and breadth of spirit and retain working relations with him.

In the 1890's Moody seemed to be establishing some sort of middle ground between extremists of right and left. Because he liked certain of the liberals as persons, he overlooked the fact that he disliked their theological opinions. Moreover, behind a facade of apparent unbending conservatism lurked his refreshing common sense which continually whispered to him that he could perhaps learn even from people who worked athwart his personal prejudices.

Washington Gladden and Lyman Abbott, having sprung from the soil of evangelicalism and having supported Moody's revivals in the seventies, continued to be his friends until his death.[44] Moody also frequently invited liberal churchmen as speakers at the summer conferences. The conferences, then, became one of the first battlegrounds in the war between fundamentalists and modernists. Josiah Strong, a proponent of the Social Gospel, Henry Drummond, one of the earliest and most popular exponents of evolutionary theology, and William Rainey Harper, New Testament scholar and later president of the University of Chicago, ranged themselves on the speakers' platform alongside Moody's dispensationalist friends.[45] The conservatives did not appreciate the evanglist's actions, and sometimes they told him so. One such incident occurred in 1893 when Henry Drummond was the featured speaker at the conference. He met instant opposition and a deputation of conference members went to Moody, urging him not to allow Drummond to continue speaking. Mulling over the request for a day, Moody then informed Drummond's opponents

43. J. F. Oates's memorandum, April 8, 1899; I. E. Brown to L. W. Messer, April 7, 1899, Messer Papers.

44. For the continued esteem these men held for Moody late in their lives, see Lyman Abbott, *Reminiscences* (New York: Houghton Mifflin, 1915), p. 479; Washington Gladden, *Recollections* (New York: Houghton Mifflin, 1909), p. 428; Jacob Dorn, *Washington Gladden: Prophet of the Social Gospel* (Columbus: Ohio State University Press, 1967), p. 380.

45. *Northfield Echoes*, 1 (June, 1894): 7–10. See also William R. Harper to D. L. Moody, September 22, 1899, Moody Papers, Powell, which invited Moody to speak at the University of Chicago.

that "the Lord had shown him that Drummond was a better man than himself," so he should go on.[46]

But as the conflict between liberals and conservatives grew, it was difficult for a man like Moody to keep his balance. His moderate feelings were mostly an extension of his personality and the private theological world that he had created, not the result of a rigorous search for theological alternatives to the increasing rigidity of the opposing camps. Indeed, it is questionable whether a moderate position, even if constructed from a sound intellectual base, could have survived for long after 1900. In any case Moody never made the attempt.

Shortly before the evangelist's death in 1899, George Adam Smith, a friend of both Drummond and Moody, and an outstanding Biblical scholar in his own right, visited Northfield. During a conversation with the revivalist the two men came to the question of Biblical criticism. After expressing hostility to the movement, Moody said: "Couldn't they [the critics] agree to a truce and for ten years bring out no fresh views, just to let us get on with the practical work of the Kingdom?"[47] Although the evangelist's words suggest a commendable desire to bring the fratricidal struggle to an end, they also show clearly his inability to understand and deal realistically with the new issues facing the church. The best he could suggest was for churchmen to ignore the ques-

46. Recounted by George Adam Smith in *The Life of Henry Drummond* (New York: Doubleday, 1898), pp. 452–53. In 1897, A. T. Pierson, an avowed dispensationalist, proposed in a moment of enthusiasm at the summer adult conference that collections be taken there for missionary work overseas that would not necessarily be funnelled through the usual denominational channels. Moody's chilliness to this proposal forced a withdrawal of the proposal the following day. Still later efforts were made, evidently with Moody's approval, to disassociate publicly the Northfield conferences with the Keswick Movement. (*Congregationalist* [August 19, 1897]; *Advance* [October, 1899]: 542, clippings in the Moody Collection, Mount Hermon Library.) For further indications of Moody's openness to views disagreeing with his own, see P. D. Moody, *My Father*, pp. 183–86; mimeographed address of Henry Sloane Coffin, in folder, "Moody Mass Meeting, Carnegie Hall, New York," Mott Papers; comments of Washington Gladden in *Congregationalist and Christian World* (November 12, 1914).

47. Quoted by George Adam Smith in the introduction to Henry Drummond, *Dwight L. Moody: Impressions and Facts* (New York: McClure, Phillips & Company, 1900), p. 30.

tions that had been raised and to engage in old-style evangelism and revivals. It was a program that fell on many deaf ears.

One writer at the time of Moody's death believed that if the evangelist had lived longer he might have become a mediator between the warring factions in the denominations.[48] In retrospect, this claim seems hardly valid. The evangelist's personal ability to bridge the gap was a tenuous achievement. Even the great force of his personal example could not affect permanently tides of sentiment that were running very deep. Thus at the end of his career Moody's public image had become something of a paradox. Still deeply respected for his personal integrity and Christian commitment, still able to charm those who gathered about him, his circle of friends remained a broad and varied group of people. But the great public acclaim of the seventies had now all but disappeared. Inability to adjust his thinking in a time of rapid change had helped to bring about his loss of prestige. Despite the achievement of successfully establishing and maintaining his schools in Northfield and Chicago and a number of other equally worthwhile projects, his last years were also a time of frequent frustration and disappointment. Perhaps it should also be said that the great revivalist's difficulties mirrored the changes occuring generally in America in the nineties as a secular and more complex urban society replaced the old order of a homogeneous, preindustrial culture. He still seemed to catch, then, something of the prevailing mood of the public, even if only negatively, as he had done more positively in his greatest moments of triumph in the 1870's.

If Moody was baffled and upset by the changing religious scene in the last decade of his life, there was always the security of warm family relations to fall back on. The evangelist loved children and his delight knew no bounds when grandchildren began to arrive. He lived to see three of them born — a girl to Emma and Percy Fitt, a boy and a girl to Will and his wife. His practice of gift-giving, a pastime that had afforded him so much pleasure with his own children, was now extended to the next generation. Sometimes it was something conventional, though charged with special

48. *Outlook* (January 20, 1900): 166.

meaning. Shortly after Irene, the daugher of Will, was born, she received from her grandfather a *Bible* with the following words inscribed on the flyleaf: "The Bible for the last forty years has been the dearest thing on earth to me and now I give a copy as my first gift to my first grandchild, *Irene Moody*, with a prayer that it may be her companion through life & guide her to those mansions that Christ has gone to prepare for those that love & serve Him on earth." There were less ordinary presents, too. On one occasion he proudly presented to an unweaned infant an unusually large cabbage fresh from his vegetable garden! Often he would leave his own home before breakfast, pick up his two granddaughters Irene and Emma, the daughter of Emma and Percy Fitt, and take them on buggy tours of his "acreage" — including visits to the cows, pigs, and hen yards. As the children became toddlers he seldom left his own place without a small companion perched beside him on the seat of the wagon or carriage.[49]

When the revivalist was away from home he wrote the children long letters talking in grown-up language about his plans for their activities together after his return. In the wintry days of early January, 1896, Moody wrote the tiny daughter of Emma Fitt a lengthy message:

> I wanted to get a letter to you before you got your first tooth. Hurry up and get them all before the hot weather comes on, for I will get you some candy and you will want teeth to eat it. If you do not I am afraid you will suck it, and that will teach you to suck your thumb or your fist as your little cousin Irene does. . . . Only think, Emma, what your mother said the other day — that I, your Grandfather, could not kiss you on the lips, because it would hurt you. . . . Did you ever hear of anything like that? But I got a kiss on

49. Date on the flyleaf of the *Bible,* now in the possession of Mrs. Frank R. Smith, New York City, is September 10, 1895; P. D. Moody, *My Father,* pp. 80–81; D. L. Moody to Irene Moody, March 9, 1897, Mrs. Frank R. Smith Collection, Library of Congress; D. L. Moody to Emma Fitt (no date), January 24, 1897, D. L. Moody to Irene Moody, March 8, 1896, Moody Papers, Mrs. Powell, East Northfield, Massachusetts.

your lips all the same, and I will get a good many more when I get home.

Irene Moody's practice of sucking her fist as well as her fingers evoked this sly comment once from an absent grandfather. "If you will count your toes some time when putting them in to your mouth you can tell about the time I will get home to see you[.] Count the big one first & by the time you get to your little toe I will be home." One of the last letters the evangelist wrote was to granddaughter Emma, in which he sent "a picture of my hand and when you write to me will you send a picture of your hand[?]" On the back of the letter was the outline of his left hand, crooked finger and all.[50]

Obviously others were also meant to enjoy the banter that flowed between the youngest and oldest in the Moody family. Late in 1895, when Irene was only three months old, her grandfather received a letter from her. She complained to him that she now had to wait *"three hours* for my meals — when I was a very little baby, I was fed every two hours, and that was bad enough." In a teasing way she continued. "Now I would like your permission to suck my fist during the last half hour that I have to wait for my meals. I just *have* to do it, but it troubles me and detracts from the pleasure and comfort, to keep thinking how it would grieve you to see me; so *please* give me your permission." The letter ended with the comment that "I must close because I am so sleepy I have to yawn all the time," and a sketch of a baby in a nightgown yawning vigorously was inked in at the side of the sheet.[51]

This playfulness with the children and the happiness it reflected was not to last long. On November 30, 1898, Will's little boy, Dwight, died of spinal meningitis.[52] The youngster had been

50. D. L. Moody to Emma Fitt, January 7, 1896, November 11, 1899, Moody Papers, Powell. D. L. Moody to "My dear little Irene," June 8, 1896, Smith Collection.

51. Irene to D. L. Moody (written by one of her parents), November 22, 1895, Smith Collection.

52. Northfield Town Records, "Deaths," p. 53. Although meningitis was the official cause of death, the small child was afflicted from birth with spinal meningocele, a serious physical defect which made him highly susceptible to infections of all sorts. This latter difficulty proba-

named for the evangelist and occupied a special place in the latter's affections. There was no doubt that the grandfather felt the loss as keenly as the parents. The fact that his round of duties had kept him away from Northfield at the time the boy died also weighed on his mind. To a close friend he wrote that he was "feeling Will's and May's loss fearfully and wish I could be at home to comfort them." As was usually the case, in this moment of family crisis his chief concern was for the welfare of those most directly affected by the tragedy. He was in Colorado when Dwight died, and so letters had to suffice in place of an immediate, personal word of comfort to the parents. The reality of his faith suffused all that he said. To May Whittle Moody, little Dwight's mother, he wrote that it was "sweet to think" that her child "was most of the time so happy while here. All of my thoughts of him was [with] a smile on his face. How bright and happy he must be now and will be forever, dear little fellow. . . . What a joyful thought to think we will meet him again and go no more out forever. . . . It is well with the child and let it be well with us." [53]

This was not the end of Moody's sorrow, however. In little more than six months his son's second child, Irene, followed her brother to the grave. In 1898 she had caught whooping cough, later to be complicated with pneumonia. In her weakened condition tuberculosis germs lodged in her body, and slowly she wasted away. In the spring of 1899 Moody toured the West Coast and took Irene and her parents along, hoping vainly that the California sunshine would cure the little girl. It was a time of prolonged anxiety for the whole family. Moody showed the strain in a letter to Reuben Torrey at the Bible Institute in Chicago. "Poor May and Will. It has been a hard winter for them and if they lose Irene I do not know what will become of them. They are so fond of children." His own feelings about his family were also enmeshed in these sad musings about what was coming to pass. He

bly should be considered a major contributing factor to the infant's death. (Conversations with Mrs. Frank R. Smith and Mrs. Mary Packard, December 30, 1966, in New York City.)

53. D. L. Moody to Ambert Moody, December 7, 1898, D. L. Moody to May Moody, December 1, 1898, D. L. Moody to Will and May Moody, December 12, 1898, Moody Papers, Powell.

concluded by saying: "I may send you a dispatch . . . asking you
to have a special prayer for her. What a winter this has been." [54]

In spite of the family's ministrations, Irene died on August 22,
1899.[55] Her grandfather lived only a few months after her. In November the first of five additional children was born to Will and
May Moody, but the evangelist died before he could begin to
plan early morning adventures with this new offspring. Although
none of the records offer concrete evidence, it does not seem
implausible to suggest that Moody's own death may have been
hastened by the pain and sorrow he experienced with the passing
of these grandchildren whom he loved so much.[56]

In February, 1899, Moody celebrated his sixty-second birthday.
He still followed a very vigorous and demanding schedule, but to
those who had known him for many years, he was clearly aging.
The killing pace he set for himself and all of his associates had
begun to have its effects much earlier. Sankey, for one, was never
able to work as hard as his partner. By the mid-eighties the burden
of the heavy schedule of meetings arranged each year had nearly
ruined his voice and forced his retirement from all but a token
number of appearances with his partner. Undaunted, Moody
pushed on, using other assistants.[57] His lavish expenditures of energy, shrugged off as inconsequential in earlier days, could not help
but exert their toll. As early as March, 1890, he wrote to a friend

54. D. L. Moody to Reuben Torrey, March 14, 1899, Moody Papers,
Moody Bible Institute.

55. Northfield Town Records, p. 55.

56. One friend has graphically described the effect Irene's impending
death had on Moody in the summer of 1899. "Again and again he
asked me to beg people not to express their sympathy when they met
him, lest it should break him down altogether." (Clipping from the
British Weekly, December 29, 1899, Moody Museum, Northfield School
for Girls.) The strongest support of the statement, however, is drawn
from the words of those who were with Moody in Kansas City at the
beginning of his final illness. During this personal ordeal, it might be
expected that the evangelist would dwell on those things that were
closest to his heart. The death of his grandchildren and the bereave-
ment of his son and his family occupied a central place in Moody's
thoughts. (C. M. Vining to A. P. Fitt, January 1, 1900, Moody Papers,
Powell.)

57. Evidence of the shift to other singing assistants is seen in accounts of Moody's work at the first student conference at Mount Hermon in 1886. See the *Springfield* [Mass.] *Republican*, July 8, 1886.

in Chicago that his work had been so demanding that he might
have to end his current campaign prematurely because he was
"so tired." He went on, "I am speaking 4 times a day & 2 after
meetings & one prayer meeting so when I get through I . . .
want to lay down & rest." A month later, he spoke to his friend
again in the same vein. Having preached "in 4 churches a day
for the past week & had 4 after meetings," he had come to realize
that "It has used me up & I must get rest." [58] During the last
nine or ten years of his life the evangelist knew that he harbored
an incipient heart ailment. Always a heavyset person, as he grew
older he put on considerable excess poundage. His great bulk
eventually forced him to buy shoes with elastic sides that ob-
viated the need of lacing and unlacing them each day. Even
though he recognized the dangers that overwork and stoutness
might bring, he ignored all warnings. One friend asserted in 1897
that he threw himself into the labors of his last years precisely
because his physical condition pointed to a shortened life.[59]

On November 12, 1899, Moody began another season of revivals with a campaign in Kansas City. He was ill even as his
work there began. His family learned later that all through the
previous summer, during the ordeal connected with the death of
his grandchild, his heart had given repeated indications of trouble,
but he had said nothing lest those close to him be weighed down
with additional worry.[60] A collapse was almost inevitable, and it
occurred shortly after the revival began. The attack was not sud-

58. D. L. Moody to T. W. Harvey, March 8, 1890, April 13, 1890,
Moody Papers, Moody Bible Institute.

59. George E. Morgan, *Mighty Days of Revival: The Life of R. C.
Morgan* (London: Morgan & Scott, 1922), p. 184; Paul D. Moody, *My
Father: An Intimate Portrait of Dwight Moody* (Boston: Little, Brown
and Co., 1938), p. 31; John B. Devins, "Dwight L. Moody at 60," *Independent*, 49 (February 11, 1897): 182. See also John Morton to D. L.
Moody, December 26, 1898, Moody Papers, Moody Bible Institute. In the
early nineties, on his doctor's orders, Moody tried for awhile to watch his
weight, taking long walks in order to reduce. Apparently he kept at it only
for a short time and just when he was in Northfield. (D. L. Moody to
N. F. McCormick, December 4, [1893?], N. F. McCormick to D. L. Moody,
December 9, 1893, Nettie Fowler McCormick Papers, Wisconsin State Historical Society, Madison, Wisconsin.

60. *Kansas City Star*, November 11, 1899, November 13, 1899; C. M.
Vining to A. P. Fitt, January 15, 1900, Moody Papers, Powell; Paul
Moody, *My Father*, p. 168.

den, but came upon him gradually. Before a doctor was called in, he was in such pain that for several nights he had to sleep fitfully sitting in a chair. Three days after he began the campaign in Kansas City he was visibly ill even to people in his audiences; nevertheless, he refused to give up his work, and preached six sermons following the doctor's first visit. For two days he had to be taken to the hall in a carriage, although the building was only two blocks from his hotel. He became so weak that a friend had to help him dress for the services. Exerting his indomitable will to the last, he refused to send word to his family until the day he started for home. Even then his terse telegram seemed understated and demonstrated his reluctance to admit that anything was seriously amiss. "Doctor thinks I need rest. Am on my way home. Have three friends with me. Will wire often." [61]

His wife and oldest son hurried to Buffalo, New York, to meet the train that was bringing the sick man home. Somehow the three people missed each other, and not until he had reached Greenfield, the county seat a short distance from Northfield, could the evangelist put himself in the care of his family. Paul, called home from his junior year at Yale, met his father. The son recalled later that his own spirits were lifted considerably on the drive to Northfield when his father chided him for having brought the slowest team of horses and laughed at the cautiousness of his young driver.

After several weeks of rest and quiet, the evangelist seemed on the road to recovery. Paul returned to school and when he came home for the Christmas vacation his father was well enough to engage in seemingly endless debates with his sons over the merits of the Boer War, a conflict that at the moment absorbed everyone's interest. Almost imperceptibly, however, the evangelist's heart had continued to weaken. A clear sign of approaching death came on December 21 when he suffered a severe fainting spell.

His last hours on the following day were typical of him, in certain ways. Although he was suffering recurrent fainting

61. *Kansas City Star*, November 17, 1899, November 18, 1899, December 22, 1899; C. C. Case to W. R. Moody, February 10, 1900, C. M. Vining to A. P. Fitt, January 1, 1900, telegram to Mrs. D. L. Moody, November 17, 1899, Moody Papers, Powell.

spells and intermittent moments when he lost consciousness, his greatest concern was the worry that he might bring to his family. Particularly he tried to ease the mind of his wife whom he knew would find this a deeply trying time. At the end he brushed aside stimulants offered to him in order that the ordeal might end more quickly for everyone. Certain that he was dying, he proclaimed at times to those in the room that it was a glorious experience, not to be feared in the least. Once he spoke of seeing again his two departed grandchildren; then he cried out, "Earth is receding and Heaven is calling," and passed away.[62]

The family held the funeral on December 26. Thirty boys from Mount Hermon acted as pallbearers, the service being conducted in the local Congregational church that Moody had attended for so many years. After the service the boys carried the body for the last time from the white frame church building, past his home and the house where he was born, and up a steep incline to Round Top, a hill on the grounds of the Seminary overlooking the Connecticut Valley immediately below and the mountains of New Hampshire and Vermont to the north. From the grove of trees where the grave was dug one could see the rooftops of the buildings at Mount Hermon two miles away. His burial spot was a peculiarly appropriate place, one that he had come to cherish both for its views of the countryside and its many personal associations. He was at rest in the place he knew and loved best.[63]

Even before the evangelist died, letters expressing concern and sympathy had begun to pour in upon the family. The volume increased as news of Moody's death was carried to the outside world. Messages of condolence came literally from all over the globe, from old friends of the family, from churches and YMCA's in Europe and the United States, and from nationally prominent men like William Jennings Bryan, Booker T. Washington, and the Presi-

62. Paul Moody, *My Father*, pp. 172–75; W. R. Moody, *Moody* (1930), pp. 536–38; A. P. Fitt to A. F. Gaylord, December 23, 1899, Moody Papers, Moody Bible Institute; Fleming H. Revell to Josephine Revell, December 26, 1899, handwritten certification of death, Dr. N. P. Wood, March 8, 1900, Moody Papers, Powell.

63. Richard C. Morse, "Family League Letters," 2 vols. (unpublished MS, YMCA Historical Library), 2: December 30, 1899; Fleming H. Revell to Josephine Revell, December 26, 1899, Moody Papers, Powell.

dent of the United States.[64] Both the secular and religious press published thousands of words in eulogy during the week following his death. All tried in one way or another to catch something of the essence and significance of Moody's life. Perhaps none was more successful than the *Independent*, a nonsectarian religious weekly, when it commented;

> He understood what was the breadth of Christian life and faith, and there was no bitterness in his soul for those who held a more liberal faith than he. What he wanted was Christian life, and, above all, Christian service. . . . For denominations he cared nothing; for Christianity he would give up his life. Every one believed in him, no matter of what faith or unfaith; all knew that Dwight L. Moody was an honest, sincere, devoted Christian.[65]

No better epitaph could have been written.

64. Scrapbooks containing most of these letters and telegrams are in the Moody Papers, Powell.
65. *Independent* (December 28, 1899), clipping, *ibid.*

A Note on Sources

The most important of Moody's personal papers have been collected and preserved by members of his immediate family. Of prime significance are the papers gathered by Mrs. Emma M. Powell, a granddaughter of Moody, who lives in East Northfield, Massachusetts. The Powell collection includes original and typescript copies of letters, sermon outlines, scrapbooks of newspaper clippings and letters to the evangelist, and other memorabilia of lesser import. Scarcely less significant were the papers collected by May Moody, the wife of the evangelist's son, Will, who lived in the family home on the grounds of the Northfield School for Girls until her death a few years ago. Mrs. Moody possessed some of the earliest letters written by her father-in-law, as well as important materials gathered by her husband as he prepared the best-known familial biography of the evangelist. Recently this collection has been broken up. Portions of the materials, including the valuable diary of D. W. Whittle — May Moody's father and a long-time confidant of the elder Moody — have been moved to Moody Bible Institute in Chicago, while other parts of the collection have remained at the Northfield School for Girls. Finally, another granddaughter, Mrs. Frank R. Smith, of New York City, over the years has kept together a small but significant group of family letters. Recently Mrs. Esther Loos, the daughter of Ambert Moody, a nephew of the evangelist who served as general manager of Moody's affairs in Northfield during his last years, added important private correspondence between Moody and her father to the Smith collection. Within the past year Mrs. Smith has deposited all her holdings in the Library of Congress.

The manuscripts in these family collections are valuable chiefly for the insight they provide into the personality and private life of the great popular preacher. They are rich and abundant in detail, indispensable aids to any student of Moody's career. These papers should not be entirely ignored, however, for the light they cast on the public aspects of Moody's activities. This is especially true of the comprehensive holdings of Mrs. Powell, and the materials of May Moody now in Chicago at the Moody Bible Institute.

Outside the family the most important group of manuscripts is located at Moody Bible Institute. The school has several hundred of Moody's letters, covering aspects of the evangelist's private life and relating to the history of the Institute from its beginnings in the 1880's to the time of Moody's death. Indispensable, too, for any understanding of the beginnings of the Institute are the papers of Nettie Fowler McCormick, a supporter of many evangelical causes and the wife of Cyrus H. McCormick, Sr. Mrs. McCormick's papers are included in the large McCormick family collection deposited at the Wisconsin State Historical Library in Madison. The secondary schools which Moody founded in Massachusetts have also preserved important manuscripts and documents. The largest portion of these materials illuminates the early days of the schools and Moody's contributions therein. At the Northfield School for Girls there is a small but important set of manuscripts in the alumni office that reveals much about the early planning of the school. Scrapbooks of letters and newspaper clippings at the Moody Museum on the girls' school campus cover a wide range of subjects, including indispensable material on Moody's revival campaign at the Chicago World's Fair in 1893. A small collection of letters and documents written by Henry Rankin, an early member of the faculty at Mount Hermon, is in the archives in the library at Mount Hermon School. These papers, combined with other file boxes of printed and manuscript materials in the archives, are most helpful in reconstructing the history of the first years of both schools in Northfield.

Moody's intimate and long-standing connections with the

YMCA are best revealed through the voluminous materials available at the Historical Library located at the national offices of the YMCA in New York City. Most of the documents there are printed sources, although the "Family League Letters" of Richard C. Morse, which speak of Moody's activities at Northfield and the reminiscences of Luther D. Wishard concerning the origins of the national student YMCA movement are important exceptions. Scattered items in the John R. Mott Papers deposited at Yale Divinity School, further illuminate Moody's impact, through the YMCA and summer conferences at Northfield, on successive college generations of the 1880's and 1890's. The archives of the Chicago YMCA, in the downtown headquarters of that organization, contain manuscripts which document both Moody's rise to eminence as a religious leader in the Windy City in the sixties, and his loss of influence in the nineties.

It should be added that diligent search for ten weeks in England failed to unearth any significant collections of materials dealing with Moody's several visits there. Printed materials are in abundance, however, and will be discussed later.

All of the documentary collections just mentioned provide information essential to any thorough and fair-minded assessment of Moody's public career. But by far the most complete record of the evangelist's public life appeared in the religious and secular periodicals and newspapers of his day. The publications of the evangelical denominations are of prime importance. By the mid-nineteenth century the weekly or bi-weekly periodicals had become one of the most characteristic instruments used by the evangelical churches to instruct and exhort the faithful. They were vigorous exponents at the popular level of the evangelical faith, and were widely circulated throughout the country. Today they remain as vast repositories of information about the evangelicals, as well as source books on the specific activities of Moody as a revivalist.

Of particular significance to this study were the following denomination periodicals: *The Congregational Herald, The Congregationalist* [Boston], *The Advance, New York Observer, New York Evangelist, The Interior, Zion's Herald, New York Christian Advocate, Northwestern Christian Advocate,* and *Western Chris-*

tian Advocate. These publications were examined systematically over extended periods beginning with the 1850's and ending about 1900. In addition the writer examined, for shorter periods of time, over a dozen other evangelical journals of regional or national circulation. Several lesser-known publications sponsored by friends of Moody appeared in the eighties and nineties. These include *The Evangelistic Record* (1881–85), *The Record of Christian Work* (1886–94), and the *Northfield Echoes* (1894–1901). These journals often offered important statements by Moody not available elsewhere, and they provided a valuable guide on almost a week-by-week schedule to Moody's activities during his extraordinarily busy last years. Files of these publications are available either at Moody Bible Institute or at the Northfield School for Girls.

In England the printed sources are almost equally voluminous. A wide range of materials, including both Anglican and nonconformist journals, is available in the holdings of the British Museum, housed chiefly in the newspaper and periodical division in Colindale, a London suburb. Deserving special mention are the nonsectarian evangelical journal *The Christian*, and its predecessor, *The Revivalist*. Published by R. C. Morgan, who became a close friend of Moody, the two weeklies are mines of information about the evangelist's activities in Great Britain from the time of his earliest visits in the sixties to his last trip overseas in the 1890's. Special mention should also be made of *The Congregationalist* [London], valuable for extended comments on Moody's revivals by the editor, R. W. Dale, and the *British Evangelist* and *The Christian World*, nonsectarian, nonconformist periodicals whose observations on Moody's activities proved especially helpful.

Secular newspapers and periodicals also devoted a great deal of space to Moody's work as a revivalist. Lavishly embellished accounts often began as front-page news and continued for many columns into the back pages. The information is repetitious and overwhelming. It also enables one to reconstruct without too much difficulty the edifice of urban mass revivalism as Moody practiced it, and to relive the excitement and stir created in England and America by the visits of Moody and Sankey. Our knowledge of Moody's theology and preaching methods is also derived chiefly from the detailed, near-verbatim accounts of his sermons that filled column after column of the major metropolitan dailies, especially during the revival campaigns of the seventies. In this study, the files of fifty-six daily newspapers were examined, representing most of the cities of the United States where Moody preached during the last third of the nineteenth century. Twenty-one newspapers published in England, Scotland, and Ireland, representing especially the principal urban centers the evangelist visited in his great revival campaign of 1873–75, were examined in England.

Index

Abbott, Lyman, 411
Abelard, Peter, 232, 233
Aberdeen, Scotland, 154
Academies, 314–15
African Methodist Episcopal Church, 280
After-meetings, 263. *See also* Inquiry meetings
Agricultural Hall (London), 170, 171
Alexander, Charles, 217, 308*n*
Alexander, Medad, 31
Alexander, Phila, 34
Alexander, Thomas, 31
American Home Missionary Society, 66
Americanization, immigrants, 73, 106–7
American Sunday School Union, 66, 102
American Tract Society, 102
Andover Theological Seminary, 147, 391
Anglicans, High Church. *See* Church of England
Anselm, 232, 233
Anti-intellectualism: in Moody's thought, 410; and revivalism, 10

Anxious bench, 143, 262
Arminianism: and revivalism, 13, 141–42; in evangelicalism (U.S.), 17–18, 141–42; in evangelicalism (England), 146–48; in Scotland, 159; and atonement, 232, 233–34
Armour, George, 202
Armour, J. F., 202
Arnold, Matthew, 183
Atlanta, Georgia, 346
Atonement, theories of, 232–36
Audiences, Moody revivals: characteristics, 272–73, 274. *See also* Middle classes
Augusta, Georgia, 279

Backsliders, 266, 267
Bainbridge, Cuthbert, 149–50
Baltimore, Maryland, 303–4, 313, 344, 345
Baptists, 65, 147–48
Barnardo, T. J., 313*n*
Barnes, Albert, 147
Beecher, Henry Ward, 94, 129, 290–91
Beecher, Lyman, 66
Belfast, Ireland, 164

Belief: compared with faith, 229
Benevolent societies: described, 17, 66; and U.S. Christian Commission, 102–3
Bentley, Cyrus, 69
Bible and Prophetic Conferences, 252, 259
Bible Institute, Chicago. *See* Moody Bible Institute
Bible Institute Colportage Association, 398
Bible work, 322, 328*n*, 330, 331*n*, 332, 397*n*
Biblical criticism, 147, 182, 188, 259, 290, 389–90, 391, 412
Biblical literalism, 125, 126, 182, 188, 259, 388, 390, 409. *See also* Infallibility of Bible
Biblical Repository, 147
Biblicism, 255–57, 392–93
Biederwolf, William, 308*n*
Biographers of D. L. Moody: amateurs, 5–8; family, 5, 7–8; fundamentalist, 7, 8; modernists, 7
Birmingham, England, 145, 166, 167, 175
Bliss, P. P., 122, 215
Boomer spirit: and evangelicalism, 68; and Moody, 61, 68; characteristic of businessmen, 61–62
Boot and shoe industry: in Boston, 44–45; in Chicago, 58–59, 60, 62; in Northfield, 27
Booth, William, 177, 313*n*
Boston: influence on western Massachusetts, 28, 29, 44; and Irish, 30; and boot and shoe industry, 44–45; description (1850's), 44, 45; and revivals, Moody, 195*n*, 197, 201, 202, 206; mentioned, 252, 306
Bourne, Hugh, 148
Bouton, Nathaniel S., 321, 330

Bow Road (London), 171
Brattleboro, Vermont, 28, 315
Briggs, Charles, 389
British Evangelist, 425
British Museum, 425
British Workman, 128
Brookes, James H., 351, 352, 406
Brooklyn, New York: and revivals, Moody, 195, 196, 197, 200, 201, 222, 264*n*, 269*n*; mentioned, 306
Bryan, William Jennings, 277, 420
Buel, Hill, and Granger, 62
Buffalo, New York, 419
Burials Act, 1880 (England), 182
Bushnell, Horace, 236, 290–91, 392
Business, Chicago as symbol of, 58
Businessmen: and Y.M.C.A., 47, 71, 72, 90; and Moody, 59*n*, 62, 90, 100, 321; and Christian stewardship, 85, 86*n*; and piety, 86–87, 88; and revivals, Moody, 200–201, 201–2

Calvinism: and revivalism, 13, 141; and evangelicalism, 17–18, 146–48; in Scotland, 159; and the atonement, 232–33, 236
Camberwell Green (London), 171
Cambridge University, 346, 359, 360
Camp, Hiram, 310
Camp Douglas (Chicago), 104
Cartwright, Peter, 3
Chapman, Wilbur J., 308*n*
Charteris, A. H., 155
Chauncy, Charles, 138–39, 157
Chicago: description (1850's), 54, 56, 57, 59, 63; history (pre-

1850), 54; and Midwest, 54–55; social structure (1850's), 55–56; boot and shoe industry, 58–59, 60; and Moody revivals, 195, 196, 197, 199, 200, 201, 202, 204, 264, 269; mentioned, 252, 303, 306, 326

Chicago Avenue Church, 130n, 252, 331n

Chicago Evangelization Society, 330–32, 334–36. *See also* Moody Bible Institute

Chicago fire, 130

Chicago Theological Seminary, 391

Chicago Tribune, 285

Chicago World's Fair (1893), 401, 423

Children, 293–94, 295–96, 300. *See also* Christian family

Christ, figure of, 230–34, 235

Christian, 128, 131, 150, 151–52, 164, 165, 425

Christian conventions, 118–19, 120, 154, 207, 343

Christian education: and Sabbath schools, 72; and the family, 295, 375

Christian family, 294–96, 300, 361, 393

Christian liberty, 238

Christian World, 425

Christology, 229–37

Church: local, and Moody revivals, 205, 206, 270, 305; doctrine of the, 246, 247, 247n; family as, 294

Church and state, 296–97

Church membership. *See* Membership, church

Church of England, 146, 168–69, 183, 187

Church of Ireland, 165

Church of Scotland: mentioned, 155, 160, 161, 162; "great disruption," 160, 162

Church of the Nazarene, 407, 408n

Circuit riders, 66, 139, 140, 329

City evangelism, 321, 323–25

City missionaries, 189, 320–21, 323, 328, 329, 330

Class distinctions, small towns, 32–33. *See also* Northfield, Massachusetts

Cleveland, Ohio, 240

Coffin, Henry Sloane, 223, 225

Commercial spirit: Chicago a symbol of, 58; Moody a symbol of, 59–60, 62

Communism, 327

Congregational Church, in Northfield, 37–38, 194, 375, 407

Congregational Herald, 86

Congregationalist, 391, 394, 401

Congregationalists: and Moody, 37–38, 48–49, 50–51, 63, 74; statistics, 65; and Illinois Street Church, 109; mentioned, 147–48, 235, 271; in England, 147–48; in 1890's, 391–92, 394

Congregational singing, 208–9, 288–89

Connecticut River, 28, 30, 193–94, 363

Connecticut River valley: economic characteristics, 28, 29; population flows, 28, 29–30, 32; mentioned, 193, 420

Conversion experience: assessed, 50, 51–52, 132, 133, 133n; and business ideals, 81–82; characteristic of evangelicalism, 66–67, 188, 260; and Sabbath schools, 72, 77

Conversions, process of, 239–41

Conversions: and revivalism, 142; and Sankey's singing,

214–15; instantaneous, 239, 241; questioned, 394
Converts at revivals, 172n, 268–70, 304–5
Conviction of sin, 239–40
Cook, Russell S., 102
Corn Exchange (Edinburgh, Scotland), 154
Cree, Thomas K., 198–99
Crerar, John, 202
Croker, Richard, 278, 395
Cross, Whitney R., 12, 18
Crystal Palace (Glasgow, Scotland), 154
Cutler, Henry F., 40–41, 368n, 395, 396, 400

Dale, Robert W., 145, 175, 425
Daniels, William H., 6
Darby, John N., 125, 126, 127, 251, 260–61
Darwinism, 182, 188, 290
Davenport, James, 138, 139
Deerfield, Massachusetts, 28
Deists, 64, 65n
Democratization, 162, 163, 182, 187–88
Denominations: defined, 64, 65–66; historical background, 64–65; statistics, 65
Depression: 1857–58 (U.S.), 61; 1873–96 (England), 186
Des Plaines, Illinois, 59
Disciples of Christ, 65
Disestablishment, 64, 65n, 139, 144, 161, 162
Dispensationalism, 21, 250–51, 252, 307, 352, 406–8
Doane, W. H., 215
Doctrine of the Church, 246, 247, 247n
Dodge, William E., 102, 103, 201–2, 205
Dow, Lorenzo, 148

Drummond, Henry, 352, 411–12
Dryer, Emma, 321–23, 331–32, 335
Dublin, Ireland, 164, 165, 167, 265
Dundee, Scotland, 154, 189
Durant, Henry, 308–9, 316–17
Dwight, Timothy, 3

Earnestness, 68
Eddy, Sherwood, 354
Edinburgh, Pennsylvania, 122
Edinburgh, Scotland, 98, 153, 154, 356
Education Act: of 1872 (Scotland), 161–62; of 1870 (England), 182
Edwards, Jonathan, 2, 137
Election, doctrine of, 141, 242
Electives, 396
Episcopalians, 2, 65, 248
Essays and Reviews, 183
Estey, Julius J., 315
Eton school, 179–80
Evangelicalism: mentioned, 1–3, 20, 87, 105; Anglo-American, 3, 19, 128–29, 131, 302n; characteristics, 17–20, 56, 63, 65–66, 67, 73, 84–85, 86n, 86–87, 105, 113–14, 136–44, 248, 297–99; and inter-denominational organizations, 17, 66, 102–3, 118, 119–20; and Y.M.C.A., 46–47, 69–71, 72; early influence on D. L. Moody, 46–52; historical antecedents, 63–64; and frontier, 65–66, 66n, 354; and moral reform, 68, 82, 102–3; and Sabbath schools, 72–74; and business, 81–88; in England, 144–49; and Christology, 230–31, 234–36; premillennialism, 252, 253n, 254; and biblicism, 255–57, 259; and the

family, 294–96, 300. *See also* Conversion experience; Denominations; Earnestness; Home missions; Inter-denominationalism; Revivalism; Voluntaryism
Evangelicals: and urban working class, 183–85; and temperance, 281
Evangelistic Record, 425

Faith; defined, 227–28; and belief, compared, 229
Farmer-preachers, 66, 140, 329
Farwell, John V., 80–81, 90, 100, 103, 107, 202, 321, 330
Farwell Hall, 94, 116, 126, 132, 133, 323, 331*n*
Field, Henry, 202
Finney, Charles Grandison, 3, 136, 141, 142, 143, 147, 148, 227, 235, 250
First Methodist Church, Chicago, 74
Fitt, A. P.: biographer of D. L. Moody, 8; marriage, 384–85; mentioned, 404
Foreign-born, 30. *See also* Immigrants
Fosdick, Harry Emerson, 401*n*
Foster, Frank H., 391
Free Church of Scotland, 153, 155–56, 158, 160, 161, 162, 173
Frontier, 10, 11, 65–66, 134, 144, 235, 287, 354
Fundamentalism: mentioned, 7, 8, 411; roots of, 20–21, 250; and Moody Bible Institute, 400

Gapmen, 328–29, 398*n*
Giddings, F. H., 394–95

Gladden, Washington, 290, 411
Glasgow, Scotland, 154, 164, 165, 189, 356
Gold Coast (Chicago), 76
Gordon, A. J., 352, 406
Gospel hymns: described, 177, 210–14; history of, 215–16; criticisms of, 216–17
Gospel Hymns and Sacred Songs, 216
Gospel wagons, 398–99
Governmental theory, atonement, 235*n*, 235–36
Graham, Billy, 1, 198
Great Awakening, 2, 137, 138, 139, 157
Greene, John C., 17
Greenfield, Massachusetts, 28, 419
Griffin, Clifford, 18
Guy Fawkes' Day, 359

Half-way Covenant, 394
Hall, Evelyn, 395–96
Hall, Newman, 128
Harper, William Rainey, 352, 383, 389, 411
Hartford, Connecticut, 192, 197
Hartzler, H. B., 339
Harvard University, 312, 396
Harvey, Turlington W., 252, 321, 330, 332
Haymarket riot, 326
Hebrew Student, 389
Henderson, C. N., 60, 61, 62
Heresy trials, 390
Herron, George, 391
High Church, Anglican. *See* Church of England
Higher criticism. *See* Biblical criticism
Hippodrome (New York), 200, 205, 229, 287–88
Historians: and D. L. Moody, 8–

Index

10, 12–14, 15–16, 17–18; and
Gilded Age, 14–15
Hobsbawm, E. J., 3
Hodge, Charles, 236n
Hogg, Quinton, 179
Holiness movements, 21, 307,
341–43, 407, 408–9
Holton, Cyrus, 38
Holton family, 31
Holton, Fannie, 362
Holton, Samuel, 44, 49, 52
Holy Ghost. See Holy Spirit
Holy Spirit, 137, 138, 143,
237–39
Home missions, 65–66, 66n,
72–73. See also City evangel-
ism; City missionaries
House of Lords, 179
House-to-house visitation, 167,
168, 170, 204
Huxley, Thomas, 183
Hymnbook Fund, 319n, 344, 369
Hymnody, 157–58, 176–77,
215–16

Illinois and Michigan Canal, 55,
58
Illinois Normal University, 321
Illinois Sabbath School Union,
119
Illinois State Sunday School Con-
vention, 120
Illinois Street Church, 107–8,
108–9, 110–12
Illinois Street mission school, 93
Immigrants: in Northfield, 30–
31; Irish, 30–31, 56, 73; in
Chicago (1850's), 55–56, 76;
and North Market Hall mis-
sion, 106–7; mentioned, 297,
299, 300
Incarnation, 231n
Independent, 421
Indianapolis, Indiana, 118, 123

Individualism: and evangelical-
ism, 67, 82–83, 188; mentioned,
284
Industrialism, 188, 252, 254, 284,
301, 307
Industrialization, and Connecti-
cut River Valley, 27, 28
Inerrancy. See Biblical literalism
Infallibility of Bible, 290. See
also Biblical literalism
Infidelity, 293, 327
Inquirers, 266–67
Inquiry meetings, 263–66, 267–68
Inquiry room, 167, 263, 266
Inquiry room workers, 265–66,
314
Inter-denominationalism, 17, 66,
102–3, 118, 119–20
Inter-denominational societies:
and Civil War, 102–3; in Mid-
west, 118–20
Inter-Seminary Missionary Alli-
ance, 353

Jacksonville, Florida, 280, 377
Jacobs, B. F., 252
Jarrow, England, 151
Jones, Sam, 202, 308n

Kansas City, Missouri, 386, 418–
19
Keith, E. G., 321, 330
Kelly, William, 251
Keswick Movement, 342, 343,
407, 408, 412n
Kimball, Edward, 49–50, 50–51
Kirk, Edward N., 49

Laymen: and Y.M.C.A., 72, 119;
as revivalists, evangelists, 140–
41, 328; and Moody's revivals,
166, 166n, 170, 171, 266, 314;

and city missions, 328; and Northfield conferences, 339, 340, 351; and American Protestantism (pre-World War I), 354–55

Lay patronage, 161, 162

Liberal Party (England), 181, 182

Liberal Protestantism, 7–8, 14, 236, 390–92, 400. *See also* Modernism

Liberty, Christian, 238

Liverpool, England, 166, 167, 170–71, 185, 189, 288

London Times, 171

Loos, Mrs. Esther, 422

Louisville, Kentucky, 201n, 280

Love of God, 228–29, 249

Low Church, Anglican. *See* Church of England

Lowlands (Scotland), 159–60

Lutherans, 65

McCormick, Cyrus H., 117, 202, 321, 326, 388, 423

McCormick, Cyrus H., Jr., 330

McCormick, Nettie Fowler, 330, 333–34, 334–35, 423

McGranahan, H. H., 397

McIlvaine, Charles P., 102

McIntosh, C. H., 126, 251

McKinley, William, 277, 420

McLoughlin, William G., 13–14, 15–16

Manchester, England, 166, 189

Mann, Horace, 29

Marshall, H. N. F., 309, 310, 310n, 369

Mason, Thomas, 40

Massachusetts, government of, 29

Mass revivalism: origins of techniques, 120–22, 152, 166–68, 170–71; financing, 170–71;

mentioned, 301–2. *See also* Revivalism

Materialism, 293, 299, 361

Mathieson, James, 171

May, Henry F., 274

Mead, Sidney, 17–18

Membership, church, and revivals, 271–72

Messer, L. Wilbur, 403, 404–5, 410

Metanoia, 240–41

Methodists: statistics, 65; and Ira Sankey, 123; mentioned, 248, 271

Metropolitan Tabernacle (London), 146

Michigan Central Railroad, 55

Michigan Southern Railroad, 55

Middle classes: and revivals, 174, 180–81, 272–73, 274; in England, 178–81; and evangelicalism, 292

Mildmay Conference, 131, 343

Mildmay Conference Center: mentioned, 127, 171, 322; and Northfield Schools, 189n

Miller, H. Thane, 215

Miller, Perry, 136

Mills, B. Fay, 202, 270, 308n

Mississippi Valley, 54

Modernism, 7–8, 400, 411

Moody, Ambert, 366n, 422

Moody, Betsey Holton: family background, 31; marriage, 34; personality, 35, 36; influence on D. L. Moody, 35, 36–37, 38, 373–74; church membership, 37, 374n

Moody Bible Institute: mentioned, 8, 97, 284, 306, 328n, 422, 423, 425; origins of, 174, 189–90, 266, 321–23; financing of, 318–19; purposes, 321, 324–28, 329–30; founding, 330–36; curriculum, 329, 397; and Student Volunteer Movement, 355*n*; in 1890's, 397–99; influence of D. L. Moody on, 399; in twentieth century, 400

Moody, Dwight L.: biographers of, 5–8; and historians, 8–14, 15; church membership, 38, 48–51, 63, 109*n*, 375; and Y.M.C.A., 46, 47–48, 69, 71–72, 80, 89, 90, 124, 128, 189, 199, 318, 344, 344–50, 403–5; and non-denominationalism, 75, 80, 106, 119; as fund raiser, 116–18, 318–19, 344; and Plymouth Brethren, 125, 126, 127, 250–51, 251*n*; as preacher, 176, 220–25; and middle classes, 178–81, 274, 276, 277, 281, 283; as storyteller, 181, 223–25; personal finances, 203; and the *Bible*, 223–25, 256–57, 259, 261; study habits, 236*n*; and individualism, 276, 278; and city missions, 320–21, 323, 324–25, 326*n*, 326–27, 328, 329–30; and college students, 346–48, 358–60; and foreign missions, 348, 349, 351, 353–54; and Keswick movement, 408, 412*n*

———— in Northfield, early life: family background, maternal, 31; family background, paternal, 31–32; influence, father, 34; birth, 35; influence, mother, 35–37; religious training, 37–39; schooling, 40–41; goes to Boston, 43

———— in Boston: Mt. Vernon Congregational Church, 38, 48–51, 94, 95; Y.M.C.A., 46; moves to Chicago, 52–53

———— in Illinois: as a businessman, 44, 45, 58, 59–62; business career ends, 88–91; and North Market Hall mission,

72, 74, 75–80, 106–8; and Emma C. Revell, 89, 96, 97; and Y.M.C.A., 100–101, 112–13, 114–16; and Civil War, 101–2, 103–6; and Illinois Street Church, 107–9, 111–12; as convention leader, 118, 119, 120–22, 129; partnership with Ira Sankey, 123–24; trips to England (1867), 124–25, 127–29; Chicago fire, 130; (1872), 131; leaves Chicago for England, 133–34

———— in Great Britain (1873–75): beginnings as revivalist, 149–53; in Scotland, 153–59, 162–63; in Ireland, 164, 165; in England, 166–68, 170–72

———— in 1880's: alters evangelistic aims, techniques, 303–7, 308, 313, 339–41, 356–58; visits England, 306, 355–62; founds Northfield Schools, 308–10, 317–21; founds Moody Bible Institute, 330–36; establishes Northfield Conferences, 339, 341–43, 346–48, 351–53; at Oxford University, 359–60; at Cambridge University, 359, 360

———— death and funeral, 419–20

———— personality: characteristics, 34, 35, 36–37, 37*n*, 62, 74–75, 77, 78–79, 90–91, 131–33, 133–34, 225–26, 261, 334, 347, 365, 366, 367–74, 376–78, 380–81, 384–85, 410–11; conversion experiences, 49–50, 51–52, 132, 133*n*, 219–20, 237, 239, 261; description of person, 78–79, 92, 217–18; analysis of, 92–96, 97–98, 99

———— home life and family: mother of D. L. Moody, 35–37,

373–74; relationship with wife, 89, 96–99, 376, 420; love of Northfield, 362–63, 364, 365, 386; gentleman farmer, 365–66; home life, 365–68, 369–71, 384–85, 386–87, 414; family relations, 372–74, 375–83, 384–85, 413–17, 419–20

—— theology: origins in Chicago, 115, 115*n*; faith, defined, 227–28; love of God, 228–29, 237; atonement, 230, 231–32, 233, 235–37; and liberal theology, 236, 409; Holy Spirit, 237–39, 409; and salvation, process of, 239–41, 243–44; repentence, 240–41, 258–59; and Calvinism, 242, 243; and Arminianism, 242, 243–44; perfectionism, 244–46, 276, 342*n*, 409; doctrine of church, 246, 247; work, 246–49; premillennialism, 249, 250–54, 276, 409; dispensationalism, 406, 407, 408, 412*n*; holiness, 408–9; biblical criticism, 409, 410, 412

—— social, economic views: affected by small town, 33–34, 42; attitude toward immigrants, 56–57, 75–76, 106–7; interest in urban poor, 56–57, 89, 96, 173, 174, 189; support of Republican Party, 59*n*, 277; tied to businessmen, 88, 90, 100, 321, 323; and Roman Catholics, 165, 371–72; as a businessman (symbolically), 178–79, 180, 218, 286–87, 300; and Negroes, 278–81; general description, 274–83, 327; on temperance, 281, 282–83; assessed, 283–85. *See also* Moody Bible Institute; Mount Hermon School for boys; Northfield School for Girls; Revivals,

Moody; Student Volunteer Movement; Y.M.C.A.

Moody, Dwight L. (son of W. R. Moody), 415–16

Moody, Edwin: as bricklayer, 32; influence on son, 34; birth, 34; description of, 34–35; marriage, 35; death, 35

Moody, Emma (daughter of D. L. Moody): mentioned, 99, 377–78, 379, 413, 414; birth, 99; in England, 362; marriage, 384–85

Moody, Emma C. (wife of D. L. Moody): ancestry, 96; marriage, 96, 97; personality, 97–99, 333–34, 375, 376*n*, 382*n*; relationship with husband, 96–99, 333–34, 369*n*, 375–76; in England, 128, 150, 362–63; family relationships, 374–75, 378–79, 381–83, 382*n*; church membership, 375

Moody family home, described, 193, 363–64

Moody, George, 364, 373

Moody, Irene, 414, 415, 416–17

Moody, Isaiah (grandfather of D. L. Moody), 32, 34

Moody, Isaiah (brother of D. L. Moody), 52

Moody, Paul D.: biographer of father, 7–8; birth, 99; mentioned, 278, 364, 366, 367, 370, 374, 375, 378*n*, 384*n*, 419

Moody, Samuel, 78, 373, 374*n*

Moody, William R.: biographer of father, 5, 8; birth, 99; mentioned, 99, 384*n*, 385, 400, 401*n*; in England, 362; at Yale, 378, 382–83; commitment as Christian, 379–81, 382–83; marriage, 384; and children, 413, 415–17

Moorehead, W. G., 406

Index

Moorhouse, Henry, 126, 152
Morgan, J. P., 202
Morgan, Robert C., 128, 131, 151, 164, 165, 425
Morse, Richard C., 345, 404, 424
Morton, C. M., 252
Mott, John R., 314–15, 354–55, 424
Mount Hermon Hundred, 350, 350n, 354
Mount Hermon School for boys: mentioned, 306, 308, 315–16, 395, 397, 420, 423; founding, 310; work program, 311; purposes, 311, 313, 320–21; curriculum, 313, 396
Mount Vernon Church, 48–49, 50–51
Müller, George, 125
Murphy, Francis, 282

Nation, 211
National Sunday School Union, 102, 111
Nativism, 56
Needham, George C., 252
Negroes, and D. L. Moody, 278–81
Nettleton, Asahel, 139–40
Newcastle, England, 150, 151, 152–53, 263, 356
Newcastle, Pennsylvania, 122, 123
New England, 55
New England Congregational Church, 109n
New Haven, Connecticut, 197
New Theology, 10, 391
New York Christian Advocate, 297, 389
New York City: mentioned, 25, 192, 242, 252, 272, 277, 294, 306; and revivals, Moody, 195,

196, 197, 200, 201, 202, 205, 264, 269
New York Evangelist, 389–90
New York Herald, 286
New York Times, 403
Niagara Conferences, 307
Nonconformists, 146, 148, 181–82
Non-denominationalism, 106, 199, 270
Noon prayer meetings: in Chicago, 69, 93, 112–13, 114–16, 263; in London, 124, 128, 131
Northfield Academy, 40
Northfield Conferences: adult, 339–40, 341–43, 404–6, 412n; and holiness, 341–43, 407, 412n; student, 346–50, 351–52, 354–55; and premillennialism, dispensationalism, 352, 406, 412n
Northfield Echoes, 425
Northfield Hotel, 397n
Northfield, Massachusetts: as D. L. Moody's home, 25; economy of, 26–27; description, 26–34, 39–40, 41–42, 192–93; and Boston, 28, 29, 30, 39, 44; social structure, 29–31; social homogeneity of, 29–30, 31, 32–33; cultural activities in, 39–40
Northfield School for Girls, 306, 422, 423, 425. See also Northfield Seminary
Northfield Schools: mentioned, 19, 174, 189–90, 308, 395–96; purposes, 310–13, 315, 320–21; financing of, 318–19; and Moody Bible Institute, 399–400
Northfield Seminary: founding, 308–9; mentioned, 363–64, 398n, 420; curriculum, 396

Northfield Training School for Girls, 397n
North Market Hall mission: founded, 74, 76n; mentioned, 76–80, 89, 310; and Y.M.C.A., 80–81; and Americanization of immigrants, 106–7

Ober, C. K., 345, 346, 349, 350
Orange, Massachusetts, 28
Otherworldliness, 276–77
Oxford Movement, 2
Oxford University, 345, 359–60

Paton, Robert, 166n
Patterson, Joseph, 102
Paul, the apostle, 243
Pennefather, William, 150
Perfectionism, 245–46
Philadelphia, Pennsylvania: and revivals, Moody, 195, 196, 197, 198, 199, 200, 201, 204, 264, 269, 273; mentioned, 244
Philanthropy, 84–85, 117–18
Phillips, Phillip, 121–22, 215
Pierson, A. T., 349, 352, 406, 412n
Pietism, 64, 144
Piety, 86–87, 275, 393
Plymouth Brethren, 125–27, 251, 406
Plymouth Congregational Church (Chicago), 63, 74
Poor relief, 104–5
Population movements, 29–30, 55–56
Postmillenialism, 249–50
Powell, Emma M. (Emma Fitt), 414–15, 422, 423
Power, religious, 238–39, 248
Prayer, 113–14
Prayer meetings, 113–14, 347. *See also* Noon prayer meetings

Preaching, 176, 225
Premillennialism, 21, 125–26, 249, 250–54, 255, 276–77, 301n, 307, 352
Presbyterian Review, 389
Presbyterians, 65, 147, 248, 271, 389, 390
Presbyterians, New School, 235
Primitive Methodists, 148
Princeton Review, 147
Professional evangelist. *See* Professional revivalist
Professional revivalist: mentioned, 136, 139, 153, 268, 305, 307; characteristics of, 139–42, 143–44, 267; purposes, 174, 305; and Moody Bible Institute, 400
Progressive orthodoxy, 391
Protestantism and American culture, 296–97
Providence, Rhode Island, 197, 345, 402
Puritan conscience, 381–82, 382n

Quincy, Illinois, 121

Railroads, 28, 30, 55, 299
Rankin, Henry B., 320, 423
Record of Christian Work, 425
Regeneration, 240, 243n
Religious census, 1851 (England), 184
Repentance, 240–41, 258–59
Revell, Fleming H., 251, 323
Revival, 128, 425
Revival: of 1857–58, 63, 69, 113, 149; of 1859 (England), 142
Revivalism: mentioned, 10, 12, 16, 66; frontier, 10, 11, 235; colonial period, 2–3, 136–39; compared, U.S. and England, 144–45; legitimacy questioned,

394–95, 401. *See also* Arminianism; Calvinism; Mass revivalism
Revivalists, itinerant, 138–40,
149
Revivals, Moody: techniques, origins of, 103, 114, 115, 120–22,
123–24, 166–68, 170; criticism
of, 138–39, 157–58, 173; assessed, 156–63, 172–78, 180–88;
advance preparations, 164–65,
167–68, 170–71, 197–99, 204–
6; financing, 170–71, 200–202;
in London, 170–72, 303, 356,
357–58; and working classes,
172–74, 357–58; converts at,
172n, 268–70; audiences characterized, 174, 180–81, 272–
73; in New York City, 195, 196,
197, 200, 201, 202, 205, 264,
269, 402–3; in Chicago, 195,
196, 197, 199, 200, 201, 202,
204, 264, 269, 303; in Philadelphia, 195, 197, 198, 199, 200,
201, 204, 264, 269, 273; in
Boston, 195n, 197, 200, 201,
202, 206, 309; in Brooklyn, 195,
196, 197, 200, 201, 222, 264n,
269n; criteria for location of,
195–97; housing, 196–97, 200,
357; and Y.M.C.A., 199–200;
publicity techniques, 199, 205;
ushers, 205; massed choirs, 204,
205; physical surroundings,
206–7; order of service, 207–8;
and local churches, 270; and
church membership, 271–72;
and Negroes, 279–80; in Baltimore, 303–4; in St. Louis, 304,
306n; in San Francisco, 304;
in Cleveland, 304–5, 306n;
procedures of, reconsidered,
303–5, 357; legitimacy questioned, 401; and Chicago
World's Fair, 401, 423

Ritualism, 168, 169, 183, 187
Rodeheaver, Homer, 217
Roman Catholics, 165, 248, 297,
371–72
Round Top, 420
Royal Opera House (London),
171
Rural-urban mixture, 42–43,
43n

Sabbatarianism, 56, 297–99, 317
Sabbath, compared with Europe,
298
Sabbath desecration, 297, 299
Sabbath school conventions,
118–19
Sabbath schools, purposes, 72–73
St. Louis, Missouri, 242, 259, 305,
313
Salvation Army, 177
Salvation, process of, 239–44
Sanctification, 21, 409. *See also*
Holiness movements; Perfectionism
Sandburg, Carl, 54
Sands, (Chicago), 75
San Francisco, California, 304
Sankey, Ira D.: early life, 122–
24; partnership with Moody,
123–24; in England, 150–51,
355, 357; in Scotland, 153–55,
159–60; criticisms of, 157–58,
209n, 216–17; as singing evangelist, described, 176–77, 209–
10; as businessman (symbolic);
in Northfield, 193–94; physical
description, 209; techniques
used in revivals, 209–11, 214–
15; ends partnership, 417
Sawyer, Henry E., 315–16, 320,
368n
Schaff, Philip, 298
Scofield, C. I., 406–7
Scofield Reference Bible, 406–7

Index

Scott, James, 166n
Second coming of Christ, 249, 251n, 252, 253
Second Great Awakening, 3
Secularism, 297, 308
Self-help ideal, 36, 178, 276, 309, 311, 312, 330
Self-help programs, 311–12, 330
Seminaries, 328, 328n, 391
Sentimentality, Victorian, 37, 90
Sheffield, England, 166, 168–69, 173, 324–25
Sin, 244, 244n, 274, 382n, 393
Slums, 75–76, 77–78
Small towns, characteristics, 25–26, 26–27, 28–31, 32–33, 41–42, 42–43, 43n
Smiles, Samuel, 178
Smith, George Adam, 412
Smith, Gypsy, 308n
Smithies, T. B., 128
Smith, Mrs. Frank R., 422, 423
Smith, Timothy, 12–13, 18, 20, 21n
Social control, institutions of, 71, 73
Social Gospel, 10, 20, 307, 391, 411
Social levelling, 32, 33n, 34
Socinianism, 232
Sola Scriptura, 255
Sovereignty of God, 234–35
Speer, Robert E., 352, 354
Springfield, Massachusetts, 192, 194, 195n, 197, 201n
Spurgeon, Charles H., 128, 145, 146
Stewardship, 84–86
Stillson, J. B., 76
Storytelling, 223–25
Strong, Josiah, 411
Stuart, George H., 102, 103, 201
Stuart, Moses, 147
Studd, J. E. K., 351

Student Volunteer Movement, 349n, 350, 351–54
Summer conferences. See Northfield conferences
Sunday, Billy, 198, 202, 268, 308n
Sunderland, England, 151, 152
Sweet, William Warren, 11–12

Tammany Hall, 278
Taylor, Graham, 391
Taylor, Nathaniel, 17
Temperance movement, 281–83
Tennent, Gilbert, 139
Thatcher, Solomon, 202
Torrey, Reuben J., 308n, 397, 399–400, 404–5, 416
Towns. See Small towns
Tractarians, 187
Tract distribution, 105–6
Traveling salesman, Moody as example, 60–61
Trotter, William, 251
Turner, Frederick Jackson, 11
Turner thesis, 11
Tuttle, Harriet, 313n

Union Theological Seminary, 223
Unitarians, 37–38, 94
United Presbyterian Church (Scotland), 156, 160, 161
United States Christian Commission, 102–3, 215
"Unsaved" masses, 172–74, 183–84, 323–24
Urban revivalism, 12, 13, 14

Varley, Henry, 128, 149
Vermont and Massachusetts Railroad, 28

Victorian father, D. L. Moody as, 16, 300
Victorian mother, Betsey Moody as, 35, 374
Victorian society, 296
Voluntaryism: in America, 3, 64–65, 140–41, 142; in Scotland, 160, 161. *See also* Disestablishment

Wanamaker, John, 200, 201, 204, 252
Washington, Booker T., 420
Weisberger, Bernard, 13–14, 15–16
Wellesley College, 309, 309n, 316–17
Wesley, John, 146
Wesleyan movement (England), 144
Whitefield, George, 2, 139
Whittle, D. W., 122, 132, 133, 215, 223, 239, 252, 279n, 351, 384, 422
Whittle, May (Mrs. W. R. Moody), 384, 413, 416, 417, 422, 423
Wilder, Robert, 349n, 350n, 353, 354
Willard, Frances, 282, 283n
Williams, George, 128
Wishard, Luther, 345–46, 347, 348–50, 424
Wiswall, E. E., 58, 60
Wolfe, Richard C., 17
Work, 83–84, 246–49
Working classes and revivals,

172–74, 357–58. *See also* "Unsaved" masses
Worldliness, 292–93
Worship, 294
Wrath of God, 228–29, 235

Yale University, 347, 378, 378n, 382, 383n, 419
Y.M.C.A.: in Boston, 46, 47–48; expression of urban America, 46–47, 48; and revivals, 69, 150, 199–200; and noon prayer meetings, 93; and U.S. Christian Commission, 102–3; national conventions, 118, 230, 344; and Ira Sankey, 123; in London, 124, 125, 128; in York, England, 150; and gospel songs, 215; International Committee, 318, 344–45, 404; and Student Volunteer Movement, 351, 354; Historical Library, 424
——— in Chicago: and D. L. Moody, 63, 72n, 101, 112–18, 403–5; and revival of 1857–58, 69; and Boston Y.M.C.A., 70; purposes, 70–71; and business community, 71, 90; and North Market Hall mission, 80, 106; and Civil War, 101–2, 103–6; and poor relief, 104–5; and tract distribution, 105–6; mentioned, 108, 109; and noon prayer meetings, 112–13, 114–16; archives, 424
York, England, 150–51